The Home Fires

Wartime Letters Written from Mother to Son.

Letters written by Helen May Price

Edited by Gregory Edwin Price

Copyright © 2007 by Gregory Edwin Price

Cover by Thor Hansen

ISBN 978-0-6151-4545-7

Printed in the United States of America. All rights reserved under International Copyright Law. Contents and/or cover may not be reproduced in whole or in part in any form without the express written consent of the Publisher.

This book is dedicated to

the memory of my grandmother,

Helen May Long Price

and my father,

Edwin Charles Price

♦

The Home Fires
Prologue

Sometime around 1967, I can remember my father and me sitting around a wicker basket that bore a Heinz gift pack calendar from 1928. It had originally held over "28 varieties" of condiments. By 1967, it held something much more valuable.

As we sat there, Dad began reading letters written to him during World War II. World War II! I had practically grown up watching it on television in some form, almost every night: Twelve O'clock High, Combat, and The Rat Patrol; I loved history, even as a child. Though the War had only been over for little more than twenty years, it seemed so ancient, yet engaging to this 10-year-old.

My greatest interest was in the cache of foreign coins and currency the basket held; their seemingly inherent antiquity and the foreign lands represented. Yet Dad's attention was on something else. Occasionally, as he poured through the letters, he would wipe his eyes and hand me something to read. Periodically, his tears would flow more heavily as he read. Conversely, we laughed over humorous post cards and read, with certain gravity, an account of the dropping of the Atomic bomb over Hiroshima. Scheduled to be a part of the American invasion force of Japan, my father was certain "the bomb" had saved his life. I knew then that this basket held treasures that I hoped would some day be my own.

Dad never talked much about his wartime service. Like a lot of the men of his generation, he heard the call to duty, perhaps fantasized, glorified or romanticized about war, until the bleak reality of its terror became his own.

I knew Dad had done his basic naval training in Virginia. He talked about having to dive off a 50-foot drop. I also knew the names of the two ships he served on, the Housatonic and the Pasadena. I was aware that he was stationed in Japan after the end of the War as a part of the occupation force. He had on a few occasions, usually around suppertime, talked about how awful the food in the service was. But the details of his experience were mostly a mystery to me.

One of the greatest personal blows of my life was when my father passed away from a heart attack at the age of fifty-two, in 1979. My mother, assisted by my two surviving sisters, had the monumental task of putting together a new life without Dad. This meant cleaning out the house, deciding what she wanted to keep and determining which things should be divided among the children.

It was during this time that I received a call from my mother. "Greg, do you want the wicker basket with Dad's old letters? If you don't, we're just going to throw them away." Immediately, without reservation, I told her that I wanted the letters and begged for them not to be disposed of.

Ten years later, while looking about the closet where the basket had come to rest, I finally sat down and closely examined the contents for the first time. It wasn't long before I came to understand exactly why my father had shed so many tears on that day back in 1967.

Neatly bundled were the numerous letters written to my father from his mother during his wartime service. It was during the course of reading these letters that I came to have a greater understanding of my father, and the family environment in which he grew up. The impact and eloquence of my grandmother's letters are something that I felt should be shared.

Helen May Long was born in October of 1897 in Shamokin, Pennsylvania to Norman Francis Long and his wife, Minnie May. She was the oldest of ten children. Married to my grandfather, Edwin Price Junior, in 1920, she had spent over twenty years on the family farm in the Bustleton section of Philadelphia when she penned the letters to my father.

These letters illustrate in detail her everyday life, her hopes, her fears, her dreams, her foibles, and her courage. They have been edited for clarity.

Gregory Edwin Price
April 2007

Chapter One

October 1944

The Price family farm on Krewstown Road in Philadelphia.

Wartime Letters Written from Mother to Son

Krewstown Road
Bustleton
Philadelphia, Pennsylvania
Thursday, October 12, 1944

Dear Edwin[1],

Today is Columbus Day and Roger[2] is at school. Granny[3] is here. She occupied your feather bed the first night, and in return has all your pants and sweaters washed and on the line. I was so happy it was a beautiful sunny day when you went away and ever since. I don't like long rainy weeks like it was last week. Granny is keeping up my morale. We have talked about everybody and everything. Pop[4] said he had his arms around Dot[5], coming home on the El[6], as her tears were close to falling. Granny said she sent her love to the two nice boys, and hope they are in step by this time. Joe[7] is feeling out of sorts ever since he came home from town, either because of all the pretty girls, or else the pace. Dad and I each had a needle at the Doctor's last night. My cold is getting better, but Pop has a fresh starter. I had a needle of liver extract for more blood. My blood pressure went down to almost normal, so that is one improvement and so I hope to keep fit. When I see you again, I hope to feel better than when you left. Everybody was very kind to me. Mrs. Spence[8] called me up again and so did Mrs. McAdams and Mrs. Delheim. We all will be very proud of you. Mrs. Spence said Edwin will make a nice-looking sailor.

---

[1] Edwin is, in most instances, a reference to Edwin Charles Price, recipient of these letters and the son of Helen May Long Price.
[2] Roger is Roger Daniel Price, also referred to as "Rog", Edwin's younger brother.
[3] Granny is Minnie May Baldy Long, Helen's mother and Edwin's grandmother.
[4] Pop or "Dad" is Edwin's father, Edwin Price Junior.
[5] Dot or Dottie is Dorthea Ems, Edwin's girlfriend.
[6] Elevated train, which runs in the northeastern part of Philadelphia.
[7] Joe is Joe Johnson, a boarder at the Price family's home. Joe works for the Baldwin family.
[8] Mrs. Spence, Mrs. McAdams and Mrs. Delheim are family friends.
[9] Uncle Charlie is Helen's younger brother, Charles Edward Long, who lived in Bristol, PA.

Dad is getting the tire tonight. Mrs. McAdams said every time she looks out the door, she thinks she is getting company because your car is in front of her house. I said, 'It will sit outside my door and two gas stamps won't go far.' I can't drive or Granny and I would have been up to Uncle Charlie's[9]. Well anyway, Granny is ironing and I must run along now to fix up pretty for Dad when he comes home to supper. I miss you. "Mom, scramble me some eggs." "Mom, is my polo shirt clean?" "Mom, Mom." So long, Darling. Be good. Lots of love and hugs.

Mother dear and all the rest. Write soon. X X X

Granny said, 'Tell the boys to blow all their troubles to the wind. Let the wind carry them away.' She sends all her love. So do I.

Mother

Friday, October 13, 1944

My Dearest Son,

Granny went down for the mail. She brought up your two letters and two for me from Aunt Kebe[10] for my birthday with two nice handmade hankies in it. Now son, I often told you not to worry over us. Be a good boy and obey orders to make things easier on yourself. A still tongue makes a wise head. Keep in mind you are there to keep Hitler and his gang where they belong, so that your sweet Dottie and your Mom won't have to suffer. Mr. Baldwin[11] said it takes boys like you and Renny[12] to protect us and our way of life.

---

[10] Aunt Kebe is Helen's younger sister, Clara Elizabeth Long.
[11] Mr. Baldwin is the Superintendent of Baldwin's Milk Company.
[12] Renny is Reynolds Baldwin, Mr. Baldwin's son.

Dr. Tumbelston[13] is going to marry Aunt Lilly[14] and Fred[15] on Dad's birthday. Dad and I are going to stand for her. Dr. T. said he was sick in bed.

Now dear son, you always wanted your hair cut short and now you got it. That is the best way, or otherwise you may get new tenants and you know we wouldn't like that. There would be no Mommy around to use the fine comb.

Wherever you are or wherever you go, one line suits me; just to know you are living is all I care about. Your letter was like sweet music and good medicine. I am much better. My arm was awful sore where I got the needle, but it is better today. I got a needle with liver extract to make more blood. I must get another on Tuesday night. I shut my eyes when he jabbed it in. It hurt for 2 days. But if it will make me better, I can take it. Dad had one for rheumatism, so Granny said I could take them too.

Dottie was down last night with Nutsie[16] when Dad was on the way up to give her the address the government sent us. We both wrote to that number (246-92-54). Maybe you will get it. Dot is coming down Saturday night. Dad asked her.

I am going to the store tonight and taking Granny to Holmesburg[17]. I had a big letter from Uncle John[18]. He has 2 stars for combat zone, 1 ribbon for Southwest Pacific Duty, one ribbon for Good Conduct and three stripes on his left sleeve, so he wasn't so damn crazy for enlisting. Besides, Uncle Sam paid all the expenses. He is on New Caledonia and is hoping to get home for Christmas. So dear, all the boys learn that home is best. You are a true, fine

---

[13] Dr. Tumbelston is the minister of the Lower Dublin Baptist Church.
[14] Aunt Lilly is Lillian Price, Edwin's aunt, and the sister of Edwin Price Junior. Her first husband was William Bissinger. Her children are Edwin Bissinger and Esther Bissinger.
[15] Fred is Fred Hamel, Aunt Lilly's second husband.
[16] Nutsie is Dottie's brother, Carl Ems.
[17] Holmesburg is a section of Philadelphia.
[18] Uncle John is John Francis Long, Helen's brother.

American boy and I am the proudest mother on Krewstown Road. You didn't hide behind the carrot tops. You keep your mouth shut and your eyes open and you will be a credit to me. No one loves you like I do because I understand you. This training is the best thing in the world for you.

It's far better having boys around than to live in the woods and still be bossed, hungry, and homesick. I have been through it all. That is why I put flowers on the kitchen table every day to make home a welcome place. Anybody can be like tooth picks of the same pattern. I appreciate fine linen, lace, flowers, my two boys and Dad. Then with plenty to cook, I am happy. Jive and tap has no allure for me. Just a hymn on Sunday and to know all is well and I am in Heaven. So Dear, be good and God will take care of you and Bless you. Dad got the tire and is feeling better. So don't worry over anything. Think of yourself.

Lots of love from all,

Mother & Dad & Roger & Joe

Brownie[19] cries for you and looks for you.

Sunday, October 15, 1944

Dear Son,

It's a cold and windy Sunday morning, but Dad is home and has us cooked out. By us, I mean Dottie and me. We were up at her house last night and brought her back here with us and she occupied your bed. Roger took her hot cocoa to wake her up, and we had waffles, sausage and grapefruit for breakfast. Now I have the roast beef in the oven and Joe is picking the

---

[19] Brownie is the Price family dog.

peppers and eggplant before old Jack Frost gets to work. Roger and Dad are up at Jonsey's,[20] putting on the new tire. Dot is in the kitchen listening to the radio and I am in the dining room. Joe brought me a nice bouquet, so I fixed them up. As you know, yesterday was my birthday. I sure did get some pretty cards and gifts. Dottie put on her card, 'From Eddie and Dottie', (perfume and hankies).

Granny was here until yesterday, so your bed has not been empty since you left. Granny, Roger and I went to the Regal[21] on Saturday afternoon to see "Home in Indiana". It was beautiful. We got more for our money at the Regal Matinee than I have seen in a long time. It was raining hard in the morning when Dad left, so he took the car as far as McAdams'. When we got out of the Regal, it was 5:30. Roger phoned from Bruggeman's gas station to Mrs. McAdams to tell Dad to pick us up. He was waiting there as we got off the car[22]. Granny left us to go home. She met Joe in Frankford[23] and I guess you know where she and Joe went. We waited and waited about one and a half hours. We were finally going home, and picking Dot up and going for my birthday supper somewhere, but we met Joe and Granny. We went in Daddy's favorite place. Then we left Joe and Granny and went on up to Ems'. We stayed an hour or so and then came home. Dot and I have been cleaning up the dishes and talking.

Now son, I guess you are in church service. Today is Worldwide Communion Sunday. So you will be busy in a good way. Dad says to please, please, no matter what you must do, not to talk back, or sass, so that in the end things will be easier for you. So please, dear, you don't know what you may go through, but I pray to God for you and wish you all the luck in the world. Much love from all of us.

---

[20] Jonsey's is a gas station owned by Fred Jones.
[21] The Regal is the Regal Movie Theater.
[22] Most likely a reference to a trolley car.
[23] Frankford is a section of Philadelphia.

I smooth your face. I love you.

Sunday Evening, October 15, 1944

Dear Edwin,

Dad just left to take Dottie home. We had a long, lazy day. It was nice out, sunshine all day, but cool. We were talking about you all day and I was so happy to know you had liberty and talked to us. Poor old Dad could hardly keep the tears back. We were different people when we got through talking to you. I was lying on the parlor sofa when the phone rang. I said Aunt Lilly was to call me up on Saturday, but I went out to forget my aches and pains. I was glad you called up on Sunday. I believe Dot will be here next weekend. If you get a chance on Sunday, call us up again. Do you know we talked for 1/2 hour? Somehow it made us feel better to hear your voice. All that Dad keeps saying is he hopes for the best for you.

We met Uncle Paul[24] in Frankford on Saturday night. He wished you good luck. Now honey, Dad is back. It's 9:30 and I guess you are fast asleep. My feet hurt and I am going to bed. Do you know this is the second letter I wrote you today? Joe mailed out 3 to you this afternoon; one from Dot, one from Roger, and mine. Dad will mail this tomorrow morning. I will walk down for the mail tomorrow, Monday, because I only had one letter so far on Friday. I was so happy to hear from you. You must realize everything is new and of course, you must start on the bottom round. Dad said to work hard and obey, and he wants to know if there is any chance of our being allowed to come down. At any rate dear, try to learn. No matter what they say, do it for your own good. "God will take care of you and His Will be done." All mothers must suffer because of those dirty Japs and that hound Hitler. Good

---

[24] Uncle Paul is Paul Engelman, Edwin's granduncle.

American boys must learn to protect us. We are proud of them all. Granny waves the flag for you all. What a day, when peace comes to the world.

Now honey, I will write every day, but news is scarce "in the sticks". The cat and dog need a chambermaid and Brownie missed you. He jumped on Dot and licked her face this morning and looked over the edge of her bed. So long for now. Nightie night.

Love from all.

Mother

Monday afternoon, October 16, 1944

Dearest Son Edwin,

Roger had luck, so he thinks. The school bus was not here at 9:30 and he has a cold. So I called him back here and now he is having a sandwich and a Pepsi. Your clothes came and we unpacked them and put what needed to go into the wash bag. I wasn't running for joy to get the box open. The man who brought it lives on Varee Road, and has four sons in the service. I thought well, the first knot is untied in the Mommy apron and it was awful hard to untie. But Dad, who is so smart, shed more tears than I did. Dot was wiping them away, so I am not as sneaky as they are; I guess we are all even.

By this time, you should be getting some letters, as I write every day. Just think. You left a week ago tomorrow. I've been in a daze ever since. Today, I tore up the parlor and it sure was a good thing I did. The moths ate two big holes as big as stove lids in the new rug under the new sofa. When I show Dad tonight, he will say I am the world's worst housewife. I sprayed 2 quarts of Larvex over everything and brushed all the furniture. They ate from the floor up through the mat. But the carpet and everything is clean. I can't understand it. They must be in the old wood.

News is scarce. Old Maria Harding[25] was buried on Saturday. She had the farm and stand above Jones'. Dad put the car in Bender's[26] this morning until Friday night. I must walk out to the Doctor's and meet Dad at 6 PM Tuesday evening to get a needle. Aunt Dot[27] will know in a week if she must go back to the hospital and get reopened.

Now son, if you travel the world, no food will ever taste like your mother's. Everybody always likes Mom's best of all. I know about that lousy saltpeter. Grandpop[28] used to overdo it in pickling the meat. But it all must be faced and if you come through, you will say like I do, I wonder how I ever did it. I wonder how I ever put up with 5 men and two bad boys, but God gives us the grace to do it.

I got your four letters all at once this morning. Hope to hear from you real soon.

Courage, strength and love.

Mother & All

Give my best wishes and lots of good luck to Herb[29]. I remember his curly hair and peg pants. Cheerio,

Mother X X

---

[25] Maria Harding was a family acquaintance.
[26] Bender's is an automotive dealer.
[27] Aunt Dot was Dorothy Noll, Helen's sister-in-law, married to Helen's brother, Robert Jefferson Long.
[28] Grandpop was Edwin Price Senior, father of Edwin Price Junior and grandfather of Edwin Charles Price.
[29] Herb was a family friend.

Wartime Letters Written from Mother to Son

Tuesday, October 17, 1944

My Dear Big Boy,

So far I have had 5 letters from you. I sort of looked for one today, but I guess you are busy learning how to be a sailor. Roger is home from school today again, as he has a real bad cold.

It's a beautiful sunny day. I have my own wash on the line and the wash man just came. I have some to iron and one bushel of green tomatoes to make relish. Roger is slicing them on the coleslaw cutter. I hate to think of peeling the onions as I have a cold and my eyes and nose keep me busy. I must walk out to the post office and pay Gallagher's[30] as I was out to the store Friday last when he came with the groceries. I will meet Dad at the Doctor's at 6. I must get another needle, but I can't tell if the other one did any good, because I have felt bad from the cold.

We have the house nice and warm and cleaned up. I got hooked anyway by Aunt Lilly. She asked me to serve the wedding feast and I said, "Oh, no, I can't do a party, it's too much work." I said, "You make reservations at Palumbo's[31] for 5 and that is less trouble for all." So she did. But last night she asked me if she could come up here around 4 o'clock to dress, so of course, being Dad's birthday and Fred's also, I will surely have to make a little extra fuss. So, I called up Williams for the flowers. Fred will pay for red roses for me, white for Aunt Lilly, yellow for Esther[32], boutonnieres for himself, Dad, and Roger, a bouquet for the table and a basket of flowers for the altar. The choir will be in practice; the pastor's brother at the organ, so maybe by the time you have a home, we will know all the tricks.

---

[30] Gallagher's was a Bustleton-area area grocery store.
[31] Palumbo's was a Philadelphia restaurant.
[32] Virginia Esther Bissinger. Aunt Lilly's daughter from her first marriage. Helen's niece.

The Home Fires

Dad mailed his letter off this morning, so you should be getting mail regularly by now. I will mail this off when I go out at 5 o'clock. I am glad it is a nice day. Roger is getting tired of slicing the tomatoes. I don't know any news. Not a flower left in the garden. Jack Frost got his work in.

Have you heard any radio since you left one week ago today? It's the longest week I put in for a long time, 18 years, but I always feel you need me and are real close to me. I smooth your face every night and walk over to say, "Well I know he's in bed and fast asleep." I guess you sleep well. I know you had a good home; but are no "lily" (Horse S--- and cabbage, that's us). Good, strong American backbones. We can work. Our hands prove that. Someday, maybe with two fine sons, I can have a fur coat and diamonds. But darling, I was always warm and pleased with the love of my two boys. Always be kind and loving and God smiles on you. I'll write more tonight.

Dot was going to wash her hair. I was so dumb. She could have done it here on Sunday. I didn't think until it was too late. She expected to walk over to see what news I had, but I guess she had letters from you. I let her read the first letter I got on Friday and the 4 yesterday from Monday she hadn't seen. I am happy to hear from you and I know you are busy and can't write. So dear, I think of you just the same all the time, every minute. Best love and kisses. I must hurry along.

Write soon. Good luck.

Mother & All   S.W.A.K. X X X X X

Dear Edwin,

I just saw by the government letter you sent. I was putting 4554 on all your letters and it's 4556. Maybe that is where your mail is going wrong. I sure hope not, as I wrote you two letters every day. Roger mailed one after school and Dad mailed one every morning. Son, I don't know how I made that mistake. It was probably my eyes, without wearing the glasses. Well, here's one addressed right. Love, love,

Mother

Tuesday, October 17, 1944

Dear Son,

This is the second letter I've written you today. I got as far as Banes Street. Mr. Gallagher[33] was there and he took me as far as the ration board. I gave them your books. It was closed when she let me in the door, and she said she would send me a receipt. Then I left your address at the minister's house and walked back and spent one hour with Mrs. Rupert[34]. After that, I went and met Dad at the Doctor's.

My blood pressure went up 20 points so the Dr. gave me two kinds of medicine and a liver-vitamin needle. My arm itches, but doesn't feel sore. It hurt some. He'll give me another one next Tuesday night. I don't know any other news.

Roger is out at church. Joe is peeling onions for the pickle I will make tomorrow. I must go on a strict diet, fruit, vegetables, and lean meat. Dad is in his favorite place. We went out tonight and turned on one burner to slow, and left the stew on high. Joe got in the door just when the pot was ready to burn.

---

[33] Mr. Gallagher was the proprietor of Gallagher's Grocery.
[34] Mrs. Rupert was a family friend.

I've got my mind on too many things. Bunny Griscom[35] goes this week and he doesn't want to, according to the English lady. Well, honey, lots of love. Nighty night. Be a good boy.

Mother

Wednesday October 18, 1944

Dearest Son Edwin,

It's a beautiful day here in Bustleton and I have canned 16 pints of relish and 1 quart of pickled onions, made the beds and finished all the rest of the household duties. Then I walked down through the garden to get the mail. Darling, it was like sweet music hearing from you. We had 4 cards, a letter and the paper. I read it from cover to cover. I know by that paper that you have every advantage to learn. I hope you can take every opportunity to do so. I feel much better today, but I am awfully hungry. How can I eat grapefruit with no sugar? The Doctor wants me to lose 15 to 20 pounds and eat no starches, sweets or fats. I must have plenty of vegetables, lean meat and fruit. So I guess I will have to do it if I want to keep fit. Maybe you won't know your fat Mommy at Christmas.

I am sure you are getting regular mail. I write twice a day. Dad takes one in the morning and then Roger mails one. I miss Roger today. Brownie has been barking and I've been looking, but can't see anyone. Mrs. Rupert gave me four beautiful roses.

Dr. Roseman[36] said he gave the fellow $50 for the new dog he gave Billie in place of Spot. Last night, he gave Dad two boxes of shells to give him. He

---

[35] Bunny Griscom was a neighbor.
[36] Dr. Roseman was the Price family physician.

said he would have given Dad $100 for Spot because after all, he kept him for two years. (Well, ain't we fools.)

Well son, I have lots of ironing to do, so I must hurry along this pen. I got the receipt for your ration books today. Dad filled his gas application out last night. Be good and ask God for the strength to carry you through. I will count the days until Christmas. What a torture. But God will smile on you.

All my love. Kisses from all.

Mother

(Enclosure – Item 1)

> DEWEY —(HOOVER'S FAVORITE SON)
> in Pittsburgh, Pa., July 31, 1944
> "AS I SEE IT, THE UNITED STATES SIMPLY CANNOT FACE ANOTHER PERIOD LIKE THE ROOSEVELT DEPRESSION."
> Under Hoover's Administration, Dewey in New York, saw long lines of Bank Depositors, Bank Doors closed, and scrip issued in lieu of money. He saw bread-lines, misery, and fear — also on street corners —
> **"APPLES" PEOPLE HAD TO SELL**
> PRESIDENT ROOSEVELT found millions of unemployed and hungry people... and through his direction they were fed... replaced misery and fear with confidence... business gained momentum... through his influence laws were enacted to bring new hope and comfort to the people of the United States.
> Our Commander-in-Chief
> is Winning the War
> Elect Him to Win the Peace!
> ROOSEVELT — STAUNCH AND SINCERE FRIEND OF LABOR, THE SOLDIER, THE FARMER, AND THE PEOPLE.

Wednesday, October 18, 1944

Dearest Son,

You know how every night, Dad asked, "Any mail?" Now it's more so. I have to read it before he eats. Hi-yo Silver![37] is going full force and I am here in the dining room as usual, thinking of you. Near or far, you have been on my mind a long time ever since you quit work. I hope and pray that whatever or wherever you are, God will smile on you. I have so much faith in you. I know that you miss us, but we miss you too and who knows but God alone. This is the best training for you. You are still my little boy. I can hardly realize that

---

[37] This is a reference to the Lone Ranger radio program.

Wartime Letters Written from Mother to Son

you are grown up and have left me. When you signed Old Nut[38] to Roger's card and I was ironing, I was thinking I could hear you and Grandpop. Old Bum and Old Nut have both left me. It seems like yesterday that you and he were scrambling around that bed and he was putting the covers on you.

One thing you have to be proud of is your home. No wonder, son. The food was the best in the world; out of the field and into the pot. You can't beat that no matter where you go.

I was thinking of all the jobs the Navy has to offer. Maybe you could get to be a vegetable buyer like Al Hermann[39] is a meat buyer at Camp Dix. But you decide what you think is best.

Dad is taking the cards down to work to show Clarence[40]. We haven't seen Dot since Dad took her home Sunday night. I guess when we go to the store Friday night we will stop there. It has been warm and nice here all day. I must go pay the phone and electric tomorrow. I hate the job, but must do the same as you. Joe laughed at "Have you a buck?" I guess you know we always helped you out.

I felt much better today. Roger mailed you a letter after school and Dad will mail this one in the morning. So here is hoping that when you have time, you will write us, as your letters are better than medicine for us. As always, we miss you, but know we are mighty proud of you. I am wearing the star on my coat that Dad bought for his mom. So I am proud to wear it for you. Nighty night. Love and hug tight.

Mother X X X X

---

[38] Old Nut and Old Bum were nicknames that Edwin Charles Price and his Grandfather; Edwin Price, Senior called each other.
[39] Al Hermann was a neighbor.
[40] Clarence was a co-worker of Edwin Price Junior at the Ford Motor company plant in Chester, PA.

Poets Corner

In a busy, Old World;
Let us never appear,
To neglect or forget
Those we hold dear.

Whatever Life may bring to us
Of Fortune or of Fame,
Whatever future years may add,
In honor to our Name,

There is a greater, richer joy,
That makes them all seem small,
A knowledge of each day well lived,
The greatest joy of all.

Bustleton Mother "E. Pluribus Unum."

Thursday, October 19, 1944

Dearest Darling Son,

Roger says hurry up. He wants to go to Baldwin's. I just got in from Frankford. I am tired and my feet hurt. It's a beautiful day. I paid the electric and bought a big Bonita mackerel for $1.25. I got 5 pork chops, "eleven points", 5 hot dogs and 2 pounds of sauerkraut. I priced liver. It is 82 cents per pound. I had the fish, so I didn't buy any.

I will write you tonight again when I have more time.

Lots of love,

Mother

Thursday, October 19, 1944

Dearest Son,

I sent you off a hurried letter this afternoon by Roger. Dad will mail this in the morning. First of all, darling, I would like to go to church this Sunday and so I won't get home much before one o'clock. But I will see Dot on the way to the store tomorrow night (Friday) and someone will be home here.

We don't know if Dad must work, so if you have liberty at 6:30 or later, or whatever time you can call, someone will be here, either Roger or Dot. I am so happy to have 3 letters from you today and also one for Dad. You know dear, we only worry about you doing what is the right thing, so you don't get punished. I was so proud of those nice letters you wrote. At heart, you are a good boy, but easily led by others.

As usual, I don't know any news, because I don't have Uncle Bill[42] telling me all the town gossip. Being on the other side of the tracks, it takes news a long time to reach me. Anyway, I am not interested in anybody outside. My little world consists of three people. They are all I think about. It is all I can do to keep going. I can't see where the medicine has helped. I still have a cold and I can't tell. I do have more color.

---

[42] Uncle Bill was Helen's brother, William Howard Long.

Now honey, about the ring. You did not answer the question. All I wanted to know was, "Where did you get the ring?" Aunt Dink[43] told me that Sissy[44] laid her ring on the sink. When she came downstairs it was gone. Snooky[45] and Byron[46] were the only ones in the house. She told Grandmom the same story and to be on the lookout for the ring. Grandmom didn't know that Aunt Dink told me the story. When she came up here on the day you left, she asked me where Dot got the ring, as Sissy's ring was exactly the same. She said, "Helen, there are rings that are alike." But I was worried, as I had never heard or seen anything. I remember admiring Dot's ring. All I want to know is where you got it. Please dear; tell me where and how you got it. That will be our secret. I will never mention what you wrote in the other letter. I trust you and love you too much. That is wonderful what you wrote. I admire you for your faith, and so, answer the question. All will be well.

Love,

Mother

I miss you too.

Friday, October 20, 1944

Dearest Son,

Well, here I am again and in a rush. It is 3 o'clock and I am still not through my work. Had a big wash on the line and went out to the Post Office and

---

[43] Aunt Dink was Lillian Ida Barnes, Helen's sister-in-law and the wife of John Francis Long.
[44] Sissy is Lillian Doreen Long, daughter of John Francis Long and Lillian Ida Barnes Long. Edwin Charles Price's first cousin.
[45] Snooky was the daughter of Robert Jefferson Long. Edwin Charles Price and Sissy's first cousin.
[46] *Byron was Byron Norman Long, son of John Francis Long and Lillian Ida Barnes Long. He was Sissy's brother and Edwin Charles Price's first cousin.

came back by 12:30, cleaned upstairs, cleaned the dining room, brought the wash in and folded it, and put the supper on to cook, and still want to do another job. So you see, as usual, the clock could still have 24 more hours on it and I couldn't catch up. I must do ironing and scrub down the front steps. I got out all your clothes this morning and looked them over. I am taking your brown suit, your last new pants (blue), and one brown pair to the tailors if we go to Frankford tonight.

Dad said, "Don't tell the boy," but you know, old dear, what poor Dad suffers. He has it in his knee. It was a sight to see him last night crawling up that railroad bank. I said to Joe, "My God, come see him." Joe and I got him fixed on the couch with the electric pad and Sloan's Lineament and he slept all through the radio noise. He is worn out. Now that he has such nice letters from you, poor old Pop will get better. So if you get this letter before you call on Sunday, don't let on I told you. He was so proud of the letters you wrote him. He took them off to show Clarence this morning. I think he has a good helper in Clarence. Dad told me last night that he heard that Ford was going to pension men $100 a month who worked there 25 years. Do you think Dad can go 9 more? If he is like Grandpop, he can. Dad is strong, but suffers with colds, etc.

Now darling, I got the home fires burning, the sauerkraut cooking, and Roger is home now early on Friday. If Dad gets the car, which he expects tonight, I guess we will see Dot, as we will stop if she is home. So until then, be good, and you will make us happy. We love you and wish you were here for supper. It's raining here.

Love,

Mother X X X

The Home Fires

I got your two letters today. And so dear, I wrote you the little poem I put in your money belt, so that when you are on Dog Watch, you can always have memories when you are cold and lonely. Just remember, Mother is with you and you talk to her and God. God answers prayers. I know. Look up at the stars. They are the windows of Heaven. Each one is guarded by an Angel, and each Angel is one of God's chosen children. They send messages to mothers. What is more beautiful than the sky? It has many moods, just like people. It sends angry winds and storms and makes us realize that God is in Heaven. So never be lonely. "Lo, I am with thee always." So sayeth the Lord, you are ever in my heart. Until we meet again, blessed be the tie that binds. Our hearts in Christian love, God smile on thee, Darling.

Love from

Mother X X

Friday Night   Dad's knee is much better tonight

Dearest Son,

I wrote to you this afternoon and Dad came home and ate his supper and then took the car out, as well as 2 gas stamps to Fred Jones[47]. He went to Ems' before he came home for supper, but Dot was not home. So he went down to the firehouse and waited for her. The Florida storm struck down here about 1 PM. Believe me, everything had to be lashed down. Joe was wet to the waist. It just started pretty bad when Roger got home. I had the home fires burning and Dad and I are not going to Frankford. I ordered two chickens from Charlie, and Dad will get a few things tomorrow night. I guess you know I am starved. You might as well shoot me and be done with it. No

---
[47] Fred Jones, owner of automotive garage, "Jonsey's".

butter, no bread, ice cream, cake, candy, olive oil, mayonnaise, in other words, all the things I like, I can't eat. The only thing I miss is the bread. I simply am never satisfied unless I have bread.

Dad will pick Dot up on the way home tomorrow night, so she will hold your bed down. I put all new sheets, blanket, and pillows on it, and shaped it up so she sinks in. She told Dad she got 7 or 9 letters from you and wrote you. I hope you are not too homesick. Honey, I often told you I was even homesick here with your father. I was homesick for 20 years, but after I had Roger, it left me. I went through torture while I worked away from home. I loved my brother Charlie so much. And now, dear, I must go through worse for love of you. I have suffered for nine months waiting for September, when you would leave me. I pray to God every day to guide you and keep you. But I have faith in God, which keeps me alive.

Now dear, you asked me about Dot. I know you, but I don't know Dot. I have only met her a few times. But I kissed her goodnight and I looked at her sweet face. I thought she is so young and my darling has picked her from all the flowers that grow. Then I said to myself, well, if he chooses her, her married life will never be cruel like mine. I will see to that. You will never know the hardships I had here, being sick and not able to work, but had to do it. That is why I think I am in Heaven now, warm and loved. It's awful to be alone because Daddy is on the road all day and half the night, and me with no one to talk to. Now I have the radio, and my children.

You see, I chat with you every day and nothing is nicer than to have a mate who likes you and the same things you like. And so I know, dear, whatever you do, I am your mother. All I want is to see you happy and settled. The only way to have a nice home like you want is to have a good start and you must save before you marry. So begin now. Now is the time. Then when you get back to us again, all will be well.

Dad ordered the Christmas turkey from the man at Ford's, so I will count the days. And if you don't get home on the 25th, we will celebrate Christmas the day you come home. I have a good icebox. So I'll say goodnight now. Lone Ranger is on. Wind and rain, I hope you are well and not out in it. Lots of love from all.

Mommy.

Dad got the car from Bender's.

Edwin, write a letter to Roger so he gets it on Tuesday the 24th, his 12th birthday. Also if you get any time, write a nice one to Dad so he gets it by Friday the 27th, the big day. Aunt Lilly gets married.

Dad said to write and tell him what you are drilling or what you must do. He would like to know about your training and your officers, and if you have made many mistakes. He was so pleased with your letters and is so proud of them. He will write soon again. Love to you from all.

October 21, 1944

Dearest Son,

All is quiet. Dad just called up from Frankford. It has rained and blown since dinnertime Friday. I have the house nice and clean and the home fires burning. The baker[48] has been in and gone. He said he sent you good wishes.

I got two letters from you today; one where you said you had a sore on your big toe. Now dear, please have it looked after. You know what foot trouble

---

[48] The baker, area baker who made home deliveries.

you have had, and perhaps your Navy shoes did it. Whatever the cause, when you have a sore, no matter where it is, it hurts, and more so on your feet.

I am glad you are getting more content. As time goes by, like everything else, you can get used to it. I've been all through it lots of times. I used to go up to Mt. Airy Deaf School and sit along the fence. When my sister Clara came out for exercise during the rest period, I would have a spoon and a glass of spaghetti or things I knew she liked. I would hurry up and put it in her mouth. One time, she pleaded to be taken home under my mother's coat. She said, "Oh Mother, I will be happy with black coffee and molasses bread." You see, we thought it was awful when we had no milk. Up there, they had a cow and didn't use any milk in the coffee nor drink any. So, the world goes on. What is one person's meat is another person's poison. Life is just what we make it to suit us.

The evening sun is trying to shine. I hope it clears up. Dot will come over tonight with Dad. We are having chicken for Sunday, so you do a good job to help keep the chickens in every pot in America. I am counting the hours. I hope to hear your voice on Sunday. So until then, cheerio, 15 hugs and 47 kisses. Love from

Mother

Sunday Evening

Dearest Son,

Today was a beautiful day, but I did not get out. It was a good thing I didn't go to church or else I would have missed your phone call, as I usually don't get home until 1 PM. Dad, Roger, Dot and I ate most of the roast chicken,

The Home Fires

and now Dad and I are alone. Roger and Dot went stepping out to the movies. Dad took them to the trolley. They will call up from Frankford and Dad will meet them and take Dot home. We had a lazy, quiet day. There isn't anything new to write about. Dad said the new gas tank is on and the car is running pretty good. I haven't been in it yet.

We were thinking of you all day. I woke up Saturday morning at 4 AM. I thought I heard you call me. I could not go to sleep. I came down to Dad. I had a cup of coffee and went back up and thought, today is Saturday and I don't have to get up for Roger. But no, I couldn't sleep. I was awfully restless until I talked to you today. I went in the parlor and Dot and I ran a race. Roger put one of those sailor hats on Dot's head. She woke up. She thought she was walking down the street with a hat on. She felt her head and looked around. She laughed. Dad had put the blanket on her. He has the home fires burning so hot that he has Dot and I cooked. We had supper and now Dad and I are back where we started. Alone. But dear, we are thankful to have something to eat and to be warm. Dad said to tell you working in the mess hall is no worse than slinging shit from the pigpen, or that load he got at Howard Smith's[49] that time. What pay? Remember, to every rose a thorn, but ain't the rose sweet? Darling, that's why I love flowers. I washed enough piss pots in my time. But God gives you grace, good with bad. So Cheerio. Lots of love, kisses and hugs.

Mother

---

[49] Howard Smith was most likely an area farmer.

Dear Edwin,

Miss Monroe[50], the library teacher, praised you to Roger. She said how much she liked you and how you used to help her. She asked Roger where you were. Some other teacher came in and she called Roger back and introduced him as Edwin's brother and made a big fuss today. So------

(Enclosure – Item 2)

---

[50] Miss Monroe was most likely the Librarian at Woodrow Wilson High School attended by Edwin Charles Price.

WILSONEWS

VOLUME X   October 23, 1944.   NUMBER 2

SPOOKS   SHIVERS
THRILLS
GHOSTS   SCREAMS

!!! MURDER !!!

Read these MYSTERY books from the SCHOOL LIBRARY!

Biggers.....Behind That Curtain
   (Charlie Chan thriller)
Blank.......Beverly Gray Freshman
   (college mystery for girls)
Burrough....From Snow to Sun
   (Good for boys)
Cleland.....Mystery at Shadylawn
   (Boarding School mystery
   for girls)
Doyle.......Hound of the Basker-
   villes & Sherlock Holmes
   for Boys
Keeler......Sing Sing Nights
   (Who was innocent?)
Kummer......The Perilous Island
   (mystery in the Aleutians)
Monsell.....Secret of the Gold
   Earring (for girls only)
Pease.......Night Boat-short sto-
   ries (Ted Moran mysteries
   for boys)
Rohmer......Hand of Fu Manchu
   (This man is a fiend!)
Seaman......The Pine Barrens Mys-
   tery (Better than a Nancy
   Drew!)
Van Dine....The Bishop Murder Case
   (Philo Vance at his best)

                      RICHARD PARKS

** ** ** ** ** ** ** ** ** **

IN MEMORY
OF LOIS RUSCHE

Dear Lois, how we miss her, Lord;
Her laugh, her cheerful smile.
But thank you anyway, dear Lord,
We had her for a while.
              JOAN S. COULSTON

** ** ** ** ** ** ** ** **

HOME FRONT

MISS LAUVER, our school counsellor, reports:
We have 18 boys on the Farm Work Program, 4 are out of school for 3 weeks and the others work after school.
There are 5 students who attend school just half a day and have a job the rest of the day.
RALPH WIEHLER is taking the course in Agriculture at the Weidner School, Broad & Olney, and enjoying the work immensely.
Three of our boys are taking the War Production Course at Mastbaum Annex and expect to go into war work in 6 months.
       JUANITA BUTTS & F. SCHARD

** ** ** ** ** ** ** ** **

BEWARE

The school nurse is on YOUR trail!! Get those physical defects corrected! It is your DUTY as an AMERICAN to keep HEALTHY.
See the gym. teachers for further information.   DEVOY

** ** ** ** ** ** ** ** ** ** **

Cottman	ANY BOY	Devereaux
Brouse Socket	over 14 years old interested in a Loretto part time job and	Summerdale
Longshore	living in these	Comly
	boundaries -- see MR. WRIGHT	

Wartime Letters Written from Mother to Son

CHATTER

.....The SUB DEB CLUB is inviting the ex-Sub Debs to a Hallowe'en party the 26th of October.
　　　　　　　　　　RITA

.....What two girls in the SUB DEB CLUB had to sing like Frank Sinatra and what girl swooned??
　　　　　　　　　　FLOSS

.....Who is the girl in Book 8 that got stuck in a locker?
What happened to Jean Cunningham's teeth?
　　　　　　　　　　ARF

.....Almost everybody in Book 6 is flaunting his Spanish. We all have the latest issue of the Reader's Digest IN SPANISH.
　　　　　　　　　　R.D.

.....In an 8A class a teacher gave two girls demerits for being happy!!!
　　　　　　　　　　ELSIE

.....Students of Book 17 are so jive crazy that when a certain girl was called on to give her formal talk, her topic was "Harry James"!
　　　　　　　　　　JUNE

..... was the boy in room 319 that wrote on the board "Kinds of Clauses" - "Santa Claus"?
　　　　　　　　　　TRIXIE

.....Who is the girl in Book 8 that had a doggie roast on Friday the 13th and has been absent ever since -- too many hot dogs?
　　　　　　　　　　ARB

.....Class motto:
"Don't fuss or bawl
　　or make a scene!
Be calm, like us-- Book 17 !"

.....JUST JIVE:
　　　　　　　　　　ELDA
If you are called "Rigor Mortis" you're a "drip"!
a creep -- a drip
a tick -- a creep that gets
　　　　under your skin
S-O-S -- Slave of Sinatra
　　　　　　　　　　MAX

****

LOST

A small red draw-string purse in the east lunchroom.
A small light green purse, on the stairs or near the girls' lockers on the first floor.
Please return to room 217.
MAXINE CORNELL
　　　DOROTHY CAMERLENGO.

"LADY BUG'S LIST"

...The boys and girls of Book 6 are supposed to have a hayride, doggie roast and barn dance-- if they ever decide on a date - and if anyone can come!

...Did you hear about the moron who always salutes the ice box? He heard it was General Electric!

...A certain girl in Book 6 is very smart. She became a junior in college on Saturday, Oct. 14!! Of course, she's back with us again; but she did get to see the Penn- William & Mary game!

...Who is this EM that insists on wearing a skull cap and orange sox???

...There is one class that practises lend-lease. Each member brings something, then they all put together and have a lunch.

****

DENNY'S DISCLOSURES !!!

...Your left eye must have a wonderful personality, because your right eye is always looking at it.

...Have you seen Howie?
Howie who?
Fine, thank you. How are you?

...Is Boo here?
Boo who?
Well, you needn't cry about it.

****

FINE REWARD

Members of Book 17 didn't have any homework for Wednesday. Miss Reilly made a bargain with them. "If you have 100 % in the PATRIOT you will have no homework for one evening."
Well, they did get 100% and the assignment was, "Homework: enjoy having no assignment! It probably won't happen again!!"
　　　　　　　　　　ELDA

****

WILSONEWS
STAFF for this issue:

JEANNETTE REINL　　ANN PARKER
PAUL DENARO　　　ROBERT HALLEY
ROY REINARD

SPEED ⋁ DAY　　BUY MORE
　　　　　　　　　WAR STAMPS

Send me your Navy paper.

The Home Fires

Sunday afternoon, October 22, 1944

Dearest Son,

I am waiting for the potatoes to get done for supper, so I will send you off a few lines for when Roger goes to church. Dot wrote you a big letter and then we both had 40 winks in the parlor. Dot was on one couch and me on the other. Now I am up, getting supper before Roger goes. We have a roast chicken with filling and mashed potatoes, lima beans, jello, etc. We had veal cutlet, tomato cocktail, dried limas, corn and baked potatoes right after we talked to you.

You sounded just like your usual self. I thought you cursed pretty much. Pal, take the orders. You know your Grandmother Price used to issue me orders every morning. Before you were born, one morning, I was sick. She was telling me what I had to do. I said, "Now listen, don't command me. In the army they give soldiers orders, but I am not in the army. My father told me when I was 21, I could do as I please and I'm seven years older." But I had to do whatever she said, sick or not. Now I have no boss and life is just as complicated with other worries. I can't seem to get rid of this cold in my chest, and this forthcoming wedding has me hooked.

Well Pal, I sent you off a letter by Joe and I will get you some candy the first chance I get, because you can have my share. No candy for Mom. Honey, give my regards to all the boys. All learners must do the hardest, dirtiest work.

I hope you "learn your lessons quick". Then you can get out of "Erringer's[51] Room". There are plenty of "Mrs. Waltons[52]" and so life goes on. Until that

---

[51] Erringer was most likely an elementary school teacher.

time, I am counting on my big boy to say "Sir", and until I see you, "I am in the Navy, Mr. Brown[53]."

It was nice to talk to you today. We would have been sick if we hadn't heard from you. So, Cheerio.

Love,

Mother (Send Roger a buck for Tuesday)

Monday afternoon, October 23, 1944

Dearest Edwin,

Here is a new week, Roger's 12th birthday and 2 weeks tomorrow since you've been gone. I can see you coming in to see your new brother. Now you are Uncle Sam's big boy and still my dear little one. To me, you are both babies. I used to think you would never grow up. All of a sudden, I had a big tall, fair-haired, blue-eyed boy, talking of getting married. Dot and I laughed yesterday. She was writing to you and I was holding down the couch and we got to talk about love. Roger asked her if she loved you. I said the love bug has bitten her or else she wouldn't be writing letters on a beautiful Sunday afternoon. She will never forget my Eddie boy. If she travels the highway of life, she can't forget my Eddie boy's soft bed. Dad calls her baby and I went in and kissed her. I used to smooth your face.

Poor old Mrs. Spence and Mrs. McAdams called me up to tell me they heard from you. Poor Mrs. Spence had called me at 8 o'clock this morning and then

---

[52] Mrs. Walton was Edwin's third grade teacher. She flunked him 3 straight years. After the third time, Helen took Edwin to school and questioned the decision. Edwin Charles was tested and promoted to 6th grade.
[53] It is unknown who Mr. Brown was.

at 2 to tell me she had such a nice letter from you. Now honey, I don't know any news. Old Jack Frost did his mischief again last night. We have a few beets left and that finishes the crop. We had too much anyway. I have a big wash out. We didn't go to Frankford Friday night, so Dad is going to run your things down tonight. We met Roger and Dot last night (Sunday) and took Dot home. She will be down here Thursday night to do my hair for Aunt Lilly's wedding. She and Roger will be at the church door, Friday night. So I am busy and tired. I must comb my hair yet. I have a big chicken on cooking.

It's a beautiful day. Three letters in the box. One Friday, one Saturday, & one to Dad. Dear, please get yourself some medical attention for your feet and cold. Honey, I would often have done lots more for you, but you wouldn't let me. Just like now. Go get your feet fixed. They will put healing powder or salve on them. Dear, write whenever you can. It helps to ease our worries.

Now dear, I will thank that nice boy who was so kind to comfort you. Don't cry about or for anything. Don't you remember a lady told me one time how beautiful our lilacs were? I said, "Yes, they should be beautiful, I water them with tears." I wouldn't want anyone to see me crying and I would steal away to the lilac bushes. I would talk to God and maybe even a bluebird. I would come back up and make the butter and cook. So life goes on. You smile and march. Say my mother is fat and sick, but if she could, she would be up front, where the American flag is flying, and proud of me. The day the sirens blow to signal the war is over, I will grab my hat and the three flags I have ready, and I will go as fast as I can. I will walk all the way to Holmesburg carrying the American flag. The day I see you coming up over that railroad bank, I will run all the way to meet my sailor boy.

So march and march, so you can be a good sailor. I am proud of my people. They come from the best Pennsylvania stock. It's boys like you and the Culps and all the rest that keeps the chicken in the pot. "No apples on street corners" do we want. We are people of the soil. From the soil, your old Grandpop made a living. We ate the best food in the world. So fight on, young and fine like you are. None better. March on.

You weren't brought up a sissy. You can wash and iron and cook. You know you used to say, "One buck, Mom" to scrub the kitchen. You can sling navy bags as well as you sling 100 pound fertilizer bags on the state truck. So dear, cheerio, I put the good in you, now is the time to benefit by it. We are for you, right or wrong. But do your best, I can't ask for more. Lots of love and kisses.

Mother

Monday Evening

Dear Edwin,

Roger is out in the town. He took your daily letter. The supper is on cooking and it is too late for me to take a rest, 5:30. The sun is so pretty, shining in the dining room, and so I will chat with you. You used to come in around this time and lay on the floor where I had to step over you to get to the icebox. So you say you look out the window and wonder what I am doing and if we think of you. Well, here is what I've been thinking. Last night I put on Dad's overcoat to go pick Dot up. The moon was so low, down over Ray's[54] house. I said the moon in the western sky hangs low and I think of you and the sweet boy long ago. For Uncle John said, in the South Pacific, the stars and moon are always so low. Looks like you can reach out of the foxhole and touch them. So I said, my dear ones, I wonder if you see the moon tonight.

---

[54] Ray was Ray Wenker, Price family neighbor.

Today I was thinking of you, and I hip hopped over the stones down to the mailbox for your letters and I said, "You can travel the highways of the world and knock, knock on every door, but you will never, no, no, never find one who loves you like me, your fat Mommy." I can hear you say, "Oh, that's 40 years ago." But you see, we always wanted to spare you life's rough highways. But war has come and your country needs you. That's what God made mothers for, to guide and serve.

I told you what the tattoo stands for. You can never erase that. And that is just the way. I have scars, deep inside my heart from hurts I have had through life. All through the years, two eyes of blue come smiling through at me. I have served my sweetheart well. Now, I look for happiness for my boys. The only way they will find it is to obey, love and honor, both at work, play and love.

Booze, cards, nightclubs, smoking and loud language never had any room in my life. I saw that in many places. Flowers and soft music and food and warmth were always a joy and pleasure. I often wonder at the talk of some women. I told you and Roger. We all know it.

Monday Evening

Well Edwin,

Here I am again. As usual, I have no news. Dad has gone off to Frankford with 3 pairs of pants, your brown suit and your brown jacket. Supper is over and the dishes washed. So I will finish this letter. But news is so scarce. I hardly know what to write about. The Lone Ranger is going full force. I cannot concentrate. Dad took back 21 beer bottles and a car full of clothes. I told him to go to Dairy Maid and get you some candy and I ordered some cookies from the baker. Roger is a pest. He has been a little bugger all week, so I am fixing him. No birthday present. No money. This year there won't be any Uncle Bill to bring in an armload. It serves him just right. I must clamp down on him, or he will just sprout out too fast now that you are not here to tone him down.

We got the Maryland roadmap. Dad has been down that way before. You are quite a way from Spencerville, where the Margerunis[55] live. Now dear, if I hadn't talked to you on Sunday, I would have been awfully worried over those Friday and Saturday letters, because of your headache and cold. No matter if they do say they only give you castor oil. That is a password. That's so every little pain you get, you are not running to sickbay. Do you have wooden barracks or tents? Do you have stoves in them or are they centrally heated? I have never forgotten how shocked I was at seeing the wreckage of what was Camp Dix after the first war. Dear, whatever the conditions, it's better than Europe or the Jap foxholes. Be brave, courage. My heart is broken, but "God's Will be done". Mother's love is beside you. I will keep you warm and lull you to sleep next to my heart. Cheerio. Love to all your pals. Have faith, courage and hope for the best. I am proud of you.

Love,

Mom

October 24, 1944

Dearest Edwin,

Honey, I hip hopped down the lane about noon and got 3 letters; Joe's, Rog's, and mine. I have all the clean curtains up, all the walls wiped, and the

---

[55] Margerunis were most likely family friends.

windows cleaned inside. A smoked neck is cooking, the devil food birthday cake baked and iced, and so I guess you know I am on the last foot, getting ready for Aunt Lilly's wedding. It's a lovely sunny day, after a heavy fog and frost this morning. The roof of your car had a thin coating of ice on it. So Old Man Winter is just around the corner. I guess you know I am not all fussed up, because I made so many parties for you and Roger. This is just one of the times he will have to miss. I hunted all over for the candles I had left from your party as I had bought two dozen, but I can't seem to find them.

I found 24 blue candles so everything is okay. I had some Halloween favors and I filled them with candy so I guess, "we have party". Well son, I must go to the Doctor's tonight again. I am tired so it's just about time for Roger to come home and I would like to get a little rest before supper. Roger must go to the shoemaker's for my shoes. Fifty cents to get two little rubber heels on them. I haven't written to Uncle John in a long time. Maybe if you get a chance, you can drop him a line. Tell him how proud you are of him, now that you know some of the training he had to go through.

John F. Long W.T. 1/C 244-79-39
N. Const. Batt. 82, Co. C. Plat. 6.
c/o Fleet Post Office
San Francisco, California

Edwin, Howard Lewis'[56] grandfather, and your grandfather (my pop) were brothers, so you come from the same stock on your mother's side. His Grandmother made the best bread in the world and after 30 years, I can still smell it and the good grape jelly. Many a slice she gave me as I was cold and hungry, coming from a long winter day at work, all frozen and with a snot nose. You are lucky. At least you have food. (I wish you were here to help

---

[56] Howard Lewis was a cousin.

blow out the 12th birthday candles.) Cheerio, darling. How is your cold?

Lots of love.

Mother

Tuesday Evening, October 24, 1944

Dearest Son Edwin,

Here I am again. I think I wrote reams of paper in World War One. But at the rate I am going now, I think I will need to buy it by the truckload. This is my second letter today, for as you know, I write twice every day. Roger takes one, and Dad takes the other. Tonight, he came back from Joe. He had the letter in his pocket as he was going to the church at 7 o'clock. Dad also wrote you tonight. We just got back from the Doctor's and he is going away until December 15th. He gave us a double dose. We each got a needle. Dad got less vaccine than last week. He said the dose he gave him last week was too strong if he had it so bad in his knee. So tonight the dose was less. He said I was worse off than Dad. He gave me a stronger medicine to make blood ,and to help my nerves. I got so tired. I told you I was going to take a rest. Just as I lay down, Mrs. Rupert came. I gave her a piece of Roger's birthday cake. My hands are getting real red from the medicine in the needle. I can see it showing through my skin. I am better than I was. My arm hurts where the needle jammed in. But I guess it all comes in life.

I haven't any news from Bristol[57] as yet. Everything was the same last Sunday. Aunt Dot was up there. Now, honey I was so relieved about the ring. I was afraid you got it from Snooky or Byron. I never mentioned the story to

---

[57] This is a reference to where Helen's brother, Charlie, lives. The "news" would be the impending birth of Charlie's next child.

anyone. So I can tell Grandmom she was wrong. It was not Sissy's ring. Is that right? I didn't say you took it. I thought maybe you got it from Byron or down at Uncle Bob's[58]. (Byron and Snooky were the only ones there when it got lost.)

Well honey, Joe went to meet Roger and I am going to bed now. I had my coffee. Many kisses. Roger is here. So long for now.

Love, Mother XXXXXXXXXXXX

Wednesday afternoon, October 25, 1944

Dearest Son,

Well here are a few lines of your usual daily letter. While I am taking a rest, I will chat with you. I got your two letters, telling me that you had your feet fixed up. I have cleaned from the garret steps to the cellar steps, put white paper over your overcoats and got your bed and room all prettied up. I am so tired. Where I got the needle last night, my arm hurts. It's 20 of 3 and I have Roger's Sunday suit to press and my black coat. Then I think I am pretty near ready except for the food. I ordered a big order from Gallagher's and will have to go to Frankford tomorrow and meet Dad on his way home. He will take the car tomorrow (Thursday), as Aunt Lilly's big day is Friday at 8:30. We will pick Dot up, as she will do my hair. When I get down to it, (a few pennies ahead) I will get something for her for doing it. You know, something pretty. I imagine she doesn't have too many pretty things.

It's a lovely October day. I don't know any news, haven't heard from anyone today. Roger will soon be home and he is going over to Joe. I read Joe's letter to him, but not the part where you said about the kiss. I am fussy about

---

[58] Uncle Bob is Robert Jefferson Long. Edwin's uncle, Helen's brother, and Snooky's father.

who I kiss or let kiss me. I knew you meant well, all in fun. Dad wrote you last night and he shed plenty of tears over you going. I often wonder why you had such a mean disposition. But I guess now you know how easy Dad was. I saw so much at home. As I get older, I knew my father was right. But we are all young once and God is always watching and in the end, only He knows the answers. So be a good Christian and God will smile on you. I am beside you on all those long night watches. Just talk to Dad and me. We love you, so smile and be happy. I wear my star for you. Until I write tonight again. Cheerio.

Love X X

Mother

Wednesday evening, October 25, 1944

Dearest Son,

The Lone Ranger is going full force and I am going to bed early. I am tired after a big day. It was a beautiful day. We let the heater go out on Tuesday. Waiting so long in the Doctor's office last night, I got cold. When we came home, Dad made a fire. Boy, am I cooked out tonight. It's 82 degrees in the dining room.

Dad just came out and asked me to ask you a question. He said you told him on Sunday you had $12.00. So why didn't you have any to send Roger $1.00? I got your box of cookies and candy ready to mail off. Dad tied and wrapped it. The cookies are so rich, I am afraid they will all be broken up by the time you receive them. Let me know. I have my feet in the big white basin soaking them while writing to you. "Two birds with one stone", eh?

I don't know a thing outside of the fact that about 15 will be here after Aunt Lilly is married. That's Dad's fault. I sure wanted to go to Palumbo's. As usual, I am hooked, but because it's Dad's only relative, I must do my stuff. I guess you know I can do my part, but Saturday I will not be worth a plugged nickel. While you are on the night watch, you can say, Mom is doing her duty too. I have been sleeping better because when I go to bed, I say, well "Old Nut", I guess you are asleep. So I tuck the covers up over your bare arms and say, "So far you are safe. God smile on you." About 3:30 I wake up and I look at the stars and I wish. I wish upon a star. They are so low this time of year. I wonder where you are and all my love goes afar. So until you hear from me again, I'll say cheerio. Nighty night. Love and kisses from us all. Dad was real happy with his letter today. Write when you can.

Love,

Mother

October 26, 1944

Dearest Son,

It's early morning and the day is breaking fair. I have a long busy day ahead. But in order not to disappoint you in your usual letter, I will write these few lines while drinking my morning coffee. I couldn't get to sleep last night. Then I dreamed that I looked in your room. It was like the door was between the two front windows of my room toward the railroad, and I said, "Dad, Edwin didn't come home last night. His bed hasn't been slept in." Then I said, "Oh what ails me? Edwin is in the Navy." I woke up. I couldn't see you, but I saw your bed like I made it up yesterday, all clean sheets. I folded Dottie's pajamas up and put them beside yours in the drawer. Then I put Friendship Dusting Powder over the blanket and pillows. So I guess I had it on my mind.

I may get your box off. Or Roger may take it. I just hate this trip to Frankford today. I will be so glad when Saturday comes. So think of me and that will keep me up and make me happy.

Roger had his cake and I put $2.00 in his card and wrote, from Dad, Edwin & Mother. He said, "What's two bucks?!" So you see, what is hardship for us is nothing to children. It should have been ten cents. Then maybe he would learn the value of money, but we all learn the hard way it seems. Now dear, about your money problem; Edwin, straight from the heart, money goes through your hands quite easy. So for Dad's sake, for Dot's and mine, send home an $18.75 Bond or a $20.00 money order.

50.00 month
-6.40 Ins
-18.75 Bond

$25.15 Balance is enough to care for your spending.

I will have a hard job paying the telephone. In fact, we will have to turn in a Bond. We have four left, after turning in seven to pay for coal and this month's car payment. It took Daddy a year to get them, one a month, so that our home is gone again. Do your part and all will be well. Your box cost $1.00 for candy and 60 cents for cookies. It all counts.

Love,

Mother

The Home Fires

Thursday, October 26, 1944 (No baby as yet at Uncle Charlie's)

Dearest Honey,

Hip, Hop, down the lane. It's 1 o'clock and I got Roger's suit pressed and on the last lap, a good stew in the pot and I still have Roger's bed to make. Then I will get ready to go to Frankford. I got the bracelet. It's beautiful and the first one I owned since I was 18. You know the broken one in the jewelry box. Dad's card came. It was unsealed and $1.00 was in it. I sealed it up. One came from Clarence and I got a beautiful one for him. While I am out I will get one for Roger. I wrote you this morning and I will mail them both with the box. I got about four letters and Roger and Dad's mail and the bracelet and the check for the four bonds and one from Uncle John. The insurance policy I will put with all of ours. Dear, the letter I wrote this morning told you about saving your money. I cried all the way up the lane. You have got too good a heart. But just like the pin you gave me, I will always cherish them and keep them. I used to wish I could buy jewels for my mother. Don't you know dear, your blue eyes are my jewels, your fair hair, my gold, and your soft smooth skin, my lily? All I ever wanted in life was nice boys. I used to wonder why you acted like you did. I pray that if you are as good as Dad, you will be okay. The only thing lacking is education. Education opens the door to opportunity. Make friends with people of standing. They can help you in this world. I guess that is why Bill Long is on destroyer escort. Dear, men higher up know where to place you. Do obey orders. I must run. But let me kiss you sweet and smooth on your face and send you all my heart's love.

I am so worried we won't get home in time for your phone call. I hope we do. Well dear, I may have to miss the Friday letter. But if I can squeeze it in, I will. Lots of love. Thanks for all.

Mother

Wartime Letters Written from Mother to Son

Thursday night 11:30

Dearest Son Edwin,

Well honey, it's nearly a new day, 11:30 and Mommy is so tired, but I want to say a few words because Friday I know I won't get time to write. But if I can squeeze it in, I will. Honey, I mailed your box and two letters as I told you. I was glad to talk to you as I told you I rushed from 3:30 on. Dad and I hurried so fast. We just got to Dot's house as she got off the bus. She had supper here. As you called, I got everything ship shape, apple pie order, flowers to nuts. Dot has my hair in dozens of curls, and two beautiful white bows tied on the white candles. Just you wait 'til you get married. You will have the finest show in Bustleton. I kissed Dot goodnight and said I smooth your face. Dear, I thought you didn't sound so happy over the phone. I think it is just too good to be true that you got so near to home. It makes your absence a little easier. Joe is still doing the dishes, and the laundry just came back. I don't know how I can crowd it in tomorrow, but if not, I will put it in the cellar. I got $5.00 worth of lunchmeat, pineapple pudding, all kinds of fancy candy, olives, pickles, cheese, rye bread, baked lima beans, homemade rolls, wedding cake, pretzels, and I made potato salad so, I guess all that needs to be said is, "I do."

So cheerio. Mommy is on one leg. Thanks a million for that beautiful gift and Dad's present. Joe and everyone have gone to bed. So, I must say goodnight too. Be a good boy. Lots of love and kisses.

Mother

Saturday, October 28, 1944

Dearest Son,

It is 1:15 in the morning. The dishes are all washed. My feet hurt and I am ready to fall in bed. So, I will make this short and sweet. Dear, I had a young, tall, fair-haired sailor boy at my table. We had 18. Dottie looked just beautiful with a white wreath of flowers in her hair and a corsage of red roses and white chrysanthemums. Esther cried terribly. Aunt Lilly looked lovely and Dot said I looked like a bride.

Everything went off to perfection. I was thinking of you the whole time. So dear, I will say goodnight. Dot will be here Saturday night. That is tonight. Lots of love and kisses.

Love,

Mother & All

Saturday evening

Dearest Sailor Son,

Old Nut, I got two letters from you this morning and they didn't sound so cheerful. What is wrong with your foot? Is it a sore rubbed from the shoes on your poor feet or what?

Well dear, it's early evening and all is quiet once more on the home front. After two busy, active days, there is now a pause, and believe you me, I need a quiet rest.

The wedding could not have been nicer. Everything turned out just wonderful. But you know there was a good captain on the lead. Dot took good care of me. She fixed my hair nicer than the hairdresser. It is still in curls. Aunt Lilly took all the pins out and made the curls a little loose and Dot said, "Mom, you look like a bride." I wrote you just before I crawled in bed this morning. To top it off, the bride and groom spent the night in your bed and Esther in Roger's. Roger was on the couch in our room and tonight, Dot will hold down the feathers. Your bed seems to be doing overtime since you left it. Esther had on your flannel pajamas. If business keeps up, I am going to hang out a sign, "Room for Rent".

Dad just called up. He said he is coming home early and will pick Dot up. Aunt Lilly got two Christmas cards from her Edwin yesterday, but not a line in them. Fred's people are very nice. Dad, as usual, acted up and so did the man aside of him. He was just as nuts. They had Brownie on a chair between them, put a napkin around his neck, wiped off his mouth and carried on. We had a busy time and I am satisfied. I am done now until breakfast time tomorrow. Dot said, "I'll see you Saturday night, Mom." She looked real pretty. Roger, Esther, and Dot sat together. So until we see you Dear, I hope your foot gets better. I got your insurance paper. So long honey.

Lots of love,

Mother

Sunday, October 29, 1944

Dearest Son Edwin,

This beautiful Sunday is drawing to a close. We had a roast beef supper & the remainder of Dad's birthday cake. I have cut a big slice for Dot to take home along with what was left. The Quiz Kids are on and I can't seem to write, but I made a wish on the moon for you. Dot and Roger went to the Circle to see Jamie. Dad met them at 6 o'clock. Now they are in the sitting room listening to the radio.

I am sending what you asked Dad for in this letter. We were all so happy to hear from you today. You seemed so much happier. We don't know what Regular Duty is, so we will, of course, be content knowing you are all right. Dot didn't have any time to write you as she was here doing my hair. We got her off the bus to talk to you Thursday night, which you know. On Friday night, for the wedding Saturday she was shopping for a new dress and shoes to see her sweetheart. Today the time has gone so fast. I slept all afternoon while they were at the movies. Dad will take Dot home when Gabriel Heater[59] is over. Granny called up. No baby as yet at Uncle Charlie's; maybe next week. She saw Aunt Minnie[60] for 20 minutes. She is not so good.

Navy licked Penn at Franklin Field yesterday. So honey, here's a kiss goodnight. Lots of love and happiness. Cheerio,

Mother

Monday morning, October 30, 1944

Dearest Sailor Son,

Just came up from the mailbox with 3 letters, 1 paper and 2 cards from you. It's 12:30. I had my lunch, put out the wash, made the beds and I must dust a little. I fixed the fires and have the roast beef to reheat, and I will take a good

---

[59] Gabriel Heater was a nationally famous radio news commentator.
[60] Aunt Minnie is Minnie Katherine Long, married to Elmer Irons. Helen's sister and Edwin's aunt.

rest this afternoon. I woke up about 1:30 AM with indigestion and I feel better now than when I got up. Dad has taken the car and so far, has two men riders and will pick Dot up about 5:45 at Oxford Bank Corn Exchange. That will be a help to Dot and company for Dad. Dad looks like a millionaire with his white shirt and Stetson cleaned and blocked for 49 cents. He has the overcoat Granny gave him cleaned and pressed and taken in in the back and his shoes half-soled. He is fairly well fixed now for the winter. He must still pay Bender and now the riders will help a little to run the car.

Dot left around 9:15 last night. She said she would write you last night. By the time you get this, I suppose you will have heard from her.

Now, "Old Nut", tonight is mischief night and I will think of you and Ed Baker[61]. That was how you and Grandpop got the names. Old Nut, you always were saying "nuts". I can still hear you and Grandpop forever. Old Bum, Old Nut, good night. My little darling, honey, sweetie, sugar tulip plumb, lots of water has gone over the old Pennypack[62] but I still remember all those things dearest to my heart. Dad was never homesick. (He never had mother love like we did. His mother had her heart in Uncle Paul.) I gave Dad more love and kindness than he ever knew. He is softhearted, but with English determination. During this war, it was a mighty good thing the English had determination or else Hitler and his gang would be over here by this time. So hats off to all the service boys. Be wise, dear. Be as smart as the next fellow. If he can do it, so can you. Try hard. I am proud of you. I brought you up clean, good, poor and honest, so carry on. I love you so much it hurts.

Cheerio,

---

[61] Ed Baker was a Price family neighbor and friend of Edwin's.
[62] Pennypack Creek runs through the northeastern part of Philadelphia.

Mother

Buggy Shephard[63] asked for you this morning. He said to tell you Jack Hardy[64] from Banes Street died in the service from illness. Did I tell you I sent your name in for the Honor Roll and Aunt Lilly's basket of flowers were sent to the Honor Roll after the wedding? (They make up for the roses that disappeared.)

Honey, I think you write lovely letters. I told you before you left that if all you say is, 'Mom, I am ok,' or 'Mom, I am alive,' or just 'Mom & Dad,' I will know you are living. So dear, I am more than happy with your nice letters.

Kisses from all of us.

Mom & Dad, Roger, Dot

**** END OF OCTOBER ****

---

[63] Buggy Shephard was a friend of Edwin's.
[64] Jack Hardy was a friend of Edwin's.

Chapter Two

November 1944

Helen May Price

Wednesday evening, November 1, 1944

Dear Son,

The day is nearly over and I will soon be going to bed. The day turned out nice after the fog. With all the shots I heard, there should be lots of potpies tonight. Roger met that fat Italian guy that used to come up to get the pears. He's the one that Dad hauled the railroad ties to West Philadelphia for. Roger said the guy had parked his car at Kennedy's coal yard and had walked from Byberry and had 2 rabbits. He said, "Every year I get rabbit on Daffy Hill." Roger said before he got up to the house he heard bang, bang. He didn't know if he got anything or not. I didn't let the cat or dog out.

The Red Feather[65] is after donations again. They wanted Dad to sign so much out of his wages. Dad signed none. Neither did Clarence. They got called to the front office. Dad said, "My wife and son give in our own community." The Baptist Institute sent me an envelope and the servicemen donation of Bustleton want a donation. You could give all your pay away.

Dad was early again at 5:20. He stopped at Baldwin's[66] for Dot. She had to stop at the A&P[67] for meat. Mrs. Ems[68] has a cold these past few days. Dad is up to his tricks with Joe. Dad is in his longies, going to get washed and shaved. Roger is in the cellar hammering.

I wrote to everybody, Bill McAdams[69] and all. I guess I will call it a day. I hope you are doing well in your guard duty. I am thinking of you all the time.

---

[65] Red Feather was a charity drive organization.
[66] Baldwin's was a local dairy business.
[67] A&P is a supermarket chain.
[68] Mrs. Ems was Dot and Carl's (Nutsie) mother.
[69] Bill McAdams was Mrs. McAdams' son. (?)

The baker told me today that his brother-in-law was dressed up for Halloween in a KKK suit and a colored man, who had "one too many", spied him. Well, that man got out in the middle of the street and ran. He said, "Oh! Lord, help me!" I bet that poor guy thought he was tarred and feathered. Well so long, my little Old Bum.

Lots of love and kisses. Nighty night.

Mother

Thursday, November 2, 1944

Well Honey,

Here is Mom again. First of all, I got the news at 8 AM that you have a new boy cousin. He's 8 ½ pounds and was born at midnight. Uncle Charlie is on the job until Granny gets there. She was at Delheim's, so she phoned me that she was on her way. She's hooked for two weeks. That's what God made mothers for, to stand by when needed. Your box of letters came, so I will put them away. No one will see them. The box was battered, but holding together.

I have a smoked neck cooking for supper with cabbage, mashed potatoes, turnips and parsnips, and a chocolate pudding made and a jelly cream roll.

Dot will be here from work. We all miss you, especially Dad. I do too. You know you were part of Dad's heart from the hour you were born. Dad and Grandpop took you away from me, but you have such a good Dad that I never minded. I love you too much, but you made me say things and get mad at you. You know now that you are away that it was only for your own good.

If you are thinking about your future and your choice is made, I am glad for your sake. Nothing is nicer than an anchor. No matter how the wind blows and how rough the steering is, if you have a good anchor to depend on, all will be well. You can weather a storm. All I hope for is the happiness of you and Dot. Take your time because life is uncertain. Smile and be happy. I look for lots of improvement in you in manner and temperament when you come home. I want to see that you have brought out the good I put in you. Our ways and customs are quiet and old. After we spent our youth in work and worry, we learned the hard way; the school of hard knocks. We want better for you.

So show Bustleton you are as good as the rest and better. When the time comes, you and Dot can put on the best wedding we know how. So save up. All good things come to those who wait. My fair-haired babies, I love you both and want the best for you. Hope to talk to you tonight.

Love, Mother

Well Honey,

I was so excited I could hardly eat supper. When you were talking first, I had Joe out to see if Dad was coming and to wave him to hurry. But Dad was at Jones' gas station getting gas. The car does 22 miles on a gallon. Dot and he just figured it out. I was so upset for fear that something had happened to Johnny Ems. Mrs. Ems was away and I sent Roger with a note. Then she called after your last call. She had a message that she was not to come up this Sunday. Dot's breath was going so fast she said she could hear her own heartbeat. But Juanita[70] said she had a letter from Johnny today.

---

[70] Juanita is Juanita Ems, wife of Dot Ems' brother John Ems. John or Johnny was Edwin's best friend.

The Home Fires

Now Pop is taking Dot home. No one is there but Grandpop Ems[71], so Dot is coming here again tomorrow night and Saturday night. Her Pop is gunning all week. He got a pheasant and some rabbits yesterday. Nutsie was out too.

The full moon is out in full force. Dot and I made a wish on it. I am so anxious to see your picture. The only thing was that I thought you should wait until your hair grew in. But, if you have your hat on, that is better.

News is scarce and Dad is going to listen to Roosevelt tonight. I think your darling looks so nice in blue. She is going to wash out her stockings and her hair tonight. I enclose what Dad said he would send. (Also $1.00.) Be good and don't take any chances while on duty. I can always understand and know that you will never forget us, but circumstance alters cases. Until I hear you or see you, all my love dear. Your little brother feels hurt and says you don't want to talk to him. So next time, talk a little longer to him.

As always, Mother

Friday, November 3, 1944

Dearest Son,

"Pest" is here yet and annoying me. I can hardly write with all the array of assortment of pens. I had a pen in my purse. I took it out to write you a letter and bingo! It was gone for two days. So I just said to him, I had a pen and now it's gone. He said, "Yes, it's in my desk." Well I made him get it. He had it all apart, to fix one of his.

Brownie has a sore eye. I have a strong suspicion it is from a hook from the cat. Those two play. She knocks down the vases and the books. I heard the

---

[71] Grandpop Ems was Dot Ems' grandfather.

piano go ping, pong, and bling. Miss Cat was walking across it. Every time I go upstairs, I think someone is moving around the furniture.

Well, the old farm is being manned by the coloreds. There are four on it now, and the usual draft evaders. They are as loudmouthed as ever. They are harvesting the circle of carrots. A big, swell car has been outside all day. I thought their boss had a new car. I sure had a surprise to see the colored lady and her beau get into it. Wonders never cease.

Roger has just left. I have a pile of work to do. No shirts for Eddie boy. I will get your clothes from the tailor's tonight. I think all your things are in shape except for your raincoat and leather jacket. I will add more to this after I get the mail.

Dot is coming again for supper tonight. Dad asked her to go to Frankford with us; so you know Mom must show off her stuff. I got pretty near all through now and the home fires are burning. The wash is on the line, a fruit cup made up for supper, potatoes up, and I got your letter.

I told you, dear, to think of me when you look at the moon. The same old moon shines down on all of us. I never saw a more beautiful picture than the full moon shining on the old Pennypack and on the Price homestead. The corn shocks and the harvest moon are always beautiful to me.

Dot called me to see it last night. Well honey, it's 12:30. I got your letter and I talked to you twice last night. You seemed so excited. If I had to go without food to pay the phone bill, I would gladly do it. Call us whenever you can. Dad breaks down every time, so talk to him the longest. Edwin, please include Roger in every kiss and letter. Roger screamed when you left. He misses you a lot.

Love,

Mother

Dear Son,

Between you and me, I know you are getting your eyes opened to a lot of things you never thought about. It's because you were guided and brought up by a good father and a Christian mother. You don't always need to go to church to live right, but it helps. We have heard of all sorts of practices in institutions, medical places, prisons, etc. I am wondering if you have come across it there when you speak of the types of boys. (Tear this up when you read it.) Be on your guard at all times. Be your own judge and take care of yourself. Don't let any bullies scare you. You know right from wrong. Always tell your troubles to your Chaplain. He will guide you and give you advice if necessary. So dear, like I told you, we know "those things", but don't speak of them.

Mother

Friday night, November 3, 1944

Dearest Son,

Well dear, it's late and Dot, Rog and Dad and I did our shopping in Frankford and then came up to the oyster house, and who came in while we were there but Mr. McAdams.

I was in bed, when I said to Dad, "Oh! I forgot Edwin's letter." So Dad said, 'You better go write him.' So here I am. I have a terrible headache. The house is so hot! We got your suit, 2 pairs of pants, brown and blues, and your jacket. They were two dollars. We took your raincoat and I got 4 boxes of camphor. So I will fix your things away. Honey, I don't know any news. I guess Dot won't write tonight, as she is tired too. She said tonight that you were such a gentleman. So I said you were raised one, but how you acted up. She said you were perfect. You've got someone who will be true to you.

We took my bracelet to Hadley's[72]. He asked kindly for you. He said Dad's friend, Bob Strickland[73], the bald-headed fellow, was doing landscape work for a year at Bainbridge. He is going to put a new catch on my bracelet. He couldn't shorten Dot's, so he tied a knot in it and now it fits and looks nice.

Well Pal, I am thinking of you every minute. I send all my motherly love and kiss you. Nighty night.

XXXXX Mother

Saturday noon, November 4, 1944
Thank Joe for that last buck.

Dearest Son,

Just received your 3 letters and I will write the usual letter, so that Joe can take it when he goes to meet Dad. I guess you will get this Sunday.

Well dear, Pop had ½ dozen raws on the shell and then ordered a big stew with a clam in it. Roger ordered a big stew, and gave Dad all the oysters. That made 24 cooked and six raw and Dad got stuck. So he put one raw in Dot's mouth. She liked it. Then Dad got stuck with the stew and Dot ate the oysters and I ate the milk and crackers. To top that off, Dot had two clams

---

[72] Hadley's was probably a jewelry shop.
[73] Bob Strickland, friend of Edwin Price Junior.

and French fries, and I had 2 crab cakes and French fries. Dot and I each wrapped one up and brought it home, as we got stuck too. We had such a big supper at home. I got up and wrote your letter as I told you. I had an awful headache when I got back in bed. I couldn't get to sleep. The fog was so heavy you couldn't see a light in Bustleton. Then an owl started to holler in the white birch tree. That got me upset. I had to call Dad. I finally got to sleep and woke up with the same damn headache.

Roger brought me coffee up. The Wenker jitney was making so damn much noise (muffler blown) that I got up at 9, but awake from seven. All the hands were finishing up the carrots in the circle. I heard the woman tell Harold[74] she topped 70 bushels on Friday. I think they got about 4000 bushels out of that circle. Today, they are finishing it up and they started on the parsnips today by the lane.

Well son, what you told me about that poor boy's misfortune reminded me of the one time Mr. Leiby, on a cold winter morning, stood up against the oven door in his underwear and the same thing happened to him. But he was home and got relief. Tell that boy, oh, for the sake of his poor mother, to go to the Doctor at once, as that is the most precious thing in life and will become infected and rot quicker than any part of your body, except your eyes. Go at once and save all that unnecessary suffering. There is no difference in any part of our body. Doctors look at you and it's the injury they are concerned about. Don't suffer when relief is so close. Those drugs they use would have stopped that burning instantly. You die from the shock of burns. No matter how small, it affects the nerves. Look at how the tomato juice just made my arms and fingers red. It hurt me so bad for a few minutes. When I used the Unguentine it took the fire right out. Always use grease for burns: Vaseline, butter, oil, any lard or any kind of grease. That time Uncle Bob got burned at the Fair Ground when he went to stick the monkey's tail in

---

[74] Harold is Harold Wenker.

the bacon fat, they poured motor oil on him until the motorcycle cops got him to the Frankford Hospital. Burns are worse than cuts. So no matter what ails you, those Navy medics wouldn't have any work to do if all fellows stayed away from sickbay when they needed help. When you boys are home and need help, mothers are on the run. Now that you have left the nest, the wings get hurt. Be brave and don't ever suffer unless it's something where you can't get help. A stitch in time saves nine. Medicine is used to help in time of need. If those guys are tough, well, a "soft answer turneth away wrath but grievous words stir up anger." That was a Bible verse I learned when I was a little girl. I never forgot it.

I wrote you a big letter and I shall be waiting to hear your voice on the phone. Dot is coming again tonight. She is going to do my hair. Well pal, I am counting the days too. The minute you hit Philadelphia, phone me. I will be waiting with the American Flag at the trolley line. I can picture you in sailor blue. I can't wait. God gives me courage. Be good.

Love,

Mother

Saturday evening, November 4, 1944

Dearest Son,

Dad is not home yet. I am through for the day and have nothing to read. I have the biggest part of the food prepared for Sunday so that it will be a long, lazy, day.

Dad told me over the phone tonight that Mrs. McAdams' mother had a stroke through the night. I heard the owl, I told you. Bad news, but of course that is

The Home Fires

just a saying. Anyhow, I don't like to hear them. I was talking to Mrs. McAdams a few minutes ago and she said her mother is in a bad condition. She was 80 last Thursday.

Well son, I seem to be running short of paper. I have used almost 60 cents worth, beside what Joe gave me last Christmas with the blue edge. I don't know any other news so far. I will add more tomorrow and mail this out when Joe goes to Frankford.

I feel a little better tonight. I took a rest after Joe left. I could hear you say, "Mom, get me something to eat." Well honey pal, we both miss each other. I hope God hears me and that we can all be happy together once again. But what good would the country be? I say I will write all kinds of cheerful letters to my sailor boy. I can't always do it. I go outside and look at the star hanging in my window and I salute it and I say, "Go ahead, you damn bums and slackers! I'm proud of my son." And I feel like hollering, "Go ahead, you Bud Wenker[75]. You are as yellow as that carrot you are hiding behind."

But, "all good things come to those who wait." God gave me Heaven on Earth. I used to wonder if I could ever be alone with my family. Now you see we never have complete happiness. My health is poor and my boy loaned to Uncle Sam, but God will take care of us. He always has. When things look darkest, Dad and I always pulled through and we tried hard because we had two nice bad boys. Now you will make us proud of you. I am the proudest mother on Krewstown Road, even if Major Dollenberg[76] lived here on the same road.

Sunday Night Dad will mail these.

---

[75] Bud Wenker was a local Bustleton resident.
[76] Major Dollenberg was a hero of World War One from Bustleton.

Wartime Letters Written from Mother to Son

10 o'clock, Monday morning, November 5, 1944

Son,

Will dash off a few lines to add to what I wrote last night. Dot spent the day with us from 12 to now. We went to see Charlie and it was Charlie boy's[77] 10th birthday. Little Violet[78] was making the cakes and believe me, she sure can do a good job of it. We had supper and then we came to Minnie's. She was the same old Minnie and that little Elmer[79] the brat. Well, I got a big bunch of chrysanthemums and my hair is tight.

I will say goodnight as I am so tired and will now go to bed. Dad is having about the 10th cup of coffee, so he will be up on the bucket all night. I was so happy to hear from you today.

Lots of love,

Mom

November 6, 1944 Put cat in the kitchen last night, Monday morning when I came down she had a mouse.

Dearest Son,

Old Man Winter hit our part of the country on a high wind...started yesterday afternoon. It gradually got colder and you know how it is when the wind whistles all night. The kitchen was 50 degrees. But I have the home fires

---

[77] Charlie Boy is Charles Long, Edwin's first cousin and daughter of Charles Edward Long and Violet Noll.
[78] Little Violet is Violet Long, Edwin's first cousin and daughter of Charles Edward Long and Violet Noll.
[79] Elmer is Elmer Andrew Irons, Edwin's first cousin and son of Elmer Grant Irons and Helen's sister, Minnie Kathrine Long.

burning and no news to tell. Pop had a bellyache all night and didn't feel any too good all night. He had the chills and he didn't sleep very well. We didn't know what could have caused it because we had home fries, salt mackerel and grapefruit for breakfast. For dinner, we had steak and onions, mashed potatoes, peas, gravy, salad with Bermuda onion, and rice custard pudding. None of that should have caused it. Now that I think of it, Little Elmer gave Dad a glass of cider. When he came home, he drank coffee and finished up the salad. You know how salad used to give you the bellyache, so maybe that's what happened to Dad.

I am so glad I did my wash on Saturday because it's too cold for me today. I couldn't sleep all night either, between all the pins and curlers in my hair and being cold. You know Dad. He never wants as many covers on as I do, so I got up and put another blanket on the bed. Then Dad said he was cold and put on his bathrobe. I said, 'Why didn't you say so, because I'm frozen?' So darn the winter. I hate it. But we had a pretty long summer and good fall. We can't complain.

Tomorrow is the big Election Day and I was going to make a day of it, go to Frankford and to vote. I told Pop this morning if it was like this, high wind and cold, I can't walk out. He will have to come get me. Dot went to Charlie's with us. I was afraid she might get scolded because her mother was sick. She had intended going home to help get the supper, but I guess Mildred helped. Mrs. Ems gave Dad, or Mr. gave Dad two rabbits. I guess I will cook them for supper. The pleasure to eat them is all Dad's. I have been wondering how Dad is. I was glad he had the car. He said he wished he could stay home, but now that he has others depending on him, he must go by hook or by crook, which was why I always depended on you to help Pop out. It seems the other way round.

I got awake at 2:45, 11:30 and my first thought was of you. I wondered if you were out. I thought you told me 7 to 12 and I was saying, my boy is out in this and it's so windy. It goes through you. I wonder if he has a warm coat. I wonder if he can get a warm drink. Oh well, war is Hell. When is it ever going to end?

I was so happy and glad to hear you took communion. Always obey God's commandments and he will take care of you. It's wonderful to have faith in God. "In my father's house are many mansions, if it were not so, I would have told you." I always got comfort from that verse.

I talked to Grandpop yesterday as I passed William Penn Cemetery. I said, 'Oh Grandpop, if anything happens to my boy, I know you will receive him with pleasure.' God forgive us all. I pray all the time for you to be spared for Dad, but God knows best. So put all your faith in God and you will get a reward from all. I am hoping with all my motherly heart to see you soon. I will add more when I see what is in the mailbox today. It's 11:30 now.

Uncle Charlie named the baby, "John George"[80] after Uncle John and Violet's father was "George". So now that is the 4th John Long. When Delaware John has his baby at Christmas, I hope it's a boy too. Bill Long is going out and Uncle John said he has only 4 letters in months. He is getting so anxious to see the U.S.A. and mail is hard to get in and out of his island. I am going to write to him today. Granny is on the job and the baby is as big as Aunt Minnie's, who is eight weeks old.

Elmer Irons[81] was so fresh and little Elmer was a terror. I guess they will never be able to calm him down. I used to think you and Grandpop showed off when we had company. But you are not in with the Irons.

---

[80] John George is John George Long, Edwin's first cousin, son of Helen's brother, Charles Edward Long and Violet Noll.
[81] Elmer Irons was Elmer Grant Irons, married to Helen's sister, Minnie Kathrine Long.

Well son, I got 5 letters in the mail today from you. I read them all from start to finish. Now I have the rabbit cooking and so I will call this a letter. With lots of love from us all,

Mom, Dad, Rog & Joe

Monday night

Dearest Son,

The evening is drawing to a close. It's getting colder and all is quiet. Dad has a cold again and he had the rabbit. I don't know if he enjoyed it or not, as he was all out of gear. He tried to drain out the water from the car to put in antifreeze. He has the car out at Benders now and Roger is with him. I will write details later. Joe is here and all is very quiet.

I don't like these kinds of nights. It seems every time there is a cold change in the weather, Pop has to be monkeying around with the pump or the car. I do hope he gets home early, as he didn't get much rest last night and he said he was cold all day. He had expected to come home and cover up, but the car must come first. So I have nothing to say.

Joe's head is touching his knees and the paper is falling on the floor. I guess I will ring off and tell you more tomorrow. Nighty night.

Love,

Mother

Wartime Letters Written from Mother to Son

November 7, 1944

Well son, today is the big day and soon we will know who will be the captain to steer the ship of state for four more years. I will be glad to get the 150 hairpins out of my hair and 4 wavers in the back. I've had them in two days now, and not a hair is out of place. But believe me; I had a job sleeping on it. Beauty and Pride killeth.

The day has broken fair and sunny, lots warmer. The high wintry wind is gone and I sure am thankful. Roger kissed me goodbye now and also the dog and cat. I thought I better write early. I haven't the cellar fire fixed yet, but it is 65 degrees in the dining room and I will soon stir things up.

I may go to the movies and make a day of it. Dad had a good night's sleep. Bill Bender[82] got the plug out and Dad put antifreeze in. Bill Bender said he liked you a lot and if you ever have the time to drop him a card, to do it. Bernie O'Neil[83] is home. Dad said Bill told him he went away a bum and came back a "man". It reminds me of the song, "There's a little bit of good in every bad little boy".

I fixed the heater, cleared the dishes, swept the kitchen, and here "is I again". I saw two gunners going up the Circle and three dogs with them. I laughed to myself. One time I saw a rabbit at the parsley bed...hot bed sash, where a pane was out. It was by my old flower garden and the grape vines were full. I was in bed. I called Dad. I said where it was. He ran out and couldn't see it. But, I yelled down, "he's still there". So Dad pulled and blew his head off. He never even sighted it. I saw one run around the hedge from the dining room window. Uncle Charlie grabbed the gun and he darned near scared me to death. He pulled before I even thought he was out. He got it.

---

[82] Bill Bender was an automotive dealer.
[83] Bernie O'Neil was probably an area resident.

So you learn to be a better shot, because you missed that rat. You didn't get on the job fast enough.

Brownie is barking so I will go see why. A freight train is all I can see. Well son, Uncle John is not getting any mail, so if you have a minute, don't forget him, and us. But drop the rest, unless you have plenty of time. I guess I will close for now. Hope you are well. "Smooth your face."

Be my nice "fair sailor". All my mother love and hugs. I miss you lots and lots, especially, "Mom, make me something to eat." Dot will never forget your French fries. Maybe you can learn to be a Navy cook.

Well, so long for now. And the "best man wins". Until I hear from you, Cheerio. Roger said call him. "Night Owl", "Old Bum".

Bye for now.

November 7, 1944

Dearest Son,

I got the letters today that you wrote on Sunday telling us you signed for the passes. I could jump for joy. I can hardly wait until the time comes. I just imagine that I can see us meeting. But oh! The parting. I am so happy to think we can get a chance to see each other once again. I don't know any news. I wrote you early this morning. When I went to vote, I mailed it.

All in Bustleton as usual was quiet. Henry Thompson[84] and Bill Wenker[85] were the only two I saw on the job back in Bender's garage. Mrs. Brown[86]

---

[84] Henry Thompson was apparently an employee at Bender's.
[85] Bill Wenker was a local Bustleton resident.

was on the job too. Mrs. Olone[79] said, "Don't forget to vote for the best man." I said, "Who is the best man?" She said, "The one you are going to vote for." But, she didn't find out whom I was voting for.

I went to the Circle to see Arsenic and Old Lace. Talk about a screwy picture, not my type at all.

Dad is shaving and all is quiet here. I am tired and sleepy, but I will stay up to hear some election news. I got home about 5. I had left at 12 and the day was fair and nice. Rog is doing his lessons. Dad will add some.

Well son, Dad got gas tonight. One gallon at Bill L.'s[87] and then had to go to Atlantic. Fred Jones was closed.

Mrs. McAdams' mother is about the same.

You have been away four weeks today. You were the fellow who was never going to get homesick. I used to get so homesick and I saw my people once a month. So now you know what I went through from 14 to 35. I was homesick for my mother until I had Roger. She waited on me hand and foot and I knew she could never do any more for me. Then my family broke up and my own boys took all my thoughts. So I know just how you feel. I want to see you and hold you to my breast once again. I never forget you are still my babies. I wish you were. Well, so long pal. Happy day. Lots of love from all.

Mother

---

[86] Mrs. Brown and Mrs. Olone were acquaintances.

[87] Most likely, Bill L.'s was a gas station.

Wednesday, November 8, 1944

Dear Son,

It's 9 o'clock. I woke up at 3:45 and I couldn't go to sleep after that. Pop called me at 5 o'clock and told me that President Roosevelt guides the ship of state. Well, I am glad for that because he kept the coal in the bin. At least he made laws so that if you did make war wages, you could still buy Bonds, instead of the landlord being able to raise the rent. Goodness knows things are expensive as it is. Women's things are beyond my pocketbook, nightgowns and slips, etc. All are beyond the poor woman's' purse. What would it be with Dewey in? He's the choice of wealth. So the best man won. Hurrah.

Of course, there is no news to write. I am going to call up Mrs. Spence after a while. It's still too early for her. I have the home fires burning and the dishes washed. I must iron a few things and make the beds. I will add more after mail time. I am so anxious to see if we get the passes. I can hardly wait to see you.

Pop is the same "old Pop on the bucket" last night. We were talking about Roosevelt and the War. I saw the news of McArthur's return to Leyte on the Philippines and I said, "Oh, if this war would only end." Pop said, "Yes. The boy has to serve 6 months after. It's been tough and he's only gone a month." So you see how he misses you too. But we are Americans. We know how to live, fight, or die. You are our hope, prayers and love. Like the song of the 4-leaf clover, God put another one in for luck. I hope you find it wherever you go. I will run along now and write more later.

Love, kiss.

Edwin, I can't understand why you didn't get any letters. I write twice every day except Saturday. If Dad doesn't go to work Sunday, then I will mail it out when Joe goes to Frankford. Sometimes I don't get mail from you for 2 days. Other times it comes overnight. Today, Wednesday noon, I had the mail you dated Tuesday. Be sure to date all your letters. Sometimes you don't.

Now listen, don't be homesick. Put your mind on your work and learn the rules. Yes, and from a mother who hates war; "Kill". You know the story I always told you about the old World War One veteran spotting the enemy and thinking of how he was once young and yet when he himself was spotted, he paid with his life. I love you just like my own life. Do everything to protect us, even to kill. I would kill anyone I thought was harming you or Roger. Those yellow rats would do anything. Always think of Bataan and Corregidor and Uncle John sweating in the SW Pacific holes for Aunt Lilly and all the mothers whose boys have gone. Learn those guns like you never in all your life learned any lesson. Then the heartaches and homesickness will end for all boys and moms and dads everywhere. The future of America, boys at Bainbridge and every other training center are in their own hands. My dear sailor boy, do your best. God gave me strength and courage to keep up the day you left. Don't worry over us. We are warm and happy to be home together. Our home on the farm was Dad's paradise. Now that war has parted us, you can understand that wooden barracks, hard beds are not in with Mom's high feathers. Yes, feathers went out of date with the bustle, but I'll still take them. So what. Think about Uncle John sleeping in fox holes...mud...wet. To Hell with War. But we've got to lick or be licked. I know you don't want the "Limeys" to have to do it all.

Now honey, I could jump for joy as I got the passes today (Wednesday). I can hardly wait for Dad and Roger. It is more than I ever dreamed of. Boy, the time will never go by. But then when I am busy, it flies. I am cleaning your bureau out, and the moths have the carpet eaten off under the corner of the bureau. I don't know what to do. I have put so much camphor and stuff around. I believe it's in the cracks of the floor. So I will give it "a goin" over, once again and hope that they don't get in your things. I've got all your things clean. When you come home at Christmas, what you don't want, you can give to Uncle Charlie. He needs them.

The day is nice, but a little raw. I have to go down and look at the cellar fire. Then I must go up and wipe the floor in your room and finish that last drawer. I threw out a lot of that junk and saved and put in a box what you wanted. Now I hope your cold has not taken a hold. Go and get something for it before it gets settled. It was awful cold up here too. I did write you, but I guess you got them all. We had four from you today. I think you are a real good boy to write. I myself go down every day at noon. I can't wait for Roger. I will see that you get candy. We will do all in our power to get to see you. Dad plans on leaving at 6AM. He has been to Oxford by machine, so we have all the maps. I guess you know I will tell Dot to be here. I will be home Saturday, so call if you can Saturday night.

Maybe Dad can't make it, but I'll be here all day getting ready for Sunday. So dear, take care of your cold. Lots of love.

Mommy

Wednesday afternoon

Dear Son,

It's a beautiful afternoon. I finished up your room and I did write you a big letter. I hope you received it. I guess you will get both of them together as I will mail them out together. At least, Roger will take them. Dad sent you a letter with a dollar in it this morning and I put one in the other letter. I told you we got the pass. I can't get you out of my mind. You must be thinking awfully hard about me this afternoon.

I guess you are wondering if we have the pass, if maybe Roger will bring it up on his way from school, but I can't wait that long. I go down every day at noon.

Well, Old Pal, I just had to feed "Crickee"[88] and then she cried to go out. So far she hasn't made any mess in the house. Old pest is curled up under my feet. He never fails to go in your room. He gets under the bed. He looks out the window. When he hears the car, he runs and cries and makes such a fuss. It's as if he says, "Pop is here, but not Edwin tonight, Mother." He runs right back and stays by your chair. When Dot sat there on Sunday, he had his paws on her lap.

We introduced Dot to parsnips and turnips. She had never eaten any before and Granny introduced her to kale on Sunday. It's bitter like broccoli, which she never tasted. I wonder what they cook, "no spaghetti" .

Oh well honey, I will close for now. I hope you understand my mail. I will write every day. You can depend on Mother, unless I am ill, then Roger will write for me.

Love,

Mother

---

[88] Crickee was one of the Price family's cats.

The Home Fires

Wednesday night

Dear Son,

This makes the third letter I have written to you today. Roger went out without the mail, so Dad took them out as he was going to Bender's. I was going to surprise Dad tonight when he opened the letter to find the pass, but as soon as he came in he said, "Did you get the passes?" Dot said you sent them. So Dot must have gotten a letter in the late mail yesterday or maybe Dad stopped there at her home. I don't know. I had your Tuesday letters today. That was fast work. Well, as I said, we will be there. Call Saturday night. Dad said to try (unless you can't) so that it's not too early or else he and Dot can't get here. Dad will tell Dot tomorrow (Thursday), so I hope to hear from you. But, I fully understand that your time is not your own. It says on the back of the pass, "not to bring any food", but I guess candy and taste of something else we could manage. Oh well, all I care about is seeing you.

I can hardly write with this pen. One time I write one way then another. I sent a Christmas card, a big letter, and a beautiful 35-cent Birthday card to Edwin Bissinger[89] with today's mail. His birthday is December 8th. It doesn't seem possible that he got to see Grandpop's home[90]. In all our talk, we never thought such a thing.

Mrs. McAdams' mother is on the last lap, just about breathing. Mrs. McAdams said she would write when she got a chance. We know what it is to "watch for the Angel to steal away". I never know how to write happy things to you, but all those things are close to my heart.

---

[89] Edwin Bissinger was Edwin's first cousin and the son of Edwin Price Junior's sister, Lillian May Price and William Bissinger.
[90] Grandpop's (Edwin Price Senior) home was in Monmouthshire, Wales before he came to America in 1871.

Roger sure did give Wenker the raspberry on the bus on account of them being for Dewey. Rog said they got so mad because Rog said, "The best man wins." He heard me say that. So the best fellow wins in everything. Try to do your best and we will be happy once again. Nighty night.

Mommy X X smooth your face X X X X

Thursday noon, November 9, 1944

Well Pal,

Today was the first I was disappointed in getting no letter from you since you started writing regular. I had four yesterday including Roger's and Dad's. I wrote you three letters yesterday, so I know you are not getting missed by me. If you are, then the mail is getting lost. I do hope you are not sick and that everything is alright with you. I know you told me not to worry, but it's hard to not see you come in the lane. We must keep a stiff upper lip. I often think about the day when I will hear sirens blow that the war is over. I bet I will laugh and cry at the same time. I pray for that day.

Well honey, I don't know any news. Mrs. Bell wrote me, but she didn't say they heard from you.

Mrs. Vera Bell
418 Glendale Ave.
Norfolk, Va.

Well son dear, it's nearly 1 PM and I am not quite through my work. Roger has to take my shoes to Frankford to the shoemaker. The Bustleton shoemaker is sick and couldn't do them. I have been feeling better the past week, but didn't sleep any too good last night. I imagined I heard someone walking in the room. One time, I heard a board go crack and "meow", oh boy! It scared it me. I yelled for Pop. He had to "chambermaid" Crickee the cat.

A little while ago, I was sitting by the stove listening to Jack Burch when Mr. Mouse came walking across the electric stove. It looked at me and stopped and then turned and jumped off. The cat was out. She got one in the kitchen, so that is why we let her in all the time.

It's nice here today. I washed Roger's flannel shirts and my stockings so I will be ready for the big day Sunday. We got the pass. I am so happy. When you get this we will be another day nearer. Until I write again tonight, I hope and pray you are alright.

Love,

Mom

(Enclosure – Item 3)

```
SPECIAL INSTRUCTIONS AND INFORMATION FOR VISITORS OF RECRUITS

1. Bring this pass with you – upon your arrival at the Main Gate you will be
   directed to the assigned reception area.
2. Do not arrive too early – visiting time is 1 PM to 4:30 PM.
3. Cameras are not permitted on the base. Do not bring gifts of food or bulky
   packages for the recruit. (Navy food is the finest and the recruits have
   plenty of it).
4. Do not make the trip if any member of your family is confined with a con-
   tagious disease.
5. All visiting is restricted to a special area which will be designated by
   sentries on duty.
6. If unable to make the trip immediately, please return this pass by mail
   to originator immediately in order to avoid disappointment.
7. We welcome your visit – we wish to make it pleasant and enjoyable, and it
   is requested that you comply strictly with all instructions in order to
   make this possible.
```

Thursday evening, November 9, 1944

Dearest Son,

I sent you off a letter this afternoon in a long envelope because I haven't any others until I get some tomorrow night. Tomorrow night, Friday, is the fellowship dinner at the church and Mrs. Rupert just called me up to see if I would come out. Mrs. Michener[91] said if I couldn't come, to let Roger come out. She would take care of him. So, Roger has just left. Dad took him, because it gets dark so early now.

Dear, I am wondering if you get all my letters, because you asked me if I got the paper you sent. I told you in one of my letters how I enjoyed it and read it from start to finish. I didn't get any mail from you this morning, so I sent Roger to the post office after he came from school and he brought me in one letter from you written on Wednesday. So I guess I won't get any tomorrow (Friday). News is scarce. I don't know anything new. I got the wash all in and dry. I am all set for Sunday. I will get you candy and I will make your pie on

---

[91] Mrs. Michener, member of the Pennypack Baptist Church.

Saturday. I will also fix you something I know you like if I can get it in Diener's. I hope you are well. I have you all pictured with that haircut. I will tell you when I see you what I think about it.

Dad brought Dot home and she said her brother, Johnny, gets home for Christmas. He is still tied to his mother's apron strings as he said he was "aheadin" straight for home and Mom. So the world goes; marriage, war, and babies, war, and marriage, always in a cycle. Dad is back now and he said he has nothing special to say, only hello, big kiss and be good. Joe says, "Hello" too. "How are you?"

I hear Bill Wenker was shooting off out in Bustleton on Election Day about Roosevelt and that nutty looking fellow that chews tobacco, sweeps up the trolley tracks and drinks a little, heard him. He punched him one and knocked him on his ass in his fine gray suit. The fellow is a little lame and like a bum. Bill has a shiner. Did Roger give them the Ha Ha.

Nighty night. Love, kiss,

Mom

Friday, November 10, 1944

Dearest Son,

I guess this will be the last letter you will receive before you see us. I woke up at 3 o'clock and it was raining bucketfuls. Roger is leaving for Wilson[92]. It's dreary and raining lightly. I am so glad the wash came back late yesterday afternoon. There was a good wind and I got them all out, but two

---

[92] Wilson is the name of the high school that Roger attends. Edwin also attended high school there.

shirts and I will dry them inside.

I don't know anything new or any news. It's raining real hard now. Are you out? I am through with my regular work now, as I left this letter several times to fix the fires, make the beds, do the dishes, and sweep the kitchen. Housekeeping is somewhat like Navy life. Routine every day, besides all the extras, such as the baby crying, when you're trying to get a little rest from the diapers, the food, the wash, iron, bake, mend, taking care of all the old men and trying to think you are smelling roses instead of horseshit and cabbage.

Soon you will smell seawater, gunpowder, and the stink of the ship. Think instead that you smell your favorite lipstick or see the mist in two beautiful eyes. It all comes in one's life. I have had all the same love dreams as you and Dot. I had mine differently than I wanted. As the years grow mellow, you look back and there are lots of harder things that hit you. For instance, 18 years through tears, smiles, sickness, fires, school, work, and then "no more guard duty". No more early breakfasts, no lunch to pack, no more time to get up. In its place is emptiness and heartache. Dear, live, love, laugh, and work while you are young, and then, when you grow too old to dream, I'll have you to remember. Remember all the happy things and plan for the best things in life. "Obey" is the way to the top. So here's hoping to kiss you about the time you get this letter.

Love,

Mom

Friday noon

Well Son,

I got your letter today, just now, telling me you had no smokes. I hope you got Dad's letter with the dollar in it. I sent you one with a dollar in it. I am hoping to hear from you Saturday night. All is well at home and all I am doing is thinking of you. I write you twice every day. Roger mails one after school and Dad mails one every morning, so you should hear from me regularly. It is still raining hard.

Roger won't want to go out to the supper tonight. If I don't get this mailed out after school, Dad will run out with it. You should have this letter before we see you Sunday. I pray God to see you. So until Sunday, love from all. Dot has a new dress to come see you in.

Suppertime, Friday evening, November 10, 1944

Well Son,

I will slip another mail in the Frankford box tonight on my way to get the meat in the hope that you get it before we see you, God willing. Now that the time is getting closer, I'm like a hen on a hot griddle. I guess you haven't much time to think. But there is one thing no man can rob us of. That is our thoughts. I know yours are with us and you are counting the hours the same as I am.

I am waiting for the gang to come home to spaghetti supper, easy and quick. The rain has disappeared. I am in hopes that it has blown itself farther away. Rain or shine, we will do all in our power, with God's help and mercy to get there. I will be a busy Mom. Tomorrow I will bake the pie and that ain't nothin'. I will do all I can do to help this war end, to the day of your return. I will do my best. That is all we mothers hope for. Crickee caught that little mouse that walked across the electric stove. I was upstairs getting cleaned up to go to the store. The phone rang and it was Aunt Lilly, and Crickee had it under the kitchen table.

Who did the nice typewriting of your envelope? This makes the fourth big envelope letter I have sent you. I will get some smaller tonight.

Oh honey, it's so warm here tonight. I am going to get off now to Frankford. Will be seeing you.

Love,

Mother

Sunday, November 12, 1944

Dearest Son,

It's 8:45 and the end of a perfect day. We stopped at Howard Johnson's at Haverford Avenue and City Line. Pop paid $6.00 for our supper and $4.00 for our dinner. I guess we are ready for bed. I was so glad you met a buddy to go up the hill with you. I saw you look back once, but I was satisfied. I think you look wonderful. If you only knew, I was so sick it was all I could do to keep myself on my feet. I took pills, aspirin, and God gave me strength to get to you.

I will cut this short. Dot took my hat off. She took my beads and bracelets off and helped me out wonderfully. So dear, I was glad to see you. Only thing was I couldn't love you enough, like when you were a little boy. Now you are a nice sailor boy. Good night for now. Pop was so pleased. Love from all.

Monday afternoon, November 13, 1944

Dearest Edwin,

Our visit is now a pleasant memory to be tucked away for the day of dreams. It is a lovely day and I am thinking of our trip yesterday.

Mrs. McAdams was the first to call, then Mrs. Spence and Granny, all wanting to know how we made out.

Bill Long came in a taxi to Aunt Dot's at 3 o'clock this morning. Aunt Dink[93], Granny, etc. were playing cards. Aunt Dink missed the bus home and Bill flew by plane to Washington DC and from there by train to see Byron, who is due home from Sampson on Tuesday. Bill must fly back to be at his base on Wednesday. When he leaves for my brother Bill's, in the west. You know where (button your lips).

Tuesday, we all expect to gather at Aunt Dink's. I guess you know I am a "busy body". I will be out tonight to see Mrs. McAdams' mother and again tomorrow. Johnny Ems' wife was there when Dad took Dot home. He stopped in. Mrs. Ems is getting Dad to take tires to get recapped where Dad got his done.

I am so anxious to know what the surprise is, but I guess I can wait. "All good things come to those who wait." I thought Howard was a nice-looking boy. I had to laugh at the lipstick he had on his chin. You tell that boy that walked up the hill with you that he took a load off my shoulder. I was so glad you didn't have to part alone from us.

---

[93] Aunt Dink was Helen's sister-in-law, Lillian Ida Barnes, married to Helen's brother John Francis Long who is referred to as "Uncle John". She is also referred to as "Aunt Lillian.

"A friend in need is a friend indeed," and to me, that was a good deed. I looked after you until I couldn't see you anymore. You looked back once and you were smiling. That warmed my heart that you two were happy going up the hill.

The hills will be long and hard. "But show you can do it," all of you boys. I saw many mothers' tears falling, but we are Americans, and you are our sons. So go forward with a smile. I got the paper and four letters.

Love,

Mom

Monday night, 10:15, November 13, 1944

Dearest Son,

Just got back from the layout and I have a terrible headache. The exhaust pipe is on the fritz and it nearly overcame us with fumes on Sunday when we went to see you. Bill Bender will fix it Wednesday night. So I am glad to get out of that car tonight. We had all the windows open.

I am ready for bed. I hope you are well and happy as can be. William McAdams telephoned from California tonight at 6:30. They told him to call once a month. He's called up three times this month. Well son, I'll cut this short. Sweet dreams.

Love from all,

Mother

Tuesday noon, November 14, 1944

Dearest Son,

Here I am again, for a little chat with you. It's a nice day. Once again it's back to routine work. I suppose you are on the same schedule, the "busy one".

Your box of letters came in today's post, along with 6 letters from you. They must have been lying around somewhere because you wrote them on the 9th and today is the 14th, yet the mail I got yesterday was written later than that. I also got two letters today that you wrote yesterday, the 13th. So you see how mail is.

Aunt Dink called me up and said Johnny is up today, but must leave at 1 o'clock. Bill must fly back at 4 o'clock and she is so afraid Byron won't get in from Sampson until too late for Bill to say "So long." Such is war, but my dear boy, I can see those things tucked in your waist and your arms around Dot. I felt kind of glad someone loved you too and that you had someone to love. That is why you are in training to make yourself fit to keep the home front safe. I told you, in the letter, I thought you looked wonderful in five weeks. What will you look like in 5 more? You are at an age where you are still growing. Edwin, I know heartache. I have been through it, like when I lived with the Grundy's and on the Main Line with the Caspar Wister Morris family. I got home once a month. I loved my brothers so much that I was homesick for 20 years. You know Dad is like all English, coldhearted, but I am warm and kind.

You will see when you get older what I mean. All Dad ever thinks about is work and sleep. He was 30 years old when I married him. He was old-fashioned and dumb. I had seen how other people lived, but I was poor and honest. Dad was very good towards the boys, who had seen Paris. They were out for sport and good times and freedom after the war, just as you will be.

So, I have no answer for you as to marriage. You ask me to look around for rings. I can advise you, but my choice may not suit the pocketbook. How can you make plans without money? I am shorter each week. The car has been the cause of it all. But we must make the best of a bad bargain. Both you and Dad always had your own way. If only you would both listen to me, we could have things easier. Dad you can't talk to, and you always thought I was against you. But dear, wherever you are, whatever you do, I am right aside you. Yes, we all say and do things. But dear, "lean on me". I talk to you, I see you. Dad says, "Why do you talk so crazy?" Well, I say "my son" I am with you, so march on. I never saw you grow up. From the time you left Jacobs School, until you left Wilson High School, you sprouted right up like magic.

I can see you getting off the school bus, the day I was in the field, when you said, "I got left down." I said you need not tell me. I know you did. What a relief on your face. And so it is. No words are necessary to eyes that love. I knew by Dad's face on Sunday, the second he spotted you. I couldn't see you, but I knew Dad had found you by the look on his face. So whatever makes you happy or sad, it does the same to me. You are one corner of my heart torn out and fashioned into you alongside of the Price. Say to yourself, for all the things my mother wanted in her life, I will make her proud of my conduct toward women, toward kindness, and toward being a genteel man. The Navy I serve will be the honor I pay my mother. So March On to Victory and I will keep the home fires burning. Always say, 'Mom, I am so tired, Mom, are you with me?' And I will say, 'Yes dear. I smooth your face and give you all my love.'

Mother

The Home Fires

Wednesday morning, November 15, 1944

Dearest Son,

Roger just left and the sun is just trying to break through over Baldwin's barn. There wasn't a star out when I woke up at 10 after 4 this morning, and to save me, I could not go to sleep again. Then when I had to get up at 7:30, I could have gone to sleep. But here I am as usual, talking to you first thing in the morning. My mind just keeps going in circles.

Pop let Brownie out at 4:30 when he got up. That dumb city dog got his nose too close to what he thought was a cat and he got it full force, once again, skunk. So he is in "jail" today until they get home tonight to disinfect him. I can hear him crying out in the truck shed and it's driving me mad. Roger put plenty of food and water there and he let him out for a run before he went to school. "Crickee" knocked down one of my real old vases and broke it yesterday.

Then the car throws off so much carbon monoxide gas that if Pop rode very far without the windows open, it would overcome him before he would get to Frankford. I called to him and told him to be sure to open the windows as soon as he got in the car. Bill Bender will do what he can tonight. My head still hammers between the tainted meat we had at that diner at the entrance to your camp road and the gas fumes. They had Dot and me licked. Never eat in there. I only ever get hooked once, so the next time I come to see you, I will have my own basket packed. Pop always objects to my fixing up anything to eat, but damn the slop you buy out. The eats cost $10.00 on Sunday and Dad or I could have eaten it all. It was tough and bad. They must have had it a month. If we get to see you again, Pop can eat in any joint he wants to, but Mom will pack the basket.

Wartime Letters Written from Mother to Son

I called Edwin, when I called for Roger to get up for school. Roger said, "Mom, you should put Ed's hat away from behind the stove. I'm the man of the house now." So I said, "I'll ask Edwin to see what he says." Whatever you say, you can answer him in a letter.

This morning I said to myself, Edwin will soon be up at 4:30 and is he out doing exercise? Is he cold? No, he sailed through mud, ice, snow, had a real bad cold and still he went to work at Sears and Budd's[94]. He ran over the fields with a bag of dry sandwiches.

So March on to Victory for the mothers of the U.S.A., all you nice boys. I still have pictures of so many of them in my mind as they awaited the arrival of their visitors last Sunday. My heart was aching for them. But God is good. It's Hitler and the Jap's rulers who want to conquer the finest country in the world. We mothers must stand by, while our boys learn how to keep well and get tough.

I hear Bunny G. and Elmer T.[95] are at Sampson. Mrs. Rupert came over about 4:30 last evening to collect for the Baptist Institute so I couldn't get out of it. This was her third time over the railroad. I like her lots.

I am expecting you to call on Thursday night. Pop will tell Dot tonight and pick up my house shoes at the shoemakers. It's $2.00 to get them soled and heeled. I need shoes, so don't at any time, buy me any jewelry. I need more necessary things than ornaments. But, I was proud to think you gave me that gift. You know, you forgot to say, "Mom, it's your birthday," even when we talked. You know it was my birthday the Saturday after you left; the Saturday night you couldn't get me on the phone.

---

[94] The Budd Company (now ThyssenKrupp Budd) is a metal fabricator and major supplier of body components to the automobile industry.
[95] Elmer T. was most likely a friend of Edwin's.

The Home Fires

I am going to call Granny at Mrs. Delheim's to see what news she got yesterday when she called Aunt Dink. I hear my cousin, Grant Culp, is in bed now from the effects of World War I. So I wrote to his sister, Nettie Tippet, to get his address. I sent her your address, so if you get any mail, you will know who she is. She is the one whose husband shot himself.

I wrote reams of paper to the boys in World War I. I guess I will use carloads in this one. Now you see how you gave that boy Marian's address? That is how Mr. Bell[96] got mine and still after 27 years keeps in touch with his wife even though we have never met. Mrs. Bell even writes to you. That is "friendship". Answer any letters you get time to.

Wednesday afternoon

Hello Honey,

I have the bathroom scrubbed, fires fixed, beds made, dishes done, and the dusting, so I hip hopped down the lane, but no letter from my baby. I keep thinking of you all day today. Some days I can work and sing a song, cry a tear or two; but today, all I do is think of you. I wonder, what's on your mind. Maybe you are thinking, "Mom has no letter today." That doesn't worry me now, as I know you are busy and not on the battlewagons. I think you are safe. Of course, I think I know the answers because of those who have gone ahead, but I put my trust in God.

You see dear, when the time grows short for the arrival of a new baby, the mother can hardly wait. She is so scared of what may happen to her with all the discomfort. Then comes the joy and gladness that she has a nice little boy. God takes care of you. With the needles and all the discomfort, it's not

---

[96] Mr. Bell was a soldier pen pal that Helen wrote to during the First World War.

like you are going through half as much as Aunt Violet[97] or Aunt Minnie. So be brave, be strong. There are lots worse things in life than Naval Training.

The joy of being together again will make us all broader and more considerate.

It's warm out now, but heavy. It had all the indications of snow this morning. You know dear, I keep thinking of the fine officer's homes near the gate and the boys appreciating the soft leather sofas. When I got on the hill in the car, I could see the long, narrow barracks and the mud, stone and fields. The polish and front is the show. I realized that when I lived in the finest, wealthiest homes in these parts where the madam's bed was inlaid with mother of pearl, but my bed was a damned old iron cot that cost about $6.95. With all the fine imported linens, we ate off of crusty oilcloth. Honey, that's why I put flowers on the kitchen table every day...flowers and smiles. I had too much horseshit. So you "aim high". Have that home sparkle. Wood and junk can pile up in any shed, but a good wife needs assistance. So make your life what I always wanted mine to be. Be proud and be up to the minute. Keep your eyes open and don't act too quickly. Time takes care of all things, but time wasted is never gained. Time and tide waits for no man. You might say Mom is always preaching, but I am only talking to you.

I took Brownie down to the mailbox and boy-oh-boy skunk is all around. The air is so heavy today and the smell sure is all around outside. The wet leaves hold the odor.

Dad has a half-pound of Limburger in the cellar. He said, "I wish the boy was here to enjoy a sandwich." He got it Friday. He said, "I'll take it to the boy." I said, "You will not!"

---

[97] Aunt Violet is Violet Noll, the wife of Helen's brother, Charles Edward Long.

Well Pal, your time will be up when you- (this is as far as I got. Guess why.)

Byron, Joe D'Angelo[98], George, Bert[88], Sissy and Aunt Dink came in. Do they look good. Byron and Joe got in from Sampson at 7 o'clock last night. They have only 7 days leave and must go back next Monday night to Sampson. It's 11 hours on the train. Byron gained 10 pounds. They looked swell. They told us all their troubles. But they said Sampson is laid out swell, but it was zero with deep snow when they left. I made tea and cake, crackers and cheese. They came up to the ration board. They got 12 red meat points, 20 blue, 7 gallons of gas and 1 pound of sugar, so they are all set for the week.

I told them to get the hell back to the ration board and say 1 pound of butter cost 20 points and they can eat that much in one week. They said the eats at Sampson were wonderful because of the cold.

Bill did not see Byron. Bill had to leave at 4 o'clock. He cried awfully. Aunt Dink said he had a break with his girl and gave back all the letters and her picture. I guess that made him feel worse.

Well so long for now pal, more later. Lots of love.

Mommy

It's raining now; better than snow. Love.

Wednesday night, November 15, 1944

Dear Son,

---

[98] Joe D'Angelo and Bert's relationship to the family is unknown.

Roger mailed off a big letter to you this afternoon and there is no news tonight. Lone Ranger is on and Dad took the car to Benders. I am real tired as I told you. I have been awake since 10 after 4 this morning. I will soon call it a day and go to bed. It rained a little, then the sun came out and now it's warm and foggy. Joe gave Brownie a bath in disinfectant, but he is still full of skunks, and stays in the cellar.

So dear, I hope you are well and happy and doing okay. Byron and Joe got $80.00 pay when they came away after receiving two ten-dollar pays and five haircuts while in camp. He left on Labor Day (September) and got home on the 15th of November. So they look fine. I called Granny and told her the news. So that's all I know. Will say nighty night and all my love. Dad got my shoes.

Thursday morning, November 16, 1944

Dear Son,

It's a dreary morning. It's raw but not too cold, with a light drizzle and no prospects of it being a cheerful day. But, I have all the comforts of home. Good food and cheerful fire; all I ask is for God to take care of all my family, one in Bainbridge, one in Chester, and one in Wilson. All have gone and left me. It's just one of those days when you don't know what ails you, but something is missing. Now you will say, "Mom must be homesick for me." The bright spot for me is expecting you to call us up tonight. I must be ready for supper when they come home, just as if I wasn't expecting the call. It's always nice at the homecoming of those we love.

When I was young, like you are now, I would go home to Pennypack Creek. All my brothers and my little sisters would be washed and combed. My little brother Charlie would be carrying big armfuls of wood. He would be so

The Home Fires

proud. He would run to me because he knew I had a little candy. I would bring pork chops or steak and my Mom would have someone run to Arlen's to get 50 cents worth of potatoes. We would sit at the table until 9 o'clock. Then they would all walk out with me to the trolley at Welsh Road and Frankford Avenue. It was always like Christmas when I went home. My Mom would bake walnut cake or make peach pie. It was always about 5 o'clock when I would get home because I had to serve 1 o'clock lunch, wash dishes and then get ready. When I lived in Germantown, I got home every Thursday or Friday so that I was like you are now.

When I came up here, I could never go out on weekdays because I had to take care of five men and two babies. Dad never wanted to go out except on Saturday night. It would be 8 o'clock before he would be done and ready. You and Roger would be sleepy and had to be carried on my lap coming and going. My legs would be numb from being tired before I started out. It took me 13 years before I was able to go to church. All I ever had was a housedress.

You asked me Sunday if that was a new hat. I had that feather since we went to Atlantic City with McAdams 13 years ago. I put it on a new shape. You see son, I have an eye for artistic things, but my purse is too flat to carry out my desires. You could have a home worth talking about. I know how to decorate and place furniture and the right combinations; but what can I do? I always have to buy clothes and shoes that are durable and lasting. Not the kind I can wear a few times and they fall apart. But, I have good taste and I am as good as "a few". Well son, here I go rambling on just for a morning chat.

I slept from 10 Wednesday night to 4:15 Thursday morning without waking up. When Dad went out, he had to call me twice. I had a good rest last night. I must clean upstairs. It's 8:45. Roger left. He wore his topcoat this morning and everything is still nice and green out. By November 23, "Thanksgiving Day", the sleet and zero weather will be with us. The coal pile has a ton gone already. This weather is mild, but we must be warm.

Dad has a cold in his throat from getting on the ground to fix the exhaust pipe. Bill won't have a pipe until next Monday. Dad fixed it so the fumes would go out of the car. Between the "old skunk" smell and all the rest, oh boy!

The noon whistles have blown. I got your short letter telling me you got Roger's sweater. I took Brownie down with me to the mailbox. The rain made him stink all over again. He is polluting the cellar today, as it is too damp in the truck shed. Joe used one-half box of soap flakes and one-half bottle of Zonite and still he is SKUNK.

Well son, news is only of home. I got two big lemon meringue pies baked. They turned out perfect. Crust a little rich. We will have them tonight when I expect Dot over for supper. I am so glad you had your feet fixed up. I am going to call Granny up. So, I'll say, pack up your troubles in your "ditty bag" and "Smile" your troubles away. Lots of love, hugs. I feel better now that I talked to you and had your letter. "No more homesick" for you.

Friday morning, November 17, 1944

Hello Honey,

It was so nice to hear from you last night; but you see, dear, your mother can tell when something is not just right, even by the tone of your voice. (Right?) Dear, I was in bed and Pop said, "Did you write to Edwin?" I didn't get up and come down. I had written you a big letter and so you will miss one mail from me.

The Home Fires

My mind is so upset all the time. I don't know. Mrs. Watson just called and asked about you. So you see everyone that I like is interested in you. I am going to try to go to church on Sunday, unless you are calling up.

It's nine-thirty and a cool, sunny morning. I must run along and get some work done; ironing, washing, cleaning. I am like you, so much to do. So March On.

I am hoping for the day to see us all together without tears, only happy days. Until then, lots of love, kisses and hugs.

Dot had the laughers on last night. I looked so funny with my hair. (Cut off the fuzz.)

Love, kiss, smooth your face.

Mom

Friday evening

Dear Son,

I was sure surprised when you called up tonight. We sure did have a nice long talk. I hope it made you feel lots better.

It's 10 o'clock and some bout is on the radio. Uncle John said he heard Roosevelt and he gets all the news from California on the radio. He said the higher ups still push him and the brig is always open for those who don't obey or who want to do right. In spite of it all, son, bite your tongue. This is War.

I mailed a letter off when I was out. So be good. Dot could not go with us. Nutsie went out, so she had to stay home with her Mom because her Dad went to the store.

Dad is going to bed so I am too. Do your duty now at K.P.[99] You will make out okay. William McAdams just got over one month of K.P.

Boake Carter[100] died of a stroke at 46.

So, Cheerio. Lots of love. Happy Sunday. Will be thinking of you.

Mom & All

Saturday noon, November 18, 1944

Son,

It's 5 of 12, but no Edwin coming in the lane at 50 MPH. Instead, I guess you are handing it out today. I wish that were me. I would love to be behind that counter dishing out food to the boys.

When you come home, then you will know how to wash and cook "not so good". I was a slave 16 long years. I served "my time". Now you know what a relief I have and how glad I am to be able to suit myself.

Well pal, I hip hopped to the mailbox and I got your pictures. They are lovely, just the image of you. Only thing on pictures, you are always so sad. Cheer up boy. You "ain't seen nuthin". Wait. You are getting hardened for what you must face ahead. You will know what I preached to you of hardship. It's far

---

[99] K.P. is "Kitchen Patrol" in the military, which is working in the kitchen. Not a desirable duty.
[100] Boake Carter's relationship to the family is unknown. Most likely he was a friend or acquaintance.

worse to be cold and hungry than to have to eat food you don't like. I ate food Grandpop bought for years. Now, I am in Heaven on Earth, as near as I will ever be. So keep your chin up. Make the best of it. The cold ocean lies ahead.

I had a nice letter from Uncle John again today. He said I should not fret or worry over you. He said to pray. He said they could hardly wait for all you young boys to get to the South Pacific to relieve them, as they have done their best to keep the Japs from the USA. Now they want a rest so bad. He said to pray for those who will never come home. That's what kills me. I pray to God to spare you. Uncle John said they go to church, rain or shine, (no seats) and sing (no music), and thank God to be alive. So dear, March On.

I am real busy and must march on to work. United we stand. Divided we fall. So stick together all, and we will have happy days again. Yes, Nettie knows I was good to her brothers in World War I. That was kind of her to say so. I love your pictures and you.

Mother

Yes, I will send a homemade cake so you get it for Thanksgiving.

Sunday afternoon, November 19, 1944
May not send cake this week. (No sugar)

Dear Son,

I was still in bed when the phone rang this morning and Pop had to yell for me. All he did was say yes to the operator. I can't understand how some people answer the telephone. I had an idea it was Granny, so I didn't rush. Well anyway, it was nice to hear from you. Sometimes, just like a flash, you stand before me or speak to me. I keep wondering what is on your mind or what you want to say to me that you don't, and so I keep thinking that I must tell you to trust in God.

I fear sometimes that maybe I have not told you enough. I know I failed when you were little. I had to spend the time taking care of the old men's wants instead of yours. That was my cross and I did my best whatever you may think of me. I had a hard road to travel. My burdens were heavy. I often wonder how I ever put up with it all. But I just say, "The Lord is my Shepherd, I shall not want." No matter what you must go through; God will give you peace everlasting. So no matter what happens, God is Master of All. Trust in prayer. Then I will know my boy is saved by God's grace and His will be done. If I know that, then I am truly satisfied. So be good and God guides you. Instead of profane language when people are mean, just say, "God leadeth me," whatever the path. I am sure no matter how hard the task, God will keep you. I know.

It is a medium day up here at home with the usual things, fires, eating, dusting, and cooking. Not much joy, except that we are thankful for health, warmth and food. We earned it by the sweat of the brow and the ache of the muscles. No one gave it to us. So now Son, on this Thanksgiving morn, give thanks to God with a free, good, kind heart for a Mom and Dad that always did their best, and they await the day of their baby's return when the War has ceased.

I always cried for my absent brother. Now this year, I must cry for all absent ones; not hysterical tears, but tears of thanks that God has spared you all for us. Never be afraid of death. God is Master of that. What is will be. Son, my heart is unburdened. Smile and March On. You are part of me. What you go through, I do too.

The Home Fires

Ease your heart and with thanks March Onward, Christian Sailor, 'til we meet again. All my love.

Mother & All

Sunday night, 10 PM

Dear Son,

We had our supper at Uncle Charlie's. All is well. The baby is fine. On the way home, we stopped to see Aunt Minnie and she made coffee. We listened to the Good Will Hour and Gabriel Heater. Then we came home where we are glad to be in the warmth.

Dad and Roger are cracking walnuts for me to make your cake tomorrow. I hope I can get it off to you. All I need is a good box to pack it in. On the way up to Uncle Charlie's, we stopped to see Dot. No one was home but Nutsie and Tom. They said Dot and the family were up the country.

I don't know any other news except that all are well. We are going to bed now. I guess you had a long, hard day. Pop and Uncle Charlie framed your picture. Uncle Charlie cut a piece of board for the back. Dad will hang it in his shop at work. I put it in one of those frames that had the birds in it by the desk. I guess you were tired tonight. We thought of you all day. Be good and you will be happy.

Love from All,

Mom

Wartime Letters Written from Mother to Son

Monday morning, November 20, 1944

My Dearest Son,

Here in the country today, Mr. Winter is giving us a taste of snow, not too cold, but raw and wet; and so I have the feeling it is better that you are inside this week. Now it is 10:30 AM and I have been awake since 3:30. I had an awful dream. I thought my own father had fallen down the steps and was dead. I heard him say, "Helen, Helen." I woke up and in that next minute the telephone was ringing. I jumped out of bed. Dad woke up, "What's the matter?" Of course, I was dashing down the steps and oh! Edwin, Oh! What is wrong? I said, "Come quick Pop, it must be something wrong." I said, "Hello?" She said, 'Could you get "guard" so and so.' I said, "What number are you calling?" She said, "Isn't this Budd's?" Well, Pop and I were a wreck. We couldn't go to sleep and now it's dark and dreary.

I have the radio on and two cakes in the oven. I can't leave to go upstairs or start in any special job because I may forget your cake. Now honey, all the news is about 6th War Loan Drive. I don't know anything new. All I have been thinking about is you and how nice looking all of Uncle Charlie's boys are. He was repairing a sled, making logs and candlesticks for Christmas. He needs pants so bad. I told him when you came home at Christmas you could give him what you picked out. Then all will be well. I hope that you get the cake okay. It's a job because I don't have any box, etc., but I guess you can eat it when you get it. I will try to send it off tonight with things that carry well, good stuff. Pop and Roger cracked the nuts. So Old Nut, so long for now.

Mom

Monday night, 5:30

Well son, I have supper cooking, sauerkraut, pork and baked limas. It's raining hard all afternoon. I went down in the rain, but no mail at 5 of 12. When Roger came, he brought 2 letters from you written Friday and Saturday, and your paper. I sent your cake 15 minutes ago. The baker is mailing it from Somerton. As it is pouring rain, I asked him to take it so you get it for Thanksgiving.

I see the piece in your paper you marked and also the menu. It doesn't sound so bad. I will be out on Friday night to McAdams' and to the store. I forgot to give the first part of this letter to the baker to mail, so you will only get one instead of two today. I am tired.

Mrs. McAdams, Mrs. Spence and Granny called me up today. Mrs. Spence said she will write when she gets a chance. The cake cost me plenty. Eighty-six cents just for the walnuts. Hope you like it.

Love,

Mom

Tuesday morning

Dear Son,

The home fires are burning. The kitchen fire was out for some reason this morning. So I have all going strong now at 9:25 this dark, dreary, lonely day. It rained and snowed since we got up Monday morning. All the fields are rivers, and all I can hear is the rain falling and the fires cracking. I guess I have come to the point where I can sit alone and dream of days to come.

The cat and the dog are my company. I had a green lollipop. I was going to put it in with the cake just for fun. I had the cake all wrapped up when I saw it. I have an awful job to keep from eating it. Pop and Joe cleaned up the cake like yours, only smaller. I didn't get any, except one tiny piece. I did want to taste it today, to see how it flavored. The cake I sent you should have been thicker, but I didn't have the right size pan. Anyway, it was a taste from home and mother. I sent you the recipe and a picture of it. First time I ever made it.

When Dad paid Heinel's[101], Elmer told him they had bought two farms in Bustleton to make an airfield, but he couldn't tell Dad where as he didn't want it to leak out. They had just put down the down payment to bind the deal that day.

The lady Granny takes care of, Mrs. Delheim, must go to the hospital every Friday now as well as Monday because her leg is worse, like Uncle Paul's. They offered Granny to stay there for the winter. I told her to stick it out for the winter where there's oil, heat, and always warm with plenty to eat and drink. Of course, everywhere you live it's one thing or another, but there are no children there and everything is so clean.

Dad and I are glad you are inside these past few days. I don't suppose "you march" this week, do you? Now you can see just what a mother with a big household must do. No matter how sick I felt, how tired, the milk had to be strained, skimmed, milk pans scalded daily. Never any let up. Toothache, earache, heartache, it was just the same. Keep going. So, now on this wintry morning, with coal to burn, plenty to eat, and myself to please, I am so thankful. I was also thankful when I read the menu on the Main Sheet. Thirty-eight thousand pounds of turkey and in Athens, Greece they died by the hundreds, daily of starvation. So my dear son, thank God you serve Old

---

[101] Heinel's was an area garage.

Glory, the finest nation in the world. Uncle John said pray, because you must be brave and you will need courage and strength. That comes from God and good living. So March On to Victory. Thanksgiving 1945 I pray God to have you all home to us mothers.

You know son, when you sit alone, go through life "on a star". You will get wise to the ways of the world. When you get out among people, you see and learn things that you never thought about. If your brain is active, you grasp it quickly. I often wonder why I know so little, but I know plenty. I never express it because my family was the kind who doesn't progress. Dad lives in the Gay '90's. I went along in stride with the times, through reading. Reading broadens your education. I read things you never dream about. Ceramics, husbandry, economics, and many things I am interested in. I have no way to express my views, because Dad would not know what I was talking about. If I was running a farm, I could tell you about soil erosion and rotation cropping. I read so much about chickens and have noted when cleaning chickens, the minute a chicken has not developed properly. I could go on and on about all sorts of flowers, their botanical names and I would make farming a paying business because I would be like Wenker, "in the know".

No matter what kind of life you choose, if you know the right people, they can always put you on the right track and help you to progress or aid you.

And so it is with love. "If you love" anyone, you always try to please them. You try to look your best. You try to do everything you know how to make them happy. If you truly love, words are not necessary. Actions speak louder than words. The eyes are the windows of the soul. They convey messages no one can read except the two they concern. So never have any doubts. If Dot loves you, you never need to ask. Actions will tell you. No matter whom you choose in God's World, no one will ever love you like your mother does. You can travel the highways of Life and knock, knock on every door. You will never find one who loves you like your mother. Winter, summer, well or sick, you are part of your mother. Only death parts. Until we meet again.

Love,

Mother

November 24, 1944

Dear Edwin,

Well, the big holiday is over and we sure spent a lazy day. I never had less to do. I felt fine up until I was to mash the potatoes. Then a spell came over me. I could only eat the chicken. After you called and Dot went home about 3, both Pop and I held down a couch in each room. Roger read a book. Joe went to Baldwin's. At 9:30 we went to bed and I got up at 9:30 this morning. It's now noon. I am through with the routine work. I am thinking about going to Frankford. I told Dot I would see her, so I guess I better go. The movies showing are lousy; none I want to see. That sort of changes my plans. I will make this letter short, as I must get dressed. We want to get off a little early. Roger is going to the Army and Navy store. I want to get some Christmas cards for England and do some window-shopping, so I will close for now. It was nice to talk to you yesterday. I will say so long. Lots of love from,

Mom and all XXXX

Friday night

Dear Son,

Short and sweet tonight again. I got home from Frankford. I went on the 3 o'clock trolley, got the meat and some Christmas cards. I met Dot. We went up to the oyster house and each had a stew. Dot and I went into the Food Fair[102]. Dad got his haircut and then we went home. Mrs. Ems was waiting for Dot. It was 7:30, so they left for Frankford.

Pop went right to bed because he had a cold, and pain in his back. So he is in bed. Mr. Wenker knocked on the door this afternoon to get your address. They haven't heard from Harold yet. I told him to write to the number on the card they got from the government and he would get it. They are as worried as we were. I guess war is awful for all people.

I will sign off now, as I am tired. It's real cold up here and raw. I am going to bed. Aunt Lilly called up. Somebody stole all her panties, bras and girdles off the clothesline while she was out on Thanksgiving Eve.

Love,

Mom

Saturday afternoon

Dear Edwin,

Joe is waiting to go, so here I am again in a hurry. No news. I got the letter you wrote after you talked to us. Maybe tonight I will get a chance to talk to you in writing. I haven't done much today.

It's a nice day here in Philadelphia. Pop is not so good. As usual, he has a cold in his kidneys. Don't worry. Dot will be with us tonight, I hope. I was cold last night. So was Dot. So tonight I will toast my toes by the fireside. I'm glad

---

[102] Food Fair was a supermarket chain.

it will be Sunday. I guess you are washing today. I've got mine dry. All my love. Write us.

Mother

Sunday evening, November 26, 1944

Dear Son,

Well, we have put in the day, which was a nice one. Pop is listening to Gabriel Heater and Roger is in bed reading one of your books. The cat is watching on the step looking behind the electric stove for a mouse. She must have seen one because she is on the alert. As soon as you hung up, I put the finishing touches to dinner. The hamburger is fried too hard. I was waiting for you to call. But, when it neared 1 PM, I thought I would proceed with the noonday meal. Then I called Mrs. Wenker. She was pleased to have word of her son. I had to cut the conversation short because of the dinner. Then Walter Shallcross[103] came in, so we had two extra for dinner. Roger is busy getting all your toys and his together. He seems to want to give them all away to Uncle Charlie's boys. I suppose it's a nice thought. He got together the marble game, the ducks Mrs. Bell sent, the drum, and the boxing gloves Uncle Bill gave you both. It looks like I have no more little boys.

Dot helped me with the dishes. Dad took her home early because her mother wanted to visit some ill woman. Now it is night and I know no other news. It was a nice weekend. Dad has a cold, which, as usual, has settled in his back muscles. I have been putting hot towels on and giving him a rub and then the electric pad ever since Saturday night. I made us a cup of broth, so I will eat that and then play nurse. So I will say goodnight with all the best love and wishes and hope that I could do something. I wish Dot could do something

---

[103] Walter Shallcross was most likely a family friend unknown to the editor.

for your cold too. I hope you feel better and get your wash done. So dear, Cheerio.

Mother & All

Monday evening, November 27, 1944

Dear Son,

Well, here I am again with nothing new to tell you. It was a nice warm day. I washed the curtains and got them ironed and up in the kitchen, so I put in a busy day. I am ready for bed. What do you think?

We got a bill in today for $20.00 for electric. Dad said, "Can't blame the boy." Well darling, I don't know a thing to say. I only think of you and I guess your wash is dry as it was a good day after yesterday's rain. The full moon is shining, so colder weather is ahead. Lots of love.

Mother & All

Tuesday 3:30, November 28, 1944

Dear Son,

The other son is saying, "Hurry up, hurry up, and get that letter written." All I have been doing today is hurrying up, because I have so many household tasks to do. I don't know which to do first. It's seven weeks today that you have been gone. It doesn't seem possible. I see by the Mainsheet, where the boys who don't graduate before Christmas may have visitors on the 23rd and 31st.

Roger is making soldiers. Uncle Charlie gave him a big piece of lead and he has 48 made perfectly. He is painting them and has 12 done. We are counting on having a Christmas as of old. Do you remember the one when the two new bicycles were under the tree? Those were the days when I had the most pleasure to hear your yells of joy.

This year, I must go through giving you to some other girl. All I want is someone to love you and care for your interests, and for you in return to do the same. The only thing is, I think you are entirely too young. You have lots to learn and you need a start that helps, and happiness to survive. When poverty comes in the window, "love flies out". Understanding and duty are far different than love. I had my share of both. I'm still sticking.

They strapped Dad's chest at Ford's. At 1:30 this morning, I had to cut it loose. He was in misery. When he got up at 4, he said he felt a little better. He has pleurisy from a cold. Don't worry though. If he was real sick, he couldn't work. But he should be in bed for a week. I will write more tonight. Hope your cold is better.

Lots of love,

Mother & All

Thursday evening, November 30, 1944

Dear Son,

I suppose you are not getting as much mail from me this week, as it has rained and Roger hasn't gotten out with an afternoon letter. I have sent one every morning with Dad. It rained all day and all night Wednesday and today until about 2 PM. Then a cold north wind came up and it gets in every crack.

The Home Fires

I have been firing up all afternoon. It's 68 degrees in the dining room with all the fires going. The paper says it will be 28 degrees by morning.

I was sewing all day. I made 5 aprons and a nightgown. I don't know any news, but I hope you are well. Dad has nothing extra.

Love,

Mom

I got your letter with the picture. No comment. The radio says snow flurries tonight with freezing temperatures. I will put the wash up in the cellar. No outside for me this winter. As I said before, no news. Only what I hear on the radio. I missed Sardi's[104] this morning. American fliers are told not to bomb the Emperor's palace in Tokyo. What bunk. They made a bomb hit on the British's Buckingham Palace. But it seems they don't want to bomb the homes of the higher ups. Poor people can take it all. Well, nighty night, sailor boy.

Love,

Mom

**** END OF NOVEMBER ****

---

[104] Sardi's was a radio program.

Chapter Three

December 1944

Edwin Charles Price, USN.

Wartime Letters Written from Mother to Son

5 PM, Friday, December 1, 1944

Dear Son,

I have put the finishing touches on the supper and will chat with you for a few minutes while I rest. I have been on the go all day, up and down, cleaning all around and shoveling on the coal. For the past 24 hours, a north wind has been sending its icy blasts along the fields.

I put out the wash and froze my fingers. I sure hate the thought of going to the store tonight. If I can get out of it, I will, because Dad is not feeling any too good. I sure am glad it's not this Sunday when we are planning to come see you. Dad needs the rest. He has the pleurisy, which is a cold that settled in the pleural cavity. He coughs so much. I don't know what to do for him. He is happy in his job and doesn't want to be bossed indoors, so I must worry along.

I am wondering if you are doing any guard duty outside. If so, I was wishing I could run with a cup of hot soup or coffee to you. But, one thing about you, you are no apartment house rosebud.

I don't know any news. I haven't seen Dottie since Sunday. I hope she writes often to you. I guess I write the most. It seems that time goes so fast when it rains. I don't work around as much, and then the dust collects, as well as the wash. I have very few shirts to iron, because the men and Roger wear the heavy ones now. I keep my things washed up piece by piece. That is the easiest and the best way. I change often; in fact, everyday. Then there is no rub scrub to do. You do the same. It is less trouble and takes less time. When things get too soiled, they are hard to wash.

Tonight, I am having smoked butt, mashed potatoes, dried limas and potpie. I wish you were here for some. I ordered 2 dozen oysters from Gallagher's and 2 quarts of milk for supper on Saturday night when Dad and Joe are out. It is easy to fix.

I got your box of letters today. I put them up in the bottom bureau drawer. Roger is here. Soon Joe will be in, so I will say so long.

Mom

Friday Night, December 1, 1944

Dear Edwin,

I wrote you at suppertime. Dad is home. We didn't go to Frankford. I got some dried beef from Gallagher's and it's tough and fine. Not a bit nice. Mr. Gallagher told me that Joe is back from the South Pacific and in the States. He will get home for Christmas. They are happy. Dot told Pop that Mrs. Mayo was at her house last night and said that Ted is in the U.S.A. and expects to get home for Christmas, too.

You asked me about the War's progress. It seems to be going bloody and strong in Europe and also in the South Pacific. Churchill says it won't be over in Germany until the summer. The A.E.F.[105] is on the banks of the Rhine. Son, meet the crisis when it comes. Get your training well-learned and then you will be able to face whatever you are called to do. I don't want to listen to war news because I get too deep. Then I break down.

Son, here is some advice. Don't worry about rings until you can safely buy

---

[105] A.E.F. is the Allied Expeditionary Force, consisting of American, British, Canadian and French forces.

them. Christmas and War are not a good season. I know your heart's desire, but I can't see how you can fill it. There is plenty of time ahead of you. So, make a right start with no debt. No matter what you do, I don't want to be an interfering mother-in-law. But, you are my son. I am only telling you the facts. You can work it out some way. The right way is the best way.

I will say goodbye for the present and hope you are well. How do you like the cold weather? I don't like it.

Lots of love,

Mommy

Saturday afternoon, December 2, 1944

Edwin,

I will give this letter to Joe to mail when he goes to Frankford. I just got two letters written on Thursday and Friday from you. I am glad you are okay. In the same mail came the phone bill. Edwin, Sunday is the cheapest time to call and in the evening after seven are cheaper rates.

Daytime calls are the most expensive per:

Oct. 22-   .35
Oct. 26-   .85
Oct. 28-   .65
Oct. 29- 1.55
Nov. 5-   1.75
Nov. 11- 1.15
Nov. 16-   .75

The Home Fires

Nov. 22-	.35
Nov. 22-	.85
	8.25
Tax	2.06
Total	$10.31
Usual	$ 4.03
	$14.34

It's not nearly as bad as I thought it would be, but enough. Dad had Thanksgiving off, so I was short and I can't send you any money today. I just paid the rent and I must have $21.00 for insurance on Monday.

We have had a real cold snap since the rain ceased. It keeps me busy taking care of fires. Roger had his hair cut at Pat's (65 cents). Now he is off to the movies. He needs pants so badly and they are so hard to get. I looked all over Frankford for corduroys. I guess I will have to go to Sears. He sure likes the sweater. I gave him your yellow scarf because it's wearing thin and the moths would like it. When you get home again, you will want a new one.

I hope you are well and doing well. I am counting the days.

Lots of love,

Mother

Are you hearing the Army and Navy game? Army is ahead 7 to 0. I am cheering for the Navy. I am so excited, plus my boys have their money bet on Navy. So have I.

Sunday afternoon, December 3, 1944

Dear Son,

Dad, Dot and I are chewing the fat. Dad is going to take Dot home now because Dot is going down to the trolley with her Aunt Jenny. I, as usual, don't know any news. Esther called up and asked if Aunt Lilly was here as she was in that wedding and did not get home until 7 o'clock this morning.

We had sauerkraut for dinner, but the pork was all fat. I was giving Dad hail. But he usually thinks he is right. I was not pleased, especially since Dot was here.

Well son, here is the $5.00. Pop is saving money well. He can help you out. I am broke and flat.

I will cut this short, as they are nearly ready to leave. Let me know when you get this.

Lots of love,

Mom, Dad, Dot, Roger

Monday afternoon, December 4, 1944

Dear Edwin,

It was 20 degrees here this morning and yesterday, but now the sun is shining full force and the home fires are burning. It's 75 degrees in the dining room for a change and I am plenty warm. Foster's Pond has three inches of ice and Roger has gone with the new skates for a try out. He bought new skating socks, so I am anxious to hear how he makes out, "wet a - -, hungry gut and frozen". Do you remember how many times you froze at the same place?

Dad sent you the $5.00. When I read over your letters, I read between the lines. You say, "Mother I will spend most of my time with you." Your letters are like sweet music to my ears. Like a melody I heard long ago. Its sweetness lingers. But I know it is only memories. You know, from the day you left me that I have seen you ten thousand times. I have seen you as many more as we sat on the rocker in the dining room. I could see Grandpop, Dad, Uncle Bill and myself sitting in that rocker holding you and letting you sleep in my lap until my legs would feel as if they were breaking. As I sat there that morning, I was glad we sat there for the memories. Then when I waved to you at the door, I went in. I screamed to the top of my voice. I said, "Oh God, give me strength. I am a good Christian mother," and in my heart I knew that was the last time you were my baby or that you belonged to me. God heard my prayer and I have not broken down since you left. Yes, tears come to my eyes. Not the brokenhearted kind because there are many sayings I get comfort from. There is a saying, "As a man sows, so shall he reap."

We have always gathered a poor harvest. So I put your life in God's hands to guide you, watch over you, and comfort you. You know the Golden Rule, if you do not heed, you will reap the harvest. God's words are true. 'No man cometh unto the Father except through me. I am the truth and the light.' So my dear son, you live your own life.

Don't worry over us. Think of us. Sure, you will never forget us, because we have protected and given you all that was in our power. You have been given kind advice. You should have the knowledge to know that two wrongs never make a right. But once wrong, you never need to make the same mistake. You dear, never need to tell me your plans. I know your mind better than you do. As sure as night follows day, I know you and can rate you and what your plans are because I know you and watched you from the hour of your birth.

The morning you were born, I told the nurse and doctor to promise me one thing. Let me see the baby "dead or alive", the minute he is born. I never saw my first son. You were in a cloth. The Doctor said, "What will it be?" I said a boy. He said, "Nurse, stand aside of the patient with the child." She gave me one look at you. I had two doctors and three nurses. I went through plenty. When I gave you up, all those things rushed through my mind. As you left, we lost 18 years of toil, sorrow, and hardship just when you could help us by your earnings. You see, God watches over us, because I have faith. You laughed at me when I went to church. I haven't been to church for three months, but I talk to God just the same. Now, you will say, "Mom, don't write me letters like this." Well my heart speaks to you. All I want in life is to see you get on the right track.

A little bird asked me this morning if I knew that Aunt Violet had Charlie arrested and in the Doylestown jail for three days "some time ago". I said no, I didn't know anything about it, but I would ask you. I remembered Charlie being absent from work for several days and I am sure that if it happened before you left, you would know about it. Do you know anything? I won't say that you told me. Of course, I can read between the lines there also. Dink is the cause of it all. I am neutral. That is their own affair, but there are two sides to every story.

I have been working hard all day. I have a wash out. I have a roast of pork, "fresh ham", in the oven with the good brown "cracklins" like you liked so much. Sweet and white potatoes, carrots and onions roasted around it, fresh green spinach and mashed white turnips are also on the menu tonight, plus cornbread, applesauce and coffee. I wish you were here, but you get a bellyful, I guess.

Monday, 7:30 PM

Well son, one hour ago I was talking to you. I was sure surprised. The phone rang once and I was just ready to sit down to a plateful. I was glad Roger got home when he did. I enjoyed my supper because I had my boys with me.

Well, I am going to listen to Vox Pop. I am glad you received the money.

The cops were out in full force at the Italian's house. Two cops escorted him to the freight cars this afternoon. Apparently, some trouble with the coloreds. I guess he didn't pay them. They shot Hap's building full of holes. Dot can tell you. She was coming home from taking her Aunt Jennie home. She was afraid. She told Pop tonight that the trolley man stopped the trolley and asked what was going on because there were so many cops at the Italian's place. Well dear, so long for now.

Lots of love,

Mommy

Tuesday Night, December 5, 1944

Dear Edwin,

I am almost ready to go to bed. Gabriel Heater is over and Beatrice Lillie is singing and getting a great hand. I guess Dad told you all the news. I was out to the Missionary at Mrs. Rupert's and was helping to make hats for the dolls for the Russians and the Indians.

I tried out a new cake recipe. Dad fed his share to Brownie. I guess you know I won't make it for you next Sunday. Well son, I don't have much news. I will ring off for now. I can't listen to Bea and write.

I hope we can come see you on Sunday.

Lots of love. Nighty night.

Mom

Wednesday Evening, December 6, 1944

Dearest Son,

You called a little earlier than I had expected, but just in time for Dad to talk to you. I waited quite a few seconds after I had accepted your call, but, as usual, I am always glad to talk to you. When I wrote last night, I told you I was listening to Beatrice Lillie, but it was Gracie Fields, the one you always liked to listen to, too.

Mr. and Mrs. North are on and I can hardly write. Dad was out to Bender's to get something done to the exhaust pipe. The piece Dad put on came loose again. Bender wasn't there, so Dad is out on the ground now working on it. He still has his chest strapped and had three prescriptions filled by the Doctor at Ford's. He should not be on the cold ground, but if it is not fixed, don't look for me on Sunday. I can't ride in that car with that gas. He said he can patch it up. I am telling you, that car and you going away sure have made me poor. But, I guess I must take it. When it comes to Christmas this year, I can't even send Mrs. Bell a present. I guess I will have to scratch. Dad is in. He said he fixed it to hold out a while.

I can't write because of the radio, so I will bring this to a close and hope to see you on Sunday. I only hope it is a nice day. So be good and God will guide you and keep you safe for us.

Love,

Mommy, Dad, Roger and Joe

Thursday Morning, December 7, 1944

Dear Son,

Roger is leaving for school. All I have done is make my bed, Joe's bed and get the fires fixed. There is no news. The weatherman said rain today, but the sun is coming up. Mother is a lady today. I am going to meet Dad at Mrs. McAdams' tonight for dinner. Roger is coming after school. We bought him a new pair of common corduroy. For some unknown reason, Pop ordered dark blue. Rog is getting so fat. He has a 30 inch waist and 27 length, so you know I can't rock him on my lap anymore. It was $4.95 for the pants. I nearly had a fit. Dad gave me $5.00 less in the pay on account of Thanksgiving out, and I still must pay this month on the car. Bill Bender's bill was $30.00. There won't be any Christmas present giving on my end of it. The man who sells the turkeys went to Delaware to see about 60 of them yesterday. Tonight, we will know if we get one. Mr. McAdams told Dad he asked for the afternoon off so he could go. We have a 25 pound one ordered, so I must figure on at least $13.00 for it. So you see, you have worry with learning and I have worry with financial difficulties. I'm always trying to make ends meet. I figured on $21.00 insurance, but I only paid $16.50 because I didn't pay on the monthly books. I had November paid and will pay on January 1st so that gave me enough for the pants.

You will say, 'All Mom talks about is bills.' But you and I used to talk things over when you were home. Roger is too young to be burdened, so I miss you in many ways. I hope to see you Sunday. I will mail this when I am out. I will shop tonight instead of Friday this week.

Bye, bye for now.

Love,

Mommy & all

Thursday Evening, 10:10 PM, December 7, 1944

Dear Son,

We are home now and I got the meat and groceries put away. As soon as I get these few lines written, I will go to bed. Dad got word this afternoon that he should work this Sunday. But he said, 'No, I am sorry, but I got passes to go see the boy and I wouldn't disappoint him.'

I had a nice time today at Mrs. McAdams' house. We had a fine supper. I tried all over to get pork chops, but there is no pork anywhere about. Mrs. Bell sent me a nice letter. She was in the hospital for an operation on her eye. She has seen plenty. Son, I will close here and hope to see you on Sunday.

Lots of love,

Mom

Friday, 5 PM, December 8, 1944

Dear Edwin,

I will have a little chat with you while supper is on cooking. Then I can write in peace, because when the radio is on with all that noise, I don't know what to say. It has been raining all day up until 3 PM. I sure am glad I don't have to go to Frankford tonight. Mrs. McAdams helped me shop yesterday. That's one job off my mind. It took me all day, up until now, to chase the dirt. I cleaned upstairs, scrubbed down the front steps out through the hall, cleaned the radio room, the dining room, pressed all of Dad's ties, washed all the scarves and put out the wash that came from the damp wash over the heat to dry.

I wrote a big letter to Mrs. Bell and now to you. I got a money order off to the bank. All my other mail is out. I still can't call it a day until after I serve up your and Dad's favorite. Mrs. McAdams' butcher gave me a Pippen sirloin steak. It's the first we had it in months. It was 33 points. It cost $1.45 and one pound of mushrooms was 78 cents. I bought fresh spinach and mashed potatoes and hurried home.

Well Honey, now I am beginning to count the hours. Dot will be here Saturday afternoon or early evening to do my hair. I will do some cooking tomorrow for Sunday for Joe. You see, I am finishing up the weekend work now.

I do hope and pray to see you on Sunday. I know Christmas is not far off. It's worse than waiting for a new dress or a new bike, or whatever one wants.

It seems like I want to talk to you and look at you all to myself, once again. I know you will have so many plans and the time will go so fast. I hope to make your visit one you will always look back to with pleasure. So hurry up, hurry up. Time, "time waits for no man". Make the most of every precious minute. Be glad you are young. Use your time to every advantage.

I feel like I lost 16 years of my life somewhere. I can't believe my hair is getting white. They say grow old gracefully. Dad always seems the same to me. You never grow old to each other. You still sit and dream. When I grow too old to dream, I'll still have you to remember.

Every time I hear "Oh Susannah", I think of you. When I hear "America" and lately, "How many hearts have you broken?" I think of you. Memories are sweet and bitter, according to your thoughts, so let yours be happy. By the time you read this, the hour will be nearer for our visit. Pray to God to guide and take care of us all.

Love,

Mom

Friday Night, December 8, 1944

Well Son,

Supper is over. The Lone Ranger is shooting it out. I have soaked my feet, read the Bulletin[106] and I am ready to call it a day. The rain has ceased, but the wind is high. The paper says it will get colder, so I guess it will clear up by Sunday.

I walked down for mail on Thursday afternoon. I was all ready to go to McAdams' and as I came up, Cliff R. came in and got gas. So I said, "Are

---

[106] The Philadelphia Bulletin was a daily newspaper.

you going to Bustleton?" He said, "Yes." I said, "Well, take me as far as the trolley." He said, "Sure." I had a nerve to ask that "Yellow". He was getting gas, so I got up the nerve. He told me Ted sent word he would arrive home about Monday to his mother's. He left the West Coast. I asked about Bob. He said his mother had telegraphed Bob about Ted's arrival. But Bob had left Massachusetts, so they don't know now where Bob is. Bob had pneumonia. He never had strong lungs.

I hope he is not shipped out. Mr. Baldwin's grandson, Edgar, is home with a hand off. He has been in Valley Forge Hospital since his return.

Well Pal, I want to wash my hair. Joe scrubbed up the kitchen. That cleans the house for the week except to go over the top tomorrow. I hope you are well and that we shall see you Sunday. So until I see you, the wind is rattling the abode tonight. No early rising tomorrow morning. No school. It's Saturday. Hope to see you soon.

Nighty night. Kiss and hug.

Mommy

Smooth your face, love kiss.

Sunday Evening, December 10, 1944

Dear Edwin,

Well son, we arrived in the house on the dot at 8 PM. We hit Howard Johnson's near Sears at 6:30 and had a lousy supper in there for $4.10. The trip, with what Pop gave you, cost us $15.00. Pop is not so good. He has a cold. We were frozen both going and coming. We saw Dot to the door. She slept all the way from the moment she left Conowingo Dam until we hit Howard Johnson's on the Boulevard.

Dear, I was so happy to see you. I thought you looked very well indeed. I hope you liked the things we brought you and that you had a good time. When you joined your mates, after you left us, Pop it seems, felt bad. I am going to get right to bed. We are frozen. Be good and you will be happy.

Nighty night. X X X X

Mom

Monday night, December 11, 1944

Well Son,

A northeast storm has lashed the fort all afternoon and Mommy has it all under control, home fires going and a good, superb supper over, and Lone Ranger, Hi-yo Silver shootin' his way. Soon I will be climbing the stairs to bed. Pop feels much better tonight. He got new medicine and had a fair night's rest. I sure was glad to see him tonight. I was so worried all day for fear he was getting another bad spell. I think he worked awfully hard on Saturday, as Clarence wasn't in, and then running here and there Saturday night. We didn't sleep very well on Saturday night. I think he was worn out on Sunday. I said, 'Pop you should not have cried.' One more look at him and Dot and I would have been in tears. He said, 'Well, I hated coming away and leaving the boy behind.' I saw so many tears down there this time that I had to get away in a hurry, biting my lips. The inside of them are sore today. I kept thinking of Dad and you all day in the rain. I kept Roger home so I wouldn't get the blues. But now, all is right again as far as home is concerned. I still love you as my baby. Smooth your face and kiss you.

I just finished looking over the paper. I see Mr. Lodge died Sunday. They took him to the hospital Tuesday when I was up at Rupert's. He gets buried on Wednesday, another first class Bustleton funeral. There's not so many left. Uncle Paul, Nelson and Brous, not many of the "boys" left. He was 74 years old, buried in Old Pennypack Cemetery. So, another big house is empty.

The baker and old Granny asked me how you were. Dot is okay. Aunt Lilly hasn't worked in two weeks. She's keeping house now for Fred. Well son, that's all the news I know. The wind is howling across the front porch, so I am going to hug the fire and go to bed. I hope you were okay today after the grub I took you. Honey, all my heart's love to you. Be a good boy for me so you can be home for Christmas. Lots of love. Nighty night.

Mommy & all

Tuesday morning, December 12, 1944

Dear Son,

I am still thinking of you; so here I am for a chat. Roger is getting ready for school. I will clean up after awhile. It is still dark. The wind rocked the bed last night and is still raging. Dad said he heard on the radio that the storm was blowing in from the west. I am going to put the radio on all day today to keep me company.

Well Edwin, it's now 10 AM. I made the beds, dusted, gathered up the wash and fixed the fires. Here I am again. I made a fresh pot of coffee. With the rain and high wind, the snow is fine. Sure enough it's a western gale. These storms are bad enough, but I think a cold northeaster is always worse. The snow is heavier from the northeast. I am wondering if you are out in your shirttail. I am in favor of military training. Even though you are away, it is a wonderful conditioner and only for the dreadful war. I suppose by the time Roger is old enough that it will be a Federal law. Boys of your age are so restless and so impulsive that you want your own way in spite of knowledge. So discipline is lax at home in order to keep a minimum of happiness and contentment.

Education is the stepping stone to success. You can readily see it by your aptitude test. You are then given an interview with a superior. He can spot your I.Q. immediately and therefore you are placed where you best fit in. I know, because I read. Dad thinks differently than I do. I have been in households where the sons were educated in Princeton, Harvard, Lawrenceville, and the best institutions of learning in the world. Not only that, but Mrs. Pearson's sons, Roderick Kellett and Wallace Kellett, who now own Kellett Autogiro Corp. and manufacture airplane parts, were officers in World War I. Rod went to officers' school at Plattsburg and got a 1st Lieutenant's commission in 6 weeks. He was in Philadelphia's own First City Troop. He got to Germany and was wounded by shrapnel. Wallace was in the Red Cross Ambulance work. First he was in Italy, then in France. Finally, he went into the very famous Lafayette Esquadrille, an airplane training unit that was of the first and best. Mrs. Pearson's son, Paul, was a C.P.O.[107] on a submarine. I could tell you many interesting tales I know because Mrs. Pearson maintained open house. All kinds of good eats were put on the dining table and loads of wounded were brought to the house to play pool or billiards and dance, those that had legs. They were brought from Grays Ferry Road Naval Hospital in Philadelphia. I know all sorts of horror tales and what you recruits go through. That was why I always said if ever there were a war, I would never give up my children.

I wasn't born yesterday. I have lived through two separate lifetimes, one from

---

[107] C.P.O. Stands for Chief Petty Officer, a naval rank.

The Home Fires

14 to 23 and the other from 25 to 47. The two years between were the love years of getting acquainted to Dad's ways. They are peculiar, but a good firm foundation of dependence. I hope in your choice of a mate, you will start out with a firm foundation. Experience will help. Take every opportunity. Contentment brings happiness. If you rush things, it never gives you a chance. As for me, I am out of the situation completely. I want to be an understanding mother. You and Pop always outbalanced me. Therefore, I told you in previous letters, you make your own plans. I've told you my wishes. Wait until the war is over. Then you will be more suited to marriage. Start out on your own, forsake all others, and live as you like, independently. Then no one can kick. This is my heart talking to you. When you come home on your visit, I want it to be the happiest Christmas possible. Don't spend one cent on me. Pins and bracelets and such don't mean a thing to me. All I want is you for our Christmas. Pop's eyes will shine like stars.

You know that old poem:

I would like to buy mother a ring,
But I am in Uncle Sam's Navy so,
I can't buy mother a thing.
But mother once told me she's happy,
just seeing me smiling and gay,
and so I will make mother so happy,
if only I get home for Christmas Day.

When Pop, you, and Roger are happy, I can cook and sing and stuff you all. I had English mail[108]. Edwin Bissinger got seven days leave to go to Irene Greenland's (your father's cousin) and to the London Zoo. Irene expects him

---

[108] English mail is a reference to mail received from Price family relatives that lived in England. Irene Greenland is one of those relatives.

there for Christmas, but the eats are scarce, no oranges. Aunt Lillie sent 6 boxes to Edwin. She put in Spam and crab meat and all sorts of canned food. They said Edwin B. is terribly lonely and homesick.

It's now one o'clock. The laundry man brought up a V-Mail Christmas card from Uncle John.

Edwin, I had a letter you wrote on the 8th (no other). Son, everything is okay. What were the things you were going to tell me Sunday? Yes, I miss you coming rushing in and our talks. You learn as you go along. My big chat is over for now. I called Aunt Lilly and read her the English letter. Esther is home with tooth trouble. Write when you can.

All my love,

Mom

December 13, 1944

Dear Edwin,

Roger just brought me up a letter you wrote on Monday. I went down to the mailbox at noon, but there wasn't any there. In the meantime, the pastor called me up and wanted your rating, etc. I gave him S/2- Edwin C. Price, inducted Aug. 28, 1944. Is that right? We are invited to pin the star on the service flag this Sunday. Pop will sure be disappointed. He has to work. Roger and I promised to go. About calling up, you better try to make it for after 1 PM if it is at all possible as I am going to church. I will tell Dad to ask Dot if she wants to go also. It is a nice day today here at home after those two days of storm. By this time, you have my big letters. I may not be home Friday if you try to call, as I must do a little last minute shopping to get Joe and Dad some little things like socks and a shirt. Dad needs ties. I will close this for now, as Roger is waiting. Dad is much better. How are you?

Love,

Mother

Wednesday night, December 13, 1944

Dear Son,

I had a telephone call. (This is as far as I got when the phone rang with your call.) The fellow said, "That you, Helen?" I said yes. He said, "It doesn't sound like you." I said, "Who is this?" He said, "Marlon." I said, "Marlon who?" He said, "Marlon Pye." I said, "Well, you must have the wrong number. This is Bustleton 1002." He said, "Isn't this North Carolina?" I said, "No. Philadelphia." I hope that call is not charged up to us. I should have informed our operator, but I was so excited. And now I am glad to hear from you and to know you are okay after two days storm.

I have all my Christmas cards ready to go out. I sure would have liked to have that radio room done up for Christmas, but money holds me back. So the house will look just the same as when you left it. You know that picture I have. "Be it ever so humble, there is no place like home."

I see all those babies and those women with tears in their eyes and so I still say, I am lucky and so are you that you have no babies coming to see you. I think I would die then. It was bad enough with Pop last Sunday, but all is well once again. This darn war has all mothers and good wives heartbroken. So I will stop here. It's hard to write cheerful letters every day. But you understand me, alone, in a nine room house, squat in the middle of 24 acres and the fellow I fought with most is 85 miles away. Kind of tough, eh?

Well pal, days are slow. Time passes quickly, so they say, but not so quickly when away from dear friends and one's dear home. Time passes slowly when alone. So never be lonely. A good friend is worth his weight in gold. I hope you have a good pal. Give love and you always get it back. So love and hugs. Nighty night.

Mommy

Saturday Evening, 7:30

Dear Son,

Here I am. Saturday evening. No date. No love. No boy. But Dad will soon be home. Roger is getting his train set up and what a time. When I go out tomorrow, I hope it is a nice day. Today, we sure had all kinds of weather, snow, sleet, and beautiful sunshine and not too cold. I put out the wash.

Wait until you read this news. I came in. Rog and I were in the kitchen. I was sitting in Roger's place at the table eating a tangerine. Then I saw a man pass the window so quick. I said to Roger, "There's a man and he's coming right in!" I jumped up and ran to the door but he opened it, as it was unlocked. It was Ted Underwood. Oh, he looks swell. He will have lots to tell you. He was reading the town paper. He got two of them and one letter from Dr. Tumbelston and he was mad. He sat down by a coconut tree, leaned his back against it, and had the town paper propped up and bing! A Jap shot a hole right through it. It hit his hand and made a small hole on his shin. He crawled into his foxhole and he was madder still. So he has the Purple Heart, two gold stars, and two stripes. He sure looks swell. He gained 16 pounds since he is in the States. He was away 27 months, nine on Guadalcanal. He came from Guam. A fellow woke him up at 2 AM and said, "Come on, you get home. You leave at 2 minutes of 4." Ted said, "Get the hell out of here," as they were always saying that. So, the truck had 5 men on it to go to the boat. When the count was taken, Ted was missing. So the Captain came, in a hurry, and told Ted. He only had two minutes to get out of the foxhole and on to the truck. There was a big air raid on when the ship pulled out. He left all his belongings and all the souvenirs he had, a Jap flag, etc. All he had was the clothes on his back.

He had all new clothes on, and he told us lots of things. His brother, Bob, is home too, but Ted came alone. He was going to do Bustleton and will be at church tomorrow.

Granny did Holmesburg with Uncle Bob and Jerry Culp yesterday. Howard Baldy read her the telegram, Bill Baldy wounded in action November 25. Pearl is nearly crazy with worry. Dot Baldy's husband, Nicky, is in the hospital 2 months also. They, of course, don't know the extent of the injuries. It's tough all around. That's all the news I know. No, Lou Hermann will arrive Christmas day. Ted told me. He was on the way to visit all on Krewstown Road and he gave me his mother's phone number. He wants you, Lou and him to get together. He leaves January 10th for Norfolk. I gave him my friend, Mrs. Bell's, address as he expects to be there 6 months.

Well son, I am waiting for Dad. I forgot to ask him if he works tomorrow. Please God, take care of you.

Lots of love, nighty night,

Mommy

Sunday, December 17, 1944

Dear Edwin,

Roger and I are in from church. Roger waited downstairs for 10 minutes. I went on up as church had started. We didn't see anything of Dot. When she left me Friday, she said she would meet us at 11, but we didn't see her. Roger pinned the star on the flag for you, and I shed a few tears. The pastor spoke just wonderfully of Ted and Bob Underwood in church and that they had good fortune to be together for Christmas and to get back to the same Sunday school. Also, Elmer T. won't get home for Christmas as he is only gone for five weeks. I do hope that you will plan to go to church with me next Sunday if you get home. I would be so proud and so happy to have you go. Please, for my sake, do go with Roger and me. Maybe Dad will have to work. He doesn't know yet.

Joe is waiting for this letter so I will run along. Dad is working. I must go get his supper ready. It's cold up here, but a nice day. The church looked beautiful, all ready for Christmas. Pop and I will be married 24 years next Sunday. I would like to have us all together to go to church as we did once before. Lots of love,

Mom

Sunday, December 17, 1944

Dear Son,

I just got through talking to you. I was so upset because I was afraid I had missed Dot. One thing I kept thinking about was that Dot failed me twice when I needed her most, the night before you left and today in honor of your star. But, that is all right by me. I can read girls like a book and I know how to read between the lines. There are so many things that experience teaches a person that words are futile. I told Pop my thoughts when he came home and so they proved true. Pop and I want your happiness at all times.

You have seen 10 weeks of outside association with all types of men. As the years come and go, you will meet all types of women. So be wise. You have all of your life before you. You know how you want a fine home. You must give yourself an opportunity. I never want in any way to interfere in your affairs, but son, if you only heed my advice, you will never go wrong. Whoever suits you will suit me. I am too smart to let anyone say I don't know my place. I know what I think and you know what you want. What you told me is the wisest thing you ever said. Stick to it. When this awful war is over, you will be able to find happiness and be more able to get on in the world. I will be real happy to see you. We can have a talk.

Until I see you, nighty night,

Mommy

Sunday, December 18, 1944 Little Billy Long has his leg broken in 3 places above the knee and has been in a cast since Friday; what he must have suffered.

Dear Son,

I wonder how many letters I have written you since you went away. I do know that I have written you more than anyone else. It's Monday afternoon and I had planned to do so much work today. But somehow I am so tired. I think if I rest up a little, I will be able to start anew. Here I am to chat with you. I don't know what to write about, as my mind is all upset. One thing keeps coming up in my mind so I will tell you what it is.

Please be careful and obey all last minute rules so that you get home. I keep thinking of all sorts of things because I know how impulsive you are and you might wisecrack or do some little thing that would deprive you of getting home. You know this is war and rules are made regardless. So please obey for Pop's sake. I smoothed his silver hair last night and he said, "Well Mom, a new week, and the boy will be home." He reminded me of old Grandpop. How he loved you so. I hate to write like this, but it's a warning.

We saw lots of things at the gate. No one gets in or out in uniform without inspection. There are many guards there. Every officer and bus and car was inspected. We saw one officer with a dame in his car and she had to get out and he had to go on.

So watch your big mouth. You talk so loud. Well pal, I may be wrong. but something in my heart says you will be home Thursday. I feel that Pop and Dot know when you will get home, but they haven't told me. You said, 'Mom, be sure and be home Thursday.' I'll be up bright and early and my eyes will be sore from looking. God take care of you and I will greet you as my fine sailor boy, the first Price to serve America from the old farm home. My son, my son, while we have each other, make no mistake, Pop's heart is big and so full of love. He said he treated Dot like a baby. You have time dear. (Plenty of it.) Be wise and think. Pop and Mom always welcomes you. So, welcome home.

Love,

Mommy

The Home Fires

Monday 5 - 10 PM, Sunday, December 18, 1944

Dear Son,

The home fires are burning and the supper is on cooking, and I'm dreaming of a white Christmas. A northeast snowstorm is raging across the fields and looks like the genuine thing. Ted Underwood said he only wished it would snow for Christmas as he had enough of jungles and heat. He has a cold because he had been going without an overcoat here for a couple of days. He had it at the tailor's as he had to get it taken in. Coming from summer in the tropics to winter is a sudden change.

I filled up the pepper boxes and somehow, I must have gotten some on my nose. It's sure burning. I just called up Gallagher's and ordered my final articles for Christmas. I ordered my order from the baker. No last minute Uncle Bill coming in loaded. I ordered one mince pie and I will bake the pumpkin and lemon meringue.

Roger hurt his ankle at school today jumping down the steps. It is quite swollen and hurts him. I put ice packs on it and he is off to Frankford with Nutsie Ems. I gave him $5.00 for Christmas presents and Pop gave him $3.40 and I gave him two before. So I am broke now until Thursday.

Here's Joe: They got a tough time getting smokes. So if you can buy any down there, you better bring them home with you as you can travel Bustleton and Frankford. Try and get any. Joe said he traveled Frankford and he hasn't had a smoke from 5 o'clock last night until just now. Miss DeKalb gave him a pack for a change.

Dad is not in yet so I will reserve this space as I sent you off two letters today. Pop took one and Roger just took one. Did I tell you Bill Baldy is wounded in action since November 25th? Well dear, it's night, and I guess Pop will have a job getting out tomorrow morning as it is still storming. Roger is home. Dot didn't come up with Pop. She went to the dentist tonight. She asked for you.

Love,

Mommy

Tuesday, December 19, 1944

Dear Son,

As long as the years shall last, I shall never forget this year of waiting. It is like waiting for you in 1926; so anxious and wondering about my baby. I won't write anymore now until I see you. Roger is taking out your license. Pop paid for his too. Rog is home from school today. He has a real bad ankle and foot. He jumped down 4 steps. We have been getting things ready for Christmas. It is bitter cold and snow, but the sun is shining warm. If it would get a little warmer, the snow would soon melt.

I got your confidential letter and the sweetest words you ever said. "Mom, you will be my girl until this old war is over." I am so glad you are getting awake. When I saw all those poor babies and the tears, I was so glad you were still free. If you have troubles now, think what it would be like to be married.

Dear, I have so much to say. You might cast it up to me in later life. Regardless of love or girl, wait until the war is over. That will give you a chance to find yourself. You are so young that you haven't had a chance in life yet. Do make a good start. Then you and your mate will be far happier. I would love to see you able to offer the finest ring made.

Have a nice Christmas. Be a gentleman. Give a present and a card and act according to your true upbringing. God will guide you. I always told you before what was best. Until we see each other, Cheerio. This is the last note until we meet. Happy Day.

Mom

(Enclosure – Item 4)

> *Straight to your door come good wishes for a MERRY CHRISTMAS and a HAPPY NEW YEAR!*
>
> *We are waiting so patient. God Bless You.*
>
> *With Love, Mother, Dad + Roger + Joe.*

December 31, 1944

This is last letter I will write for another year. You see I wrote quite a few and I am still keeping it up. I was so glad to hear from you just now. It took a load off my heart.

I walked in by the piano and implored God to keep you safe and well and I thanked God for letting me be so near you once again. I put you in God's keeping. I know it's war and before another New Year dawns, may God give peace to all hearts, all over the world. I pray as the bells ring out.

I never forgot one New Year's spent here long years ago, when I was so in love. I thought the dark hours of midnight would never come. I paced the floor of that little room, where all the love, sorrow, and death took place in the past 20 years. I lived a lifetime in that little room. The night my two boys and the dog spent in that bed last week will never be forgotten. My memories are sweet and bitter.

The world goes on. What we find and how we live matters to no one but ourselves. Our lives are empty or full. My pages are full, with more to be written. Please God and the end will be good.

I hope you are feeling lots better. The States are the pie and cake. No matter where you go, Old Glory goes with you. So does my love, Pop and Roger's.

You were awfully nasty to your little brother that last night. You didn't care about anybody but Dot. Pop and I got sense, and you put Dot in a position. I hope for the best, that all is well. So, until I hear from you, love from all. Cheerio. Nighty night.

Mommy

That is our secret.

END OF DECEMBER

Chapter Four

January 1945

(Item 5 - To find a fifth one fold as indicated)

Wartime Letters Written from Mother to Son

New Year's Day, 1945

Well Son,

Here's the first letter and first chat with you of the New Year while I wait for Dad to come home from work. What a day. But, I have gone through some almost as bad. As Ruth Long said, each time she goes through trouble, she thinks she can never face it again, but when it strikes we must go on. I am not alone in heartache, as millions the world over are torn apart today by this cruel war. I made no New Year Resolutions. I prayed for peace to the entire world and asked God to watch over you all, every boy, everywhere.

The home fires are burning and the kettle is full of good food, so I thank God for that and the fact that I heard your voice today. To know that you serve, that's it's warm and you have food; I am thankful for all that. It helps to keep my chin up.

Pop is out in all this weather. It sure is blowing and raining. The only news I know was I called Mrs. Spence to say "Happy New Year" after I talked to you and had the dishes done at 3 o'clock. She was still in bed. Pop thinks I am awful not getting up until 7:30. He doesn't know what a good wife he has to keep him clean and warm. You live and learn is a true saying. You are never too old to learn. I learn every day. I know you are a good boy when I hear tales of others. Make me proud of you in Bustleton. Don't worry, keep well and save all you can. Find a true pal. God will smile on you. Trust in God at all times. Pray and you will come through. So until I hear from you,

Nighty night,

Mommy

(The fifth one!)

Tuesday, January 2, 1945

Dear Son,

It's nearing suppertime and I have been taking it easy all day. It has been awful windy and cold, but the sun has shone all day. I have been firing up hard on the coal pile and here I am for a chat with you. I bundled up. It took me five minutes down and five minutes back from the mailbox. Boy, was my face cold; no letters either. When Roger came in from school, he brought me three from you. They sure sound homesick. I know what it is like. In the old days I used to come from Grundy's or Pearson's and it took three or four hours by trolley. I would no more get home, when I would have to start back. Here you are in Bainbridge. Just think how wonderful it is to be able to talk on the telephone. I went up to your room and looked out the window at Fisher's cows. The little old phone wire was swinging in the winter wind. I said, Oh! You precious little wire, what joy you have brought me, all the way from Bainbridge. Isn't it a wonderful thing how it can carry your voice?

We must all face hardships. Then when we get older, we try to spare our children all we suffered. When you were so set on going at 17, I wouldn't consent because I wanted to spare you. When the time came for you to go, it took one corner of my heart. That took me four weeks to get over and $13.00 to the Doctor, not to mention what I suffered. But God gave me strength. Yet you wouldn't tell me when you would get home even when you and Dad knew. God was with me again. I knew. I prayed so much for you. I got on my knees and begged God to hear me and thanked him over and over. God is good to us. Trust in him, my boy. Jesus never fails.

One thing I want to say, I don't want to be downhearted and blue. Think of all the nice times we have had and what a good Dad you have. I tried over and over to help you meet life. The only way was the hard way. If millions of others can face it, so can you.

Stick out your chin, take it with a grin. Uncle John said the States are cake and pie. So get hard as you can. When you are old and gray, dear, you will still have memories of how you threw tomatoes at each other in the field and yet when you wanted a taste before your eyes the guy said no. I saw bread and fowl burned up and milk poured in the sink. I was 16 and my little brother Charlie and the rest were hungry. So goes the world. On and on. But, God Bless Old Glory as she waves high on American shores. She will never die. Her sons are loyal, brave and true and will always defend the red, white, and blue. There will always be homes when boys like you fight on. Sail on. God be with you. Dad is okay. So am I. Hope you are. All love from,

Mommy

Tuesday Evening January 2, 1945

Dear Son,

I called Baldwin's about 3:30. The girl said Dot had not come in to work. She guessed Dot had too much New Year spirit. I said, 'Oh no. She always works.' Carl told Roger she had quit and was working at McClain's in Bustleton. I will let you know any other news. Pop waited for her until a girl came out and said she hadn't been in. I will let you know anything I hear. It should be down to 12 degrees here tonight. Burr. Love,

Mom

January 3, 1945

Dear Son,

It's 48 degrees in the dining room and I am all wrapped up and waiting for the coffee. It's so dark at 7:30 that I hate to get up. What about Dad and you getting up so much earlier. I can't see to dust and it's too cold to wash. The wash man has not been here since before Christmas so I must get down to washing before the weekend. Dear, the home fires are burning strong and it will soon warm up.

I remember the days when, biff, biff, the doors were opening every second, in and out, Uncle Paul, Uncle Nelson, Uncle Bill, Frank, Pop, Grandpop. They used to drive me crazy. You were in a basket on the kitchen cabinet all wrapped up. It's a wonder you ever lived, but I did all in my power. I was in bed. It was cold in that big barn room, so today, I am going to move over to your room. Pop said he didn't like your bed. I said it took you a long time to find that out because we slept in it from the time we got married until you started to sleep in it. Pop said, "I like this bed better." He says it is the best one he ever slept in. His feet don't push the boards.

I had said my prayers and I said, 'Oh God, please give my boy peace of mind.' Tell him I am talking to him and wishing for him. Then the phone rang. I hardly heard it. Pop didn't hear it. I tell you I was sprinting very carefully through the dark until I got to the bottom step. I put the light on in the parlor and I dashed to the phone. You sounded so much better. I went to sleep and didn't wake up until the clock went off.

Roger is getting ready for school. I have my coffee. It's been two years today since Uncle John left. I don't know how Aunt Dink carries on. He has been in the South Pacific for 18 months. Today is Aunt Kebe's birthday. That is how I remember the date Uncle John left.

I had a card from Uncle Bill's girl, June. Their new address is 448 W. 118th Place, Los Angeles, California. His store name is Louisiana Fish Co., Vernon & Central Ave., Los Angeles. Look in the California phone book if you should happen to get near there.

Roger has gone off to school. I cleaned the kitchen and I will close this page. Perhaps I will write one later, after I get the mail. Pop doesn't like to write. Did you hear how he pushed it off to you last night? Well you can always hear from Mommy.

Wednesday afternoon

Well Son,

I wrote you a letter this morning and Roger and Nutsie took it out a few minutes ago. Nutsie said Dot is at McClain's and also that she got a special delivery letter from Budd's today. But of course, he didn't know what it was about. I sent a note to Dot asking her if she heard from you and your new number of the barracks. I didn't get any letter from you today, but your driver's license came, so I will enclose it in this letter. I sure do hope you get home over the weekend.

It is 5:20 and I have the home fires going. I think it has warmed up a little. It's 70 degrees in the dining room and that's quite a change from this morning's 48 degrees.

Oh, well. I paid $21.00 for insurance and I am broke until tomorrow night. It's a short pay this time with Christmas and Saturday out. The coal man called up and said he had two tons for me. I couldn't take it, as the bond check has not come through yet. He said they didn't do any bookkeeping, so he would hold it until early next week. It's $27.00. I ordered 2 tons for the heater. It must be ordered 10 days ahead, so believe me; housekeeping has its problems, especially where finances are concerned. I never have been able to pull up since we got the car, and you left. Pop would rave if I wanted $40.00 for bed clothes or a new rug for the radio room or new paper. But $38.00 for new tires and the $30.00 repair bill for December is nothing.

I have almost decided to go get a job at Budd's. If other women work away from home, I can too. I will have 25 pairs of dirty stockings lying on the bureau like Aunt Dot instead of one pair of holes. Roger is the only drawback or else I would be up to Budd's. That railroad would get me down; up and down in the snow. I would go right out tomorrow. But then I say, why should I punish myself when I have three men to work for me? Ha, Ha.

Well son, I will add more later. Maybe Pop or Joe has some news. I am weary. I have not been out since December 24th to church with you. I was proud and happy that day to sit near my sailor boy. God Bless you.

Life is cruel and tough when one is poor, so take advantage of every opportunity you possibly can.

Pop went up for gas and Dot was asleep in the chair. Her mother said she was going to Baldwin's tomorrow. I guess she told you all the news. They said you got her on the phone.

Pussycat, Lizzie Bit, is sick. I guess she was looking for "bundle". Anyway, the poor little thing is sick. Out catting all night requires "pay".

Joe treated us to ice cream. Pop got it at Jones'. I see by tonight's paper where all carrot top hiders must be called to service between 18 and 25. But I guess Cliff will still be around next spring. Harold W. bought a big farm north of here, near John Patterson, I believe. At least that's what Ray told us on Thanksgiving Day. They were not going to farm this place this year, just put in grain.

Son, I hope you get the driver's license I have enclosed. Dot got my note and a letter from you. I got none today.

Snow is due here tonight. Pop said, try for the high school work. He would be so happy and it would help you out. It would keep you nearer the States longer, so consider it. Do your best at all times. Love from all. Hope you get off Saturday. Nighty night.

Mommy

Thursday morning, January 4, 1945

Dearest Son,

I just hung up from talking to you. To hear your voice makes my day happier. I hope you feel lots better now that you have talked over your troubles with mother. I still say I hate the war, that I love my country, but I prefer us being together. I failed in training you, but I never failed in teaching you the good things. How can people be so mean as to say no to anyone who needs help? I am poor because I fed every bum who came to the door, took them in, gave them warm food, dry stockings and did everything in my power to help people. Even though it didn't cost those fellows a penny, they would deny you medical attention. I even think I have a touch of it. I bathe my eyes every few hours. I can't work in the dark with the lights on and it's a dark and dreary day. I have the kitchen done. I am held back all the time for lack of funds. I would like to clean the inside of my big closet, but no "Kemtone". I have taken the things out so many times, but put them back with the old walls. It all looks the same. I must make myself content and carry on. After all, all I think of is you, Roger, and Dad. We have plugged along this far and we still have plenty of time left to enjoy a little of life. I have it better now, than ever before in my life. Yet I must suffer and grieve because of this awful war.

Edwin, I hear footsteps, up and down the front steps. It scares me so bad. It sounds just like a human. It's the cat. The dog barked so loud and ran in. I put all my trust in that dog. I so hate being alone. I miss your car dashing in at 50 MPH. "Mom, make me something to eat! Mom, Mom." No one ever asks me that but you.

Now Son, I will go upstairs and straighten up. When I come down, maybe I can write more.

The home fires are fixed and it's not as cold as yesterday. The Christmas tree still looks and smells nice, so I will leave it up, with a wish you get home again to see it within the month. I emptied your stocking yesterday. The tangerine was getting soft.

I went for the mail and there wasn't any. That was at 12:30. While I was eating a sandwich and drinking tea, the mailman came. So I went down again. I got two letters from you and the phone bill. Oh boy. It will almost knock Pop over. It's $31.41. I don't know how we can pay it, but somehow we must. After Pop sees it, I will send it on to you. One call was $4.95. That was the Thanksgiving call.

If Roger goes out, I will mail this off. I hope you got your license. I forgot to tell you this morning that I sent it off. The sun is out a little and it has gotten much warmer up here. I hope you have a song in your heart. Be glad you are inside. Smile. It is the thing that goes the farthest toward making life worthwhile, that costs the least and does the most; just a pleasant smile. You be brave, be good. God will take care of you, stand beside you and guide you. All will be well.

Lots of love from all.

XXXXX   Mom

Thursday Evening, January 4, 1945

Well Son,

Roger mailed a letter off to you. Here goes another. By this time, you should be getting regular mail. Each time I talked to you, I forgot to tell you I sent off your driver's license this morning. Yours and Dad's came together yesterday. It sure did get lots warmer and I am glad of that.

I have hamburger made like the dried beef, mashed potatoes, and a big Bermuda onion for supper. I also have jellyroll, coffee, cheese, etc. Here I am waiting for the return of my workers, but one won't rush in, "Mom, Mom." I miss you. I do hope and pray you can get settled. It would be so much nicer and easier if you had certain duty. To get shoved around is not so good. You can see what an education means. Also it's who you know that pushes you along in this world. You know that cooperation with fellow mates goes a long way. They pass the word and it's not always the good word. All I can say is don't disobey. But don't let "Hitlers" overrule you either. There are lots of Hitlers in this world, but they don't last long. Sometimes, the little fellow is licked. But if he is right, he will come out on top. He who laughs last, laughs best is an old saying. It proved true about the tomatoes. Life goes on, war, babies, marriages, and deaths. Each one lives in a little circle and no one cares except those concerned. I care for you and therefore I am interested in all you do. You are a difficult boy at times and good as gold at others. You go through an adolescent age and when you return, you will be a man. You will wonder at some of the things you did.

The incident of the pillowcase will teach you to be spotless. That is how I want you to be. I kept you spotless and your bed too. No dog was clean enough for our home. Time changes all things and the clock of life is wound but once. No man has the power to tell just where the hands will stop. God is the master of our fate. Trust in God to guide you and give you courage and strength to carry you through your training and duty. If you are earnest, he will hear your prayers. Don't forget.

As you said, there is a right way and a Navy way. So do the Navy way and you won't go wrong. Every letter I write, I am lecturing. But what I put on paper, I have told you over and over. So, the flowers still bloom. The sun still shines. Smile.

Joe is home. Next will be Dad. I will ring off for now. I want to hear all the news from you, so write when you can. All you need to say is Mother and I know you are alive. Until we see each other, God bless you my baby.

Mommy

January 5, 1945

Dear Son,

Here are a few lines now as Roger is going to get his haircut. I have been so busy all day and still have much to do since it's Friday. I gave the kitchen a good going over and cleaned out the closet in the cellar way. Roger and I made a big fire and we had to watch it. Rog had the broom and I had the kettle. We didn't want to get the grass started, as it was a clean sweep. We made out okay. It's 26 degrees up here today. I will write more tonight. I had two weeks wash just came back, so I will make this short and sweet until tonight.

All my love,

Mother

Friday afternoon, January 5, 1945

Well Son,

It's 5 PM and Roger just came back from getting his hair cut and taking his

The Home Fires

back wheel to get a new one from Alburger. It will cost him $3.00. He has $2.25 left from his Christmas money. I have worked hard all day. Roger said he heard Benny O'Neil has gone A.W.O.L.[109] and Hockey Miller is home. Mrs. Gallagher told me today that Joe goes back this Wednesday to San Francisco. So I guess there will be more heartache this next week in Bustleton.

I couldn't get to sleep last night. I am tired now, but I don't want to lie down or else I won't sleep tonight again. I have soup on and some home fries for Pop, and two cans of fish in tomato sauce. The sun has been shining all day and the dirt sure flew. I cleaned four baskets out of the kitchen closet and one out of the cellar way. Each time it gets a little less. Maybe you can fix things up like I want them when you come home. Or maybe we can get a nice big old country house and fix it for our own. Maybe.

We got the bond check today for $37.50. Twenty-seven of it goes toward two tons of coal for the kitchen range. I often heard coal called black diamonds. They used to call the 4 o'clock express to the coal regions The Black Diamond Express. I used to wonder why it was called that. But now I know. Coal is almost as precious as diamonds. When you shovel it in, it costs so much. I would much rather be warm and burn $13.00 for coal than to be sick with a sore throat and suffer and end up giving the money to the Doctor. All I pray for is to be comfortable and to have this war end.

Be careful what you say and do. I know you will have God for your guiding star.

We had supper so I will be getting along to bed soon. Dot told Pop the news of your conversation about the fireman job. I think Pop seemed pleased. Whatever you get dear, this is war. You know Sherman said War is Hell, but

---

[109] A.W.O.L. is a military acronym meaning Absent Without Leave.

that ain't half of it.

Well tulip plum, the Aldrich family is on the radio. Henry wants meatballs and spaghetti. Homer wants french fries. They are lost on the side of a hill in a snowstorm and they find a hat and it has cherries on it. They are funny.

Well son, I will sign off now, as my legs are getting cold. So honey dear, all my love and best of luck, my sailor baby. Nighty night. Lots of love. Kisses.

Mommy

Saturday Evening, January 6, 1945

Dearest Son,

The day is drawing near early evening. I don't need to cook. I have the home fires burning good. It is very cold here today, but nice. Roger came in from Alburger's and he was frozen. It's a still cold, no wind. That helps. I told Pop and Joe to fix the fires this morning as I was going to have a day of rest and Miss Lizzie Bit came up, "meow" at 5 AM. I had to get up and come down as we had left her in the kitchen all night. I knew she was asking me to let her out. I called Pop and he had the radio going so loud and was putting coal on the fire. So, I had to get up. She was going to "feather her nest" in the middle of your bed. I got her and came down. Do you think I could go to sleep after that? No. So I cleaned out the drawers in the dining room desk. There were tax receipts from 1895 to 1938. Grandpop paid out some money for taxes. Pop had $31.00 out for taxes, dues, bonds, insurance, etc. That is why the poor man is always poor, because he is taxed with the rich man.

It's 5:15 and Roger must go to the shoemaker for his school shoes. It will cost $1.85. I gave him a bite to eat and I have a cup of tea here. I had a letter from Uncle John, in 8 days. He is in the hills of New Caledonia. We don't know if he will get sent on or get sent home. He had turkey for Christmas. He said our cousin, Ollie Culp, is on the same island. So, he will go to see him. Uncle John's wife, Aunt Dink, went to Delaware today to see the baby.

I will say I miss you calling today. I hope you are well, my dear. With all my love, Nighty night.

Mommy

Saturday Evening, January 6, 1945

Dear Edwin,

Roger mailed you a letter around 5:30 and here goes again. Dad is not home yet. He has to get the meat tonight because it was too cold for me to go out last night. Did I tell you I had a letter from Uncle John today? He said he got your letter and to put 6 cents air mail on them because it takes a month or more to get free mail and 3 cent mail. He hadn't any letters since December 8. He wrote that December 28, so I got it in record time on January 6 (air mail). He said he is okay and still in the hills of New Caledonia. He had turkey and all the trimmings for Christmas. He heard Ollie Culp is on the same island, so he will hunt him up. I sent his letter to Nettie Tippett so she can tell the news to Ollie's wife.

I found your new white sailor hat only yesterday in the closet. Pop said he knew you forgot it. I went in to wrap up your new brown shoes and to see if your clothes were okay from moths. I was sure surprised when I saw your hat. You hadn't said a word to me about it.

It sure is cold up here tonight. I will be glad to see Dad. Roger is in the cellar and I get lonesome. I didn't even have one phone call today, except Dad tonight. Roger has been in the cellar most of the day and he is dirty and cranky. He doesn't want to bring up the coal, just like you. But you learned since you left my feather bed, eh! I had one letter from you today, but as of yet, no money order. I probably will get it Monday.

Here comes Dad now. He brought home all the things to eat. He lost one of his riders yesterday, as he moved to Jersey. Pop said Dot may walk down Sunday. It's awful cold up here. Pop gets his new tires on Tuesday. We must turn in two more bonds for coal. That leaves us with four. Edwin, when did you quit Budd's? We can claim you if you didn't make $500, which I say you didn't. When did you quit Budd's and how long in 1944 were you there? Okay, so long. Nighty night. Hope you are okay.

Mom & All

Sunday, January 7, 1945

Dear Son,

The countryside looks like a Christmas card. The icy fingers of winter have clutched all the branches of the trees and I assure you, I don't like it. I will be happy when I see Dad. I hardly know how the poor old dear does it. Traveling so far daily is hard. When you have the load to carry, the burden is not light.

I have been holding down the couch all afternoon and the home fires are burning. Joe and the three pests are on the job. Rog, Brownie and Lizzie Bit are pestering me. Surprise! Just now, 5:15, Ray Wenker came in with his boy and Allen. They knocked on the door and said, "Here's your ice cream." I opened it and a letter of business was in it from Uncle Bill saying Quigley's was open Sunday and was just "around the corner", etc. We are waiting for Dad to come home for supper. I was glad Ray broke open the driveway.

We have had supper, so I will finish my letter. Maybe you will call up tonight. We had sauerkraut and then the ice cream, not such a good combination. Pop is shaving. Joe will do the dishes after he gets through. Pop said you should have been driving today. There was a big fire. A church burned down at 22nd and Tioga. Dad saw the companies there. I heard the Blind Gospel Singer telling it.

Well Pal, I am going to be like the bears and the groundhogs tonight. I am going to bury myself under the wool blankets. I wish I could tuck you in, but I guess Dot will be the next one to tuck you in and smooth your face. I hope she does it with as much love as I have for you. Write when you can. Take care of your eyes. God will be your guide. I love you. Nighty night.

Mom

Monday January 8, 1945

Dear Son,

Today Mr. Winter had us snow and ice bound. There was no school bus and so Roger and I were exploring the attic storeroom. We found our scrapbooks. Yours seems to be the best one. I went through my Dad's old valise. It was full of old papers from 1871 to 1876. I tell you, we sure have some junk up there. Some of these spring days, I hope to get up there and make a clean sweep. I have so many clippings cut out. The scrapbooks are so dear. You know how we like to look over the old ones of Grandma Price's family. So who knows who will look over ours?

Well dear, the Lone Ranger is on and Pop is asleep as he had a big day. Joe is asleep too. I will soon be going to bed.

Mr. Gallagher called me up. He said Joe met a fellow in the South Pacific named Henry, who said he knew you and used to go in Gallagher's with you. He said he lived on Krewstown Road. He sent a message with Joe to his mother. I asked Cliff and Harold if they knew where he lived, but they said no. The phone book lists two Henrys in the 9500 block on Bustleton Avenue. I am wondering if you would know who he was. I told Mr. G. I never heard of anyone by that name being there with you.

Well, I don't know any news. I sent word to Dot about your eyes. Pop didn't meet her tonight. He told her not to wait after 5:45, as he might be late. He was late, so she wasn't there. The driveway is better, but it was snowing most of the day.

Mrs. Spence just called me up. She said Sun Ray Money in the News called up Mr. Russell and he said he had just turned off his radio. Do they have electric? He missed out to the tune of $90.00. He told the fellow he had three sons in the service and he could use the money, as "farming" wasn't doing so good just now. She said, "Oh, wouldn't Mrs. Price be surprised if they had called 1002". Yes.

I listen nearly every night, but it would be the night I miss. F. Jones got a cablegram that the English wife was coming to America. Okay.

Mom   XXXX

Monday, January 8, 1945

Dear Son,

Now it's time for my afternoon chat with you, because I talked to you on the phone. When I went away from the phone it was snowing hard. But, it didn't last long. The coal man was coming in with the two tons of coal, and I was going to call them up and order a ton of briquettes to help out the heater coal.

I want to say I am so thankful it was nothing more serious with your dear eyes. My, how glad I was to get your money order. Poor old dear said, 'Don't rob the boy, we will make out somehow.' I tell you son, Pop and I live for you two boys. We have done all we could for you. You caused us many sleepless nights over worrying about that car and drink. You never fooled Pop or me. Now we must worry over this damn war. I guess we are never quite happy or content no matter how old we get. Dear, I could write a book. Someday when I rock your babies to sleep, I will sing that song, "When I grow too old to dream, I'll have you to remember."

The day you were going to run away, you were about as big as Elmer Irons is now, and it was a Saturday morning. I ran out under the maple tree. I was all stove polish and you went half way up the field to the railroad and I said, "Go on! In five minutes I phone for the police." I went in and you came right back. I don't know where Pop was, maybe huckstering, I think. I'm glad those days are over. I went through some tough ones. I can't think that you are almost a man and away on your Uncle Sam's land. On a New Year's Day, 18 years ago, Uncle Bill came in and you were in a basket on the kitchen table and you "cooed" for the first time. I was so proud of you. Uncle Bill said, "I would be the happiest man in the world if he was mine; do you mind if I am nice to him?" I said no. Yet when you are fighting for your country, he didn't say a nice thing to you. I can't understand it. But then dear, they are memories to put in the volume called life. What is written on the pages concerns no one but us four. No one cares for us like we do for each other. When you fell off the bicycle and got hurt, that hurt me. When you crushed your thumb and I held you all night, you said, "Mom. Do you feel it in your elbow?" Yes. Whatever hurts you hurts me. So smile and then I can smile too.

Lizzie Bit made one jump. Wee, wee she got the mouse. Believe me, that cat earns her space on the parlor chair. She sure has caught some mice since she is here.

The ice is melting fast. I must run along now, baby. I thank you for the money, which is a wonderful help. Cast your bread upon the waters and it's returned twofold. Bye.

Love,

Mommy

Tuesday Morning, January 9, 1945

Hello Son,

On a winter morning here I am for a chat with you. Roger, Dad and Joe are on their way to school and work. You, I guess, are up since the "wee sma" hours. Here, I am alone in flesh, but not in spirit, because I am talking to you. Brownie and Lizzie Bit are the sole rulers of the house. I am not going to do much work today, just a little mending and a little ironing.

I've got the home fires burning. Since I wrote the above, Juniata called up from her home and wanted to know if Dot got home okay last night. It's no wonder Pop couldn't see her after work. She went down there Saturday. Juniata said she took her as far as Wilmington on the way home. I do know you were planning on going there on a weekend leave. I am wondering if it was a gag to test me out to see what I knew.

I assure you dear, no one interested me. I have lived too long, off the highway, to be bothered about other people's whereabouts. Pop saw Underwood at Ems on his way home from getting gas. So I said to Pop, Dot is free. She has a chance while you are away to find her own mind. I still say, wait until the war is over. Then is the time to decide your future. This way, when two fellows are after the same girl, whichever one you choose after you get married, it's the wrong guy. Then you must pay the rest of your married life. Although I know nothing about Dot, or her whereabouts, I have not seen her since the night you were home. As you said, weather makes no difference when you are young.

I hope your eyes are lots better. I hope you get settled. Please God, end this war. Until I see you, I will write tonight. You are my baby, so all my love and more.

Mommy

Maybe Dot wasn't home. Juniata said it was late when she left her. Don't worry.

Letter 2
Tuesday Evening, January 9, 1945

Dear Son,

I received two letters and the Main Sheet. It was so nice to hear from you. I read the Main Sheet through and I only laughed at one thing. It was the fellow using his neckerchief for a handkerchief.

I had a surprise today. Aunt Minnie called me up and she is at Elmer's sister's house in Mayfair as Danny Boy has a mastoid infection. They almost lost the little darling. Little Elmer has swollen glands. Aunt Minnie felt better after she told me her troubles. You know how you need me. Well she did too. We both felt better after we gabbed. We gabbed for one hour. She is staying there until Thursday.

I see by the paper where you rate liberty weekend after one week of duty and 2 liberties in 4 weeks. If you don't get on draft, you may rate this weekend. I hope. Did I tell you that Roger was on his knees praying and said, "Dear God, make it snow all night and all day tomorrow." I said, 'Roger you mustn't ask God for trifles. How would Dad get out to earn our food?' He said, "Mother, it's right from here," and he pointed to his heart. Nutsie Ems was going to pray for the same thing. They had that made up so the bus wouldn't get through. It came along at 9:15 on Monday morning, but they were back home by that time.

I thought of the day that Dave and you found the money. I made you go back to school, but he went on home because they had nothing to eat. I often wonder where he is, in Federal Naval Prison I guess, just because he was in love and homesick. He stayed away. A.W.O.L. I know what it is. I wasn't allowed to quit or my brothers wouldn't have enough to eat. I have been fighting 30 years to keep body and soul together. I'm still going, but not as strong these last two years. I realize you gave me $30.00. It was expensive talking. They say talk is cheap, but it doesn't seem so when it costs $45.00 for us to say hello, how are you. Yet, I would go hungry to pay it. I will write more later. I have pork and beans in the oven and so an easy supper. I am waiting patiently for my loved ones' return. I like to see them home around the fireside. Then all the world is well with me, but with one missing, I am not content.

Edwin, Roger forgot your letter to mail this afternoon, so I will send both out with Pop tomorrow morning. I am sorry. I must hunt up some paper, so I will finish this up. I wrote you a big letter this morning. Write whenever you can. I love you dear.

Mommy

Wednesday morning, January 10, 1945 I think Byron is getting home this weekend. He is in Rhode Island. $12.00 carfare.

Dearest Son,

You sure got me out of bed this morning. I shut up the kitchen fire and went down and coaled up the heater. I took coffee up to Roger, made a fresh pot and came down and fried scrapple from Comac. It was nothing but buckwheat flour and corn meal (never saw a hog). I made my bed and dusted around. Now I am set for the day. My head is dizzy and light today, so I will take it easy. Pop gave me "hail" at 5 AM. I put the pork and beans in the oven at 1 PM on Tuesday and the electric oven was still on when Pop came down Wednesday morning to go to work. But it was only on 200 degrees, so that was a help. My kitchen man is going to get H. tonight, as he did the dishes, made the coffee, and that proves he didn't wipe off the stove.

He says, "Now, don't I always?" And he insists on taking over. "You get out of the kitchen, I'll run things, you look at the paper." So, I will tell him he won't get a reference when he goes from the farm, if he can't take charge and keep the situation under control because the "Captain" has to bail me out because of the "rookie's" mistakes. Ha Ha.

Well Pal, the two week's Christmas wash is not back yet. Another big one has been ready to go out since last Saturday. I called them up after I talked to you and gave them H., but it doesn't do any good. After this war, I will have myself a new washer. It would pay me now to have one. It's $2.00 and more a week for laundry, and I must wash all the silks and fancies anyway.

Fulmer Street is one sheet of glass ice. I need the money, but I can't get to the post office, (me fall down and go bang). We will have to turn in two more bonds for heater coal. Then I hope that Dad doesn't lose anymore time, so we can catch up a little. There are two more payments on the car. I must pay one now which was due on the 3rd and then one more. With the $40 repair bill, it will be 2 more months. By that time, the junker will probably be ready for the heap.

I am going to write to the Bridge Land Company. Twenty years ago, we bought from them. I am going to tell them they can't swindle me. I will report them to the F.B.I. The lots were $514 and Pop paid $445 and one lot was supposed to be won free. Therefore, they gypped us. Since we really paid $445, it entitles us to at least one lot. I'll let you know what I hear when I write, when they answer, and they will answer. Well son, when you have written as many letters as I have, you will know what to say. You sure do finer than I ever expected. Keep up the good work. Make Dad proud of you. Carry on. You are young and in a good place to learn. Never steal. You see how good I brought you up. So be good. God will love you. So do I.

The Home Fires

Mommy

Wednesday Night, January 10, 1945

Dearest Son,

Here is Mom again. There's nothing new to write about. The only thing I know is that it sure is cold (10 degrees). I am in the warm, thank God. Lone Ranger is on and I sure have a tough time to write, but baby, all I know is home. My head is dizzy these two days. I am mighty lonesome for someone to talk to, although I sure did enjoy talking to you this morning. I wrote you one letter today.

I heard Dot just got out of bed at suppertime. Pop said you should take your time. There are plenty of girls who would love to write you every day, especially if they wanted you for a life mate.

Somehow, Pop is disgusted. I told him to do his own writing. He wants you to go to school if it's any way possible. Then you can be in the States, no matter where it is. Then you can also have a trade. God will guide you. We love you so much. We know what life is all about and we want you to profit by our experience.

Pop is snoring. Roger is yelling, "Pop, you are not listening to Lone Ranger." They and Joe were frozen all day. Not me. I hope you are in the warm. K.P. never killed anybody, although the hours are long and dreary. Just thank God you are in the good old U.S.A. Sunny Smile is on. It makes me think of you.

All day long, I've been singing this song:

You always take the sweetest rose
and crush it 'til the petals fall.
You always break the kindest heart
with words you can't recall.

So if I broke your heart last night-
It's 'cause I love you best of all.

Perhaps the words are not just quite right, but love is a strange thing. It strikes young and old. Once it gets a hold on you boys, what it does to your life, you know the first stings when you get no letter. I love you today, tomorrow and yesterday, forever and ever my son.

With all my love. Nighty night.

Mommy

Edwin, one time I read a story about a murder mystery. An old fellow like "Old Benny" used to go about the countryside and gather nuts. It said he impregnated the forests and he knew all the goings on and if they could find him, he could solve the mystery. So I quickly hunted up the dictionary to see what "impregnated" meant because I thought that was a bad word. Every time I saw Old Benny, I thought of it. Every time I see a letter like this and you ask questions about Dot, it reminds me of it; impregnated, going into.

> He impregnated the forest.

> He went into the forest gathering nuts and news.

The Home Fires

So, I don't go after news. I am a poor one for that.

Thursday morning, January 11, 1945 All Pop's love and Roger's. Joe talks about you and misses you Old Nut.

Dearest Son,

Well, two mornings straight you got me out of bed. I have the home fires going full force and my coffee beside me. Roger is getting his breakfast. I made my bed after I talked to you and combed my hair, which is in bad need of a set. But my hairdresser is on the loose end these days. Pop is not going to stop at Baldwin's any more. I do think Dot could have called up, but young people never think. So far today, there is no new word. The only thing that concerns me is the coal pile. I ordered two tons for the heater two weeks ago. I called up again yesterday and he said no for two more weeks. I would freeze to death in this weather if we didn't have the old kitchen range to toast our toes on. This house sure is a humdinger to heat. I often think of the old days, when Uncle Paul was the fireman. The truck shed was cozy and me freezing.

I dreamed last night that I heard two boys screaming. I yelled for Dad and I ran. I saw two men running around a hill. One was John Raynor, a drunk from Frankford, and old Grandpop Price chasing him. I said, "What's the matter?" Johnnie R. said, "Look at the black eye he gave me." He was all beat up. Grandpop said, "I'll teach him to cheat me at cards." Uncle Paul and he and Grandpop were so mad. Grandpop was going to throw him in the creek and Pop and I wouldn't let him. All Grandpop kept saying was, "I'll teach him never to cheat me." Funny, Grandpop hated cards. He never played them in his life.

Later Thursday morning

Well Son,

Here I am again. "All I do is think of you". It sure does ease the separation by being able to talk to you and get your nice letters. Just think how Aunt Lilly must feel, not even getting but one letter in 9 months. I think he is still a "load in the pants". She should fix him by not writing to him, but a mother's love follows you the world over, where all else fails.

I am back again with a fresh cup of coffee. I can't eat a thing. My head is quite bad. I guess I will have to start in with the Doctor treatment again. I am not sick, but I have not an ounce of strength. I can't even hold up my arms to fuss with my hair. But I can rest and that helps me a lot. The main worry I have is getting the food from the store. Pop hates to bother with the books and I miss you going to the store. I hope and pray that peace will soon come to all and that we can start the next 20 years of my ending life with peace together. I am better off now than ever in my life, but I must suffer this war separation. For God to keep you safe is the wish of

Your Mommy XXXX

Thursday Afternoon

Dear Edwin,

Well son, it's twice in one day to talk to you. The knot must sure be tight in your Mommy's apron string. I am happy it is. I think you have gotten a little more sense since you left home. You've found that every rose has a thorn. You finally admitted that Pop and I were right in not signing you away sooner. Every year you learn more. Those that go before, pave the way for those who follow. Your Pop and I traveled the rough road and so we always wanted it paved for you. So you pave it for Roger, Carl, Thomas and the Charlie Long boys. When they grow up, they can point with pride to all the boys who served when the call came from the hills, and from the valleys came a stirring call for men. Yes, March On Son. March on to Victory even though your heart is breaking. Laugh, clown, laugh and remember, down on the farm, the home fires burn and love awaits the return of our sailor son. Cheerio love,

Mom & Dad, Roger & Joe, Carry on to Victory.

January 12, 1945

Dear Son,

Perhaps these few lines will follow you. Here is a big kiss and hug to warm your heart from the first girl who ever loved you. I am thinking of you this cold January day and I was somehow thinking of John McCullough.

The coal men are here putting in a ton of coke. It's the first coke ever put in the cellar since I've lived here. If coke from coal is like rayon from silk, then it's no good. I hate rayon. I like cotton far better.

Roger said, "Mom, you look like an old lady." I have two pink eyes this morning. I wonder where I got that? I have felt a touch of it all along. So, I have bathed them with boric acid solution. This morning they are showing up a little.

I said, "Roger, perhaps Edwin is beginning to feel some of the longing and heartache I have suffered for a year, knowing that he would finally leave us." Now you know why Pop and I were upset when you and John Mc. were going to New York at age 10 to explore the world. I'll stay down on the farm with those we love. There's only four in our world and each one is precious.

Old Granny went to see Minnie. She got my letter so she came to Holmesburg and saw Charlie Smith, who was home for Christmas. He got ten days extension from Alaska. Granny had too much spirits, by the way she sounded over the phone. Minnie sure was glad to see her. I must call up Deiner's about the meat.

Well son, Thank God I just talked to you, so I won't add any more to this letter.

Cheerio, be good, be kind and God will guide you.

All the luck and the best wishes of your dear little brother, your old Dad and fat Mommy.

Love- Love- Love

Monday night, January 15, 1945

Dear Son,

Before I get settled down for the evening, I shall chat with you. We had a favorite supper of yours tonight, meat beef pie, coleslaw, etc. I was in hopes of you getting home. Now as evening is drawing to a close, I am giving up hope. It was so nice to see you once again. It makes me feel like living all over. As you already know, the fields around look snow and icebound.

All I know is cooking, cleaning, and keeping the home fires burning. I keep looking out the window across the fields at nothing. I sure saw a welcome

The Home Fires

sight Sunday evening at about 5:30. When I drew the curtain back, my heart took two skips when I saw two loves "coming my way", happy in the cold and snow with red roses.

Dear Son, It's now Tuesday morning and you can see I got as far as the above when the back door opened ever so softly and my two loves surprised me. It was like a ray of sunshine on a cold winter night. Then this morning getting up to call you at 3:30, I often wonder how I ever put up with the Prices. It takes cast iron nerves. I am in my usual place and so glad and happy you got in on time. I am worrying about Dad being out in this storm. It seems to me this is the worst blizzard this winter.

I left Roger in bed. I kept thinking of the old slave. He told his master he had a rhyme made up and now he could go free. So the master said, 'Let's hear it.' The old slave had been out in the storm and he was so glad to get in. He had said the rhyme so many times to himself. "A storm from the Northeast is not fit for man nor beast." The old slave said, "Master, I am free. A storm from the Northeast is not fit for man nor dog." The master said, "Slave, you get back to your work. You had your chance."

You see son, one word can change a life. I never said words to change mine. I stuck through Northeast and all kinds of storms. A good ship needs a good captain and the crew must help to guide the ship. A mother's hand needs help to guide her household. Be a good rudder and sail on to Victory.

Love,

Mommy

Thursday, January 25, 1945

Dearest Son,

Pop keeps saying, "I wonder where the boy is tonight?" and asking if I heard from you. He felt better after he knew you got back on time. Dot called up around 9 to see if I had heard from you. She said she almost froze walking down the pike as it was 2 degrees. Believe me, I been firing up since 2:30 AM as you know Pop said he nearly froze his feet. He couldn't get any coffee until he got to Chester. He said half the shop was late because of frozen up cars and cars turned over. Baldwin's radiators froze up on the third floor and broke and leaked all over. Joe had his hands full and he said he was cold all day. The dishes are cleared away and Pop and Joe had a shot to get warm.

I've been thinking of you all day and as usual, no news. I can't write because they have Mr. Keene on. Your bed is going to have two new occupants tonight, Dad and Mom. It's warmer. Roger has a cold. He nearly froze waiting for the school bus, which came by about 9:10. So he slept all afternoon. I am in hopes you will get this letter soon after your arrival so that you will know all is well with us.

Mrs. Bell asked if you knew that boy's name. I shall make this letter short and say goodnight for now. I hope to hear from you real soon.

With all my love,

Mom, Dad, & All

Friday, January 26, 1945

Dearest Son,

If you are going south, you won't know how cold it is up here. I don't think it was quite as bad as the morning you left. I didn't crawl out of bed until 9 o'clock. As usual, I got awake and up when Dad went. He sure did some churning to get started this morning, but the old wagon was faithful. Pop told the men if he wasn't on time, they shouldn't wait. I called up Kennedy. He said no coal in before next weekend. So I had to order another ton of coke for $15.00. I think he sure gives us a dirty deal. Believe me, if this war ever gets over, he won't get my trade. I ordered that coal a month ago.

I was talking to Mrs. Spence and Mrs. McAdams yesterday. Otherwise, I know no news. Roger has a real cold. He has been in bed two days. Up and down. Me, well, I had a good night's sleep in your bed. It's still the best one in the house. So, I will stay there the rest of the winter. I hope you had a fairly comfortable trip. Of course, we will be happy when we hear from you. I will stop here to see what the mail brings us.

Pop bought a big, fresh mackerel, 2 pieces of fillet, and one pound of shrimp, 2 dozen eggs, 2 boxes of tomatoes, and I have a chicken and a half pan of scrapple. I guess we will make out this weekend.

I have the house good and warm and most of my routine work done. We also had our lunch. Now, I will finish up and I will finish this letter tonight. Maybe I will hear some news.

No letter today, love. No letter today. So here I am again. It's still mighty cold. That's the big news at home. We put out some bread for the birds, and the three fat crows rule the back garden. All Roger keeps saying is "Oh! What a good shot." By the time he gets your rifle and gets out the back door, the crow family is sailing to Fisher's woods. He says, "Mother, they smell me. They must." All he is interested in doing is getting the goat house fixed for the pigeons. If he fails this term at Wilson, well, no pigeons. He missed more school this term than all the time he missed put together at Jacobs. So long for now. Lots of love.

Mommy

Friday, January 26, 1945

Dearest Son,

Evening is here and still very cold. Brown was over and looked at the pump at last. It needed a new valve and minor adjustment. The new baker said he was in bed and bang! He said his boiler split open and the smoke door blew off. There was $250 worth of damage and no heat.

Mr. Gallagher was just in. He brought me 100 pounds of potatoes for $5.00. He said he didn't know when we would get any more. He said he spun out near Fisher's this morning and had to get pulled out. Pop is wondering where you are by now. Aunt Violet called to find out if you got off. This is the third letter sent to San Francisco. I hope you get them okay. I sent out some requests for seed catalogs tonight. Uncle Charlie said he will miss you and asked Aunt Violet to call me up.

Roger has a real cold, sore nose, and I guess we will be going to bed very shortly.

Pop thinks there is some dirt in the gas line. I told you he had a job starting this morning. When he picked up his first rider, the car wouldn't start. So,

The Home Fires

they pushed it down a hill and it went. Tonight, he was a half hour getting out of Chester. He called Bill up. So far, Bill has not called back. It's so cold. But we will keep our fingers crossed.

Pop bought a Bonita Mackerel and we had it baked for supper. It cost $1.54, but it sure was delicious. I have read the evening paper and have a fresh cup of coffee. I could eat some ice cream. I'll go out and get some snow. I did it many a time when I was a kid. I put it in a jar and shook it with sugar.

Edwin, I hope you had a nice trip. Until I hear some news, I am thinking of you and will be happy when we hear from you. So until then, Nighty Night. All my love.

Mommy & All

Johnny Ems just called up and asked me to send Roger over to tell his wife he can't get home until 1 PM, so Pop has to go.

Saturday, January 27, 1945

Dearest Son,

You sure must have gone some by this time, and I wonder if you have any church service on the train. I guess you are tired of riding by this time. If anyone had ever told me I would let my little boy go to California without us, I would have thought they were crazy. This is something like a dream.

I got a ton of coke for $15.00, the first thing this morning and the damn liar Kennedy got three cars of coal in. I guess he wanted to get rid of the coke to make room for the coal. There is an embargo on all freight beginning today. It will last three days so war material can go through, because the fruits and vegetables are perishable. There's no use shipping them in, in this zero degree weather. Thursday was the coldest of all. I shall never forget that cold morning as long as I live.

One other real cold morning that I'll never forget was when I was not quite sixteen, frozen and hungry on Welsh Road Hill where Uncle Bob lived. I had to get up to get myself out to work and there was no fire. So I thought, 'I'll put the window up and if the coal oil explodes, I'll jump out the window.' I poured the coal oil out of the lamp on green wood. I didn't get a chance to jump out the window. It just went "puff" and knocked me against the wall and blew out upstairs, across Mom and Dad's bed and out of the chimney hole for the stove upstairs.

I got up at 2:30 on Thursday to fire up so the house would be warm for you. I was wondering what you were thinking as you stood against the stove in your sailor coat. When you come back, I hope your disposition is changed for the better. I kissed your hands and you were so disgusted. I was just as disgusted with you. All the hardships I went through for you. I didn't say anything, but I was so mad at you. I took the five dollars Pop gave me for shoes for Christmas and you bought that coat that was too big. I don't know what promises you made. But, that is the last money I am going to give you. From now on, you take care of yourself. Learn the value of money. You wrote me a letter to remind me of the money you gave me. I gave it all back. If you don't have any money and you can't get along, well, do without.

I paid the $31.42 telephone bill this morning. Pop went out at 4 o'clock and he churned away until 5 o'clock with that car and froze in zero weather. Think over all the things you done in the past year and see if you can do better yourself. No more nagging from Mom and Dad. You are on your own. You are my life and soul. From now on, you can love me a little. Like I told you before, you can travel the highways of the world and knock, knock on every door, but no one will run and let you in and be as happy to see you and know you are safely home. See how much money you will have to get that fine home and have all you want. You won't get up at 4 AM for Dad and me. I want you to understand. Make no mistake. Don't tell me you are homesick or all that ails you, or you are lovesick for someone you have to coax. I wasn't born yesterday. I will make a good mother-in-law.

Cheerio.

Mom

Sunday Evening, January 28, 1945

Dearest Son,

I wrote you this morning. Supper is now over. Kate Smith is singing "Don't Fence Me In". Mrs. Bell said she has been in her house since before Christmas and she knows what they mean when they sing that song. Roger was up to Harry's again for the third time and didn't get the pigeons yet. He said Harry got down by the bed and prayed. He is burned up because he didn't get them. I think Harry is giving him the run around. The girl who lost the wallet was here. She was sure smart and educated; Spanish. Her father is an officer in the Navy with 13 years in the boiler room. She sure was an interesting girl and gave Roger the money ($1.05). The weather man says snow mixed with rain, temp 36. I heard Pop and Roger talking about you, wondering where you were. Roger asked Pop how far it was. Pop said too far to suit him, 3000 miles. Do you realize that's as far across the Atlantic to England? I guess you won't see England on this trip. We hope wherever you are, you are well. We think of you and love you all the time in our hearts. All Pop tells you is to lend no money and be good, and you will come out on top. The town paper is out so it may follow you. I will send your new address to them and $1.00 for 1945. John E. is home today, so Rog said Dot called me up Saturday morning and said she had your card. She may walk over today, but I guess it's too cold. Lots of love. Nighty night.

Mommy

Monday Evening, January 29, 1945

Dear Son,

I received your card from Chicago. You sure made good time to that point. I guess you didn't go the southern route. I also had a letter from Uncle John, who said he signed up for four more years. He said he makes more than Bill, Byron and Edwin, and then some. He will have some money when he comes home. I also had a letter from your Aunt Mildred.

Today, I seem to be in trouble all around. The day started out with a terrible sleet storm. Tonight, Pop got over at Wenker's drive to let F. Fisher pass and he got in the gutter. Nutsie Ems came running. We had our supper. It was 6:45, so Joe, Roger and Nutsie went with shovels and he got out. Now he is out at Bender's. There's trouble with the fuel line.

Aunt Lilly called up. So did Mrs. Spence and Granny. I told Granny I was mad at her for repeating what I told her what you and Dot said about Minnie's baby. She got mad. She said you and Dot were liars and that she never said anything to you or to anyone. She raised the devil and blamed it all on me. She said I never gave her anything and carried on. She said I was jealous of her. I believe she had one too many. She cried and said I made her cry and would never forgive me. You know it will be a rainy day before I ever repeat anything again. I didn't want to get in any fight the other night, but you and Dot did say it and I did repeat it. Granny was so mad at Dot and especially for Dot saying you got married that day. She is burned up.

I don't know anything pleasant to write about. Roger is up to H.T. after those pigeons again. Nutsie is with him. If he comes home again without them, I will be just as pleased.

Johnnie Ems is home again tonight. I won't write any more because I don't know what to write about.

Granny is all puffed up with Al. She says Al is going to buy a home and give it to her for a birthday present. I hope he does. But there must be a string somewhere. I may be wrong, but cards and drink are bad company and I may be old-fashioned. Like I told you, see the world and don't worry over us. See what a fine home you will have. Maybe I can come and rock the baby. Your wife will make supper for me and you will coax me to say yes or no. So long for now. I know you must be in California by now. Nighty night.

Mom & All XXXX

January 30, 1945

Dearest Son Edwin,

Well son, one more day left of the first month of the New Year. What a cold, stormy one it has been. Pop has traveled along pretty good with the car. I sure will be glad when the bluebirds sing. Yes, I had your card from Chicago and two letters from Denver, Colorado. Yes, Denver has a cold climate. I guess you were amazed at the Rockies. Colorado is a place where they have a good high dry climate for T.B. patients. Never in all of God's world did I ever dream you would be going west. Strange things happen in this world. I told you, Bustleton to you will always be home, the finest place in the world to you. But your country calls and you answered. I am so proud of you. I pray all the time for God to guide you. If you are at your base, you probably have some of my mail, for I have written every day. I think this is letter number 8.

I talked to Aunt Lilly today. She had a big letter from Irene Greenland in England. Irene said Edwin B. got to her house January 6th for a few hours leave. A knock on the door at 10:30 and he had to leave early the next morning. Edwin is at Ascot, England, 20 miles southwest of London. They live 20 miles north of London. That is only as far as Dad travels 38 miles each way to Chester. She said Edwin always had the poker, poking at the fire grate (open fireplace). So she said, "Edwin, you like to poke at the fire." He laughed. He said, "Yes, we don't have these kinds of fires in America. They went out of date with the Pilgrims." She said it was her turn to laugh.

I guess we are many jumps ahead of what you will see and hear about in travels. Telephone to my brother Bill, maybe he can get to see you or you can phone from his place if you get any liberty. All I ask is that you are a gentleman as I have taught you to be, and I shall be proud of you, my sailor son. I do hope you have a nice pal and mate. If you find a good friend who you can talk to, the time is not as long or as hard.

Pop and I are still occupying your bed. The bed is swell, but I don't like hearing the wind singing through the passageway between the truck shed and the house. Man oh! Can that sing a mournful tune along around 3 AM, just about the time Pop gets up. When I first got married, I used to get mad at Pop at some of his habits. I used to say to him, "You exasperate me beyond endurance." When he would be working in Heinel's, he would get mad at something he would be doing and he would say it. The fellows would stop and listen to him. When he told them those were the words his wife used, they could hardly believe him.

When you were waiting for him on Thursday morning to take you, he just kept his one pace. That is all I kept thinking. You got so impatient. I used to get the same way. "You exasperate me beyond words," my endurance is worn.

I used to wash the supper dishes, take a bath, and bathe you and Roger. You would be all dirty. Roger would shit the pants. All the powder would be off my face from sweat and still Pop would be peacefully sitting with his feet in the basin until he was ready. You were both hungry and sleepy. So, I started to sit home on Saturday night. Now, after all the joy of wanting you to get big, I am still more alone than ever. That train ride took you too far for me to smooth your face and tuck you in. So be good. Be kind and you will be happy.

Love,

Mom XXXX

January 31, 1945 Dot said she had your two letters and two cards yesterday. Love to you. She called me up today.

Dearest Son,

Here is another real cold day, down to 6 degrees. I guess by this time you're in San Francisco, where the fog is. What did you think of the Sierras and Rockies?

Last night, the full moon was sailing through the sky. The sky was like big snow banks and big dark clouds. When the moon would sail behind the dark cloud, you couldn't see it. I would say, well son, I know the moon is there, beyond the cloud. Someday, my son will come sailing in that old lane.

I wonder if you ever think of that awfully cold morning you went away. I know you like it warm. Yesterday I had your two letters from Denver and today I heard a lady say over the radio that it was 20 below zero in Denver. If that's the case, you can be glad you're going on to California where you surely are by this time. Each time I heard from you, I was surprised you were so far away.

Roger got promoted to grade 7-B. He had to go back today to return a history book before he could get his report. He came up to a G- in two subjects so I am satisfied. He and Nutsie were together all day today.

It sure is cold here tonight. Kennedy promised us a ton of coal Friday. I heard from Uncle John today. He got our Christmas cards on Jan. 21st and the town paper I sent December 1st.

All is well. Pop is okay. John Ems phoned Dot. Dot phoned me to tell his wife not to go home today as he hoped to get home again tonight.

So long honey,

Mommy and all

****END OF JANUARY ****

Chapter Five

February 1945

Helen, Roger and Edwin Price Jr.

Wartime Letters Written from Mother to Son

February 1, 1945

Dearest Son,

These few lines are in a hurry. It's 2:45 and Roger and Carl Ems are eating dinner. It's still very, very cold here. You left me one week ago today. I had an awful dream about you this morning. I dreamed you got into some awful trouble (in the English Royal Navy).

I was awake with Pop at 3 o'clock. When he went to go at 4:30, he couldn't get the jalopy started, so he fooled with it until 5 o'clock. Then he had to hoof it off to the trolley. I called Mrs. McAdams to be on the lookout for him. I called her up at noon and she said he got there on time. So I called Bill Bender and they towed the car out about noontime. (I guess there was ice in the fuel line.) So tonight I guess Pop will be later than ever getting home. There's always some worry.

Mrs. Spence called me up just as I started to write this letter, so I had to lay it aside. Now it's 5:15. Joe is home. I have a little piece of rib beef on cooking. Pop got it from Hoover, where he got the turkey. So I have the cabbage and potatoes on too.

Roger is out with Carl all day. I have sent you about 8 letters and today one came back for two more cents and it was a real thin one. I do hope you have gotten my mail. I am so very anxious to hear how you like California and all about your trip. Was it wonderful? I want to tell you, dearest son, that I received the pillow top today. It is one of the most precious gifts I ever received. I know you read that beautiful verse and I knew that was in your heart. I cried when I read that. The colors were so lovely. I put a pillow in it right away. I had just cleaned your room all up and put the new blue blanket on the bed. I powdered the sheets and I put the pillow in the middle of your bed. I can't sleep in your room, so tonight will find Dad and me back in our own room. Dad doesn't like the bed and I don't like to hear the wind singing between the truck shed and the house. I can hear the back door rattle. So cold or not, back we go tonight.

I tell you, it's one sheet of ice all over. The wash man came today for the first time in two weeks. He walked up. Bill Bender went mighty slowly. Gallagher is coming in with an order. I tried at Gallagher's and the Post Office to get a check cashed today. They would do it, but no money. The Post Office told Roger to come back this afternoon. As you know, today is rent day. That doesn't leave much left. I will add a few lines after supper when Dad gets home to see what news he has. Joe said he was talking to Dot tonight. She got your mail.

Well son, it is nearly 10 o'clock. I will add a few lines. Pop had to walk home. He didn't see Bill Bender and the car was not done. So, he is going with McAdams again tomorrow. Roger found a swell .22 rifle in the gutter up Krewstown Road. He and Nutsie cleaned all the rust off of it. It is a nice real heavy one. I do hope you got my mail. I sure will be so glad to hear from you. Pop is calling, "Lizzie Bit, Lizzie Bit." We all send our love. Nutsie said Dot got her pillow top and it's lovely. Thanks dear, but honey, look out for yourself. I love you, just like the verse. Nighty night. Your own,

Mommy

February 2, 1945

Hello Son,

The ground hog saw his shadow, so we have six more weeks of winter. And winter it sure has been here in the east; as you know, I told you in a previous letter. Roger is off until Monday on account of promotion and as usual, Mother is the lady. Pop had to hoof it off to the trolley and a big freight held him up this morning. I thought if that were your long legs, you would be just one step ahead of the freight.

The chief concern at home is the coal shortage. Kennedy has promised us a ton by Monday. We, of course, have been good and warm, but with a worry we can't get any more. Roger is having breakfast and it's 9:30. The home fires are burning and I have the usual cleaning up to do. Pop called Joe to come up to your room to see the pillow top. Pop leaned over the foot of the bed. Joe stood there, and of course, you know he can't read. So I had to read it out to them. When I read your Denver letters to Pop at the table, the tears ran down Pop's cheeks. He makes me cry.

The American flag was a beautiful sight to those men whom the Rangers rescued from the Japs in the Philippines. Look at that beautiful flag and say, yes, my mother's tears are in your stars and I will help to keep you flying. Keep up your good work, no matter what the odds. Fight on. March on to Victory. I shall ever be proud and grateful to all the boys who left their homes; from the hills and from the valley came the stirring call for men. You said, 'Sir, I will enlist. Mother will you sign?' God saved me from doing that and called on Dad. So serve and do your best. God will guide you, if you have faith. All my love,

Mommy

February 2, 1945

Dear Edwin,

I wrote you a letter this morning. Roger took it out about 10 AM. It's noon now. Nutsie and Roger brought me the mail. So you are in California. You didn't say what the weather was like. I do hope you got all the mail sent to San Francisco. I sent about 12 letters.

I got your tax from Budd's today. I will send it or whatever Dad says. We may fill it out for you. You earned $620.88 and paid $86.20 tax. So, I think you get a refund. Let me tell you another headache. I paid $31.41 last week and the new phone bill is $31.81. I sure don't know how it will get paid. The last call from Perryville was 40 cents and one on January 5 was $2.60. So I am sunk.

I hope you get all my mail. I write 2 and 3 times a day. I have put 6 cents on them. Some came back. So long for now. I will write tonight.

Love,

Mom

No news of Byron. God Bless Him.

February 3, 1945

Dearest Son,

I had a dream that Mrs. Watson was trying to get me on the phone. The bell wouldn't stop ringing. I woke up. Man, oh, man was that phone bell ringing. I was out of bed with one throw of the covers, one look of the clock, I said,

"Edwin is on the phone, Pop, and away I ran." The dog was barking and running in front of me in the dark, down the steps. I had a chair full of clothes. I came through the parlor. I liked to break my two toes against the chair. It was a second when I heard your sweet voice. I would have been so happy, but you cried. I could hear you saying goodbye, goodbye, as I was hanging up. I was so sorry I didn't wait until you had hung up. My dear son, only God will help us. I wrote you so many letters since you left. I hope you get them.

Roger is going up to see Uncle Bill and will take this. I just called Dot. The man told me she is not at work. I got your pillow top, so did she. I talked to her several times on the phone up until now. We had three letters; two from Denver and one from Treasure Island. The pillow is precious to me. Thanks darling. Please take care of yourself. We are all well. Write the news.

Love,

Mom

February 3, 1945

Dearest Son,

Another one of my letters came back this afternoon. So, I put it in a new envelope and sent it off to you 12 cents airmail. It is 5:30, Saturday, and Nutsie and Roger are in the cellar. Nutsie is housekeeper today. He said he had his orders. Mrs. Ems, Tommy, and Dot went down to the bus to meet Juanita and Mildred, who have been down in Maryland since last Friday. Tommy needs shoes. Dot is going with Juanita to Virginia to visit Juanita's mother for two weeks. Nutsie told me. I cut off the nightgown I made and Dot wanted her pajamas, so I sent them both with a letter inviting her over and telling her to write you. I told her you called 3 AM Philadelphia time, 12 western time.

I was so glad to hear from you. I have been sick and nervous all day because you cried. I could hear you saying goodbye. Now dear, I would just love to fold you in my arms and kiss you. You had no time for that when you were home. I got down on my knees beside you and my heart was broke. If you don't brace up, it's hard for me. You were such a difficult boy, but I tried hard to show you the right way. Nothing will please me more than to have this war over and you settled down. This past year has been an awful tough one. I was so in hopes this war would end. With all the different troubles, it's hard travelin' and I always wanted the best for you.

Edwin, don't worry about going to see Uncle Bill. Pop said, save your money. Be sure and let us know if we should make out your tax returns. The way I figure it, you should have a refund. We sure need some help with the phone bill. We have turned in 6 bonds for coal, phone, and insurance since Christmas. Pop has put $70.00 on that car since Christmas, counting tires. The riders haven't helped to pay it off. I have the blankets to pay for. Save all you can so you can get a good start.

Nutsie is going to mail this out. This makes three today. I do hope you get my mail. I love you dear. I love you more than you can tell. God guide and keep you safe for us.

Lots of love,

Mother

Wartime Letters Written from Mother to Son

Sunday noon, February 4, 1945

Dearest Son,

Back home here, the sun is shining bright and 30 degrees. That is some relief after the zero weather we have had for the past three weeks. I have a big shad in the oven baking. I usually say, that is my first spring dinner. Anyhow, I can make believe it's spring even though the fields are still white with snow. I often had my "little" sailor boy pick me a bunch of daffodils when it was snowing and the March winds blowing. Somehow, I don't have a flower in the house. I always had some begonias blooming, where I could nip off a few for the kitchen table. Today, I just have a pretty blue dish of your great-grandmother's in the center. I have flowers in my hair, artificial ones. But I can still say make believe. I didn't get to church. Pop got up at 7:30, brought us up coffee and it was 9:30 when he got through his bath. I had the usual (dried beef). Aunt Violet was the good fairy that helped me out.

Pop had a fight in Deiner's last night. A new butcher wouldn't sell him a pound of dried beef. He said they didn't buy it for a year. Pop said, yes, he had bought it for five years. Finally Ed, the boy like you, waited on him. He got it.

Roger says Fred Baker is home for good with a medical discharge from the Navy and a crippled leg. Also, Corduff is home for good on a medical. They never were much good if you ask me, and they're two more headaches for Mrs. B. in that shack.

I don't know any news. Dad and Joe are working on the car. (No brakes this morning.) Pop put in the thermostat, so now we have heat in the car. I often think of the old days when we rode in the Model T. That's the one you and Grandpop set on fire and when the gas tank blew up, it shook Bustleton.

What must Berlin be like? I wonder how they like our style of fighting.

Son, my Pop would never let me go to Hawaii with the Grundy family. That's why I lost out, as they went somewhere warm every winter. My Pop didn't trust the Japs. He used to tell me how they treated women. So don't trust anyone or feel sorry for the enemy. Remember, shoot to kill. Count all as love from,

Mother XXX

Sunday Evening, February 4, 1945

Dear Son,
Supper is over, the dishes must be washed and the "maid" is out. So mother is on the job. Dad is fireman today. He is off today, the first Sunday in six weeks. One of the Russell brothers is home. I don't know if it is Matt or Jim. I also hear Byron Hickman was rescued from torpedoing. Each day brings news of someone. I am thinking of you and wondering how you like California. By this time, it is mid-afternoon where you are. Are you on liberty? It sure is a dull day here. It looks like rain all afternoon. We cleaned a lot of the junk out of the cellar. We burned up a week's trash and took cans out. We cleaned out the drain and, on account of the weather, Pop had Joe wash the car windows. No one called up.

Pop went for gas, so he took the horns up to Ems'. He was talking to Mrs. Ems, who had just put out a big wash. The poor woman has a houseful with John and Juniata. I guess she is doing double duty now that they are all away. Johnnie did not get home the last time he phoned for his wife to stay. Mr. Ems saw the ship was gone. She left the next day and took Mildred as there was no school on account of promotions.

They say the Frankford Theatre is like an icebox. Some of the schools and amusement places have no coal, although the churches mostly have coal in. Some are meeting in just one classroom on account of the freight embargo, which has been put on twice now to let war freight go through.

Since Pop is not working today. I guess it will soon get caught up. It does put some people out. Mostly, the poor people burn wood or coal oil and never had enough money to fill the cellar with coal in the summertime. This is War. So I am willing to eat carrots and beets if it will only get over and our boys get back.

Son, it's either hailing or raining. I don't know another thing to tell you. Roger is here and all the talk is of pigeons. Nutsie and he worked all afternoon fixing them up and they played checkers. Pop and I held down the couch; me in the parlor and Pop in the radio room. Now I will finish and do the dishes and listen to the Good Will Hour.

Roger says it's hailing. And he said, "Joe, lend me a buck." Joe said, "No, it's Joe *give* me a buck." So long my darling. Mrs. Ems told Pop that Dot went to Virginia. Nighty night. Hope and pray you are getting my letters. Kisses and love from all,

Mother

Monday, February 5, 1945

Dearest Son,

It's Monday noon at home and it's a dreary, cloudy day. I've gone through the house and had some lunch while listening to Sardi's. Now I have on the Jack Birch Show. Roger got off to school after a nice holiday. It sure did sleet and rain. Everything is one sheet of ice. The home fires are burning and "Baby Brownie" and Lizzie Bit are keeping me company, otherwise all else is quiet and I am thinking of you. It's still early out your way. I haven't anything new to tell you. Pop wrote you last night. I guess we both wrote you the same news. Roger said to tell you the fleet's in. Littleton, near Jacob's school, is home, also one of the Russells, and so each one "blows the main down".

Rog is going to Frankford to pay $15.44 electric bill and get a new ring book. He bummed a dollar off Joe. "Lend me a buck, Joe?" Darling, today I heard Bobby Philippino say on Sardi's program that he was the happiest man in the world because all his people live in the northern part of Manila. He hopes his mother will cook a good chicken dinner for General MacArthur. I guess there are many more hearts to be happy when at last the war is over. Wherever you are, your Mother's and Dad's love follows you. You are never alone, dear. Don't ever get lonesome for us. Just talk to us and know we are part of you. All we want is life to be made safe and brighter for you and everyone. Joe helps us out and he sure is a good fellow to all of us. He takes good care of Dad and helps him out wonderfully. So don't worry over us. Just take the very best care of yourself that is possible. Then I can feel that God will guide you. Until we are together again, lots of kisses and all our love.

Mom, Dad, & Rog

Both Dot and I had a card from the postmaster in Salt Lake City, Utah, that a post card is held there for 2 cents postage, so I sent a 3 cent stamp to get mine in a letter.

Monday, February 5, 1945

Dear Edwin,

I asked Joe what news he has. He says what news has he, all we know is work. Roger says Bernie O'Neal is still home. Roger has the Constitution to learn. What a headache. He has ten amendments to write.

Pop is out at Bender's getting the brakes fixed.

Pop just got home, so I will tell you what he says. Bill can't fix the brakes until Wednesday night. I hear Dave Tumbelston is at Quantico, Virginia and that his wife is at the parsonage with two kids. One is hers and the other is supposed to be her sister's, and "another on the way". I guess Dave is hooked. You stay single and don't let any of those far west girls smile on you. Pop says to tell us about the place if you can, and how you like it. Is the food any better or different? How is the weather? Pop is calling the cat Lizzie Bit. I sure named her. Joe and Pop are glad to get home in this weather.
We will all be glad when it's spring. Mrs. Spence sent her love. Drop her a card when you get time. All our love,

Mom, Dad, Roger & Joe (3 letters today) Nighty night.

Mommy

February 6, 1945

Dearest Son,

Well, it's almost bedtime and we have spent a dreary, long evening together. Nutsie is here. Roger had supper up there and didn't come home until 7:30. I received your letter that you wrote on February 1, with your picture. It sure pleased Dad. I guess you are going the limit now that you get liberty and burning the candle at both ends, and not getting enough sleep to take care of yourself.

My dear son, I don't know any news to tell you except that it is warmer. Mrs. McAdams told me that William expects to get home sometime soon.

Pop laughed when he read your letter saying you were in mess hall. Also, Pop says please be careful so that you are not penniless and without funds.

Joe, Pop, Nutsie, Roger and I are here. I have been cutting out pictures for a scrap book and not doing much work today. Did you get lots of my mail? I wrote you quite a few. I'll say you and your mate look swell. How I love you. Be well and keep well. All my love.

Mother and All

February 7, 1945

Dearest Edwin,

By this time you are surely getting some mail. It seems I have written so much that I have no news left or nothing to write about. I am anxiously awaiting a big letter from you telling me all about your trip. It's awful hard to write when you don't get out or don't hear any news. I ask Joe, anything new? No. Roger and Dad? No.

Dad is out at Bender's in hopes of getting the brakes fixed. It's not quite so cold here, but still plenty of ice and snow around. I haven't heard a word from anyone.

I did Roger's long division and he says he used to subtract. So I said yes, and still I can't get him to do it. Oh well, my children were never wizards. I guess they will learn sometime.

I am weary tonight. My heart is heavy and so I can't write. When I have a big letter from you I will feel better. Tell me all about your work. Are you getting along with your mates? Tell me what you saw on your trip. There are so many things for you to write to me.

Mrs. Spence and Mrs. McAdams called me up today. Same old story, how are you? Goodbye. I think of you all the time. Tommy Ems was here with Roger. I will say nighty night for now. Dot went to Virginia as I had told you. I got your pictures today. Pop said your hat was too much on the side. Roger was pleased too. Dad's picture of you was better than mine, but not as nice as I think you are. Okay dear, for now. All my love to you. Your own,

Mommy

February 8, 1945

Dearest Son,

Evening shadows are falling. Supper is on cooking; smells good. It's time for a little chat with you until the rest of my family comes home. It has rained and snowed here all day. It's dark and dreary. I have done some washing and the usual cleaning. I was pasting some pictures in a scrapbook I started in World War I. Mostly cooking pictures. I am still weary of the house and thinking of you as usual. It's just 5 o'clock here and mid-afternoon where you are. Roger got the ice and snow off the walk and back porch when he came in from school. That was the first we have been able to remove since you left.

Aunt Dink called me up today. She said she had the blues and she was wondering how I was. I was glad to talk to her. There's no farther news of Byron as yet. She wants us to come down. She got a big wooden box from Uncle John with some beautiful shells, a Jap's hat, a Jap shovel, and a

The Home Fires

beautiful ashtray from a Jap's quarters. She said everyone in the neighborhood was coming in to see them. Uncle John said to be sure and keep everything and another box is on the way. Outside of that, there is no special news. I will wait until Dad comes home to finish this. Maybe he knows some news.

Roger said Biddle is home. I guess Wenker is too. I framed your picture you sent me in the frame on my bureau. It's the one we gave Dad that time that he didn't like. I took it up with me when I went to bed last night and I took it out of the folder and it fit just fine. When Pop came up, he had his glass of water and he stood his on his table and he said, "I want my boy." I said, "I beat you, look where I got mine." He wasn't so pleased when he saw how nice mine looked, and so today, I took Granny's picture out of the frame and put yours in it and stood it on his table. I looked at that painted road and I said, "Son, the only road that counts is the road back, the one that leads to home." The picture you sent Roger is here on the sideboard. I have looked at it all day and that nice smiling face of that dear boy. It warms my heart to see his arm around your neck. I have said many times today, God smile on those two. That boy must have some little token of kindness in his heart for my boy to put his arm around his neck. I know you are never lonely for companionship.

Pop has the little picture in the wallet Dot gave him. It just fits. I still haven't any for my purse. I missed it off the sideboard today so, I said, "Pop, have you got my small picture?" He offered to give it back. I said, "No, Edwin will get his picture taken again, a small one." Edwin, I will close here. No letter today. Please write. Pop asks every night. Lots of love from all. Nighty night

Mother XXXXX

Wartime Letters Written from Mother to Son

Friday, February 9, 1945

Dear Son,

Just a few hurried lines to you now as Roger is going to the Post Office to mail a money order. I got the big letter, and it's a wonder. The box was open on both ends; the string all in a knot, ready to fall off. It's a wonder I got it and the paper. I sure am disappointed not hearing from you. I got only 4 short letters since you left. Yes, we got the pictures. Dad said he thought hats were for your head and never knew they hung them on your ear. When Aunt Mary wore her hat on the back of her head, she had everybody laughing at her. I suppose hats are made to wear at any angle that suits us. When you get your picture taken, act sanely and natural. None of them suit me and I still want one for my purse. If I get any I like, I will have it enlarged, like Uncle Bill's. I will write later this evening. For now, be good and behave. Hope you are okay. Lots of love.

Mom

February 9, 1945

Dearest Son,

Still ice and snow hereabouts, but it sure is a welcome relief to have it 38 degrees. Kind of eases up on the coal pile, which is sure sick looking again. Two tons a month is hard on the pocket book. Still, in all, it is much better than last year. Ten tons used so far and three tons of coke. I am still good for 4 more O.P.A. allotment. I am in hope of doing two more. I will sure be glad to hear Mrs. Robin chirp.

I have only been down to see Aunt Dink for a little while. That is the only time

The Home Fires

I have been out since Christmas. I am getting house weary and will be glad when I can doll and primp to walk to church. I would liked to have sent you something for Valentine's Day, but I don't get out. I think it is foolish to send candy. If there is anything special you want me to send, I will try to do so. As usual, all I I know is work, eat and sleep.

Roger told me that John Reese is home. I read in the paper where he had completed his 50th mission over Germany on Christmas Day. Roger says he looks like a picture. Have you heard any hometown news? Mrs. McAdams got your address card yesterday. I do hope you are well and learning your work. Aunt Violet said she would write to you if she had your address. If you get a chance, drop a card to Aunt Minnie Irons, Street Road & Murray Street, Croydon, Bucks Co. RD 2, Penna. She always asks for you. Sam Thomas came to Dad today and Aunt Kebe called me up last night. She told Sam you were home and had sore eyes. Pop told him no. I guess he didn't know you were home at Christmas because he didn't see you and she mixes everything up. If you have any time at all, write to them and mention how you enjoyed yourself at Christmas and that your eyes got better. I am so damn fed up with the whole family mixtures that I am sick of it all. I know I won't ever get mixed up again.

Granny always repeats and stirs up too much. I am sorry you ever said anything to me about Aunt Minnie. I have had so many heartaches over conditions in past years that I should never have mentioned it and known better. I guarantee it won't happen again.

Lone Ranger is on. I can't write. You are gone two weeks. I will sure be glad when I hear you are getting my mail. So until I hear good news from you, I love you lots.

Wartime Letters Written from Mother to Son

Mom & All

Saturday Afternoon, February 10, 1945

Here ,it is 4 PM. I am alone and along about this time on Saturday, you used to come racing in at 50 and my hair would stand on end. I would wait until you were in to see what kind of a humor you were in before I would say anything. Sometimes you would lie on the floor, between the door and the icebox and say, "Mom make me something to eat." I would have to step in and out over you. Now I am alone. Roger is out with Nutsie serving papers. I gave them both their lunch and off they went.

Boy, oh, boy. You should see how fat and big the crows are getting. They sure have a fat living from the bread and potato parings this winter. Roger has gone out so many times for a shot, but as soon as he gets set, off they go.

Today, I had a short letter you wrote on the 4th and then the only real letter you wrote was Feb. 6th telling me you received three letters. I sure wrote you, two and three times a day, so you would get some mail. I even wrote the day you left so you would have mail when you arrived there. I guess the mail is held up somewhere. I was so glad to get the pillowcase. The verse made me cry, for I know you read it. I have the new blanket on your bed and the pillowcase on a pillow in the center of your bed. I framed Roger's picture of you with your pal and put it on his bureau. I put Pop's on his table, and the picture of the married fellow and you. I still need some small pictures of you by yourself.

I still don't know any news. If the weather is nice, I am going to Holmesburg on Lincoln's Birthday, as Roger has no school. If you have had any letters from me, I have told you all I know. Now, I never saw an orange tree; but I have been told that brides choose orange blossoms because they are the only trees that bear fruit leaves and blossoms all at the same time. They continue to blossom while bearing fruit. As you know, fruit trees here at home, apple, pear, etc., blossom, and then the blossom falls and forms the fruit. So orange blossoms are the bride's flower. I had a wreath of them when I got married (on my head).

Well son, it will be a long evening. Joe has been home and gone. I am washed and curled. I have the house shining and so I will find something to read after this. I read your paper all from cover to cover. You sure must be in some large place. Of course, you know your mother follows all the news and knows about all places. Any little place I never heard about, I always look it up in books and magazines. I read about San Francisco many times and the Golden Gate. I saw lots of pictures of it. I was so glad to hear from you. Keep up the good work. I will make you some French fries when you come home. You can cook for me. What do you say? Love from all.

Mom

February 12, 1945 Lizzie Bit is missing since Saturday night when Roger left her out.

Hello Son,

Today is good old Honest Abe's day. There's no school. It's just like a real spring day, only there is a pile of snow as high as the back porch. There's ice and filthy dirty snow all over. The city of Tacony is sure a filthy sight of ashes and water. Everybody is trying to open up the gutter to let the black water run.

Dad, Roger and I took all day Sunday off. We left here at 12:30 for Aunt Dink's. When we got there, she wasn't home. We met Howard Baldy and

Pop took us on to Uncle Bob's. We just got there as they were about to have their dinner; spaghetti and meatballs and two heaping meat platters full and a spring salad dish of lettuce, sliced tomato, cucumbers, scallions and radishes. It was a picture. We sat down and sure enjoyed being with them. Rog and all the kids went down to the movies.

Before we were through dinner, in comes Pearl and Howard. They had Bill's letter and his purple heart. A nurse in Pittsburgh, Pa. packed it up for him. He is doing okay. And who do you think is in the same hospital in England? He said, "Where you from soldier?" He said, "Bustleton." Bill said, "Do you know Eddie Price?" He said, "Sure, lived on the same road." It was one of the Bittners. You know Leo's brother. Leo drives for Kennedy, the coal man. Mrs. Bittner works with Aunt Dot and they now live on Welsh Road. He has one eye out. Another of the Bittners is home with a medical discharge.

Then Pop and I went down to see the Fetters. We hunted all over Howell Street in Wissinoming and finally found them. His sister was there and her husband. Georgie came with his wife and we stayed about two hours. They invited us for supper, but we were meeting Roger at 6 so we didn't stay.

We went on up to Dink's. Aunt Dot and the Baldys' were there. Aunt Dink made us supper. I felt cheap eating off of her, but she insisted. We got home here at 8:10. We had a big day. I got Granny a card for her birthday. I am not going out today. Pop insisted on me going out today. It's so bad walking. Roger had his heart set on going with Emsie, and so here I am pretty well through my work. I still have to get combed up.

I hear they are going to celebrate Granny's birthday at Charlie's, but I am counted out. There's no way for me to get up there. Besides, no booze for me.

The Home Fires

George Fetters got out the whiskey and coming fast. Pop had two, but I soon got out. They live near Comly Park. You know, up by the 66 line. I don't know any other news. I didn't send any letter yesterday (Sunday), but sent two on Saturday.

Son, don't fail to write any chance you get. My letters are Dad's and his are mine, as you are of our flesh; equal. Pop said, after a while, I guess Edwin won't want to write at all, but don't kill him altogether. We miss you enough. So write whenever you can squeeze it in. Until I hear from you, all my love and write Dad. Dot is not home yet. Nutsie was here Saturday evening with us. He is a nice little boy.

All my love, dear. XXXX

Roger, Joe, Mother and Dad

February 12, 1945

Edwin,

I had a letter from Uncle John. The Red Cross never notified him. The first word he had about Byron was what I wrote him. He hadn't heard from Aunt Dink in 3 weeks. Today, Aunt Dink got all of Byron's clothes. I had your card from Salt Lake and three letters. The letters were from February 5th, 6th, and 8th. So I guess that is the last you wrote, as today is the 12th. I will write tomorrow.

Mom X X X

February 13, 1945 Valentine's Day is Granny's birthday. Remember the party we had? Well, the blizzard is the same today, one day ahead.

Wartime Letters Written from Mother to Son

Dearest Son,

I guess you had a lot of reading to do getting so many of my letters at once. I always look for the date on the envelope and then I read them in order. The bus just picked up Roger and it's 10 of 9. You are just about getting breakfast; and by the time school is out, Roger will just about get home. A real blizzard is raging after two days of spring-like weather and after the sidewalks are just about getting cleaned off from a 4-week spell of winter. I imagine your weather is about on a level with Washington DC., but they say San Francisco has lots of fog.

Edwin, a lady on Welsh Road has a big barn full of pigeons. Pop thinks it's Margerum's old place. She told Roger and Nutsie they could have all they could catch. With no school yesterday, they walked with the express wagon to get them last night. They worked for three hours and got six pigeons. They were a half hour or more getting home, pulling the wagon through snow, ice and water. They were up and down trying to catch the birds. Nutsie drank 3 glasses of water when he got here. Pop and Joe had gone to bed and I was waiting and looking for them. They had got in just before you called. Then Nutsie had that long walk home. They had served the papers and stopped in. I said, come right back and I will invite you for spaghetti supper. Pop got home early (6 PM) and so we ate. Then Roger and Nutsie came and he sure likes his spaghetti. Lizzie Bit came back at 5 AM this morning (Tuesday). She was gone since Saturday night. The spaghetti wasn't as good as I usually make, but I still have some left for tonight. When the phone rang, I was alarmed because I had talked to Mrs. Spence, Aunt Lilly, and Aunt Dink.

I didn't tell you, Aunt Dink got Byron's clothes home in the afternoon with the sea bag and hammock. She was too upset to open it. She also had mail from Uncle John. All he said to her was that he was too upset to write. In my letter, he said, he had not heard from Aunt Dink in three weeks. In her letters was all good news about Byron being home. He got my letters in the same mail. He shed the first tears since he was over there. He said he had been happy that morning because he was thinking it was his and Dink's 23rd wedding day. He said the Red Cross had not notified him and he will tell me what he thinks of the Red Cross when he gets home. And so, I was the Red Cross that broke the sad news to him. Thank God for that, because I wrote him a fine letter. But that don't heal the heartache.

Dearest, I was so happy to hear you. We had a little difficulty getting connected. I waited about 5 minutes. Roger ran for Dad to get him up. Dearest, I knew what war was and so I spared you as long as I could, but be a brave boy. God will give you courage and strength. Pray to God to be your guide and hope. You know you are missed and loved by all of us.

Mother   X X X X X X X X X

February 13, 1945

Dear Son,

Here is the second letter for today, and as usual, there is no news outside the fact that I received your two air mail letters. There was one for Dad and one for me, which of course, we all share the same. I see you were not pleased with what I wrote. I could still tell you plenty more and yet you would have to learn the hard way, just as your letter said. You were out and did not get up when you should have. You can't burn the candle at both ends. After all, I told you strip tease and all that simple stuff takes your mind off of good work and things that will be of benefit to you. I have gone through so many heartaches that I just can't stand any more. I was worried all day because you have no money. Still, I can't say a word, because I know you will never have a cent. Because you count double and you never save. You must put a certain amount away or else you never have it. Edwin Bissinger has thirteen 25 dollar bonds and one 100 dollar one in our safe, and all the ones his mother has not brought up here. You are in since October. I haven't seen any bonds. I don't know what you signed for. I know that Bill McAdams is paying $100 to get home by train and $1.00 for each meal. If you did get any time to get home, you wouldn't have any money. I know I couldn't send you any. I haven't paid the second phone bill yet and we have four bonds left.

My heart has been broken since Christmas. I haven't been able to catch up. I worry about you all the time. I said when you left me the first time that I gave you to God and Uncle Sam. All I do is pray for your own good. To me, you are a baby and life is a hard master. You are gone from my protection. You must stand on your own. How you do it is entirely your own life. As long as I live, you can share everything I have. But sometimes you ask the impossible. Both Dad and I have done all in our power for you. Show us now what you can do. Yes, you can make sacrifices. My dear boy, please learn before you get too old. All I can say is God guide you, keep you safe for us and pray.

All our love

Mom

February 14, 1945

Dearest Son,

Today I didn't even get a letter from you. I sure felt bad all day that I was not able to get one to you in time for Valentine's Day. But what I miss on a Valentine, I send you every day. I like those kinds of things. I made a big shirred one for on the dining room table out of red crepe paper and white lace paper doilies. It looks nice and I keep thinking of you. We had your favorite supper, steak, mashed potatoes, peas, gravy, sliced tomatoes, & a big pot of vegetable soup. I made 2 apple cakes. Roger almost ate half of one. So that was our Valentine party. I guess Granny is looking for us all, but here in Philadelphia, we had an awful sleet storm with snow first. Everything is one sheet of ice, so driving was tough, and walking was out of the question for me to get up to Uncle Charlie's, where she is celebrating her birthday. She is still sore at me because I haven't heard from her since.

Pop got smashed into by a Ford man this morning with no insurance. It wrecked the right front fender. So Pop must get a new one. It was awful bad driving. So the junker will do until spring, then I guess it will be ready for the heap.

I don't know any news for I can't get out. I asked Joe. He said all he knows is work. I asked Nutsie. He said nothing. So all I know is the weather. Lizzie Bit is back and she has been a pain all day, eating her head off. Well dearest, here is all my love. Be a good boy and do what is right. Do it for me. Until we meet again. Cheerio, "My little baby Valentine". I still have the one you made at school.

Love,

Mother and All

Thursday, February 15, 1945

Good Morning Son,

How are you, this bleak, cold, dark, winter day here at home? I can't open the back outside door. Rain and sleet froze it fast. We have to use the front door until I can get at it later in the day. Roger is eating his breakfast. I fixed the fires and I have my coffee here beside me on the dining room table. I must clean upstairs this day and iron the heavy shirts I put in the cellar yesterday. Then I will call the Mayfair laundry about 9. They have my wash for two weeks now. I need Pop's 10% wool longies, as he only has three suits and we need the heavy stockings. Roger is practically in his birthday suit for want of underwear. He wore out what was left of yours. I bought him two long suits, size 32 and they are now too tight. He is growing so fast.

Son, we sure have had a terrific winter. I will be glad when the lima beans are in the pod. But you know the old saying, if winter comes, spring can't be far behind. I once saw a good movie that had that theme. I think it was called, "Wintertime".

Later-

Well son, here I am again. A big freight going by went over some caps. It made me think I was getting shot. All is so quiet here with the cat and dog and me. When Baby barks, I nearly jump out of my hide (skin). I must run along now as it's 9:30. I have the kitchen done. I want to get up and clean the upstairs and get back down at 11 for Sardi's program. I will wait to see if Roger brings any mail. I will write just before supper. I cannot write when Lone Ranger and Radio Hi-O is going full blast, so I will write in the daytime. Nutsie said he expects Dot to get home this Sunday. Dot said on her card to me that the scenery was beautiful, but "no place like home".

Thursday 12 noon

Oh. Son dearest, please don't ever send me a Special Delivery letter again. I am still shaking and trembling. I even went to sign it Helen M. Long. I had to rub it out. I don't know what made me do it. I sure thought you were in trouble. When I saw the telegram, uniform, hat, I ran to the back door. I told you it was stuck. I tried to kick it open and I looked. Then I saw he must be at the front door. The dog was running in front of me and barking so loud. I tell you dear, if I am alone and a telegram comes, you know I will drop dead on the spot if it has bad news about you.

I pray all day and all the time for strength, for courage, and hope. Before you ever had to go to war, I never wanted war. I knew what Grant, Jerry, Tommy and Paul Bell told me about it. I never let Paul down in letters. I wrote to him, just like I write to you. He always appreciated my letters. I told you on the phone and I also told you in a letter, that I got the big letter that was in the box. The box was all broken. I send you an air mail, every day by Dad. Roger often takes out an extra one. I always send one Saturday morning. If Dad doesn't work Sunday, well, I don't always get one off. But dearest, I write you all I can. I got two letters on Tuesday and none since until this special one now. I sure was a wreck until I had it read. I am still crying; nerves.

Son, it is a million times better for you to be in mess hall, than a fox hole on K-rations. It may not be so good, but thank God you are in the States. Look at poor old Dad, up at 3:30 every morning. All he gets out of life is a smoke and a bite to eat. Think of me and why I hate the farm. For 16 years, I could not go out unless I asked Grandpop. I never got off the place sometimes for 8 or 9 months. All I knew was cook and scrub. Yes, I had desires, but I knew I was licked and so I had to carry on. Now you have to learn life. You are complaining about your sweetheart not writing. Well, the world is large. You know I told you what you do at 16 will not suit you at 25. Be a good boy. Do your work. That helps keep me going. All I can say I have told you so many times before, I love you. Your welfare is ours, Pop's, Roger's and mine. So be good.

Love,

Wartime Letters Written from Mother to Son

Mom

Dear, I always trusted you. I brought you up never to steal and know when you had gone the limit. I have great faith in you and Roger. You must learn to be content. We can't bring this war to an end, so we must pray for God to guide us. If you get to Los Angeles, for my sake, be a gentleman. Don't drink and curse. You accuse me of showing off with Dot. You know in your own heart we always had flowers on the table and around the house whenever we could get them. Just show people what a fine boy I raised. Someday, I will tell you why. Just make me be as proud of you as I am. I always stuck up for you to others. So don't let me down.

Mom

February 15, 1945

Dearest Son Edwin (and not Eddie)

This is the second letter today. Look at the date always. Then you can keep up with the mail. I wrote you at noon telling you about getting the Special Delivery letter. I am still upset. It's now 4:30. Roger has gone to Ems and mailed your letter out. When he came in from school he brought me three letters from you, 2 were air mail and one free from the 10th, 11th and 13th. You told me in the 13th you sent a special. If only I had gotten that first. You see the only difference in the special is you put 23 cents on it. I got the special at 12 noon and the air mail at 3:30, both written the same day. Well son, I feel so much happier now that I have had three big letters from you. A kind act is never forgotten, like that fellow giving you a lift. There are some people in this world born to help and be kind. Others are only mean and hateful, cold and selfish. That is why I always kept "nagging" to make some degree sink in so that in life you could meet the situation. I put lots of faith in you and I understand you. I recognize your good points and your faults.

Whenever we have had any difficulties, I could read you. You know I can read people so well. I knew exactly your traits; some mine, some Dad's. I could tell each action. You are dominated by old Mrs. Price's side, like Uncle Paul. Then again, I could see plenty of my people. They say, "The apple never rolls far from the tree." Pop could be far smarter than he is. But, he acts so dumb. He has lots of his father's ways. He lets on he doesn't know people. He pays money without a receipt. He gets on and off that couch a hundred times; let's on he is asleep and is really listening. Well, I could keep on and on.

It's much warmer here, but there's still ice on the walk and steps. It didn't melt very fast. It's 80 degrees in the dining room with the cellar fire damped off. The wash came back. I hung it up and I finished the upstairs. I talked to Mrs. Spence and Aunt Lilly. I have the table set for supper.

My dear boy, I have written you so much. I am always thinking of you. I told you many times over, when I write, it is my daily chat with you. Along about this time (5 PM), I begin to look for you coming in at 50 MPH with the shoes swinging and swaying. I dust off your pictures. I talk to them and the days and hours pass into another world. I think as long as I live, I will never forget the first day and the last day you left home or the day you came in from boot. I could not have waited another minute for you that day. All the things I planned to say and I couldn't speak when I saw you. I often picture your return. Wherever you are when I hear the war is over, you know I will fall to my knees and thank God. It's just as hard for sons to be away as it is for mother's good boys, thinking of home, mother and dad and all the loved ones. If they don't, well, they are selfish and tough. God loves all those who are kind to one another. To me, you are still my little boy. You grew away too fast, just when things were going a little easier. But, it will broaden your mind and educate you more than books. Knowing different types of people will make you what you want to be. It's an opportunity you would never have money for. "Travel is an education." So my dear, keep out of trouble. Cultivate friendships that can elevate you. Self-educate yourself. March on. March on to Victory. Then we can all live in peace and free from fear. So my darling, what more can I say. I love you. I am beside you in thought. God keep you in strength and spirit for-

XXXXXX Mommy and all

REASON FOR LIFE

I don't know how to say it, but somehow it seems to me:

That maybe we are stationed where God
wanted us to be.

That the little place I'm filling is the reason
for my birth.

And just to do the work I do; He sent
me down to earth.

If God had wanted otherwise
I reckon He'd have made

Me just a little different; of a worse or better
grade.

And since God knows and understands all

The Home Fires

things of land and sea,

I fancy that He placed me here; just where
he wanted me.

Sometimes I get to thinking as my labors
I review,

That I should like a higher place
with greater tasks to do.

But I come to the conclusion; when the
evening is stilled:

That the past to which God sent me is the
past he wanted filled.

So I plod along and struggle in the hope
when day is through,

That I'm really necessary to the things
God wants to do.

And there isn't any service I can give
which I should scorn,

For it may be just the reason God
allowed me to be born.

Edgar A. Guest

Son, I always kept those verses in mind. They keep morale a lot when it gets low. Just remember, "Do our best", and keep going and all will be well.

February 16, 1945

Dearest Son,

Here, it is almost noon. I guess you have almost put in a day's work and are ready for a second breakfast. I have listened to Sardi's and had my lunch. All the fires are damped off as it is quite moderate. There is still ice and snow in some places. It went fast yesterday and the sun was out bright until a while ago. It has clouded up and looks like rain. It sure is mud all around. But it will still get cold. Old Man Winter has his back broken, I hope. Here I am, for my usual morning chat.
I wake up. I look at the clock. I say Edwin is in bed. Edwin's getting up. I wonder if Edwin got paid. Pop said, no money will keep him at the base and get him some rest. Everything happens for a purpose. Like I wrote you yesterday, it gives you an education in life. No money, no bread. With two babies to feed, life is a worry. A warm dish of food and a bunk to rest in is worth the work.

Oh, boy! Mommy is a lady again for four mornings in bed. Four days in a row, we get up when we feel like it. What a break. I have been getting this winter with holidays. Well dearest, I must iron and finish up my work. Roger is a good boy, so I didn't read him what you asked. I said is Roger still "a good boy?" Edwin, Roger did not get any letters from you. Dad got his. He said he would try to write on Sunday.

The wind is kicking up. Maybe that will dry things up. I hope you are well. Try to be happy. I will write more later today. Lots of love from all.

Mom, Dad, Roger & Joe   X X X X X X X X

I walked down for the mail. I will try to send you your shoes on Saturday if I can find a box. I will write tonight. Roger got your letter today. Don't go to see my brother without money and do not call him collect. Love, Mom (Friday afternoon 16th)

Friday afternoon, February 16, 1945

Dear Son,

Roger mailed out the letter I wrote you this morning. Here I am again. I got the shirts ironed and the house cleaned up except for the kitchen (a buck will do it, Mom). Maybe Joe will do it after supper. The sunshine sure muddied up everything today; regular mud flats and rivers.

Mr. Gallagher brought in the groceries. I went to the door to call the dog. Bang. I got locked out. I called to Mr. Gallagher. He got out of the truck and we got a crowbar and pried open the window on the front porch. It sure was stuck since it had got painted. He climbed in the window for me. I sure was glad. I had a pan in the middle of the stove. It just so happened that Roger got back around 4:30. I sure would have been sunk. I would have had to walk over to Joe without a coat to get his key. Thank goodness it wasn't cold. Mr. Gallagher said his Joe is home again for 30 days then is to go to Virginia.

Nutsie said Dot's mail sure is piling up from Eddie. We expect her home Sunday.

I have two fresh mackerel to bake in the oven and six pieces of fillet of cod to dip and fry. I have some mashed yellow turnips for a change, and lettuce cut up like I fix it. I guess that will keep them fit. I haven't set the table yet, but I have it all in readiness to start. I usually get things ready too soon. You can never depend on Dad. Last night it was 6:30. The night before, we were all through by six. I try to be ready for 6 or else we go ahead and eat. I don't like to eat without Dad, as that would be two missing. I don't know any news. I will look your shoes up and send them off to you. I do hope you are well. Be content and then you will be happy. We can't always change things. So, until I see you and smooth your dear face, I love and kiss you, hug tight.

Your old Mommy X X X X baby dearest love.

Sunday, February 18, 1945

Dearest Son,

Here it is 1:30 Sunday, and I have been thinking of you for hours. We had a deep snow, the hard, crisp kind that is good for sledding. This is after two spring-like days. I told you I was in hopes that Old Man Winter had his back broke. Lo, and behold, Pop said Saturday morning, "Well Mother, it's snowing." By dinnertime, Elmer Irons had all he could do to get in. They brought the three children to me to mind while they went out shopping. They sure were good children for a surprise. Little Elmer was sure good and the baby was an angel. Minnie is having her class of 12 women on the 21st. She is making everything red, white, and blue for Washington's Birthday. They got new shades for the house and spent $45.00 for inlaid linoleum. They had a good afternoon in Frankford. They had just got up here when you called up. Dad had been up bright and early in hopes you would call today. He sent Roger up before 9 o'clock to see if Dot got home yet. Dad is going up again about 12. If you call, you will know all this. I want Joe to take this letter when he goes to Frankford in hopes that you may get it by Tuesday.

The Home Fires

Well darling, I got a good dinner on. The house is warm. I had a nice bath. I dusted up and Joe scrubbed the kitchen. Now he is cleaning out the car. He takes great pride in keeping the car clean, and he sure knows how to do it. It was 10 o'clock when Aunt Minnie left last night. Roger and Carl didn't get back until 11. A lady on Welsh Road is giving them all the pigeons they can catch. They must go to the barn at night to get them. So far they caught 11. Elmer showed them how to make a trap and they went over with it last night.

Dad said he would write soon. You know we love you heaps and heaps and wish that you will do all you can to be careful. God will take care of you.

All our love,

Dad, Mother, Roger, Joe, and all your friends

February 18, 1945

Dearest Son,

Here is your faithful old "girl" for her usual chat, although I had two others today. I sent one off with Joe and one hour ago we talked to you on the telephone. I sure wonder where you are reading this. I will always have you on my mind. Because you are a fine, young man, you will ever think of home. People who never want to go home haven't a worthwhile one.

My dear son, I could never write any more than I have in the past. The only thing is this; in every line it holds you close to me. All my love is yours. Here I am as usual, like we used to talk to each other. Edwin, you came in that lane at fifty! "Mom, you're crazy". Well, I guess I am crazy over you. God bless the boys who know how to speed. They are the winners.

Keep your eyes peeled for your old Uncle John's 82nd Battalion, Sea.Bees and for Johnny Ems and Bill Long. I hope you meet up with one of them. Don't be ashamed to hug them for their mothers as a special greeting. Tell them all the news. We are all well, all have plenty to eat, we are warm, and so all we ask is the return of our loved ones.

Nutsie and Roger are gone again to see if they got any birds in the trap Elmer showed them how to build. Dad, as usual, is holding down the couch and listening to Kate Smith. The show is a real good one. I am enclosing a picture of what I think is your pin-up girl, Dorthea. Nearest thing I have of her. So my honey chile, I'll say, be good and then I will be happy as ever and ever. All our love,

Mom, Dad, Roger, Joe

February 19, 1945

Dearest Son,

Today, I am alone. It's Monday and all are off to work and school, so I have my coffee beside me and now for my little chat with you. I tuned in Sardi's and the radio went off. It went off yesterday too. But, Dad got it playing again. Now it's off and I won't get any news until Pop sees if he can fix it. I sure was glad to hear from you again. Pop waited all day, then he went for gas and to see if Dot got home. He had just gotten back and he wasn't in the house yet when you called. I know this will be all stale news when you get it, but I must have my little talk with you each day. The only thing is it's so long for you to answer back. Mom, "That was forty years ago." I often heard about funny stories. Pop said, "I have to do it for the boy." He's running for your girl, three times, to see if she is home. I wonder if she will ever run for Pop. You never can tell, but it tickles me. Some people you know, son, never worry over anything. She is young and it's a good thing. People can go away and forget the world.

The snow is heavy around and I have a few pieces to wash out. I will finish this later, as I expect to hear from you tonight. We have asked Dot for supper if she gets home. I got a long day to put in, so I will take it easy. I wrote to Bill and told him to keep his eyes on the lookout for you. That is Uncle John's Bill. I hear there was a fire at Florence Beyer's house on Sunday morning. Joe said he saw all the furniture out on the porch. I haven't heard any details. I don't know if she was in church at the time or not. Joe said he heard the fire company go out about eleven o'clock.

Monday Evening 7:30

Dearest Son,

I read in the paper where the fire was at Selma Copeland's. It burned them out while they were at church. Marie James lives in the apartment. That must be her furniture on Florence B's porch. That's why Joe thought the fire was there.

Well dear, we just finished talking to you. As usual, I was worrying about you being on time for 7 o'clock, not thinking of the difference in time. I think you must be getting nearly all my mail when you got the one about the fellow smacking Dad's fender. He ordered another secondhand one from Bill Bender. Today we got the notice for the new license. That's 10 more smackers. If business keeps up, we'll go to ruin.

Son, I shall be looking after all your things the best I know how. Please save your money and then when I see your head coming up the railroad bank or the taxi, I will run and take it all off of you. What do you say? Heaps of love and luck.

Mom, Dad, Rog, Joe & All

February 20, 1945

Dearest Son,

Well son, I just hung up the phone from talking to you. The time sure does fly. I did not expect to hear from you. I thought it was Mrs. McAdams, as Mrs. Spence had called me at 8:30. I am just about finished my work. All the fires are fixed. Lizzie Bit has a "beau" calling her. But I guess you know she stays right in. Aunt Kebe said to Tom the alley cat, what you mean "alley cat"? So Granny showed her some walking the back fence. She said, G.D. they keep me awake. Granny sure laughed. Nothing would wake those two up.

Well, I don't know anything new. Keep sending a letter to Dad. We both read them. Pop sure is a humdinger. He never wanted any harm to come to you in any way. He thought he would be so proud and so happy if you turned out a good boy, as Uncle Paul was always finding fault. Grandpop had great faith in you. What an ordeal to get you raised. Now we still have to worry. But, down in own my heart I think it is a wonderful experience except for the danger. I put you in God's care. You and I stood together and took Jesus into our life and so I know that God's Will be done is my faith and hope. You know, baby. How many girls would come to a farm and work as I did? I did it because I knew what a good man was. It kept my faith and hopes high. I look to the day when we are a happy family together in some little home where Pop has his black raspberry bushes and our chickens. Dad and I haven't too many years left according to time. Whatever is our lot, I thank God because all you need do is look around. I have read books of all places in the world, things I never talk about at home. I can keep up with the best. All I ask for is comfort for all, health for Dad, and your return. It's a big order, but God will hear me and do what is best. I will write when I come home tonight.

All our love,

Mom and All

February 20, 1945

Dearest Son,

It's 10 after 9 and Pop is on the warpath with Roger trying to get a light strung out from the kitchen to see to put the chains on the car. We left here at 7 o'clock to go to Frankford to see Walter. We parked on Harrison Street. I took off my galoshes and left them in the car. We walked to Frankford ,but there were no radio stores open. And lo, it started to snow and we couldn't find the undertakers as there are 4 on the same block. After Pop punched doorbells all along, we finally found it.

Now the truckshed had something wrong with the light. They have blown out three bulbs from the kitchen connection and still no light to fix the chains. They have all the back kitchen doors open. I can feel the cold coming in the kitchen window. The snow is deep and snowing faster. Dad said he heard on a radio where a big storm was coming in from the west. I guess we will be snowed in by morning.

Dearest, I wonder where you will read this and maybe the bluebirds will be singing by the time you get it. Carl and Tommy were here when we came back. They had to get home. I said, 'Boys you better start.' It's 9:10 now and so I guess you are eating your supper for tonight. I talked to you this morning. Dot is not home as of yet. Pop is mean as all. So, tonight I will go to bed. I told Dad not to worry over getting home tomorrow night, that is, if he gets out tomorrow morning.

I have plenty of potatoes, onions, sauerkraut, fish and meat, and flour to bake biscuits. "Mom, are these biscuits hot?" So long for now, my dearest. I hope you are okay. I hope to hear of your new destination soon. Nighty night.

Love,

Mommy

February 21, 1945

Hello Son,

As usual, here I am for our little chat today. It's still early in the day for me. It's 10 o'clock. I suppose you are just about getting over breakfast on today's date. But when you are reading this? Where? Today, we look out on a picture of winter wonderland as I wrote you last night and told you we were out in the snowstorm. It didn't last all night, but the trees are all heavy and on top of what we had on Saturday, it sure has me snowed in.
I sure know Dad had a hard job driving to work as it was so hazy. You couldn't see a light in the town. You know all the shops in Frankford have no lights in the windows. You can't tell if they are open or not until you get up to the door. It sure looks odd. Last night was the first time I was out in a snowstorm in 20 years. Pop had to take his hankie and try to knock the snow from our overcoats before we went into the undertaker's parlors.

Walter looked fine and young, like our own Grandpop improved. He was in a fine brown suit, much like your gray, and a brown shirt and tie. The flowers were lovely that we and Aunt Lilly put together. Aunt Lillie and Esther and

Anne Rigger came together. Fred didn't come. Nor did I see Bill Bissinger. We were home here by 9. They probably came later. Walter had a stroke and died in Frankford Hospital. He was there from Tuesday to Saturday, so he was a tough old guy. He came here for years for Grandma Price's rice pudding. She showed me how to make it. She made it like they did at Grundy's, and I never tasted better anywhere, or half as good.

I have the home fires burning and tomorrow is Joe's birthday. I will make him a cake. I will wait to finish this letter after I see if I have any mail from you. Roger had a card and I got the two letters with the masthead. Roger and Carl are great friends. I will write later. Enough for now.

It's after 2 o'clock and no mail from you since the specials I told you about on the phone. The snow is melting fast, but it's still cold. It's only 13 degrees. I got most of last week's ironing done. I still have 2 shirts for Rog and 2 heavies for Dad, so I will finish up before getting supper. Roger is going to Baldwin's, so he will mail this. All my love and hopes to hear from you.

Mom

Thursday, February 22, 1945

Dearest Son,

Well, the home fires are burning. Roger is still in bed. All is quiet, and here I am for our little chat. I know you are thinking of us special today. I have an angel cake in the oven. It takes 60 minutes to bake and uses no shortening, which of course, is rationed, but it does take 7 eggs. But dear old Joe is worth it. Pop took the radio to work yesterday. He stopped at Bond, but they wouldn't fix it for 10 days or more. Burns Washing Machine Co. told us of a place in the 5000 block, so Pop went there and it is to be done tonight. I sure will be glad as I do like to listen to Sardi's at 11 and the news that follows. But here I am. It has rained since 4 PM yesterday and still we have that misty fine foggy rain. Everything is ice and slush. Pop is going to get the radio, then stop and get ice cream for the cake. That will be Joe's party.

News! Pop will pay the last on the car, but still owes for the repair bill. It sure has been a headache. Roger is going to pay $31.81 telephone when he gets up.

I woke up at one o'clock and I could see you so plain. I felt in my heart you were leaving our country. I said, it's 10 o'clock on the west coast. This is the first night, since you were born, that I didn't have any idea where you were. Since you went away, I would say that Edwin was at a base and was pretty nearly comfortable. But last night, I put in an awful night talking to you. I want to stop that. I guess I wouldn't love you if I didn't wonder where you were. I do think that you are going through the biggest experience that you ever faced. Dear, please "save". Put so much away just as if you didn't have it. If you get time off, you can't come home if you don't. Edwin, it takes $100 to come home quick and comfortable, and $1.00 for each meal. That would be $12.00 without any extras. It would cost the same to go back.

Please, I do expect to see you by the Fourth of July. But, whatever comes or goes, be content. Then I will be happy. As of yet, I haven't received the record, or Dad the money you sent him. Dot is home since Tuesday night in the snow. I haven't seen her or heard from her. Roger is up now and I must get his breakfast. Lots of love.
Mother and all

February 22, 1945

Dearest Son,

I wrote you a letter this morning telling you it was Joe's birthday and that I had an angel cake in the oven. The cake is out and looks swell. You know the pure white kind with the hole in the center. I am going to ice that chocolate. Now I have a two layer chocolate devil food cake in the oven. I will ice that white. I made one for you when you were eighteen and I made one for Joe. I made one for Dad's birthday and gave nearly all of it to Dot.

Nutsie came over after I wrote your letter. He and Roger and I had fried scrapple. I was paying their way to Frankford to pay the phone. They were half way to the railroad tracks when I phoned the operator to ask her if it was open. Today is a holiday. She said no. So I ran to the front and called them. So they took a kettle of soup over to Joe and they are gone two hours now. They gave me back your letter. I guess Pop will mail out two tomorrow.

Well boy, it sure is pouring rain. As soon as the cake is out of the oven, I will go finish up upstairs. If I go up now, I may forget the cake. So here I sit talking to you. It's 1 PM. I have a good piece of pork on cooking and soon I will put in the sauerkraut. Pop will be late on account of paying off the car, etc. We may eat before he gets home. You never saw how foggy it is. You can hardly see the toilet. It sure is pouring rain. If only it doesn't freeze. We are to get a ton of coal Saturday. Pop gave me $13.00 for it. Bill B. said he would fix the car fender next Monday. Pop called him last night. I will finish this after Roger comes home to see if I got any mail from you. Okay.

Well son, it's now 4:30. Supper is all ready, except the potatoes. The pork is cooked and the table is set. The house is hot and the cakes are iced. Five white candles were all I had. Joe is 55. Nutsie and Roger are in the cellar. I dried them and gave them something to eat. Now Nutsie must go in the rain to serve papers. A river is running down our lane. No mail today; holiday. So long.

Wartime Letters Written from Mother to Son

Mother & all

February 22, 1945

Dearest Son,

I guess you will say, what ails Mom, writing me three letters in one day? From now on, date all your letters. I sure was surprised to talk to you tonight. I was pleased that Dad got in just in time to talk to you. As I told you, it has rained here all day and is foggy. What a long drawn out day. I sure was happy to hear from you. I guess you are in some warm spot reading this. I guess you are so happy to get this mail. Hello my darling baby. Smooth your dear face. Mommy is standing right aside of you and nagging you. Mom is saying, do your best and then she will be happy as all her life has been a long, hard one. Now Mommy is saying she has a big, fine son and he is seeing some of the world. So my dear, what else can I write? I haven't been out anywhere.

We had the cakes and Nutsie was here with us. Pop as usual was nag, nag to Roger about washing his hands. So I said, 'If you keep on, I will get away from the table.' It's the same old story. Nutsie said he got a licking last night and his mother hit him with a big stick. I used the hair brush once. Not often did I lick my boys. That's why they don't mind.

When you come home, I guess you will at last be a "man". For now, I only think of you as "my oldest boy". And so, time waits for no man. It passes quickly or slowly according to our surroundings. I have never had enough time. The clock could have 24 more hours on it and still I wouldn't have all I wanted done. But now I am a "lady". I got up at 9 AM as Roger has no school until next Monday. Nutsie and he are out again tonight for more pigeons. They have a tough time catching them. I don't know what they want them for, maybe just a hobby.

Well dearest son, it's great to meet, hard to part, you are the darling of my heart. If you love me as I love you, nothing can ever make us part. I trust in God. All my faith, hope, and courage are yours. As I stand and chat with you, squeeze my hand and say, hello Mom. Until I press you to my heart, all my love.

Mom, Dad, Rog

February 23, 1945

Dearest Son,

In these parts, it's the first time the snow has been cleared away since you were home. It rained and rained and you should see the mud. I guess it will be June before I can wallow through it. Still, it has its advantage because it has warmed up. Now dear, I guess you know this day has meant something in our lives. I just couldn't sleep thinking of you. I said to Dad, "Dad, we got something to think about today." He said, "Yes. Tell the boy we are with him." So I walked the gang plank beside you. I kept saying to you, March On to Victory.

I don't know of any news. I only know the sad kind of different boys. Simons, who married one of the Hamilton girls is missing. One of the Hattles won't come home and so it goes each day. It makes my hair a little whiter, but God gives me strength and hope. Sometimes I get mad at myself. I don't know anything to write especially when I write you three letters in one day as I did yesterday. I also had the pleasure of talking to you last evening. I sure was glad Dad got in to say hello to you. I didn't expect him so early. I said to Joe, "Is that a car?" Brownie barked. Joe said no. I said hurry and look. Sure enough it was Dad.

Well the last payment was made on the car. He said the repair bill is $80. I nearly passed out. I sure am in a rut over that car. Roger and I have no shoes. No underwear. It's a good thing I guess that I don't get out.

Now as for Granny's birthday, I told you that we had a few words. She was going to be with Al and I was sore as hell. When I found out she was up at Bristol, I left them alone. The bottle and they could have a better time without me. Then the weather was so bad and Dad will not go any place at night. So I am at the mercy of my family. You wouldn't take me and neither will Dad. So the damn car is of no use to me. I'll be glad when we don't have it.

I will write more later after mail time. I still have all my work to do. Roger and Nutsie are going off to Frankford to pay $35.81 for the telephone. I will write more later. I hope you get off with good luck. Just think you are on a vacation. Until I write tonight.

Lots of love,

Mom & All

February 23, 1945

Hello Son,

It's now supper time. I have leftovers warmed up, hot biscuits made and the ice box cleaned out. Friday and tomorrow, we will have new food. This is the best day we had for many a day. We had sunshine a good part of the day. That's the first for week. There's a good wind going. I put the wash out on the front porch. It's all dry but for two pieces. I washed out a lace tablecloth and

Roger's gym shorts. They will soon dry.

Joe is home and getting up the coal. Aunt Dink called up. She heard from Bill and Uncle John. I guess Granny is up with Aunt Minnie since Tuesday night. I guess she helped entertain her ladies last Wednesday. I got your package of letters today and Pop's letter with the dollar. I got a friendly letter from Mrs. Getz. She said the Boyds were up there during the summer.

Well son, that's all for now. Hope to hear from you real soon. Lots and lots of love.

Mom & All X X X X

Saturday Afternoon 4 PM, February 24, 1945

Dearest Son,

I can't see the car coming in doing 50 MPH this afternoon. Along about this time on Saturdays you usually came in. "Mom, make me somptin' to eat." I sure wonder where my boy is. I wonder if you're sick. By the time you are reading this, I suppose you will sure enough be a salt sailor. Did you cross the Equator? You know they say you are not a sailor until you do.

Joe has been home and left for Frankford. Roger, Carl, and Thomas had their lunch packed and their canteens filled with hot coffee. They left about 11 o'clock to go fishing. I guess they must have had some luck, as I have not seen anything of them since. I am beginning to look for them, too. It looks like I have no little boys any more.

It is windy and cold here today. The mud is drying up and so are a few of the heaps of snow lying about. The boys now have about 30 pigeons and they are kept busy with them and the papers. The four day holiday has not been much good, as the snow and rain has had their feet wet inside and out and their clothes wet and muddy.

The coal came this morning. It was $13.29 and the phone bill is paid. I sent in three bonds, which finishes up all we had. There're seven calls from California. The tax is so high on those calls. I expect the bill to be about $70. That is a hard knock on the finances. Just you wait and see if you pay my phone bill. But, I think you are worth that much to me.

I got your income from Supreme. It was $219. They withheld $22.70 tax. That makes your income still under $1000 for 1943 and 1944, but I will file that also. They were kind of long and drawn out sending it, as it must be in before March 15th. That will keep you straightened out and no worry about it when you come home.

I got up about 8 o'clock as I expected the coal to be delivered and it came at 10:30. I ironed up all the clothes and I just got through. I will write a little more when Roger comes back. I won't know if I got any mail from you or not so, until later.

Well dear, I wrote you earlier. Now it is 5:30, Saturday, February 24th. Roger and the Ems boys just came back. I got 4 letters from you and one from Uncle John. I had a letter written one week ago from you and one from the 22nd. I guess that was the last one you sent out. Just think. I got it in two days, whereas the others took a week via airmail. Edwin, as of yet, I have not gotten the record or watch. I did get the round bundle of letters

Uncle John says he doesn't think he will see you as he is too far in at present. He said you will have it good compared to those who went out first with no food, no nothing. He said we now have the finest fleet in the world and plenty of supplies coming in. Thank God. The boys in Blue are coming through and now you are one of them. I know you will be an honor to Dad and me. You are now. I can't say anymore than I have told you so many times before. Smile and do your share. We love you with all our hearts.

Edwin, the fishermen came home smiling. Each had a great big fish on the end of their lines. I was sitting at the window. They came so happy. I said you never caught them. They are too big. Then they told me some kid gave them to them. They were ocean fish. Kids sure do funny things. While I was gab, gab, I left the door go shut. Locked out again. I said, well I guess the third time I will be locked out. Roger got in the front window. Here I am alone again. They went off to serve the papers. The sun has been out all day, but windy and cold.

I got all your kisses and all your love. I think you are a fine boy to write like you do. I know the love is in your heart, because Dad and I put love into your heart. You won't find none better than old Dad. Dot is okay and we know who she is. You were a wise boy. You will have everything to be thankful for once you come home. No bread lines. Roosevelt says to buy bonds. They are our guarantee against bread lines. Dearest, we'll pull through somehow. Lots of love to you, dear, while you are reading. Here's a hug and kiss. Love from all. Your own,

Mommy

February 25, 1945 Sunday at home. For a change, no snow, no wild winds; but oh! the mud. As usual, a quiet day so far.

Dearest Son,

Here I am as usual for our little chat. It's now 12:30 and I did not get to church, oh! Several good excuses, but I have listened to the radio services. I have wondered if you took the opportunity. I know that as I am writing, you are somewhere you have never been before.

The pork and lima beans are in the oven. Joe is polishing your car. He sure knows how to do it. He hauled away all the trash. Dad opened up the drain down in the field. This past rain sure played havoc with the lane. It made it quite bad at the turn in. I guess every rock along the drive has been carried down there. I was thinking. I wonder how many loads have been put in that drive in 58 years since the Prices have lived here.

I sit in that big chair up in your room and I look out the window. I can only see as far as the mail box. I never see a soul I know. I did think I saw Uncle Paul yesterday, but he usually goes the other way to the bus. Roger and Carl have 31 pigeons now and I believe Carl is coming down around three this afternoon. I don't know what's on the program, but Tommy and Carl and Roger were still with the pigeons at 11 o'clock last night. They said Mrs. Ems fried the fish. I have not seen or heard from Dot. The boys said she was back at work at McClains'.

Aunt Dink called me up Friday. She said she was going with Sis and George to Delaware over the weekend. George hasn't seen Johnny's baby yet. She said Al sent Granny 65 white carnations for her birthday and that Granny was up at Aunt Minnie's. Other than that, I don't know any news. Joe will mail out two letters to you when he goes off to Frankford.
I will write tonight again for Dad to mail in the morning. All is well. Hope you are too. Cheerio.

Love,

The Home Fires

Mother & All

Sunday Nite, February 25, 1945

Dearest Son,

Like you say, I am stuck for news. It's the same old thing. It was a nice sunny day and not so cold. It brought out the first visitor of the spring. Harry Thompson called on us. I sure was amazed and surprised at his intelligence. It has been years since I heard him talk. I sure was surprised. He used such good language. He asked me for your address, so I gave it to him. I guess he will be writing to you soon.

Pop wants to write a few lines:

Well Son, Old Pal. How are you making out by this time? It sure was good to talk to you the other night. I thought when I was coming home that you may call up, but I had three stops to make. I had to stop at Heinel's and at the radio shop to get the radio. One tube went on the bum. That cost me $4.30. Then I had to stop and get gas, so you see, I did not lose any time getting home. I am so glad I did not miss you. Well pal, take good care of yourself. Don't be scared. I know that it is easy for me to say that sitting up here, but we must hope for the best. Try and study all you can and do what you are told. I think you will come out all right. God will be with you. I will write you some more when we get your new address, so I will say so long for now. Mother will take over. God will be with you.

S.W.A.K.

Well Baby. I am through the dishes; for you know on Sunday night my maid is out. Dad took Harry home and then he brought us some ice cream and I gave them a light supper. I am now going to listen to Mediation Court and then go to bed before Gabriel Heater shoots his gab. I have a headache all day and have been busy cooking.

Tomorrow, I will be alone again and wishing it was Sunday and calling my son to get up for breakfast. I wrote you this morning. Joe mailed them out and so I will say nighty night and Cheerio.

Lots of love from,

Mother, Brownie & All

February 26, 1945

Dearest Son,

After I wrote you last night telling you what a nice spring-like day we had, Dad put the sash on the hot bed, getting the ground to warm up for the new season's plants. Today it sure is a traditional blue Monday. It has been coming down steadily since early morning. The fields and drives sure are mud flats. You know where they had the carrots trenched behind the lilacs? They came up there over the drive with the tractor and trucks. You need hip boots to get through the mud there. I don't see how I can walk out to the trolley. Down by Jimmy's chicken house, it's a river. Soon, I guess I will be complaining about the heat. It's a warm rain. At least I have all the fires damped off and I am sweating.

I wrote to Mrs. Bell. I had a letter from Aunt Katie, so I must answer that. Today Elmer Irons Jr. is seven years old. I haven't heard from Granny. I was wondering if she was still at Delheim's. I may call up after awhile. I don't know any news, so I will wait until after mail time to finish this.

The Home Fires

Yesterday, being such a nice day, I thought Dot might walk over. The boys didn't come over either and they had a date with Roger at three o'clock.

All we do is talk about you. We sure will be glad when we get your news. I had one of my usual spells today. I can hardly work. I can't carry up the coal so I am taking it easy. I ironed all the clothes up last Saturday and I don't have any starched shirts, only one or two for Dad. So I will go over them.

Monday afternoon: well son, it's still pouring rain. I got three letters from you including what you said was your last one as you got out and two on telephone stationary. Yes, I have all your letters. Three were written on February 22nd. I hope to hear from you soon again. I got your post card of the Golden Gates. Love from all.

Love,

Mother & All

Tuesday, February 27, 1945

Dearest Son,

How I looked for your record. I had the needle in the player and all ready to go. Well, today it came and though I am a good mother, I can curse when I want to. I called that jerk bastard mail man all I can think of. He took it and cracked it to get it in the mail box. But, it was sort of flexible and I managed to play it. My dear boy, you need never worry about not being able to talk. Professionals can't do any better. I sure think it is swell. I can hardly wait until Dad hears it.

It is 5 after 2 here and I have ham and cabbage for supper tonight. The wind is blowing a 40 mile shake, but the sun is shining bright. I have all the drafts closed on the fires, but they are going right out the pipe. It rained all day yesterday. Through the night, the wind came up. At 3 AM I woke up. I could smell the coffee cooking. I said to Dad, boy the fire must be going right out the flue. And so it was this morning. It rained from 5 AM to 10:30 when it started to hail. Then it stopped and everything is mud. I can see signs of spring. The green wheat is starting to come up. The grass looks a little greener, what I can see of it.

Here's a news item. Fred started on his tantrum all week. So Aunt Lilly sent Esther out to have the cops near, and she put him out last night. She said that's the end for him. The cops came back about 1 ½ hours later and said they had taken him away. Aunt Lilly said she couldn't tell me over the phone, but he has bad habits. I guess she will go back to work. I warned her. She is never willing to heed my advice. I never tell her wrong, nor you either.

Any boy who can be as kind and thoughtful as you should have a high place in this life. It sure is funny that as much as Aunt Lilly wants love, that she can't find it. She is too dumb to know she will never find any as good or true as Bill Bissinger. Edwin, you can travel the world. You will never find perfection. Even children are not perfection in the sight of their own mothers. Love is not blind. But love overlooks. Unless you can overlook faults in others, we cannot love or be happy.

Yes. Grandpop put your pigeons in the pot. I am making some pillowcases out of torn sheets, and mended Dad's overalls, so I must run along. I haven't felt any too good the last few days, but when the sun shines, I will be okay. Roger is going out to the post office to get a money order for the license for your car so that will be settled.

One of the white pigeons is out. Roger is heartbroken for fear it won't come back. As of yet, they haven't things fixed up right on account of the bad weather.

Well dearest, Joe will laugh when he hears you say keep up with the dishes. Joe is better than three maids. I wouldn't give him up for 6 women in the house to do my work. Neither would Mrs. Baldwin. So he can do the dishes and I am thankful. (A buck scrubs the kitchen, Mom!) When you come home, you might have to scrub your own kitchen eh?

Dearest, write to Pop. He sure talks about you and misses you. So long Pal, honey, sweetie.

Love,

Mom & All

Tuesday afternoon, February 27, 1945

Dearest Son,

If you don't get any mail except in a bunch, you sure will have a lot of letters to read from me. Here I am for my usual evening chat. I took Dad and Joe in to hear your record as soon as they finished supper. You sure have to listen close to hear what you say. Joe got a kick out of what you said about letting the girls alone. Well, Gabriel Heater is on with the news. I guess the whole world has its ears tuned for Berlin's fall. It sure is some war. We all hope it gets over soon.

Well darling, we have another first class funeral in Bustleton; Charlie Heyer died this week. So I read in tonight's paper. It said he died after a long illness. Also, in the rain this morning, the motorman who runs the early morning car that Dad used to get, Charles Larkin, killed a man with the trolley near McAdams'. Pop saw the tie up on his way to work. He stopped and saw it was his motorman. Pop asked him if there was anything he could do. He said no. They had sent for the red car, so he was dead. He ran in front of it at the stop and the motorman failed to see him in the rain and kept on going. Well, I don't know anything pleasant.

Roger had a busy time as several of the pigeons got out. I guess you know he was sure in a state. I can't write on account of the news, so I will say nighty night for now. As I wrote you today, Roger mailed it when he got the money order for your car license, so that's sent off. I hope to hear from you. As of yet, I have not received your watch. I'll let you know. Lots of love from all.

X X X X Mom

Wednesday, February 28, 1945

Hello Son,

I guess you know I am not sorry to write the last day of February, although it was the very best winter I had on the farm. I still had the worst worry. So it goes to prove that we can never be completely happy. Of course, it was a real cold winter, but I had the doors shut most of the day. There was no one to keep biffing them open to let in all the winter. I secured all the windows and the front door with weather tape. We burned five tons less coal than last year and the winter last year did not give us nearly so much bad weather.

The home fires are fixed. Roger has gone off to school and it's very, very cold here today. But the sun is shining. Before noon I guess it will be mud again.

The record is only paper. Dad wants me to write to them to see if I can get another copy. I played it two or three times this morning. I caught on to something new, tell mother to smooth my face. Yes dear. I wake up, as the moon is in the full this week. I woke up. I got up and looked at the clock. I thought, oh boy, there's Pop and it's ten after seven. But it was 25 of 2. I said, 'Old moon, you are supposed to be more beautiful in the Pacific sky and so low, but it's the same moon my boy will see. To us you are more beautiful when you come up over the fire house and we look at you on the fields of home.' Wherever my boy is, Dad and Mom's love is as true as that full moon. It is always there. Maybe you can't see it, but you know it's there. I did tell you that I love all of God's wonders. The moon, the stars, the rain, the snow, it's all in the heart. They can be cruel and yet beautiful. So it is with love. It's cruel and kind. Don't think it's possible? Like you say on the record, Rog, go to school, be a good boy. I wonder if I ever told you that. You can go to school every day. But if you fool around and don't pay attention, you might as well be home. As you go through life, you learn. You see now where the boys are that took education seriously. They are the bosses. So it is all through life.

I had a little discussion with Mrs. Spence. She asked me how much I get from the government. I said nothing. She said why not? I said you can't get an allotment from the government if you are in good circumstances, where your husband has a war job. So yesterday she called me up. She said she wanted to tell me how mistaken I was. That sailor fellow Pat who goes to see Florence, his mother gets $78 a month and his father works for a war plant and his two sisters. Then she went on to say that Marie Bogan's brother is in the Navy and Mrs. Bogan gets $20 a month. So, of course, by that time, I knew the answer. I said, yes they send that out of their pay. That's not a government allotment. Well, she said, what else is it? The government pays them. So she said, Oh. You mean to tell me that you are going to let Edwin blow away all that money every month? I said after he pays out insurance and his bond. Oh yes she said. So do those boys. I said maybe they make more money than Edwin. She said Pat was in 6 years. So, I said, all boys are not alike. But I get mad at other people always trying to run my business. But for your good, for my good, and for advice, I know it's nice to have plenty of spending money. For all in our good Lord's name, please, please, listen to my good advice. Please. You will get extra money now that you are away. Make out an allotment of 10 to 20 dollars a month to me. I can save some for you, and buy a few things I need so badly for the house and myself. Roger is without clothes. You know it was all I could do to keep up the car. I still have that big repair bill to clear off. I know, and so do you, that whatever port you are in you will spend every cent you get your hands on. If you don't want to make out an allotment, send home a bond a month. Then you will have something to get married on. When the time comes for a $125 baby bill where will you get it? Because what you earn will only pay the rent and buy the food. So make 1945 your new start for the future. I shall not write any more about it ever. But you see what happened at Christmas. It will be the same all your life if you don't listen to me. As of yet, I have had no Bonds from you and no insurance policy, but two papers saying you signed for it and your signature. So please dear, help shoulder the burden. You are young.

Lots of love,

Mother

Wednesday Noon, February 28, 1945

Dearest Son,

Well, here it is dinner time. I wrote you a letter this morning. I listened to Sardi's, part of it, as Dot called me up and so I talked with her for nearly a

The Home Fires

half hour. Of course, we talked about you. She said she had a letter from you yesterday from California and she wanted to know if I had the record yet. I invited her over. I said I looked for her last Sunday as it was such a nice sunny day. She said she was in bed most of the day. So, I have my coffee and here I am for my little chat.

Roger says I shouldn't waste so many stamps, I should leave the letter open all day. I know if it is too heavy, it will come back and I can't write at night with all that bull on the radio. I like complete quiet and you know it. I would rather write when everyone is away. Then I can be alone with my thoughts. I write to you just what I think. Dot said, "I'll call you up this afternoon." Someone must have come in. So, I don't know any news. I am going to call up Aunt Lilly to see what's new. Dad and Joe are okay. Roger and I have a little cold, but otherwise, everything at home is just the same. I washed out the flannels and put them on the porch line, but the sun went back in. It's dark and gray and cold. Looks like more snow.

Dot said the kids down there were in swimming and all she wore was waist and skirt. She said before she got home she was shivering. What a difference in the weather. She said she was homesick after two days without a drop of milk, canned or fresh, and coffee, black as mud, cooked all day. I guess there is never any place like home, no matter how humble. After what you see on your travels, you will know you have a palace to come back to. I try not to think too much. Just keep up and save. I know I have faith in you. I always did have and so I hope and pray all the time for all.

I called Aunt Lilly. She said nothing new. She sends you love and a kiss. It's hailing, so I must get the things off the line, fix the fires and will add more lately. All my love.

Mom

Well son, it's night and we are having our coffee. Soon we will go to bed. I don't know any more news. Dad and I would like to know how much money you are getting now that you have left. Uncle John said he got your letter. Please don't worry over us. We are all okay. We don't want you to be without money. Dear, I am going to bed now. It has rained and sleeted all day and it's cold. So I smooth your face and kiss you good night. I hope you are feeling better by now. All our love,

Your Mother and all, kisses love.

**** END OF FEBRUARY ****

Chapter Six

March 1945

Edwin Charles Price, USN.

Wartime Letters Written from Mother to Son

Thursday, March 1, 1945

Hello Son,

Well March came in like a lamb; woe is me for the end. You know the story I told you about looking up in the sky for lions. The sun is shining very nice all day. It's now 5 o'clock. I didn't get to you this morning for my little chat, but here I am.

Your watch came about noon with the Main Sheet and the Town paper. I have my glasses on and I got so interested, I forgot to listen to Roosevelt. I was all tuned to listen in and that quick, I forgot it. Oh, I guess I will read what he said in the paper tonight.

Anyway, yesterday we had a sleet storm. It left everything icy this morning, but now it has warmed up quite a bit. I have me a stew on cooking. I am trying very hard to make it like you and Dad used to get it when you were our boy on the huckster route with Dad taking you in the lunch car. I have garlic in it and I sure do hate to smell it, but Dad doesn't like the meat pie, and my baby is not here to help me eat the crust. So, I will try my best to please Dad. He always says nobody could make it like that fellow. I will let you know how I make out with it tomorrow. I have been busy all day ironing and cleaning, so I have everything under control now.

I said I better tell my baby what I know, which is not much, only that it was a much better day to bury Charlie Heyer, as it sure did rain and was an icy one yesterday.

As you know, we are talking about you and wondering when we will get your new address and a letter. It's a week tonight that I talked to you, but somehow, it sure seems longer than that. But then, I miss you most along about this time, expecting to hear you coming in at 50 miles per hour. Oh well, I am not alone; and a new era will dawn where life will be roses and dew will be like diamonds and all will be well. Little Elmer Irons sings 'I got sunshine in my heart,' so you sing it too. No room for the devil. I got sunshine in my heart. That is the spirit you and I must have. Then the gray clouds will roll away the cobwebs.

Say, I see by the town paper that Harry Jones' wife has a baby daughter. I don't know if she brought it here after she came. I must catch up on that news. I don't hear anything since you left. Well dearest, all is well. May God keep you safe and well is the wish of all.

My love,

Dad, Rog, Joe, Mom

Friday, March 2, 1945

Dearest Son,

As yesterday was the first day of the new month, I decided to number my letters in a way that you can keep track of what I chat about and also if any are missing. I hope by this time you have gotten over being seasick, as that seems to be the main thing Dad talks about. It is now nearing 5 o'clock and I am tired. It's Friday here and the wash came home, so I hurried and put it out. It's nearly all dry. Along with my other work, I am all in, so I have the table set. The remainder of the stew from last night is warming up along with some leftover cabbage. Dad got $1.00 worth of steak cod. I have that breaded, but I won't fry it until the last minute. Joe is not home yet. Here comes the baker, so I will add more later.

Here I am again. The day has been a pretty good one with sunshine most of the day and lots warmer, 44 degrees in Philadelphia. I have the fish frying now. I was talking to the baker, but of course, I never ask any questions, so I don't know any news.

I cleaned out the bottom part of the corner cupboard in the radio room. It sure was about time. I would sure have been ashamed to let anyone see my neglect. You would have laughed to see me throwing away all the old corset stays, pure whalebone ones and sets of them that were still in the paper, not to say anything about the moth that was an old pillow top. Well it's done, and what a help. Before summer comes, the third story is due for a general overhauling. Out it goes. What a lot of stuff to hoard. It's no earthly good. The first day I feel good, I am going up there before it gets too warm.

Son, I don't know a thing to write about except to say hello and that I love you. I will be happier when I get your new address or hear from you again. I told you in yesterday's letter that I got your watch in good condition. You should have kept it. Dad was all for my sending it to you. I think it was nice you sent it back. I will say cheerio. All my love, Edwin. This letter may be delayed as all I have is a 3 cent stamp. Roger will go to the post office Saturday.

Love,

Mom & All

Saturday, March 3, 1945

Dearest Son,

Letter No. 2 only has a 3 cent stamp on it, so if it is not with your mail call,

The Home Fires

you will know that you may get it later. Dad mailed it out on his way to work this morning. Here I am, sticking an extra one in because Roger is going off to the post office. Today it is pouring rain again. Your old Grandpop told me a lot about the weather. I sure know he never missed it much. He said the full moon always governs the month's weather. If it's real cold, expect cold, hot, the same, rain, the same. So the full moon had a cloudy circle around it. As I looked at it I said, well full moon, you are in the rainy quarter. Spring rains for March instead of high wind. We have had three big rains since. It started last night about eleven and it's still running.

Roger is invited to a party over on Banes Street or Cole Street at Mrs. Bender's niece, Nancy Maxwell's. It was her mother who told me you made her hair stand up the way you sped through Bustleton. Well, you know what I told her. They are the boys that are now making the enemy flee or else.

We, of course, are talking about you at every turn. Dad said you were on his mind so much yesterday. We are wondering about all the where's, why's, and how's about you. Did you get sick? Are you on the job? Is it hot? You know. How long will it be before we hear from you? I said three weeks; so I will let you know when I do. The papers and your watch are the last we heard so far to date.

Well son, I pressed Roger's blue corduroy and I must iron a few shirts. It's Saturday and all the usual things to do. So, I will say so long for now. I am writing every day. You can keep account of the letters by the date, as I started to number them the first day of March. That way you can read them in order if you get a pile all at once.

I send all our love to you. I do wish my hairdresser would come around and fix my hair. I haven't seen her since you were home, but I did talk to her on the phone as I told you. Well, our little chat was a happy one.

Love,

Mom

Sunday March 4, 1945

Dearest Son Edwin,

Here it is Sunday noon. Joe is scrubbing the kitchen for me. I have a great big shad in the oven. Last night, something happened to Brownie. His right hind leg started to shake. He cries and can hardly get up. At 5:30 he came crying to the bed to Dad just like a human. His whole body was trembling. So Dad rubbed it for about an hour. When Dad pressed on a bone down near his tail, he cried out loud. So Roger and Dad have now gone to a dog and cat hospital over on Frankford Avenue in Mayfair. We called up first. We couldn't get an answer from the one here at Oxford Circle. I will let you know in my letter tonight how he is.

Joe brought me two lovely, fragrant gardenias last night. I have them on the dining room table where I am now chatting to you. I did not get to church. It's raw out and dreary.

Dad saw Dot last night at Deiner's. She talked to him and said she would be over today sometime. Perhaps I can write you some news of interest.

Baldwin's got a new Ford. Carl and Tommy were here last night. Rog and all went for pigeons. They got one each. They were here while Mrs. Ems and Dot were in Frankford. The boys said they went down to Hadley's to get their repaired watches. Dad said Hadley moved to his old home on Griscom Street and his shop is in the front room. The place where he was was sold. I guess Dot will get a surprise when she gets there and finds him moved. Dad said a sign was on the door.

I didn't get up until 10 o'clock. My back has been bad all week. I didn't feel like sitting still too long.

The sun is trying to come out and the wind was up last night. I guess you can tell me lots about the weather when I see you. Just do like I told you, dearest, and keep the sunshine in your heart, no matter what the odds. Don't let anyone or anybody get you down. Think Mother first put sunshine in my heart. That is our motto, what say? Will write later.

Love,

Mom

Hello Baby,

Here I am again. It's 7:30 and Kate Smith is on with Private Hargrove of "See Here Fame". The day turned out nice and sunny. We had a fine dinner and a warmed over supper. Dot spent the afternoon with me. I played the record a couple of times and we talked about you and her trip to West Virginia and just common place talk. There's nothing new except that her mother got a new coat at Lane Bryant.

I am going in now and listen to the court cases and then to bed. Brownie is much better tonight. Dad gave him a hot Epsom Salt bath. He rubbed him with camphorated oil and gave him two kinds of pills. I guess he has some of Dad's rheumatism. But he is much better. I am glad. You know how Dad moans when he gets it. The poor little baby sure cried. He is a baby. Lizzie Bit is out looking for a beau. Pop said, "Go ahead catting you, Bit." She came in this morning, kind of run out and slept all day and now is out again.

Well dearest, your love looked as sweet as ever, pretty blonde hair and pink rose dress that I like. I love fair girls. I will close for now.

All our love,

Mom & All

Monday morning, March 5, 1945

Hello Son,

Same old thing here at home. The sun is trying to shine and I had the hall window open upstairs. I could hear lots of birds singing over in those pine trees across the railroad tracks for the first time since Christmas. I see the men are taking out those parsnips here, along the left side of the drive and they still have the colored woman with them. She sure is a good worker and tough. I wish my health was like that; but I guess everyone is suited for their task. Outside of that, I don't know a thing.

Brownie is better and he sure is a baby. He is here beside me. Roger and Dad gave him his pills. He takes them just fine. He sure is a sissy. To tell you a funny one, believe it or not, I told you how Dad rubbed the dog's back and he gave him hot Epsom Salt packs just like we do for Dad. Poor Dad had the rheumatism so bad in his hand and wrist that he couldn't sleep all night. I said maybe the Epsom Salt brought it out in Dad's hand. (We sure had to laugh.)

Edwin, I wrote, "We sure", then I didn't know what I was going to say. I heard a noise. It sounded like the third story door opened. Brownie growled. Then he barked and ran in the parlor. It scared me darn much; I forgot what I was going to write. I sure hate to be here alone. My nerves are so bad all week. I can't stand any noise. I had a lovely Sunday. We had such a nice dinner. Dot spent the afternoon with me while Dad held down the couch.

It's now 10:30, so I am going to listen to Sardi's. I have the house pretty well cleaned up. Joe scrubbed the kitchen yesterday. I fixed all the fires. I will add a little more after the mail comes, although I don't expect to hear from you for three weeks after you left. The time will seem so long. I guess God knows we are together in thought and spirit. The miles don't separate our hearts or love, does it? I smooth your face baby. I'll never forget that record. Well baby, it's night now. Gabriel Heater is on with the news. There's nothing new. I am thinking of you and hoping to hear from you. Lots of love from all and lots of kisses.

Mother & all

Tuesday, March 6, 1945

Dearest Son,

Roger is leaving for school and the rain is falling in bucketfuls. Dad said he put in his tulip bed at work yesterday and before he was through, it was hailing and raining, but he got it done. That saves him extra work.

Here I am, back again for our little chat. I am all through with the regular household work. I made the beds, did the dishes, brushed down the walls in the kitchen, fixed the fires and powdered my nose. It's 9:30 and time for my second cup of coffee and our chat for the morning. How are you today, son? You know I don't like too many rainy days. If I had some paint, I would do up the kitchen. If I had some Kemtone, I would do up the sitting room. And so it goes. If I had some dress material, I would make some housedresses.

Remember the day I was so happy to see you coming 50 miles per down Fulmer Street? You picked me up when I thought I would never get home. Roger was going ahead to get his express wagon to get the load we were carrying. Well, that is one of the reasons I don't get to Frankford more often. I am so loaded with bundles.

I sent to Patton for to give Dad's seed order. I also expect the insurance man. Mrs. Spence called me up yesterday and she said did I know that if Edwin made an allotment of $10.00 a month to me, the Government would match it with $10.00? She said, 'Don't think I want to butt into your business, but it's nothing to me,' etc., etc. Well I said I don't know anything about it. I almost got into words. I do hope you are well. My main reason for telling you these things is to say that you have an opportunity now to save. If you don't, you will find life harder later on. Now is the time to save to get your start.

What do you think? Bud Wenker did not even take his time off when he finished boot. He went right to school. Young Billie was telling Roger yesterday. They went down to see him twice and he doesn't want to lose any time in getting a rating. He must not have been as homesick as you thought. I don't know what he is qualifying for, but I bet he will go high. His mother said he intends to go to college after the war is over. He is lucky. Please, for my sake, get that good conduct card, as you never did get one at home or school. So surprise me, please. It was funny on Sunday. Pop wouldn't show Dot your picture. He was afraid she might see the next fold where he had you and the girl. On Saturday night, the two "old hicks" bought me two gardenias. They sure smell so lovely and fragrant. I had them in the ice box. So I put them out on the table. Roger asked, are these flowers real? I said, smell them. He said, 'I do; but Dad said they are only paper. Mom put perfume on them.' With this rain and heavy heat they sure do smell. Each night I set the dish in the ice box. That keeps them fresh longer. One is starting to turn yellow.

The Home Fires

I hear a bird singing so sweetly out in the pine tree. I have to go see what it is.

Well, I couldn't see it. Down in the lilac row and over in the woods they sure are singing a new tune. I guess spring is just around the corner. As soon as the warm sun comes out, I guess the daffodils will pop out, but, there's no little boy and Grandpop to sit in a cold wind picking a snotty nose. ("Daffy down dilly" came up in the cold, through the brown mold, although the March breezes blew keen in her face.) I can see you running and Grandpop on his knees, legs under him. Well, time changes everything. Now you are one of Uncle Sam's wagons. Water boy, water boy, I'm goin' to tell your mammy.

You are a man now and all you must do is account to Uncle Sam; but I'll take you back as a "bad debt". "You still owe me" and no more "Buck will scrub your kitchen, Mom." I used to scrub it every day. But those days are gone. Younger hands will have to bend the knee and take over, just as I did for Old Mrs. Price. I am tired and sick of it all. I love to work, but when you don't have anything in life to work for, you just go down, down. So I keep you for pride, for you, for Dad, for Roger. If you don't return love, that makes life empty.

I read over your letters and I say how different they are of you. I still smooth your face and think of you as my baby. I know you are past all that and able to make your own baby, but I want you to have a chance in life first. I want you to be free and enjoy yourself. With it all, it's like Dave D. told you. Work a little, play a little, save a little and you will find the world a finer place. I had a big chat. I guess I might as well go to bed. It's real dark and I am lonesome. Can't you rush in at 50 miles per hour and say, "Mom make me somethin' to eat." Okay dear. Lots of love.

Mom

Hello Edwin,

It's 12 Noon now and Aunt Dink just called me up. She told me Uncle John got his wrist broken. I don't know how, but it is 165 miles to the nearest hospital from where he is. They were taking him there for x-ray, etc. Bill wrote and said not to worry if Aunt Dink didn't hear from him. He was leaving where he was.

Googy Smith and Francis Smith met in Belgium. Wasn't that something for them two to meet? Charlie, the other brother, is in Alaska. He was home for Christmas.

Mr. Patton was in about 11, just as I was going to listen to Sardi's. The phone rang lightly several times and I said, 'Hello.' Finally, I dialed the operator. She said, 'Number please.' I said, 'The bell is ringing.' She said they were working on the line. I hung up. It rang again. I answered. It was Aunt Dink. She said every time for 15 minutes she got the busy signal. So you never can tell. She was going to come up today, but it is raining so hard. I told her to come up and stay for supper. George works at Budd's and he can come right here. Then Dad can take them home after supper. She said George worked six Sundays straight and a young fellow asked him if he could work in his place as he is married and needs the money. So George said sure. He didn't like Sunday work anyway. Aunt Dink said God was with George. The fellow touched a live wire. It threw him 35 feet, burned him black and he was dead when he hit the floor last Sunday. Dink said Byron must be missing a year before he is declared dead. Then they get that pay also. Uncle John said she should not sign any papers without reading them over and not to run to Washington or Rhode Island, to let them come to her. Dink said she was out last Sunday and a Naval Officer was at the house.

She didn't get to see him, nor did she get any message except that if she wanted to see the chaplain to send back the card they sent her. She said Charlie and Violet, Dot and Peach, and Howard and Pearl were there on Sunday evening. She said Valentine's have the store and Uncle Charlie's house up for sale. They want $5,000 for Uncle Charlie's house, so they are looking for another house up that way. I guess they will go a long way before they find one, especially with 7 kids.

Well, I think I have written you a lot of news today. I hope to hear from you and am anxiously waiting. Until I do, I send all my love. So does Dad. He asks every night. 'Hear from the boy?' I said last night, "Now Pop, give him time." He said, 'Well it's getting long, Mom.' I said I know. So dearest, here's to hoping you get all my mail.

Love,

Mom

Wednesday morning, March 7, 1945

Hello Son,

It's 10 AM and I still have the beds to make. I have been at the fires twice and I still have a few dishes to wash, but I thought I would have some coffee and chat with you for a little while. I sure have been on the bum the past week. I have a little cold in my head and my blood pressure is high. Last night, I was up a dozen times, so this morning I have no go. Here I am son. Where are you? I am beginning to look for a card with your change of address. So far, the last I heard from you was the paper and book of Treasure Island. Now I have my coffee here and I picked up the ink bottle. Wouldn't I have been in a mess if I took a drink out of that?

It has rained all day and night for two days. It's still running off the roof, but has stopped. It's a warm spring rain and it's hot in the house. It's 75 degrees in the dining room. So I went to the front door and smelled a little fresh country air. I left the door open a crack and as soon as my back was turned, out went Brownie. He is gone about 15 minutes now. "I guess the books need going over?" Fisher's have 3 dogs that are here every day. Yesterday, one is so fresh it comes up on the porch. I guess Brownie has gone to call. The big Sis. He can't jump up on the bed. Roger had to get up this morning when Dad left to put him on the bed. I called Roger, as Brownie had made such a fuss. He couldn't make it. I said I told you in the first start, you want a dog? I am no chambermaid for a dog or cat; so wait on them. You know it's just wonderful to have pets and plants and flowers if someone else does the work. I am a lady now, not the money kind, so I am going to take life easy. No one to say, 'Mom make me somethin' to eat.' I miss that and I hope for the day when you can eat my French fries. (I stuck you the last time you were home.) I don't know any news. That darn dog is not back yet.

Sardi's is on now and Brownie is back. Uncle Corny said the shack they bought on the installment plan is always damp. Why? Because there is a dew (due) on it. Said he keeps the hogs in the back bedroom. Tom asked him if he knew that was not sanitary. Corny replied, 'If tis so, haven't lost a hog in 8 years.'

I had crackers and milk for my lunch. I have my coffee here again. The beds are made, dishes washed and here I am to finish our little chat. I paid $22.19 insurance yesterday and must send a money order to the bank today for $18.00. I guess if we live long enough, we will get there. There are five paydays in March, which will help a lot.

We had a small letter from Sarah Rowley's oldest daughter, Beatrice, 49 years old and unmarried. She said they got the letter I wrote December 31st on February 16. All the news is nothing but war. The Ohio River is flooding western Pennsylvania. Schools are closed and Portsmouth, Ohio is worst hit. Pittsburgh is flooded. I still say Philadelphia, Bustleton, U.S.A. is good enough for me. All I ask is health and a little home comfort and I am happy. As I told you before, I don't know any news whatsoever. I will write more later.

Well dearest, it's now night and the radio is going full force. They put 7 truck loads of cinders in the lane just before supper, on piles. Pop just about got in. Ray Wenker called up and asked Pop if he would spread them around. Pop and Joe are down at the mailbox spreading them and it's dark. Pop said it would be better for him getting out in the morning. Pop got the car license plates today, V.5. 205. I think that's the number.

I am getting awful anxious to hear from you. I feel a little better tonight. I had a rest today. I smooth your face and say nighty night and send all my love.

Your own Mom

Thursday, March 8, 1945

Dearest Son,

It's 11:45 and I have been on the go ever since I got up. I cleaned upstairs and fixed the fires and had a bite to eat. I've done all the usual daily tasks and now I will have my little chat. I kissed your big pictures and Byron's and Bill's and I shed a few tears. Today is Bill's birthday, and also the birthday of my grandpa, John Long. He would be 98 years old today and Bill is 19.

The sun is shining nice, but it's snappy and cold. Dot called me up to find out if I heard from you.

Sixteen heroes of the 4th Marine Corp are at Treasure Island today. I sure pray for all those boys. Dot said her mother had a book yesterday (March 7) from you from Treasure Island. I sent the card to Pepsi Cola about the record on where I can get one remade. If it was a good record, I would play it every day. Dot said George got his first class rating and he sure is happy. I invited her over to lunch after work on Saturday and to do my hair. I said, 'Dot, you sound as if you are quite near me.' She said, 'Well I am only across the railroad.'

Mr. Patton brought the seed, so it looks like we will have a garden. Dad said he heard he has only five days a work week beginning this week. So he will have Saturday and Sunday off. He said he and Joe must make a little extra money. It looks like they had enough supplies in Dad's line.

I guess Roosevelt settled the day when he was with Churchill and Stalin at Yalta. The city of Cologne, Germany is finished. Patton's 3rd Division is crossing the Rhine. I guess the Heinies know what it's all about by now. (What's the strongest thing in the world? A roll of toilet paper. It wipes out hundreds of thousands of Heinies a day.) Bad Mamma.

Well son, I don't know a thing, but horse shit smells. I guess that is okay if you like horses. As for me, give me roses, lilacs, gardenias, honeysuckles and apple blossom time and I love it. I have my hair curled and nose powdered. My hair is silver on the sides. Hurry up. I hope I hear from you real soon. Roger, Dad and Joe say hello pal. No bucks. Cheerio from all.

Love,

Mom

Friday, March 9, 1945

Dearest Son,

It's 11:30. Sardi's is over and I had a bite and my coffee. I've gone through the usual work of the day, as well as the wash on the line. The sun is shining nice for a change, but the air still has a frosty feel, so much so, that I had to put on Ted's white coat. How are you, my dearest? Pop thought he had me this morning. I put your letter on his plate every night. While he is listening to Gabriel Heater, I usually go up with Roger. When you first went, he used to say, 'Did you write to the boy?' Every night he would put the letter on his plate. You saw it when you were home. Well, he stopped asking me. So Roger said, 'Mom, don't close up the letters you write until night. Then if there is anything new, you won't "waste" another stamp.' So I write you mostly in the morning. Last night, I forgot to put your letter out. So, Pop called me as soon as he got up. He said, "Come on Mother. Write to the boy." I said, 'Ha, Ha. Don't fool me. I write every day.' He said, 'This is one you missed.' I said, 'No, it's in the drawer.' He said, 'Come and put a stamp on it.' I said, No, it is all ready.' So he got it and I said, 'Now Dad, they won't make any more paper when I forget to write to my firstborn.' He said, 'You can't write to him.' I said, 'No, but the first one I had to call my own. Now he belongs to Uncle Sam.' All we do is talk about you and wonder if you are all right and wonder how you get along and wonder where you are and so the days pass. It's been two weeks since you left.

The heroes were coming in to Treasure Island yesterday, over 200 of them. They had been away 2 and 4 years. The interviewer asked one fellow what he thought when he saw the "Rock" (Alcatraz). He said, wonderful, perfect. The interviewer said if a famous prison looks wonderful, you don't need to tell me what the Golden Gates look like. The G.I. said, "If my folks are not listening in and anyone in my hometown hears me, please tell my folks that

I'm nearing home."

All the boys were waiting to hit a telephone. They were being interviewed on a tug or some sort of vessel bringing them in from the ship that had brought them home. I was saying, 'Oh, if my boy was bringing them home on his ship, or Uncle John, would I be proud.' I was crying and cursing at the same time. I can't listen to the radio.

The airplanes seem to be having a busy time around here all morning. The dog is still not right. Lizzie Bit has an increase coming. She is curled up here.

Well, I have been down to the "little house". Will you ever forget that cold morning you hated to go? I am waiting for you to come home and say, 'Mom I can get a loan from the government, so come on, we are going to get that good farm and you and I will have to manage. So Mom, you do the counting, Pop do the bossing, and Roger, Joe, and I will do the work. Dot will run the truck and tractor. I'll mind the baby and cook and get the wash out. Think you can do it, or no Mom, we can't take "Gail" on a farm. She must live in a row house.' Ha! Ha! Poor Edwin can't live on a city street!!! Oh, for the rolling sea.

I heard two good stories on the radio. One was "Anything can come up a Country Road." The other was "The Home Stretch" about 2 sea captains, coming home to London after three years at sea. It sure was funny.

Well me lad, I still have the dining room to do so I will say "au revoir and bon voyage" for now and will finish later. Don't forget, I got sunshine in my heart. No room for the devil. Jesus shines in my heart, so keep smiling, my love, and all is well. All is well. See you later. Smooth your face and kiss me son. Though night covers all, and fortunes may forsake you, sweet dreams will ever take you Home. Home to the one who loves you dearly. "So smile for me, Seventh Heaven."

Mother

Saturday, March 10, 1945

Dearest Son,

Here it is Saturday about 2. I was listening to the radio. I was hurrying up to have everything spic and span. Had home fries, deviled eggs, string beans, beautiful fried fillet and shrimp salad with slices of green peppers and coffee, tea and jelly roll. Miss Dot was supposed to come from work at 12:30 for lunch and to do my hair. Roger and Carl came in about 1, so I said, 'What time does Dot get through?' and they said, 'She "ain't" comin' for lunch, she's goin' with Mom to the store.' Well that's okay. But I think she could have called me up. Young people today don't have the manners I was brought up with when you make a luncheon date. They said she would be here later. I hate that kind of business.

Roger went up to Uncle Bill's today, the first since the week before Christmas. He gave him $10.00 and said, 'Where have you been so long?' He showed him a new $100 note and he said, 'If I thought you knew what to do with it, I would give it to you.' Roger should have said yes for clothes.

I had a nice letter from Uncle John today. That's 2 this week. He fell and broke his wrist on a stone. He said he wrote to you four times. He heard from his Bill. Aunt Violet called me up from Bristol today, where she was shopping with Norman. Little Violet was taking care of the kids. Uncle Charlie is deferred until June. They are looking for a house, as theirs is up for sale. She said the hospital bill for little Bill's leg is one hundred dollars. I told her to hold out for a thousand dollars or more, as little Bill's leg will always be crooked. That's a big concern, who can pay it, as they are insured.

Well, Nutsie and Roger are cleaning up around. A pack of about 15 dogs are roaming the place. Brownie is still on the sick list and Lizzie Bit is in my rocking chair. I will close for now, dearest, and go get cleaned up. Nutsie, Roger and I sure had a good lunch. I am looking for you coming in at 50. Pop lost the gas cap last night. Where did you put the spare one? Hope you are well. Haven't heard from you yet.

Love,

Mom and all

Sunday, March 11, 1945

Dearest Son,

It is Sunday afternoon and the same old thing, quiet with no company as of yet. Dot got over at 6 PM Saturday night and she and Carl stayed until after 11. We listened to the radio and laughed. Dot did my hair, so I have been to church. I met Dave Tumbelston and his wife and her little boy, a real curly head. They got a house in Quantico, VA at the base and so they are leaving Bustleton next week. On Saturday night, they are giving them a party in Alburger Hall. Each one is supposed to bring a gift. It's a secret to Dave. Margery Dudley told me to come. Dave's wife expects the stork and so she wants to get settled. Dave will be stationed there at that marine base. You know Bill Tumbelston is a major. They have some pull. Dave has been two years or more in the South Pacific, so he deserves to be home.

Dot said she was going to church today. Her mother got a new coat. The old man had a load on and busted the fender, etc. on the station wagon on

Friday night last. That was why Dot had to go to the store yesterday afternoon. She did say she would come over today, but I haven't seen her yet. She said, I'll see you about 2, but it's after three now. I stayed dressed from church. I thought if she came early enough, I might get to the movies. But now, I am going up and get my things off.

An Army Chaplain issued the sermon this morning. He told us lots of things. Well, Joe is rushing in. He must get back on the job. Mahlon and Dan Brown met at Guam through the Red Cross and had their pictures taken together. Mrs. Brown showed them to me. The pictures were sent with a Mother's Day card. Today is Aunt Lilly's 39th birthday. I sang Happy Birthday to her over the phone. That's all the news I know except that I saw my first robin of spring on the railroad bank as I walked home from church.

Lots of love,

Mom and All

Monday, March 12, 1945

Dearest Son,

Here I am. It's after 7 o'clock and I am tired. I went to Frankford at 11 and got home at 5. I looked at all the windows, but didn't see any Easter bonnet to suit me. So I got a few things (garters). That's the first since the war is on. I also got two pairs of stockings and a comb. Then I took in the movies. It was Keys of the Kingdom, a stirring picture of Catholic missionaries in China. It was dull and not to my liking, but a lengthy picture and interesting. I met Doreen Price and came home tired, had supper, helped Roger with math, and now they are listening to Hi-yo Silver.

I don't know any news. I went up to Uncle Charlie's Sunday night. He wasn't home. He was at Aunt Dink's. Violet was there and the kids. Nothing new. Granny called up from Delheim's while I was out. Roger was home from school and he answered. So here I am for our little chat with nothing to talk about. I am getting anxious to hear from you. All is well here and hope you are too. So I will say nighty night as I am tired and don't know of anything new.

I told you Uncle John had a broken wrist. Fell on a stone. I had two letters last week from him. He said he wrote you four times. The Red Cross never notified him about Byron. So dearest, all my love to you. Smooth your face and hold you tight. Mother, Dad and all miss you. Everyone asked for you yesterday. I was proud to see your name on the church honor roll in gold letters. Cheerio.

All my love,

Your own Mommy

Tuesday, March 13, 1945

Dearest Son,

The sun is shining nice and bright, but it's still cold and raw. It's nearly 1 PM and I haven't accomplished very much so far today. I sure am at a loss to know what to write about. But here's another letter just in hopes that you may receive mail at intervals. I want you to have letters from us, even if they don't contain any news of interest. You know all our love is with you and that you are never alone in thoughts; for I am with you always and so is Dad.
Brownie Baby is sick. He is a pretty sick boy today. His hind leg has the rheumatism or something. He can't keep it still. Dad is going to take him to

the Doctor's some night this week.

I had an Aunt Emma. She was one of my mother's sisters. She was young and she married Phil Palmer, who was an Italian. That was a disgrace in those days to marry a foreigner. Aunt Emma got spells like Aunt Mary. Well, Phil had run away from home and he finally got to America. When I was Roger's age, I used to play the phonograph (Victrola now). We had a record and it was called "Where is my wandering Boy tonight. The boy of my tenderest care. The boy who was once my joy in life. Oh! Tell him I love him so. My heart overflows. My story he knows. Oh! Where is my boy tonight?" I used to see Phil with tears in his eyes and I used to say Aunt Emmy, 'Why does Phil cry when I play that record?' She said, 'You ask him.' So I did. He said, 'Every time I hear that, it makes me think of my mother.' Well I said, 'I can write,' (he couldn't read or write). 'I'll write and tell her where you are.' He said, 'No. My mother Italiano, no understand English.' Today I found myself singing that song two or three times. God is in my heart and my love for my boy is there too. I am like all mothers. Faith, hope and courage. Lots of hugs and kisses.

Mommy

March 14, 1945

Dearest Son,

Sardi's is on from Denver, Colorado and they say it is 79 degrees there today. He has a 94 year old lady there. I talked to Aunt Lilly. She wrote to Fred asking for a date for Friday night. I can't understand her.
Poor Brownie put in two real sick days. Pop took him to the Doctor's last night. He gave him three kinds of medicine. Pop had to take him in the cellar and give him the "monkey", just the same as a person. His temperature was

105 degrees, so he must go back on Saturday night. You would feel sorry for him. Pop is so (you know) he can't remember what the Doctor said was wrong with him. All we can do is treat him and hope he pulls through. He hasn't eaten anything for two days.

The sun is shining and I have two tablecloths to put out and a few more things to do. Joe has a cold. He went to Dr. Roseman last night too. Lizzie Bit makes a bee line for the center of your bed every morning, so I am going to fool her for a few days. I will close the door. It's funny how they hunt the soft, cleanest places.

Aunt Dink called me up last night. She wanted me to go down to Aunt Kebe's today, meet Granny and go "busy body" to Front Street. I said no; as I had been out on Monday and I still am not over it yet. I hear Al has bought a house in Granny's name about three blocks from Aunt Kebe's, with 5 rooms and a bath. I hope it's not another case of Fred and Aunt Lilly. She knows her own business best. Well son, I also heard that Dot left M.C.C. and is back at Baldwin's. Nutsie told Roger yesterday. Dot is close. She doesn't tell me much. Of course, I am only interested for your sake.

Well dear, I'll say bye, bye for now. Lots of love.

Mom & All

March 15, 1945

Hello Son,

I feel like singing for joy and saying Hello Sweetheart, darlin', sweetie, sugar, tulip, plum, for today I heard from you. Seven letters from February 26th to March 7th mailed Sunday, March 11th and received today. They were just

The Home Fires

like reading a book.

Last night, I dreamed I had a letter from you and on the outside was a picture of some camels and I said, 'Oh My God! He is in Egypt. Now that is the last place I ever expected to hear from him.'

This morning Roger coaxed me to let him stay home from school, so we spent the whole morning outside cleaning up. I told Roger my dream. I said, 'There's the mailman. I'll go down for the mail.' Roger said, 'No, I'll go.' He went on his bike, so he was up in a jiffy. He shouted, 'Come on, Mother, your dream came true, 7 letters from Edwin.' By that time I was sweating and I said, 'Oh, come on the front steps and help me open them.'

I was reading the last letter and Roger said the phone was ringing. I ran in. A man said, 'Mrs. Price?' I said yes. He said, "How are you?" I said, "Who am I speaking to?" He said, "Can't you guess?" I said, "No, not quite." He said, "I just called to inquire about your health." I said, 'Since I do not know who is calling, I'm not telling.' He said, 'Don't you know?' I said, 'Yes! I suppose I talked to you many times before. Did you get back from the North Atlantic?' He laughed. It was Uncle Bill Long. So, I had two surprises today. I can hardly wait for Dad to get home.

It's five o'clock and Dad is stopping off to pay Heinel's on the eighty dollar repair bill. The car still throws gas or some smell that makes my head ache.

I was up to Uncle Charlie's last Sunday night. That's the first since last Christmas I was out except to see Walter S. laid out.

Now dearest, I hope by this time you have mail from home. I have written every day since you left home at Christmas or since you left Philadelphia. Dear, the pictures are out for the present. Good pictures cost money. Be content with the little ones you have. Your brother left the Marshall Islands and we don't know where he is just yet. Dad said we will write any news we know of brother. He is just fine. Uncle John is still in the hills of New Caledonia. Bill left Pearl Harbor and said he was going towards his Pop. I also told you that the Brown Brothers met on Guam through the Red Cross. Dan was loading and Mahlon came to where he was. They had their pictures taken, but I told you that before.

If you hear any news of where brother R. is, or Uncle J. let us know. We understood everything about your letters. If every boy would write as good as you do, we wouldn't have to worry like poor Aunt Lilly. No letters from Edwin Bissinger for months. Also, you know Mr. McAdams had one nephew killed and one was missing. They got word that he is a prisoner in Germany now.

I think it is just the finest thing that you looked after the officer's quarters. Take every opportunity to work and gain knowledge.

As you go westward, you get a day ahead of us. Are you a member of Davy Jones' locker yet? I must get a map.

I am so thankful to God and so glad you didn't get real sea sick. Eat all the fruit you can get, and bacon, butter, chocolate milk. They give you what you need for that oppressive heat.

When the beautiful moon sails the sky, look for the one who loves you. They are as true as that moon. Will close for now.

Love,

Mom & All

The Home Fires

March 16, 1945

Dearest Son,

Here it is Friday night and Gabriel Heater is on with the news. Aunt Lilly was here for supper and is still here beside me. She did my hair. It sure was a real warm, spring day for a change, one that gave us the spring fever. I had one more letter from you today after getting seven yesterday. You told me you have not had any mail from home. I do hope that by now you have had some of my letters, for I know how anxious I was to hear from you.

I guess you sure know what an ocean voyage is like by this time and what the heat is like. Now dearest son, no one in this world could be any happier than I am to have such nice letters from you. And my dear, if anybody makes fun of the way you talk, well you suit me. I know that you have had every opportunity to go to school. You did your share by helping to keep the "welfare" from our doorstep. Now you are serving our country. You are still young. God knows all the answers.

Well dearest, I read all your letters over two or three times and I can't see anything wrong with any of them for there is love in every line. All I do is hope and pray for your safety.

Dearest, I had a beautiful letter from Pepsi Cola saying to send back the record and they will be too pleased to make a new disc free of charge.

Aunt Lilly has left now and I am going to bed. All my love. I saw Dot and talked to her several times. She is back at Baldwin's again. They wouldn't give her a release. Keep up your good, nice letters. I love all the mistakes because you are part of me and perfect in my eyes.

All our love,

Mom, Dad, Rog, Joe

Saturday, March 17, 1945

Dear Son Edwin,

Here at home, it is 6:30 Saturday morning. I just couldn't sleep. That's always the way on the mornings that I don't need to get up to get brother off to school. I guess these old hicks are so used to rising with the crack of dawn, that when the eastern sun peeps over the horizon, nothing can hold us in bed. When Dad calls me at 4 with the radio going hot stuff, mother is set for the day.

Aunt Lilly has Dot's wavers in my hair so tight, she has me almost scalped. I had to lie on my belly to get any comfort. I came down for my coffee. I have a most delicious cup here aside of me and I will have a little chat with you and then go back up until Rog is ready to get up.

Of course, I don't know any special news; outside of the fact that Underwood is on the job, at least three times this week. Sunday night, I saw him there and Dad is so mad. I told Dad there are no strings on either of you, which is as it should be. It's a privilege to have friends. But the thing is, this is a raw spot because of the circumstances. You know son, the fellow who has the most money is always the winner! There is an old saying that, "All is fair in love or war." But that is far from being true. You may roam the world and yet the love that follows you is from the heart of her who loves you. You can meet many who say those "three little words". No matter how sweet they may sound, none is ever as sincere as a mother's words spoken in harshness, because you are a part of her. Half of the world never knows how the other half lives. You found this out in six short months away in the world that life on the farm was milk and honey. Like that home life you knew, money could never buy the experience you are gaining. All you need to do is keep your chin up. I told you many times never to be homesick or lonely. The carpet of blue above your head is your guide. Grandpop stands behind one of God's windows, just as he sat at our kitchen window looking out towards the West. He is your watchman now. Never be afraid. Ask God for comfort. Everyone in the world is scared at times, and of many different things. God pulls us through if we have faith.

Dad brought home a big sack of oranges last night. They are the finest ones I have seen since he huckstered. They are sitting on the floor by the sideboard. It keeps me thinking of Christmas in days gone by when we had oranges by the crate and popcorn and everything. The sideboard couldn't hold another dish. We used to think we were poor and yet we were the wealthiest and happiest. I know I always fixed, decorated and cleaned and flowers are still on the kitchen table. Little boys used to bring me spring beauties and ferns and pansies and daffodils. That is why mothers grow old gracefully and content. When a boy writes such nice letters home to Mom, Dad and Rog, then some of the good is showing. Whatever life's burdens, we have the comforting thoughts and remembrances of happy times on the farm, far away from all that damn noise, hustle, and bossing. So save your money and we can still have a place called "Desired Acres". I am going up now. I will write more this afternoon. Love dearest darling, big hug, baby.

It's noon now son, so I will add a few more lines, although Nutsie was here. He had been at the barber shop. Rog had left at nine o'clock so they missed each other. He said he didn't know anything new. I said to tell Dot I send my regards. I still have some work to do, so I will write later. But, before I forget, Brownie is much better. Dad is hurrying home tonight to get him to the Doctor's before nine. I don't know if I am going out to the church or not. I hate to walk out. It's quite warm here the past two days. Birds are singing. I saw another robin yesterday in the maple tree. Dad drained the antifreeze out of the car last night. I guess spring is right around the corner.

Dearest, it's now 3:30. Joe is home and I talked to Mrs. Spence. Joe is going to take this letter out. So my dear little boy, I love you, hug you and miss you in every line I write. Keep your chin up. I am proud of you and so is Dad. All of us. So keep it up and don't let anyone make you mad. God is on the side of a Christian Sailor lad.

Cheerio X X X X

Mom & All

Sunday, March 18, 1945

Dearest Son,

I am listening to the Answer Man on the radio. I was at church, and came home to smoked butt, cabbage, and sure was hungry. All the women were out in full spring beauty. Some of them sure looked like 1890. The hats are sure funny. You should have seen Mrs. Erwin's white head with a lilac sailor. Dr. Stoudt's wife looked as if she had hunted out Mrs. Lodge's attic. Did I laugh! So far, I have not got mine. Pop got his new Easter bonnet last night in Frankford. It's gray and cost $6.00. You ought to be home. We'd go to Lane Bryant and you'd say, "Mom, I'm gonna tell Dad how much you paid for that hat!" It was $12.75. It's still one of the prettiest I ever had, eh? Pop liked it.

Mrs. Laubenstein asked me for your address. Elmer T. is out of San Pedro, California on a shakedown cruise. He hasn't had any mail from home, but they hear from him, and so it goes. Dad got one of Russell's horses. Joe and Dad had to pull him and the harrow. Boy oh boy. Dad had a stick. Joe jabbed him in the rump with a fork. They are just about getting through now cleaning off the patch.

Ford's will plow sometime next week so Dad has got the spring fever again.

Say, what do you think? We had two real hot days, 84 and 88 and the warmest St. Patrick's Day ever known. It sure was welcome to me. I looked all over the Atlas. It has all the routes from San Francisco and how many miles each one is and where the day changes. If you meet up with Roger, let me know where you saw brother or where you heard from him last and what he was doing. Uncle John is in the hills of New Caledonia. Below the equator that is, off the Australian coast.
He is doing okay, getting all good things fresh to eat. Lot of French settled there.

It's 5 after 4 now and Joe took the plug home. Dad is going now to meet Joe, as he has to go do his work. Dad made a fire and took all the rubbish away. The place looks nice and clean now.

Well dearest son, I've been thinking of you so much today. Did you get to church on board ship? Did you sit still? Well, I guess you will have sea legs and are old salt by now. I send all my love to you. So does Dad and all the rest.

Carl and Roger are sprouting their wings. They are invited up to Violet's birthday party today. All they talked about all week was the girls they met up there last week. We got a few hair ribbons and a poem book, etc. and I did them up nicely. Roger made several pins like the one he made for Dot. Young Violet just called up to see if they were coming up. I was so dumb I didn't wish her a happy birthday. But, I sent cards etc. with Roger like I used to for you. Yes, I will send something for you for Dot's birthday if you say so. I gave her supper and also $1.00 for doing my hair last week. She didn't want to take it. It's worth that much to walk over and it saves me going to Frankford and it's done to suit me. It saves me time. I hope to see her and have her do it up for Easter. I will say bye for now. Lots of love. Lots of everything.

Mom & All

(Enclosure – Item 6)

—Photos by Jack Snyder, Record Staff Photographer.

LOVE BLOOMING: Watertender 1/c Myles Armour and Phillis Fragel on a Fairmount Park bench prove that Hollywood stars are pikers when it comes to high-powered osculation.

Hottest Winter Day Baffles Men of Science

'It Might Be Gremlins,' One Declares as Mercury Soars to New High of 84; Atlantic City Jammed With Heat Refugees

The weather yesterday continued to baffle the world of science and to gladden the hearts of the laity as the thermometer again zoomed to mid-summer temperatures.

"Might Be Gremlins"

One gentleman of science thrust his head over the top of his ivory tower, wiped his brow and sighed: "Unofficially, I just don't get it. . . . It might be gremlins."

Another allowed himself the comment that "after January, it's certainly coming to us. But where from is something else again."

The weather bureau, somewhat firmer, announced: "It's a flow of warm air from somewhere in the South."

Hottest Winter Day

Wherever it came from, it was the hottest winter day on record, reaching 84 degrees at 1 P. M., smashing Friday's high of 82.

It threw Atlantic City into the vacation jitters as trains arrived well packed with pleasure-seekers

Wartime Letters Written from Mother to Son

Monday, March 19, 1945

Dearest Son:

At home here we are having a light spring rain. Dad has the plot all harrowed and cleaned up around. It sure is a refreshing look after the long winter months of snow and ice. I talked to Aunt Lilly this morning and she said her Edwin left home for the service two years ago today. She tore off all the paper in Edwin's room yesterday (Sunday) and so I am thinking of the time you and I did our radio room. "Whew." Now it needs it again.

The McAdams' came up about 4:30 yesterday and they were only here a few minutes when Aunt Minnie and her family came in. Little Danny Boy sure is a sweet baby. I can't get them off my mind all night and today because when I took that baby from her, I could hear the baby breathing heavy. Before she left, I said they all had the whooping cough. I put my hand on Elmer's shoulder and I said, Elmer, don't go to work tomorrow. Take those three babies to a doctor. I am not a nurse, but if those three children don't have it, well then, I never saw it. The baby has a running ear and he sure was turning his little head. His lips got blue when he coughed just like yours used to get when you had it.

Roger told me that they had three fire companies there on Saturday. Little Elmer's face was all red and I said he's sunburned. Minnie said no. That's from the fire. But she didn't tell me all the excitement they had. Elmer was burning off his field. Minnie said Elmer was cutting up the tree you cut down and he was saying, 'Edwin, this sure is a tough tree to cut up. Edwin, I ought to leave this damn thing until you get home to finish it.' Minnie said she wondered who he was talking to and she stood at the window and listened. She said he sure was talking out loud to you.

Mrs. McAdams, Minnie and I were laughing, as little Elmer is worse than you and William put together. To think how we were sitting so peacefully on a spring afternoon and worrying about you both.

I put on a swell supper for Minnie and all we did was talk about you. Roger was out sprouting to Aunt Violet's, so there was no one but Dad and Mom to rule the roost, no chicks to pick and fuss.

It's dark and raining and I'm listening to Jack Bircsh and his songs. It's 12 noon here. I had my lunch. Now I am having my little chat with you. I still miss you more than ever. Dad put the car in Bender's this morning and so don't you know it would rain when he has to walk home tonight. I am supposed to go to Frankford and up to Holmesburg tomorrow. I hope it's not raining like it is now. I don't know any news other than I have written you. I do hope and pray for you all the time. Yesterday, we were talking about boys and how the different mothers take the news. Minnie said, "Why make a fuss? You can't do anything and after all, it's only routine. There are millions of others." I said, "Send Elmer or Danny away and see if you think it's just routine." It's a wonderful thing to have hard hearts and tough nerves, but I'll still take home and love and children and let the rest of the world go by.

I lay on the daffodil hill one day in spring when I was young and had a heavy heart because I was married only five months and Dad was so very ill in Frankford Hospital. I looked at the white clouds floating through the blue sky and I talked to God that day. I got up feeling like a new girl, for the clouds were rolling by. I knew life was the same way, clouds and sun, and beauty where we looked for it. That song was popular; Let the rest of the World go by. And I did. I found that there is no place like the peace and quiet of the countryside, and one you love. You never are poor. Richness and beauty is in all you can look at from the top of the daffodil hill. And so I look for a white sailor hat and two long legs coming over the bank and all is well. All is well. That's all for now.

Lots of love,

Mom and all

March 20, 1945

Dearest Son,

It's 5:15 PM and I am home and tired out. I sure had a great adventure today. I had more trolley rides up to Holmesburg and home. I met Mrs. McAdams in Frankford and we had lunch together. It is so warm we had to take off our coats and carry them. I met Mrs. Laubenstein on the trolley and she took me into her house and gave me a cool drink of seven up and then I came home.

It's now seven o'clock. We had supper without Dad. I just phoned Mrs. McAdams and she said he had to work a little later. So I guess he will be in soon. Here is a bit of news I heard today. The Hermanns' bought that stone house next to Heller's Hotel lot. Where the Lovetts' live, they bought the double house and are going to remodel it and fix one side of it for one of the sons and sell the place here on Krewstown Road. Mrs. Laubenstein's son asked for first chance, but as of yet he has no answer. I went to Aunt Dink's and she wasn't home. I am tired and I will be glad when Dad gets home.

One of your letters came back today. It has an 8 cent stamp on it and needed 4 cents more. Edwin, Uncle John sent me a pale rose, silk handkerchief with a souvenir of New Caledonia embroidered on it. It looks like an outline of the island done in dark blue thread on the rose. It's lovely.

The Home Fires

He said he is okay and still in the same place.

Well dearest darling, I hope you are okay. Elmer T. writes awful blue letters home, so his Granny told me. He can write, but he hasn't heard from home. So I do hope you get my mail.

I am always thinking of you and wonder if you saw the sun cross the equator. It's 7:38 here at home. Spring was due, but instead, I think the sun must have gotten twisted because it's like summer. The cherry blossoms are in bloom in Washington D.C., the earliest in 18 years. The fire company sure is on the run with grass fires. But Lou and Edwin are kinda slow on the job this year for the field on the upper side. I guess you have it plenty hot where you are. Blow, wind, blow and send my sailor home to me. Lots of love, hugs.

Mother and all

March 21, 1945

Dearest, Dearest Son,

After a nice lovely spring day yesterday, today is just the opposite. It rained all day and now it's cold. Dad had to start a fire in the heater. All this after we sweated and had no covers on the bed, just sheets.

Gabriel Heater is on with the news. I sure would love to hear from you. It's a week ago tomorrow since I had your eight letters. I can't write much tonight. I have a headache and so I am going to bed right now. The only news I know is that Granny's friend, Elsie Ford, called me up today. So did Mrs. McAdams. Roger said Johnny Ems hit Philadelphia again, came home, and then went down to get his wife. Other than that, I don't know anything. I spent a long lazy day. I didn't do a thing. I love you very much. I hope to see and hear from you, so keep your chin up. You ought to hear Gabriel Heater tonight. He said Winston Churchill is going to shoot Hitler one hour after he is captured. Let us hope somebody does. Whatever the punishment Hitler gets would be too good for him. God will see what he metes out to him, when he comes to judge.

Darling, here is my happy page. Sunshine in your heart puts it in mine. We all send our love to you. Carry on. I am proud of you and your name. Don't let anyone make you mad. Don't take anything to heart. The world contains all kinds to insult or be kind. So think of Mom and Dad, who loves you, and God to guide you. You don't need anything else. So cheerio.

Love from Roger and Mother and all. XXX

Write when you can.

XXXX

March 22, 1945

Hello Son,

Well, it's still raining, a two day spring rain. Everything is green and lovely, but I guess this will finish the magnolias and cherry blossoms. The yellow forsythia bush is just starting to bud, but the flowering almond is not started yet. That never blooms here until the first of May and then you know we always have a week of northeast rains.

There isn't a single thing I know of to write to you except the weather and to say hello. I talked to Aunt Lilly and Mrs. Spence today. I cleaned upstairs, have the fires fixed, the soup pot on for Joe and the icebox empty. Meat is getting scarcer all the time. But of course, I have always managed to get what I need. So I am having the soup and a big pan of raw fries; and that is my limit of news; housework, the same old story. I don't want to miss a day, as I must have my little chat with you. I sent the record back to Pepsi Cola today. I put it in the same wrapper you sent it in and then put white paper about it. It cost three cents parcel post. I hope they send me back a good one.

I put clean covers on all the tables and cleaned it all up nicely. After Easter, I think I will tackle the radio room. I wish that while I am so tired and up on the step ladder, that in will walk a tall sailor boy, my son, and say, 'Mom get down out of there. Let me do it'. But I guess that would only be a dream, for I would hear this instead, "Yes, for a buck, Mom!"

Did I tell you that I gave Rog a buck last Saturday to scrub the kitchen and he did a real fine job? So now, I have two maids, one to scrub and one to do the dishes. Soon I will be a real lady. I used to wish for the day when I wouldn't have much work. Now I wish I had all seven around the table, cooking and yipering and yelling. Then I would be younger. Time is slipping fast. I guess I will be a Granny when you come home to stay. Dreams are cheap, but no one can share them. So for now, lots of love,

Mom

Friday, March 23, 1945

Dearest Son,

Here, it is suppertime. While I am waiting for Joe, I will write you a few lines. I did not have our little chat early this morning, as Friday is a busy day on the farm. The day broke sunny and fair after two days of cold rain, and what a help. I got the wash back around noon, dried. I mostly ironed off and now for a few minutes pause.

The steak cod is sizzling golden brown in the pan. I also have mashed potatoes; raw canned tomatoes fixed as you like them, peas, a big, sliced, Bermuda onion, and sliced pickle. So all is ready. Dad is stopping off at Heinel's again tonight, so we won't wait unless Joe is much later.

It's now 6 o'clock. Rog and Nutsie are monkeying with the power motor. They had it going, but it won't run over the ruts without stopping. In the meantime, they ate a large raisin pie. Cliff R. was in today. He is digging out the gas tank. They are taking it up to the new farm in Trevose. He said he expects to get called any day now. Bud W. is taking 16 weeks school at Bainbridge. He comes home on weekends. H. Wenker was selling his own house for 18 months. Some Doctor made a down payment on it. He is asking ten thousand for it. Bill Bender was telling Dad that after he made the deal with the doctor, he changed his mind about selling it. He said his wife didn't want to sell it, etc. But I am not so damn dumb. Because Flora Boyd told me if you taught school in Philadelphia, you had to live in Philadelphia, and Trevose is in Bucks County. I ain't as dumb as I look. She doesn't want to stop work. While she works, she is her own boss and is independent of the Wenker gang. She is a nice girl and too smart for them.

Oh well, dearest how are you? I hope you are getting my mail. We are getting real anxious to have some news of you. But, God is good to us. So I hope all is well. All is well at home. No real news. This is just to say hello to my darling. Love from all. And so I'll be seeing you. Smooth my face, Mother. Cheerio.

Mom & All

The Home Fires

Saturday, March 24th, 1945

Dearest Son,

I guess you know I am real happy today. It's cold, but the sun is in my heart. I had four letters and Roger got one, mailed March 17th. So now according to things, you see, I got mail twice weekly, March 11th and today got the 17th, which was just one week coming. I think that is swell. I was getting anxious and you still say don't mail, what I write. Well love, Pop insists that I mail one every day, and like I told you in other letters, I had one with F.P.O. 128 and so I guess you will get a good many letters. I try to number mine, beginning with the first day of March. In that way, you can keep track of them. Now I have told you all the news I hear daily.

I have seen Dot once, since you left and talked to her a couple of times on the phone. She is working back at Baldwin's. Underwood has been there quite a few times, and so I don't know what is what. With young girls, they don't want to be bothered with old people. We are not interesting.

I love company and I keep thinking all week how I can see you bringing me an Easter plant, ever since you were big enough to carry one home. On two occasions, they were very special. One was when it was so cold, and you had a hole in your pants, and you nearly froze, and the other was last year when you sat at Dot's feet and told me you asked her to marry you. Well perhaps I am wrong, but I do still think it was best until you return. Then you will be better able to care, love and keep a wife. I still can't get over how dark your hair got. I love blonde hair and I want to be a nice mother to anyone you may choose. There is so much going on in this world that one half never knows how the other half lives. I wanted my life to be sunshine and flowers. I always made flowers all about, for beauty. Love, food, and children are all that counts in our world. A little circle of four, and all else to forget.

Now dear, I always told you everything. I met our dear friend at the Holmesburg Bank. He said, how about taking a trolley ride. So I did. He gave me one hundred dollars to buy my new Easter bonnet. He got thin, and I think ten years older. That was the first I had seen or heard from him in eight months. He had on Grandpop's glasses, a heavy winter overcoat and it was the first day of spring and 80 degrees. I told you how we had several warm days. So I guess you know Roger and I are going Easter shopping. Maybe we can get our pictures taken after all, and our teeth fixed. He sure is good to us and loves us. I still think he is our only friend "in need". He has never failed us in all the years. I didn't say a word. He said, "I haven't seen you for so long. I would like to give you some money." He had three 100 dollar bills that I saw, and a roll of 10's and 5's. He handed me a $100 bill. I said, 'Oh! I can't take that money.' He handed me it all. He said, "Do you want smaller money notes?" I said I wouldn't know who would change it for me. So he gave me eight $10 notes and four $5 notes. I kept laughing to myself. Clang, clang went the trolley. Clang, clang went the bell. I was on the El twice and in and out of 8 trolleys. So Rog said $10 for each one. Pop said he'd go trolley car riding any day for that much. Now only we four know it. I didn't tell Joe that I met anyone Tuesday when I was out. But Dad and Rog knew where I was going, as I told you in a previous letter. I had a phone call the day I got your first 8 letters. So you know now that Easter is perfect outside of not having you.

The dog is better and can run and hop once again. I got a nice big rice pudding cooked. Tomorrow is Palm Sunday. I shall say special prayers all week for the boys and lots and lots for you.

Love,

Mom

March 25th, 1945
Palm Sunday

Dearest Darling Son,

Well I guess you know I sure am thinking about you today, because it was on a Palm Sunday Eve that you and I were baptized. God has shown his mercy and love to me since then; and so I thought of you doubly all day today. It's a beautiful day here at home. I have the table full of yellow forsythia bell and Mrs. Rupert gave me two white and one lavender hyacinth and they smell so fragrant.

Dad and I just had a nice supper. Roger is with Thomas Ems. John Hussman, his wife and Granny were here today. Dad and Joe made a flower garden all the whole length behind the barn, so I guess I will have some flowers. The altar of the church had baskets of pansies all the way across, but no one was baptized today. Roger said Norman Brown is getting baptized next week. I haven't heard of anyone else.

Major Bill Tumbelston was wounded at the Iwo Jima Battle. Margery Dudley told me today. Everyone asked for you. Pastor Tumbelston said to send his best wishes to you. I see your name is on the roll downstairs. Bob Underwood was in Sunday School, so Rog said. I didn't see him. Outside of dinner and church, I didn't do much else except look at the paper. Roger and I are going on our usual spring shopping trip. I went to Frankford Saturday night. Cost me $1.75 taxi to get home. I bought Roger a pair of black shoes, "men's size" 6 1/2. Cost me $1.00 more for the half size. He wore them to Sunday School this morning. They rubbed a blister on his big toe. The car is still in Bender's, so I had to walk each way. It's a long story.

I am thinking of you all the time. Hope you are well. If you can get anywhere near New Caledonia, try to get the Red Cross to help you meet Uncle John if possible. All is well.

Love,

Mother

Monday & Tuesday, March 26th & 27th, 1945

Hello Honey Darlin, Sweetie, Sugar Tulip, Plum.

Here I am, way behind with out little chat, but as ever thinking of you. All tuckered out. Too much Easter bonnet parade. Rog and I didn't lose the pocket book, but we sure ran our legs off. Strawbridges first; "hats" no good. Bought Roger a suit there, somewhat like your gray one, except that it has more blue flecked through it. No damn good, but hooked, as usual, cash $16.95. Better than I expected, but he is growing so fast. I got 5 dresses, three for church, and two for the house. I paid as much for the house dresses as I was used to paying for the church dresses. I got two pairs of shoes. Brown pumps and the black "old lady kind".

I was sick when I left home yesterday, but worse last night and still not over it. I got the daffodils and hyacinths on the table and spring in my heart. So all I wish for is you. I had all God could give me for Christmas, and so Easter is the first holiday without my firstborn. But, your Easter basket will be fixed with no candy. Candy is hard to get, but if Uncle Sam's boys get it, I am satisfied. All I ask God for is bread and a drink. If it will end this war, I am for it. America is so wonderful. I always had plenty and more to eat, but I had to work hard for it. Dad is planning on getting the ground plowed up tomorrow.

I can see you coming in at 50 miles per hour last year and jumping out of the car and coming over to talk to me, while Dad was marking out onion sets. I believe Dad is going to put in cantaloupes where you had the watermelons. I still have the preserved rind. No one ate it yet.

Now, I must tell you, we went in Gimbels, Adams, and a shirt store and finally found neck size 14 youth shirt for Rog. They were $3.95 a piece. Two are plain white, one check, blue and gray. So you see, $1.00 for a 25 cent tie. Then we wound up at three 5 & 10 cent stores. Went to Lane Bryant, couldn't get any shoes there, so home to Frankford. I got them in Dial, near Circle. Walked to Sam's the Tailor with the suit pants, then back to Oxford Pike. Rog ran over to White Tower and ate four hamburgers on the trolley. Got home 7:30, nearly piss the pants. All day, no go. And now for the hat, it's a lime green sailor with a flower garden in front in shades of lilac, lavender and orchid. Also, lime green gloves and silk bag, the same, earrings that I'll wear with my breast pin from you with the green stone and my light suit and brown pumps.

Dot sent word she would be over Saturday to do my hair. Then I will ask her about getting the picture taken. Pop says we must get it done. And so my Darling, wherever you were on Easter, my heart was beside you.

We are to give $1.00 for each star on the flag, to go to the Red Cross. When I give mine, it cleans up my hundred. But I can always get plenty at the same place.

So dear, until I write tomorrow again, I hope and pray, and send all my love to you. So does dear old Dad. Rog has the week off. He went fishing up to Uncle Charlie's. Carl and he packed a big lunch. They are not back yet. It's supper time now. So Cheerio.

Love,

Mom & All

Wednesday, March 28th, 1945

Dearest Son,

At home here, it sure is an ideal spring morning. Dear old Dad is home and Ford Motor men are here plowing up the plot behind the house. Dad is sure happy. You know how he loves the earth; and to get it ready. For then he knows the pantry will be full in the winter harvest. He is always looking out for us. The onions sure are growing in the cellar. Dad has all my flower seeds in.

So we are off for a good start for the new season and I hope to put in an extra leg under the table for when you get home. But, if you don't eat any more than you did at Christmas, then I won't need to cook. French fries are out now. You didn't eat all I made for you.

They are singing "Springtime in the Rockies, once again, I'll say I love you." That was Mr. Leiby's favorite and it takes me back to the harvest days, when we had everything to make "mother's hair gray". But, they are still the happiest days.

Today, I have a full table with Dad, 2 Ford men and Rog. I have fried country sausage, mashed potatoes, oven stewed tomatoes, sweet corn, summer salad, scallions, and baked lima beans in the oven since 8 am. I put in a pan of biscuits and a 4 quart rice pudding that tastes like ice cream. How I wish you could share it. Like I said, I'll put an extra leg under the table when I see those two long legs coming over the railroad bank. So call me up when you get to Philadelphia.

I am waiting for the biscuits. Then I will call the men. So I will write more later. Maybe I will hear some news. Carl is here. He brought me one flounder he caught Sunday. Cheerio.

The day has been real warm. It's now supper time, 5:30 and the ground is plowed, disked and harrowed; a perfect day. Dear old Dad laid on his back in the sun and he was happy. Now the work begins, cow peas first, then onions and so on. I gave them beer and ginger ale and plenty good dinner. And now tonight, I am all warmed up and have potato soup for Joe and me. I will finish this up while waiting for them to come home.

I don't know of any news except that I was lazy all afternoon. Talked to Mrs. Spence and Aunt Lilly. All they worry over is what I got for Easter. I got mine. Let them worry over their own. I hope to hear from you soon again. I hope you have all my letters by this time. Well pal, I guess Easter will be another year away when you read this.

All my love,

Mom

Thursday, March 29, 1945

Dearest Son,

Here, it is supper time and I am just getting down to our little chat of the day. I have a flounder in the oven baking for Rog, a nice big fellow that Carl caught, and a pan of spaghetti, cheese, meatballs, a summer salad tossed together and rice pudding. I am waiting for them to come home.

I fixed your Easter basket and Roger's. I put the little table where the desk was between the two windows and I have them on there. Roger bought two plants and I put one in each basket. He dug and potted some daffodils and I put them in the baskets also, and some forsythia I put in a small jar. I put that cut paper around them and it looks lovely. I shed a few tears.

Dot called me up and said she would be over Saturday to do my hair. I am glad for that. Well son, I don't know any special news. The day was real warm, but it's getting windy and looks like it shaping up for rain. I am all pressed up and ready for Easter, so I hope it doesn't rain. We left out the kitchen and heater fire the last few days. I hear Dot got a new suit and things. She didn't tell me, but Carl did. She was going out to lunch and it was then 1:30, so she didn't have much time to talk. When she comes in Saturday, I will ask her about the picture.

Well dear, I must run along and I shall pray special tomorrow, Good Friday. God be with thee, guide and keep thee safe. My darling, all my love,

Also Dad, Rog, Dot, Joe, Mom

Friday, March 30, 1945

Dearest Son,

Here it is Good Friday. It has been a beautiful, glorious day. Tonight I have gone outside and the sky is real pretty. And you know the full moon governs the weather.

I have all the daffodils fixed all over the house and all cleaned up, groceries in, and you know Mommy. I am thinking of you hard tonight and a fair-haired girl and a pink hydrangea, and a boy on the floor at her feet. Those days past have been long and a worry. But as God shed his light on the world; may it shine brighter in the days to come. I was already to go to bed and I realized that I had not written to you. My chat today is slender, just to say hello and ask how is my baby. I guess you are sure thinking of us, just as we are of you. You, of course, know where we are. It's tough going to bed and not seeing you or knowing where you are. But I look at the moon every night and when the clouds hide it, I say I guess Edwin sees it or Edwin is in bed or Edwin is getting up. For now, I am too mixed up on the time and wonder all about you. But God is good and so on this Blessed Good Friday, may God hear our prayers and send peace to the world.

Dearest, the radio is on and I can't concentrate. I will say nightie night and send all my love to you and a big hug. Big kiss and so darling, Cheerio. Mother and All. Baby, I love you dearest.

Your Best Girl, Mom

Happy Easter Day.

****END OF MARCH****

Chapter Seven

April 1945

Krewstown Road: "Every time you went out you took a rope and shovel."

Wartime Letters Written from Mother to Son

Easter Sunday April 1, 1945   Pop fooled Joe, Rog and me as usual.

Dearest Son,

Here it is mid-afternoon of a beautiful Easter day. Got just this far...when in come the Boyds and another lady and little boy. I made two lemon meringue pies and Dick saw them on top of the icebox. So I guess you know I cut one. They have just gone and so here I am for our little chat. Your sweetheart came over last night and did my hair. Just as she got here, we had a rainstorm. Lightning blew out the lights and blew the kitchen bulb and the big one in the dining room. It didn't last long.

I made a lunch for Dot. Roger went up, but he is home here now. No one is home there he said. He looked so nice in his new suit today. Dad and he went to church with me. I wore my black coat, but it got real hot. We have a fire going and we are cooked.

I had on a big pot of vegetable soup and all the extra trimmings. Aunt Lilly was supposed to come up to the church. But I haven't seen or heard from her yet.

Little Dick weighs about 200 pounds or more. He sure is a size. Dad bought me a beautiful corsage, one white carnation surrounded with lavender sweet peas, just went with my hat. Dear old Dad knows his stuff. Aunt Dot was to come up, but she is not here yet. Well, "money makes the mare go", and so I will spend a lazy evening. Joe has gone. They cut most of the grass behind the barn and sure are getting things done up nicely.

I heard Admiral Nimitz's message on this Easter morn. Dad and I are wondering if you were in that mass of 1400 ships in the China Sea. We both said special Easter prayers.

The Home Fires

Well dearest, it's now 7 o'clock. I guess Dot won't walk over now. She got a new powder blue suit. We asked her about getting her picture taken. She has hers taken and awaiting to send to you.

Since I started this letter, I had a house full of company again. Howard and Pearl Baldy and Marge and her husband Joe and the two babies. The oldest boy is sure a picture. Marge is sure beautiful.

I have been sick with a terrible cold like when you went to Bainbridge. I stood outside gabbing when they were plowing the ground. I guess that's where I caught it. It's 85 degrees here in the house and I am sure cooked.

We had two letters Saturday. One written the 21st and one V to brother. I don't know any news. Bill Baldy is back with Patton's 3rd Division after being in the hospital 100 days. That's over three months. He has since been in Holland, Belgium and now Germany.

Well dearest, I hope you can fix up the Easter baskets next year and all the world has peace. My darling on this Blessed Easter, a big hug, and all our love, and God watch and guide you.

Dearest my love,

Mom & All

The 5 calls from California were $71.84 and the other two were $21.00.

Wartime Letters Written from Mother to Son

Monday April 2, 1945 (V-Mail)

Dearest Son Edwin C. Price, 246, 92, 54.

This is the first V-Mail I have ever written to you and I got this off the table in church yesterday, Easter Sunday. I did not know the printing was on it until I opened it just now. It is raining a soft spring rain after a most beautiful warm Easter Sunday.

I have looked over the morning papers and done the usual work. It's now nearly eleven and I have my second cup of coffee beside me for our little chat for the day, in hopes this letter reaches you quicker.

Dearest, the papers have plenty of news of Pacific doings. Be brave. Dad and I are beside you, helping you, so do your best. God stands guide and your brother helps us too. Do all in your power. Be brave. Mom smoothes your face.

Call on her to wipe your brow and love you forever. My darling, I love you forever.

Mother

Monday April 2, 1945

Dearest Son,

Now you see I wrote you every day in March and numbered the letters, so you should have 31 letters for March. I will start to number them now for April so you can keep track of them when you open them. Also, I wrote my first V-mail letter to you this morning. I won't number them, but will slip in an extra

The Home Fires

one now and then in hope you do get them. I will be so happy when I get the word that you are getting my mail, because ten days sure is a long wait. But, anything pleases me. You don't need to write anything. All you need say is Dad, Mother, and I know you are okay. But war is Hell. Dad and I are listening and reading so we are satisfied not to hear anything mentioned. "No news is good news."

Well dearest, I write so much that I know nothing of interest. Dot did not get down Easter Sunday as she promised. But you know dear, I understand all young people.

I made a kitchen fire again, because we are having a fine, spring rain. Like I told you yesterday, I have a real bad cold and can't "talk", all in my voice box. Nutsie Ems had it so bad and then I got it.

We read in the paper that when Germany's defeat is officially announced, six sirens will blast at 5 second intervals and three hours of celebration will follow in Independence Square. If the sirens sound after 7 PM, it will be celebrated the next day at 11 AM. So I said, 'Well Nutsie, I would love and kiss you if they would only blow now.' I said I have a sore throat, but I would hug you any way. He said, 'Mrs. Price, I wouldn't mind. It would be worth getting a sore throat from you if they would only blow this minute.' We both had tears in our eyes.

I feel you so close to me this day, darling. I am with you in this tense and troubled time. God speaks to us, so keep the faith. God has a mansion in the sky and I trust you to Him. So have a little talk with the Lord and I know then that "All is well"; and comfort us both. Now stand on the step and tell me how short I am. And let me smooth your face, and then kiss me. I know you can "go on". Stand the heat. The American flag is my pride and the Star in my window my pride. God Bless you All. Kiss, love, hug.

Well Darling,

Our little chat each day is a comfort because I can tell you some of the things in my heart. I am going to rest all afternoon, if I can, on the parlor couch. I wish you could put the Vicks on me.

A lady was here to see me yesterday, Easter Sunday, and she said she had gone to the movies to see Fibber McGee and Molly. When she came home, her neighbor lady was at the door and she said, 'Sally, come in quick; but sit down first, I have a shock for you, but it's a pleasant one.' She said, 'In the kitchen, someone wants to see you.' Her son, home from three years in New Guinea, etc. All she said was Charles, Charles. She sure was surprised as she didn't even know he was coming home. I would like to see you home too, but as you are only a new one, I guess I must wait my turn.

Dearest, I will finish this up later. Maybe there will be some mail.

Darling, there were 3 letters today, love. Am I glad. One has the card in it. Tell your buddy, he shall be my boy too and I shall pray special for him every night and day. I am so glad you got assigned to a ship. I hope and pray for you all. I have a cold, but all is well. God is your guide. I am beside you. So are Dad and all.

Mommy hugs her sailor boy.

Monday April 2, 1945 (V-Mail)

Dearest Son Edwin,

I sure hope you get my mail. This makes two V-Mails and one regular one today. Roger just brought three letters. That makes 18 in all so far including the one with the card enclosed.

Dearest, I hear Ed Baker is in Italy. Edwin Bissinger is still in England. Bill Long is in the Pacific area and still on the same ship. Uncle John is at New Caledonia. There is no more news of Byron.

D. Price got locked up for disorderly conduct in Rhawn Street Drug Store.

Dot was here Saturday night and did my hair. John Ems is at New York. He had 38,000 cases of Scotch whiskey and was drunk all the way home.

Dearest, I wrote you 31 letters or more in March, one every day. Dad is home on Sunday. We went to church on Easter. The car is in Bender's two weeks now. Your telephone bill was $71.84. Maybe you can help us out a little with a money order. What about your bonds? We have none as of yet. Edwin Bissinger never writes Aunt Lilly. Dearest, I am glad you have good ship mates.

Love,

Mother & All

Tuesday, April 3rd, 1945

Dearest Son,

It's nearing 5, and just the time I am looking for you coming round the bend doing 50 miles per hour, but no Edwin. "Now Mom, you're crazy. I was comin' in slow, you only think it looks like fifty," and the dust going towards

Russell's in clouds.

Well, here I am for our little chat. I did not hear Sardi's or Listening Post. I just had tuned in when Aunt Lilly called. While talking to her, the kitchen door opened and in came Aunt Dink, all in blue, like the blue birds. The violets are in bloom across the railroad, so Aunt Dink said. The daffodils are yellow on the hill. By Sunday, the lilacs will be in bloom. So you know, this is the earliest ever known since I came to the farm. I have been here 20 years this June. Aunt Dink sure came on a good day. I have this cold and spirits low. We sure did gab, gab. We cried and laughed and I made a date with her, Aunt Dot, Akie's mother, and Mary O'Connell to go see A Tree Grows in Brooklyn at the Fox. I will try to arrange it.

Aunt Dink said that Sissy and Timmy went to Atlantic City for Easter on Saturday and Jeano (Fats), Bert, Wilson and George will go Sunday morning. They were all to sleep at Aunt Dink's. Jeano said he would sleep at home because he had to go to early Mass with his Mom and Dad. So the other two boys got in bed with George. Finally, Bert got up and went down on the couch. He said he got so cold that he put his overcoat on and piled the sofa cushions on top of himself and still he was cold. It got cold in the night. Aunt Dink said, "You dumb bugger, there's 17 coats hanging out in the shed and kitchen". She made them a good Easter breakfast. It got so cold here that Dad started the heater at 6 AM because I was sick with this cold. By Sunday noon, we were opening the front and back doors.

Along about 2:30 AM Jeano called George and Bert. George went in to Aunt Dink and called her. She said, what do you want George? He said, come on Dink. Get the Flag. Jeano said it came in over the radio, the war is over. (Aunt Dink has the American Flag to raise on the pole. No matter what the day or hour, all the people will run to her yard and celebrate.) So Aunt Dink jumps out of bed, grabbing her shoes and house coat. All the lamps get lit and Jeano hollers, "April Fool". Those boys were fit to be tied. They lifted up the window, and they were grabbing their pants and shoes. They said, you S.B.! We will go off to Atlantic City now and leave you. You better go to Mass.

Dad fixed the telephone and called Joe up from the field and said Baldwin wanted him. I was upstairs. Dad hid in the radio room. Joe comes in, Hello, Hello, Hello? I yelled April Fool. Was he mad! Dad laughed so much. He fooled me four times. I said you always got me out of bed. He said, I would have, but I knew you were sick.

Well dearest, the coffee and potatoes are cooking. It's so quiet here. All you can hear is this pen scratching. It rained a gentle rain all night. Everything is so green and beautiful looking. Mrs. Spence called up to see how I was. Rog has gone to see Uncle Bill. He is not back yet. He wants to buy 25 baby chicks, 6 weeks old, 25 cents apiece. So he went to see his pal. Dad took your letters down for Clarence to read. He shed real tears when he read where you said we would have a little home with a white fence. He loves you so much. He said, "I'll get along. All I want is my boy." And so, may God keep you safe.

Mother & All

Tuesday, April 3, 1945 (V-Mail)

Dearest Son Edwin,

I just finished writing you our usual daily chat letter. In hopes that these will reach you first, you know that I write you every day. As I told you so often, I sent 31 letters in March, one for each day and every one with eight cent airmail stamps. I shall put 6 cents on these in hopes they may reach you and trust that you are well. I am getting your mail. I had three lots.

Roger was up to see Uncle Bill. I told you in the letter I just wrote. He got a ten spot so I guess he will get the 25 chickens. I also told you Aunt Dink spent the day with me.

Well my darling, Joe is here. Dad is coming. Bill W. is down at the end plowing for the Victory garden.

We have everything in order and are working hard. My cold is getting better. I do hope you are getting my mail. Aunt Lilly wrote you today. Everyone sends love and best wishes to you, my sailor son.

Love,

Mom & All

Wednesday, April 4, 1945   I write you everyday. love, Mom

Dearest Son Edwin,

It's 11:30. Sardi's is just over. I only listened to part of it. After a high of 76 degrees on Monday, the drop is down to 40 degrees. I just got through making a fire in the heater and fixing up the kitchen. We have about two days supply of coal for the heater. I will burn up the trash and a little wood on chilly days and "fence me in the dining room and kitchen".

Bill Wenker plowed up the Victory garden plot last night, but I guess Eddie won't push the wheel hoe this year for him. He asked Dad about you last night as Dad took a walk to the mailbox to get out a wasps' nest. I asked Dad, 'Will they come back?' He said, 'Well some of them won't!' So, he was talking to Bill. You see we got plowed a little early and that means working it over as we have had several rains. Ever since Sunday it has been cold and mean at night. But Dad has been doing fine with the hot seedbed. All is coming up, tomatoes, peppers, salad, celery, eggplant, cabbage and some flower seed. Have the rhubarb all cleaned and hoed and Dad put some fertilizer on it Sunday night and spread the onion sets out for planting. Now Joe, Dad and Rog must get busy to put the chicken wire up for a fence. Dad is planning on putting passion flower vines all along the chicken fence and holly hocks behind the tool shed. He has it all cleaned up back there. Joe started a big round flowerbed, but now I am thinking he will just have to let it go.

Rog is buying 30 chickens and I sure am happy for that. Maybe we will have the chickens ready for the pot. Rog said, no, I am going to raise pigeons so I can have some for the pot when my brother gets home.

Well darling, the day is dark and dreary and I get so lonesome. So here is the time for our little chat. My cold is getting better. I don't know any new news. Like you say, all I know is hello and so long. I sure would like to paint and get new oil cloth for the kitchen and tear up the rooms and refix. But, my hands are tied. "Money makes the mare go." I guess no matter what income I have, like everyone else, it's never enough. But I would always make a sacrifice when it comes to those I love. Dad and I do love you. And like Aunt Dink said. She gets defiant when she looks at Byron's picture. He was young and never knew anything about life. Dad and I always knew you would have lots to learn about the world. We saw some and I read plenty and so I always wanted to keep you my baby. It's a long hard struggle once you start out on your own. Dad and I would do all in our power for you. We did not want to burden you before you knew what life was all about. You can feel free to go with whoever you please; that is the best way. Then, when you are ready to settle down, you will not be restless. You will know who you want. So my dear, when peace is here, we will all be happy again. I will write a V-mail later today, but for now must hurry along to finish up.

All my love,

Joe, Dad, Rog, Mom

Wednesday, April 4, 1945 (V-Mail)

Dearest Son,

I write you a V-Mail and a regular letter every day and also send them with air mail stamps in hopes you get some mail. I worry so much about you not getting any mail, that I have been repeating the news over and over hoping that by this time you surely have had some news from us. We are all well except I told you that I had a cold over Easter, but we went to church happy as we had a letter on Saturday from you. We all looked nice. As usual, Mom never let the crows set on us or any special occasion, did I? I sleeked your hair and I picked you nice ties. We went off and Dad said, 'Fine holiday.' We weren't all four in church. I think of you all the time. So does Dad. The garden looks green and beautiful. We have a new flower bed with pansy plants and tulips. All is well.

All our love,

Mom

Wednesday, April 4th, 1945

Second No. 4 letter today. Darling, to keep the letters straight, so you can read them in order, I am numbering all I write the same day with the same number. I wrote one regular one and a V-mail already today, but that was this morning.

The Home Fires

So now, Rog is home from school and brought March 25 & 26 letters and one air mail from you. I was so happy and so glad to hear from you. Still my baby has no mail, but dear, I sure have kept this pen busy. I wrote 31 letters to you in March, not counting the Easter card and extras I slipped in. Now dearest, I have written three letters a day since I had your U.S.S.H. address, dear. I know Dad will be so happy. If only you could send us some money, especially by April 24, so we can pay the telephone bill of $71.84 for 5 California calls. The other 2 were $21.82. Dear, the last call was $15.00 without the tax. But somehow we will pull through.

I am so glad to hear you have a good boss. I know that if you cooperate and be a good boy, that all will be well. Dad and I are so proud of you. This is a wonderful chance and start for you.

My dear son, no Mother or Dad anywhere can ever do any more for their boys than we have tried. We know you came from a good clean home and you wouldn't be satisfied with food anywhere in the world. No one ever made pot pie, meat pie, cherry pie, hot salad or brown cake like my own Mom. You know, for twenty years I used to send the ingredients to my own Mom to mix up the brown cake for Christmas. I can cook to perfection. Grandma Price showed me how to make a 4 quart rice pudding and it tastes like the best ice cream when it comes out of our wonderful ice box. Grandpa Price raised hogs of 400 pounds with 60 pound hind legs of ham. And now with this war to go peddling for a couple of fatty pork chops when I often saw Dad and you eat 16. I bought $5 worth of eggs for Easter and two gallons of vegetable soup. It's all gone. I have a smoked butt on cooking, coleslaw with homemade dressing; Dad's favorite. All the fellows want to know is what in the name of heaven we did with the eggs. Dad and Roger ate a dozen before they went to bed last night, after a full course supper. I gave the fellow who plowed the ground a pint jar of green tomato relish. I know it is good. I made so much of it. The next morning, he ran to the fence to Dad and said,

"My God, Price, get your wife to write out that recipe for my wife. She wants to make some of that relish right away. It's the best we ever tasted." So I said to Dad, the darn fool doesn't even know what it was made from. Where would she, in South Philadelphia get green tomatoes now to make Green Tomato Pickle? But that's the modern woman.

Now dear, you sure have set your heart on pictures. I told you Dot has hers taken awaiting your word. The pictures are so costly that at present we have all we can do to keep going. The car has been in Bender's garage two weeks now. Dad will write you the details. I did not get any bonds and do not know how much you have allotted monthly for them. Also, we have two papers stating you took out insurance and named us each as beneficiary. Is that supposed to be the policy? It does not say policy. Dear, you should have all these things looked after because of the beats of today. You know how they got Dad and me on the pump. There are so many legal technicalities that the poor man never has a chance.

Now darling, I hope you are well. Take care of yourself, your feet and all personal things. Always remember what I told you. Be satisfied. God put you in the station you are wanted in most. Be proud of Uncle Sam. All kinds make a world and a good Dad welcomes you home and loves you. Give your pal a kiss for me and tell him I said to take care of each other and so all is well.

Mother

Thursday, April 5th, 1945

Good Morning Son,

I am here with you for our little daily chat. Rog has just left. Brownie is growling. It's a cold, dreary, heavy, rainy day. But we have had such unseasonably warm weather that everything is green. They have all the grass cut; except the part from the path over towards the goat house. Joe got down on his knees and cut with the sickle. It's a foot high and so beautiful and green. We should have "Old Topsy" or Bill Goat in there. He would soon chew it off. The flowering almond bushes outside the kitchen window are in full bloom. You know they never bloom until May and then we always have that three day Northeaster. You know where I always tell you the same story. A storm from the northeast is not fit for man nor beast. Well, enough about the weather. It just puts me out of gear. I used to love a rainstorm; I could make a roaring fire to dry out things and then mother got to work on the cooking.

This is the time for the new asparagus. Pop got three handfuls. I saw a fat fellow yesterday. To me, it looked like Mike Rowley in a sailor's outfit. He came all along the bank clear up to the lilac row. So when Dad was tramping around on his way in from work, I sent Rog to call him. He said why didn't you chase him? So I said, 'Well Dad, he had on a sailor uniform and he is welcome to anything that grows.' Dad said he guessed it was that fat Italian man from South Philadelphia, as Mike Rowley is in the Pacific.

Bob Underwood came up on the same trolley as Dad last night. He got off at his home street. He never even spoke to Dad. So Dad said he didn't bother. Dad is so mad. Of course, I don't know what to think. You told me about sending a letter. Dot told me Saturday night she had a most beautiful letter from you and she was going to bring it over Easter Sunday for me to read and to see her new powder blue suit. Same color as that top coat she has. Well, I didn't see or hear from her since. I am always so glad and so happy for her to do my hair. I offered to pay for it, but she will not take it. I would still have all the trouble of getting ready for Frankford and it would not be done any better. Dad knows that Bob is there a good many nights and we have seen Dot out in the car. Dad said that she is not being true to you; but of course, you are not her boss yet. But Dot said to me Saturday night that she turned her ring around on her finger. She said, 'Ed said I wouldn't keep this ring on when he gave it to me.' Then she said, 'I'll keep it forever.' I felt so happy in my heart; because I knew the understanding you and I had about the ring. Now I guess I should not tell you all this, but you are a part of me, and what concerns you is my share too.

You and I always had a little chat now and then. Now I am in my velvet robe, hair in papers, and I like to have my coffee and my talk with you or my day is not started right. I was going to wash out a few fancies on Tuesday, but Aunt Dink came, so they are still on the chair. I guess they will keep. I lay in bed Easter morning thinking of all the past ones and how Dad went to Mayfair and got Besser's up to get you a bigger suit. And how on the first day of April, I stood you on the kitchen chair by the window and dressed you all up and I taught you the poem out of the Nursery book of Verse. Do you remember how you got up in Assembly and said it?

On the First Day of April.

Alone, Alone, I went into the woods and sat on a stone.

I sat on a broad stone, and sang to the birds.

The tune was God's making, but I made the words.

Alone, Alone, Mother I love you, but I'm not alone.

The birds and the bees,

the flowers and trees

are all about me and soon I see my Home.

The water and sea

the ship and me are not alone.

My mother's love follows me.

I kept adding all sorts of verses to it, and as you wrote, you were sitting on your bunk thinking of us at home. So you see, God sends visions to a mother's heart. She lives always in memories of happy or sad times and she can feel your presence.

You wrote, hold the kiss tight. You see it was Easter Sunday and you said, here it was Saturday night and you wondered if I was alone and if Dad was in Frankford. Now I see I have made a mistake because it was Palm Sunday when you were thinking so hard of home. I wrote you I had Dot here on Easter eve and we had the thunderstorm. The eve before Palm Sunday, when you were wondering if I was alone, I wrote you that I was in Frankford. I had $100 in my purse. We had supper in Rialto. Dad was just as simple with the girls as ever. Dad had two, big carry all bags. Mom was loaded down with bundles. Dad & Joe went into Ewald's to get a short one. Me, you know, hurrry, hurry. I said, 'To hell with this lugging. My feet hurt.' Pop dashed back in to get two bottles of beer. I sailed across Frankford Avenue. A taxi came out of Paul Street. I hailed him before Dad got across. I threw in the bundles. Joe threw the beer on the floor and home we came, $1.45. I gave him $1.75. I had no change. It was worth it. But that bastard car of ours, we never have it when we need it. Easter Sunday, I was so sick. I had to walk to church. I nearly passed out last night when Dad gave me the V-Mail letter to read that he wrote for you and it said it was costing $150 for the repair job. I said, 'Dad, it's just as always never spend a nickel on the house, but the Goddamn barn or horses or cars or piles of shit that cost hundreds or the goddamn telephone bill, or any other bill; I am going to worry no longer.'

I guess you will say, Mother, but dear, I could write volumes. If you and Dad don't make the effort for the home, what can I do? This winter has sure turned my hair gray. I see the white lilacs are out over the outhouse. All I look forward to is the sunshine, spring, and your return. When I see the birds coming back, I say to myself, the fledglings will come back to the home nest. So long for now, darling.

All is well.

Love,

Mother

Letter No. 5 Second Part
Thursday Afternoon, April 5th, 1945

Dearest Son,

It has rained and blown all the day. I have the home fires burning and I guess you are wishing for a cool breeze. I waited to start house cleaning this week. As usual, it is some kind of thing. I did hope to start in Monday, but I just could not carry two gallons of Kemtone. So I must wait until we get the car, which we expect this weekend.

I just called Aunt Lilly. She is almost through hers, well in fact, she is just finished. She did all of her upstairs. Fred is still away. Edwin, Granny just called me up. She has the house in her name, and is finishing it all through with paper and paint. She expects to be in it in two weeks. She is working her head off and praying that God will let her live in it. She said she is going to make a will and leave it to Charlie. He has seven children and needs help. So now you see, Aunt Minnie, Aunt Clara, Uncle Bob have their own homes and Uncle Bill has three. That leaves just us, and Uncle John. So you better get busy. Well darling, she said Al gave her flowers. Some other guy bought Clara flowers, but Sam Thomas never gives her a nickel. If you don't buy flowers for your sweetheart, some other fellow will. Always keep that in mind. The way to keep love in bloom is with flowers. I always told you that you can't catch flies with vinegar. Use sugar. And so it is with women. They fall for sweet words. All women are not alike. I am cold and proud. But I like kind words. Being of the old-fashioned type, you can't buy me. One hundred dollar notes, candy and food don't gloss over the mean disposition or selfish way of some people. My Dad said to be a one man woman and so I tried to always be that. I had plenty of temptation. Sweethearts and friends are different. So my dear, are my boys to me, all my world. I have seen the good and bad of life. I am content and happy with Dad, you and Rog. That's all that counts in this world, the ones we love.

Your Mom

Thursday, April 5, 1945 (V-Mail)

Dearest Son,

I sent off two regular letters and now this in hopes that it reaches you first. As you know, I write you every day and hope by this time you have heard from home.

I wrote to Uncle John today and told him the day's news. Pennsylvania miners are on strike and a Louisiana town is flooded, not to say anything about the black market. I am sure glad one guy got it. It was the man Granny worked for. You met him last summer the day Pop ran out of gas. His wife bought a dining room suit for $850 and new rugs. I said, yes, the German Polish can buy it because he is cheating the people. I told Dad last night how he sold a big steak to a woman for no red points. Tonight's Bulletin says Judge Welsh gave him 32 days in jail and fined him $250. He got off a little easier than our meat man. I hope they get them all. They are making a fortune and we poor people got to like it and fight to live.

Love,

Mother

Friday, April 6th, 1945

Dearest Son Edwin,

Well son, as usual, I am just about through the morning routine. I still have plenty to do and I am also thinking of you. I put a big wash out. I didn't have any soap flakes or powder and with our hard water here, it sure was difficult to use P. & G., which is the only soap I could ever get any results from. After such warm weather, all the white lilacs out, the flowering almond, and the daffodils. Last night, the weatherman predicted frost for tonight. I have the fires going full and just am not comfortable because the house gets damp after two days of high wind and rain. The old grandpops and grannies are sure right about the weather. March came in like a lion and goes out like a lamb or just turned the other way. That's what it sure did do. The full moon also governs the month's weather, and that was true.

The Home Fires

Dad said if the frost comes tonight, goodbye all the flowers behind the barn. Rog has a flower bed made between the edge of the hedge and the crooked maple tree near the iron post where I put the clothes line. He made it round, then drew a cross through it and put daffodils on the cross parts and pansies in between. It looks very nice. The lilacs will even be too early for Mother's Day, the 2nd Sunday in May. They are ready to sell for this Sunday when Rog hopes to sell a few. He got some boards from Baldwin's. They are going to put up the wire from the barn to the goat house for a chicken yard. It costs $25 for a hundred 6 week old chicks. Rog ordered 32. That was all he had money for after he ordered the feed. He expects the baker to bring the chickens today. He took the crate on Wednesday. I sure hope we have luck with them. Pop said, "Are you keeping the pigeons?" He said, "Sure, so I can get Mom to make that pot of soup for Ed."

I am not half done my work yet, as Friday is a busy day, and yet I wanted my second cup of coffee and our little chat. The only thing is it takes so long for you to answer me back. "Mom, you're crazy. I wasn't doin' 50. Only looks like it to you."

Ted Malone said a fellow got him to the airport with military escort in a jeep, 30 seconds before the plane took off for home. Ted said, America. He closed his eyes after two blocks. God Bless all the boys. Come on home and make all the villagers take notice that from now on, the boys will run America. Dear Dad and I can eat scrapple and I can continue to scrub and wipe because Dad is still tops, an honest, good, hardworking farmer.

Mr. Delheim has to set 32 days in jail and pay a $250 fine. I said that isn't half punishment enough. The lizards and bugs and sweat won't crawl on him and he won't sleep in a hole in the ground. I only wish he had to stay in jail as long as my poor brother has to stay in the jungles and as long as you have to sweat in a ship hold. But they can have their steaks and chops and

$850 for a dining room suit and all new summer rugs. Whenever I see them I won't forget. I'll say, what good is all that when you are a black market traitor to our sons and brothers and nephews and cousins. I haven't had a piece of butter in the house since you were home. It's now 26 red points. And I love butter. But dear, I often drank black coffee and had dry bread with salt on it. I also had great big gobs of homemade butter and the thickest of cream. No matter. We live as honest, upright Christians and God will be good to us. I thank God every day. Never be lonely or homesick. I often told you that. Look at the stars. Pick out one that you think Grandpop sits on. And say, 'Grandpop, I am doing my best.' Grandpop will say, "Old Nut". Grandpop's little darlin', honey. Are you warm enough? And then you will know that love never fails. It's always beside and near you. You can feel it no matter what others do to you. You have our love, our thoughts, and we always understand. So forget any hard knocks you may get and know your Mom will smooth them away and love you forever and ever. I hope you like the pictures I sent you. Hope you are getting mail. And so darling, I must run along now. It's 11 o'clock.

Cheerio,

Mom & All

Friday, April 6, 1945 (V-Mail)

Dearest Son,

Now it's evening and Dad, as usual, is listening to the Lone Ranger. Joe is doing the dishes. So, here I am. I told you in my regular letter all the news I know. Johnny Ems was home on Wednesday. Juanita left yesterday. Old Mr. Ems is pretty bad. He is bedridden. Dr. Getty has been there 3 or 4 times this week. It's old age. I guess Mrs. Ems has her hands full.

Well dearest, Rog was so disappointed. The chickens are all roosters, so we are getting them anyway for the table and it's a cheap buy at that. I was paying Charlie S. $5.00 for two hens and now we are getting 32 roosters for $8.00. I will shine cooking those, so hurry home. Mom will save some to roast for you. Well dearest, I don't know anything. The letter with the pictures came back for 4 more cents, so I am sending it in the same mail as this. Cheerio.

All our love,

Mom & All

Saturday, April 7, 1945

My Darling,

Oh! My dearest, if only you are getting our mail. Pop wrote you and I am writing you every day. Now, today here at home it's a lovely spring day. The lilacs are in bloom and everything is green and beautiful and there is no sailor boy to say, "Mom make me something to eat." I just finished up our lunch dishes and Rog is scrubbing the kitchen. I am all in. We were outside for about two hours. We dug all up behind the house here and I planted a row of that striped grass and some ragged robins; and it is tough on me. I can't work outside any more. Well, I see a truck up at the Club. Looks like somebody moving in. Darling, it's nearly 2 o'clock and I guess Joe will soon be home.

I still have some wash to take in off the line. I don't get the wash back until Friday afternoon. That makes a lot of weekend work. I cleaned all the scraps out of the ice box. I got two big mackerel to bake for Sunday and new potatoes and dandelions. Pop wanted dandelions, but we can't put a bacon dressing on them. We can't get bacon. Things are getting a little tight. I sent the last three bonds in this morning to help pay the telephone, $71.84. Edwin B. got three bonds this week, which makes $550 in bonds in two years. Dad said we would save anything you send home. We need your help so badly, but we want you to save. As yet, we have no bonds from you. Dearest darling, I trust you and know you are doing your best. All my heart's motherly love goes out to you. I hold you close. I got the new record today. It's wonderful, my baby. I love you.

Mom

Saturday, April 7, 1945 (V-Mail)

My Dearest Son,

My heart aches for you because you are not getting any mail as your letter of March 27th states you have not had any as yet. Now my darling, in hope everyday that you surely have some mail, I tell you the same thing over and over. All is well. All is well, darling. I love you so much and I pray to God every day to speed some word to you. I sent you 31 letters in March besides all the extras I tucked in and it's a week today since I have been sending V-Air mail. I sent you stamps and pictures.

Dot was over and we are all doing fine.; Joe the dishes, Rog the kitchen and Mom a lady.

My dearest baby, all my love,

Mom

The Home Fires

Sunday, April 8, 1945

Dearest Son,

It's the most beautiful day and the lilac row is one picture, just in bloom. I went to church, walked each way. The car is supposed to be done tomorrow night. Dad got the onion sets in, peas, string beans, spinach, beets, salad, and they worked hard all day. The place sure looks clean and nice. They took the gas pump out. So things look kind of bare around.

Darling, Mrs. Tumbelston has gotten ever so much better since David got home. The Pastor said this morning that she will soon be able to come home. I am so glad because she was always so nice to me. This war sure does strange things to people. I know that everyone will be glad when it's over.

My darling, you have been on my mind so much because the last letter I had so far was written on the 27th of March and you still say you had no mail. I prayed for you and all today. I feel so much better when I know you have had mail. I sure have not failed you dearest. I have told you every item of news. I ask Rog, Carl, Dad, Joe, of any news I can write the boy. You know I am not out and I don't hear any news. Rog saw Dot today and Mrs. Ems, but don't know any news. He helped wheel hoe; he covered and made hills.

Dearest, we had our supper. Not too much. There was no one to cook for. A little for Dad and a little for Rog, and Joe is out to the movies. My cold is nearly better, but I don't feel extra. Tonight when I hear Mediation Board, I am going to bed. Pop is out putting the sash back on. Rog is doing his lessons and I haven't heard anyone. I didn't get to see A Tree Grows in Brooklyn. Tomorrow, I hope to start spring house cleaning. So I will say, all our love, all our hopes. I am so happy you write when you can. As ever, my love and prayers for you and all. Your dear old mother smoothes your face.

Love,

Mom

Sunday, April 8, 1945

Dearest Son,

Two letters today and every day for a week. You will have a book to read when I get through as I wrote you so many letters. I pray that by this time you will surely have some mail from home. Dad wrote you the other night and said he would write once a week. My dearest, I can't write when the radio is going. Bill Baldy is with Patton's Army and Uncle John is still at the same place. Bill is like you, on the move, but still on the Starr. So, my dear, all is well. Lessons and farm are all I know. The weather is perfect today and I hope you are well. Pop is having a fight with the cat. Cheerio.

Love,

Mom

Monday, April 9th, 1945

Dearest Son,

Here I am for a few lines. I am behind today for our little chat. It's a beautiful day here at home with all the beauty of spring about. It fairly takes your breath away. From here to Frankford is God's own country with the azalea, tulips, and all the colors of the rainbow. I got the Kemtone, but I didn't carry it home. They are going to deliver it on Thursday, so I got that settled. And darling, Meet me in St. Louis, meet me at the fair. I thought of it ever since and I can't get the tune out of my mind. I thought of you all the while I was seeing it. I kept remembering Home in Indiana, but St. Louis has lots of singing and dancing in it. Clang, Clang went the trolley song. It was sure lovely. I am tired and all in. Joe is doing the dishes. Pop is going out to Bender's.

Here is some news. As many scrapes as you got into, I never knew you to get licked. Roger sure looks pretty tonight. He came up to the railroad to meet me and I near passed out when I saw him. He has a big, thick, busted top lip, a fat nose, a lump on his forehead and a big bump by his ear. He said a fellow from Somerton is the one he got in the fight with. He said the boy was bigger and he fought outside the school yard before the bus left. He wouldn't tell me what the fight was about.

Roger got his chickens today and so that is all the news I know. I do hope and pray that you have some mail. All I do is think of you and hope and pray that you sure are well. My darling, I love you. I smooth your face and kiss you goodnight. So does Dad.

Your Mom and Dad

Tuesday, April 10, 1945

Dearest Darling,

It's another beautiful day here at home and just high noon. Had a bowl of your favorite potato soup and was thinking of you all the while I was eating all alone and listening to Gil Martin and the news, and saying he (you) never wanted to hear the news; and I am so eagerly listening to every word of the

Pacific news. I was thinking of the days when you worked on the farm and made $12.00 a week. Everyday we listened to that program of the Beer Barrel Polka and I thought my, how fast he grew. I used to wish that your brother was more your age. But this morning and last night, I said to him that I am so glad, now, you are not old enough and yet I remembered what Mrs. Hermann said that Saturday we walked down the lane with her. You'll be in it before it's over, you wait. Then I'll tell you what I think of God. I often think how sure I felt that it would be over before you had to go.

Darling, fate plays funny tricks on our lives. I often used to wish for such a day when I would be alone. But no Grandpop, no Edwin, no Uncle Bill, it's funny how life goes. Even to Uncle Bill, who came in for over 20 years. Wars are terrible. They not only take our sons, but separate families through work and many other things.

I thought I heard kittens. I got up to look, but Lizzie Bit is curled up on the parlor sofa. I smacked her off the middle of your bed this morning. Yesterday, after I was out to the Circle to see Meet Me in St. Louis, I came home and the dog had the spreads all torn up on all the beds. Dad said you should love him because he is hunting for you. Thinks maybe you are sick. Well I said, "If I was, what could the dog do?" Dad loves that dog and cat. He is so pleased to think the dog takes such good care of me.

The lilacs have the house smelling so nice. I took down the curtains in my room, washed down all the paints, scrubbed the floor, turned the carpets around, washed the windows, all the pictures on the wall and brushed the wall down. So that is the house cleaned. I turned the bed between the windows and I will try to finish up the upstairs this week. I am so tired now, so I came for a drink of coffee. I have the curtains washed, so I thought I would have my usual chat with my baby and drink my coffee and rest up. I planted one small passion vine in a pot to give to Mrs. Rupert. Next Sunday,

I hope to get up to the cemetery.

On April 15th, it would have been my Dad's seventieth birthday. The poor old dear died too soon, before he had a chance to enjoy life. Granny expects to get into her new home by two weeks. Her address is Mrs. Minnie M. Long, 320 Fremont Street, Kensington, Philadelphia. She got a bedroom suit for $185. Uncle Bob and Aunt Dink were to wallpaper last Saturday. Aunt Dot quit her job. I haven't heard the details.

Well son, you should have seen Roger. He looks pretty. I said, 'Well Edwin got in a fight when he left the country. Said he had a busted lip.' What next? Me, Dad, or Joe, always three in a row. Well dearest, I hope you get my mail, hope you are well. Be good.

All my love. Kiss,

Mom

Tuesday, April 10, 1945 (V-Mail)

Dearest Darling Son,

I had a letter from you today written on April 2nd, the day after Easter. Yes, dear, I have answered all the questions you ask me in every letter. I hope you have had some mail by this time. I know you sure would have some reading to do. I sent you a picture of Rog and me taken before Easter. The letter I got today told me that you saw Meet Me In St. Louis. I told you in the letter I wrote you that I saw it yesterday all by myself. I can't get the tune out of my mind. Do you remember I sang it for you and Dot when you were home? I sure was happy to see such a nice picture. I like those kind.

Well, supper is nearly ready. All are home but Dad. He won't be happy when he hears the car is not done again tonight. He will write you all about it.

Dear, I hope you are well. Keep up for my sake. I love you.

All our love,

Mom

Wednesday, April 11th, 1945

Dearest Darling,

Yes. You are my Edwin and Dad is my Eddie. It sure breaks my heart to know you have waited so long for mail. But darling, you are close to me because I wrote every question you asked me. As a mother, I love you more than ever, because I can read some of the things I taught you are coming out in your letters. Like how you didn't like to go to church and that far away place where God stationed you, for reasons only known to Him, you knew your Mom and Dad felt you beside them, looking at your gold watch, and wondering when the pastor was going to shut up. You told me you said a prayer on Easter morn. Did you get to any church service? Dearest, you can pray no matter where you are.

My baby, I had a little accident. I was going out to the toilet and I had a plate with some gravy bread on it for the dog. Somehow I fell down. I, as usual, fell on my right knee. I always catch myself going and tore $1.25 stocking knee out. But worst of all, I twisted my left foot. I heard a bone crack. Dad and Joe ran and it took the two of them to get me up. I couldn't lean on my right knee. I had house cleaned my room. It took me five hours to scrub the paints and clean it. I was so proud at how nice it looked, but I was so tired. I laid down for a half hour before supper. We had a roast of beef, the first beef in months. It was fifty-five points. I had that in roasting, mashed potatoes, and the asparagus that Dad had gathered. I rested while the supper was cooking. Joe and Dad went right into the garden, so I did the dishes and I had to go to the toilet before I finished them. The pain was so bad. I said, 'Oh! Let me lay,' but I finally got in and I cried all night.

At 1 AM Dad got up and was putting on his shirt and tie. I said, Dad? He said, 'Yes?' I said, "Where are you going?" He said to work. Why? I said. It's only one o'clock. 'Oh,' he said. 'I thought I heard the alarm go off.' Then I fell asleep until the alarm went off and my foot felt a little better. This morning I soaked it in hot Epsom Salts. I can hardly step on it. It doesn't pain like it did, but I got sick over it. The cold I had seems to be going through me in my throat and ear, then in my nose and now in my back and bladder. Dad said, 'Old age creeping up.' Maybe.

I had planned to house clean your room "as if it needs it", but I'll give it the once over and take the curtains down. I may stain and varnish the floor. You tracked in white paint near the closet when you were white-walling your car tires. It dried on and left a white mark as big as a quarter. The closet and bureau I don't have to touch as I have all your things done except your leather lumber jacket. I tied that in a muslin bag and I put 10 boxes of camphor balls in the closet. I had put a new blue blanket on your bed last Saturday. I found two big moths on it. So I took it off and put it in moth balls in the box. I am going to take the rug up. It is a dull day today, so I am not doing anything. I'll get my kitchen done and all by Mother's Day I hope. I am going to Kemtone the kitchen. So I guess you know, same old mother, chasing dirt.

Here is some news, darling. I got three letters from you today, the last one written Easter and a Bond for $18.75 for you marked March. So I guess they will come in. I will put them safely away for your start. So dear, I hope you get a good one. I can't find that place on the map I have, but my brother is doing okay. All is well.

Love,

Dad, Rog, Joe, & Mother

The drawing of the sailor was swell.

Wednesday, April 11th, 1945 (V-Mail)

My Darling,

It's almost supper time. I had a nice rest. I washed and combed and I'm ready to serve Dad a good supper. I told you in my morning letter about hurting my foot. I kept soaking it all day and it feels lots better. I crawled around the dining room floor, as I could not stand on it. I stained the floor light oak and I will apply varnish over it. I want to get it all done by Mother's Day.

Now my darling, Bill is still in the Pacific on the same ship. Aunt Dink has an idea that Uncle John may be getting home. He is trying to tell her something about thirteen. She has not heard from him in two weeks.

My dearest, I am so proud of you. Do your best. I love you forever.

All our love,

Mom, Dad, brother & Joe

Thursday, April 12, 1945

Dearest Son,

I see by the date that tomorrow will be Friday the 13th and so beware of walking under ladders, etc. Dear, the white lilacs and the lavender ones are the prettiest I ever saw them. I had a letter from you today, written on April 3rd, so that is good work, and telling me that at last you had mail. Seven letters from Treasure Island, so you see dear, even though you told me not to mail the letters, I went right on sending them out every day, because I had hopes they would catch up with you somewhere.

I laughed at the drawing of the sailor mopping up. He has nothing on me. I mopped up the third floor today. I did a half ass job, as usual. But I still hauled out three bushel baskets.

At 4:30, I got all in. My leg above the knee is quite sore in the muscle and my foot is still sore. But, I can get around better on it today. The steps sure play havoc with me.

Dad and Rog are going to see Meet Me in St. Louis. Roger fooled around and Dad just called up to see if he is coming. He is meeting him at McAdams. We still haven't the car. Something went wrong after Bill had it all together. Dad and Rog will get supper at the usual place. I know they will enjoy it all. It's pay night. I told Dad I had your letter. Mrs. McAdams said William is getting home this week, the first in over a year. He is still at Ocean Side, California. Old Grandpop Ems is up out of bed again. Doc Getty was there four times last week; but he is out on the stand selling lilacs again.

I am waiting for Joe to come in for supper. I did the dining room floor. Everything is piled in the middle, so I will be glad when I get done. I got the

Kemtone today. I am so happy for that. I love to clean up. I need a new pen.

Well dearest, I haven't heard from Dot since the night before Easter. When I get my house cleaning done I will give her a call because she may come over and do my hair for Mother's Day. I hope so. Rog planted a big clump of daffodils and gave them to her for Easter.

The dog is better and the cat is ready for the second lot; so spring is here. I don't know anything new. Granny is busy getting her house in order. I haven't seen it yet. I am still cross. Aunt Dot just quit work, so I hear. Uncle Bob wants her home for the summer.

Well honey dear, do your best. Soon the Russians are to shake the hands of the Americans in triumph over Berlin. Twenty-seven years too late. They should have done that in War One. But we all live and learn. May God give us peace and security for your generation to come. I love you, I miss you, I am proud of you. And I will cook for you, as of old, my baby.

All our love,

Your old Mom, Dad, Brother, Joe, Dot and All

Thursday, April 12, 1945 (V-Mail)

My Dearest Son,

Well dear, I wrote you a few hours ago. Joe and I had supper. I had been so busy all day and so I said to Joe, 'Oh! I was going to listen to the news at 6, but I forgot.' So at 7, I thought, I'll listen to the Unseen Advisor, but I was ten minutes late. I tuned in and I couldn't get the Unseen Advisor. I thought, now what? I was ready to turn off when something caught my attention. Well, I tell you, dear, it sure was a shock to hear our President had died at 3:35 this afternoon at Warm Springs. I know that Dad will sure be shocked. I feel like I have lost a loved one. I know we have lost our greatest and best guide. Dearest, I feel very bad over it. I pray to God for all and Peace. My darling, I love you. Be brave and carry on.

All our love,

Mom

Friday, April 13th 1945

My darling,

Busy as a bee today and could keep going. Still have an hour's work to do, but Joe is in control of the kitchen, so I came to have my little chat with you. Yes, I am behind time today, but you know me, get started and want to get finished. I did all of the ceiling I could reach pale yellow, and all one side by the radio peach, and the back where your chair is. So I guess you know the kitchen looks like a new place. Joe is doing the ceiling over the stoves. By tomorrow night, I hope to have it all done. I washed the curtains in between. After I finished up at 4 o'clock, I ironed them. I am dead tired now. It's nearly 8 o'clock. Pop is out. I guess he's hunting asparagus. We got quite a nice lot. Dad knows where to look for it. This pen will hardly write.

Well dearest, I had three nice letters from you today. You are a good boy to write us. That means so much to us. My darling, I told you if you didn't get time to write and you just put Mom, Dad, then we know you are alive. My sweetheart, Pop is your pal, and all we pray for is the safe return of all the boys.

I listened today to the radio. I will write more tomorrow. I don't know any news. Dad has still not got the car and he will write you. Yes, we got the watch and your new record, and so all is well.

All the world mourns our beloved President. I put the flag and the U.S. Navy black hatband over the picture I have of the three together.

Love,

Mom

Sunday, April 15, 1945

Dearest Son,

Well it's 6 PM and it seems it's the first moment I had since last Wednesday. I worked so hard Friday and Saturday on the kitchen and still did not complete the job. On Saturday, I spent the entire day in the kitchen. I listened to the Roosevelt funeral procession from the time of the train's arrival until his casket was taken into the White House and I thought of everything. The stores were closed and Dad had to go to Uncle Bill's, so we had sausage for breakfast and hot dogs for dinner. Aunt Minnie came and she came again today. I took care of her two boys while she went to see her little girl, who is in the Frankford Hospital. We don't know what ails her. Something has happened to her legs, but it wasn't infantile. They have her under observation. Edwin, these pens are so bad, I simply cannot write.

Carl is here. He is such a nice boy. I can't get a word of news out of him. Old Grandpop is up and around. Mother and Dot are okay. Dot got your letter and that is as much as I know.

Pop will get the goat house turned around. Today, the place was such a busy place all day. I did not get to church. Ben Barber & John Keenan are working up the place all day with two tractors and cars coming in and out.

They would not let Aunt Minnie see Ruthie today because she cried so much last night and wouldn't eat any supper. Aunt Minnie looked in the door at her and it nearly broke her heart. I gave them coffee and dinner, so Elmer Irons took us up to the cemetery as today would have been my Dad's 70th birthday. It was hurry up, hurry up and so I fixed all the flowers here at home on the table for Roosevelt, Byron and Dad. I put their pictures on the small table and filled flowers and the American flag.

On Saturday, it was a glorious beautiful day and I worked and worked. I had a blanket out on the lawn. About 3 o'clock, it started to get dark and I went out and got the blanket in and man oh man, a 60 mile gale blew up, the trees bent and I was alone in the house. But the gardener down at the end was working and John and Ben and another man working here, so I sure was glad I wasn't on the place alone. The rain came in the pipe on the kitchen stove; black water ran in on the new paint. Dad is not through yet. I got a bite on cooking and so I will call it a day. Don't worry over anything, son. I love you. All is well. I love you, so does Dad.

Love,

Mom

Monday, April 16th and Tuesday, April 17th, 1945

Dearest Son,

Having had no stamps, I will combine Monday and Tuesday writing. Worse yet is the pen. When I get out to Frankford, I will surely buy myself a new one. Since last Octobe that old pen sure has written some letters.

Rog has to go to the post office this afternoon, but it's a cold, rainy day so it was put off. I started a fire in the heater a while ago, burning up the junk and trash around. Dad cleaned out the truck shed yesterday, burnt the old tires and all the junk. The flames went so high, he darn near had the telephone and electric wires on fire. Dad got the wire up for the chicken yard and two rows of salad and 2 of early cabbage in. This rain sure is good for them to start. Tonight, he was going to put in the dahlia roots, but I know he will be tired and won't work out in the rain.

Well, it's near five and I got on the usual pot of soup for Joe and me. Dad and Rog don't care for soup, so they get mashed potatoes, corn, and half smokes and a few odds and ends from yesterday.

Dear, I don't know any special news. All of America was in mourning. All the stores were closed and no commercials on the radio. Most of all the programs were canceled and only church music, organ music and sacred music played ever since our pilot's death. Dad and I were sure sorry about it. We put our whole faith in Roosevelt, but we hope and pray President Truman will carry us through; no apple selling. Roosevelt sure kept the wolf from our door after the wolf had gained entrance, he was hard to lick, but Roosevelt helped us conquer him and with God's guidance, our destiny will be Victory and bring those we love home. So darling, do your best. Mom knows what you go through.

Well darling, it's now 4 o'clock Tuesday and it's raining quite hard since all day Monday, and now most of Tuesday it has rained. There's nothing new I know about. I still have only one stamp so I will send a V-mail out by Dad and keep this letter until Rog gets stamps.

Mrs. Spence called me up a while ago and asked to come up next Sunday if Dad will meet them at the trolley. So I guess next Sunday is all planned. I took the lace curtains down in the dining room today. I washed the windows and so I will get ready for the summer, cleaned up about. I guess when Spence sees my kitchen, they won't be so pleased because we didn't get the stuff from them, but I couldn't help it. They are too far away. I still have a second coat to put on half of it. Joe doesn't paint to suit me. He doesn't apply enough paint. Yes, I go over it two or three times and then one coat is enough. But Joe smears it out.

Dearest, I found one air mail stamp I had given Roger. He started to write you but didn't finish. So I will send this letter out. I am trying to write this with one of Uncle Paul's pens. I will try to go to Frankford on Friday, so I will try to get a new pen.

Now dearest, we owe 4 x 18 at the Land T. Bank. Dad owes 4/72- Heinel's repair bill- 21.00 a month. I am thinking of making a loan again at the bank and paying Heinel's in full. Then instead of having to put out 21.00 a month, I will only put out 18/39 18.00. Then it won't be so hard to meet. Maybe then we can see our way clear later. As you know, Dad can't get the title until the bill is paid. I am so God damn fed up with Heinel's, it ain't funny. They will never hook me again. Pop is so damn easy. I'll let you know in the next letter. Hope you are well.
All my love,

Mom

Haven't had a letter since you wrote April 6th.

Wednesday, April 18, 1945

Hello Dearest,

Well here I am for our little chat. It's 5 o'clock, supper on cooking; not much, just cabbage. But I guess we will make out. I am all cleaned up, flowers in my hair, lipstick (showing off Mom). There are flowers all around, lily of valley and violets. On the dining table are iris and lilac. I am more than tired. I've been putting finishing touches on the kitchen, and varnished the floor in the dining room. You know I did have half of it done and I had to do it over because the stain was two different colors. So I had to do it over. It never pays to do a half ass job. Well, same old thing to write about. It's rained for 2 days. Today, the sun was shining all day. It was a little on the cool side, but I have left all the fires go out. Thank God.

Dad has the car on the road again, and riders. That will pay Bill Bender. I sent the letter to the bank asking for the loan. I told Dad just what I wrote you about Heinel's and I told him I sent the letter off. He is the usual calm old Dad. He didn't say a word. I want to save your bonds and ours. I told you I had one for you from the government and you have the one from Budd's. So that's a start. Ed B. has $560.00 in bonds. Well dearest, I hope we get a place of our own, but you must have 1/3 down. I keep on wishing and hoping and getting "old lady", so my life is in Dad's and your care. See what you can do for me.

I know one thing. I got the house spotless. Rog has his chickens under control. Dad has a good start on the garden. I guess we are set for another season. My darling, I had two letters from Uncle John today. He said he had not heard from you or Bill. He is still on New Caledonia and hopes to get home this year. He wrote on Good Friday, March 28, and I just got it today, April 18. It was a much longer time coming than it usually is.

Old dog is on the run. We showed him your picture this morning and he licked it with his tongue. Rog said, "You kiss him." We sure laughed about how he smeared the glass. Old Lizzie is on the increase again. It beats all how business keeps up. Aunt Lilly said she wrote you today. I also had a letter from Getts in Scranton asking about you. They said they had not heard from you since February. Edwin, that letter Uncle John sent you, you should keep. That had a trip over the Pacific across the U.S.A. and back. It sure has traveled. Everything is okay. No letters from you since April 11th, Dad is getting anxious again.

So long for now love, my baby, hug tight.

Mom

All of us- Joe, Dad, Rog

Thursday, April 19, 1945

Well Darling,

It's 5:30, almost suppertime. The sun is shining and I have a big wash still on the line. It's cold enough for a fire, which I made this morning. Could stand one through the house also, but while I am working, I am warm enough. I'm just about finished up in the kitchen and the dining room floor has a little to go. The ribbon in my hair, ½ dozen dresses, shoes, everything shows signs of paint. I still have the inside of both closets in the kitchen to do. I must be in good humor to do them or out the hell goes all within. I sure have moved and cleaned up some stuff in 20 years.

Mrs. Roosevelt needed Army trucks to move her stuff from the White House after twelve years. God Bless her. She left an up to date kitchen and all things in modern order and also left her good housekeeper there to show the new First Lady, Mrs. Truman, all the pointers.

Dear, I just had a phone call for Dad saying McAdams case is supposed to come up Monday. It sure has been postponed a lot.

As I wrote in my two previous letters, I got the papers from the bank today. They don't fool around, so I filled them in and Dad has to sign on the dotted line. I will pay off those beat's $85.00 repair job, which you know they never did that much to the car. But, I'll tell you, I will never again consent to Dad having any dealings with them again. If you send me any money, I will do what I think is best. I expect to go pay the big phone bill tomorrow.

I had a letter from Uncle John yesterday. He said he hopes to get home this year. Darling, my favorite war correspondent, Ernie Pyle, gave his life on the Pacific front.

Well dearest, Carl is coming for supper. I just invited him for spaghetti. Joe is home and Carl is going to serve me the Bulletin. He gets a $25.00 War Bond for 12 new customers. Joe said Rose's father died this morning in Reading. One more news item, Bill McAdams is expected home from California tomorrow. I will let you know later. So long for now, Dearest. I kissed your lips tight on your picture this morning.

All my love, baby. No letters today.

Mom and All

.

Saturday April 21, 1945

Dearest Son,

The Home Fires

Here it is 7:30 and "old hick" had to get up at 6 am. The damn dog is howling. He's on the loose again. He is a wonderful pet. I guess that's why we have him. He gets ramming around and he doesn't know his ass from a hole in the hedge.

I went off to Frankford yesterday afternoon about 4 o'clock and it started to rain, but I had an umbrella. I met Dad at 5:30. I had the meat bought and I don't think we will get any more for two weeks, as I have only 20 points left. But you know Mom can eat scrapple.

Dad and I had supper in Frankford, came up to the Food Fair and finished our shopping and then stopped at McAdams. William got home yesterday at 10:30. It took five days to come from California. The train fare cost $70.00. He sat up all the way. It cost $20.00 for meals and then tips. He looks wonderful, but was tired out. His mother was going to take him to the city today to get a new uniform. His uniform blouse was like Johnny Ems', too tight. He did not look as nice as I think you did. He has a First Class rating now and is in the Amphibian Outfit. He has an arm cherron that classes him with the Marines, Navy and Army.

I am still in my night shirt tail. So I must hurry along as I have the house in apple pie order. Mrs. Spence is coming tomorrow, Sunday. I have a great big, fresh shad to bake, new potatoes, asparagus, scallions, endive and cucumbers and all that goes with it. I also have a big 8 pound Bolar beef roast, so we will not go hungry, and a homemade, lemon meringue pie.

I will write later.

Love,

Mom & All

Saturday, April 21, 1945

Well darling, it's now high noon. I sure have been working, but still have pies to make. I tuned in the news and a rest to finish our chat. There is a boy singing, "Old Faithful". It sure makes me sad. It's 48 degrees here in downtown Philadelphia, so I made a fire in the heater. There's just enough fuel for tomorrow.

Lizzie Bits had a big black beau courting her last night when Dad and I came home. She was out all night. Now she is curled up in the middle of my rocker. Now dearest, here is all I know.

Did you hear about the baby just born in Philadelphia, like an animal?

No, gosh. What kind of an animal?

Well, it has a dear (deer) face and a bare (bear) ass!

(Pop's latest)
Hello, Mom is on the air and I sure wish I could hear you say 'Here I come at 50, Mom. Get me my dinner.'

Well my dearest darling, I hope I get some mail today. Pop says we will put your money away that you send. I paid the phone $71.84 yesterday. That's off my mind now.

Darling, I love you, hug you.

Mom & All

Sunday, April 22nd 1945

Dearest Son,

Here it is after 10 PM and I guess you know, my feet hurt, and I am ready for bed. But I must say hello and tell you the news. Mr. & Mrs. Spence have just left and Dad is just back. He took them to the firehouse. I sure had a big supper at 4:30 and it was 7 when we got up from the table.

Pop loaned me his pen just now, and it is just as bad. Can't write slanted, I must write up and down this way. You know Pop, the backhanded writer.

We sure had a surprise at breakfast time. A nice car came in and up to the door came Ted Underwood, up from Norfolk. He leaves at 11 tonight. He just had a weekend pass. Bob is at a school in Connecticut. Ted is going to see my friend in Virginia, Mrs. Bell. I gave him her address. He looks fine. He gained ten pounds.

I started to read your last letter to Mrs. Spence and I had to add my own words when I came to the part about her. But Dad told her a thing or two. Leave it to him. Dad is so busy. He said he would write you real soon. He worked all day in the garden. We had a fierce storm here Saturday afternoon again. That's two Saturdays straight. Around 5 yesterday, Rog and Ems' boys got soaked. It got real cold. The radio went on the fritz this morning again.

We are really anxious to hear from you. All our love,

Your own Mom and Dad and all

Wartime Letters Written from Mother to Son

Monday, April 23rd, 1945

Dearest Son,

Here I am for our little chat. It's a nice day, cold, fire going, kettle singing. I don't know any more than when I wrote you last night. Just finished up the usual work. I had a cup of soup, a cup of coffee, a piece of lemon meringue pie, and now for my siesta. How are you? Happy, I hope. All Dad and I and Roger do is talk about you. We miss you most at meal time and tip toeing in, shh to Brownie, "That you Edwin?" We live and hope and pray for all and go on waiting. I've waited for you with anxious moments before, long years ago. It's almost the same sort of longing and anxiety to know if all will be well with us. Before, you were within and you are still within my heart. As ever, I love you, smooth your face. You know I thought that when I touched your baby face, it was finer than any silk or velvet I had ever touched. And so through the years, I loved to smooth your brow. When you started to get fuzz, I knew you were no longer my baby, but my big boy, ready to make your own babies. Postpone that day until you have had a chance in life. All I asked God for was to give you a chance in Life.

Son, I am lonesome today, no radio and no company. I miss you at times like these. But I am proud of you. Dad will write. He's been so busy. We are all pretty good. The chickens are doing swell (cat got three). Roger will write. He's busy with pigeons, chickens, lawn and lessons.
All our love,

Mother & All

Here is how I painted the kitchen. The border is the same as the dining room.

The Home Fires

Mother

(Encl)

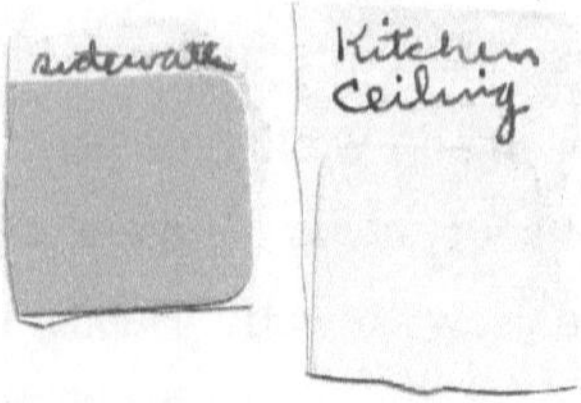

[handwritten notes: "sidewalk" and "Kitchen ceiling"]

Tuesday, April 24, 1945

Dearest Son,

Well, the month of April is nearing a close and I never thought I would be writing you so many letters; I just think I don't know any news. If you were home, you would be rushing in. I would say, "What's new?" and you would say, "Oh, nothing." Then when I would be surprised at some bit of news that Uncle Bill would tell me and I would tell it at the table, you knew it. So now, I will chat with you, even though I have no news.

Four walls can't talk to me. All I know is the weather, the housework, and my feelings. Here, we had a frost Sunday night; 35 degrees. Pop left the hot bed sash up. It just about ruined the tomato plants. He was going to set some out on Sunday. It was so cold and the wind was blowing. I told him there is plenty of time. You see, the spring heat is six weeks ahead of time.

The lilacs are all over. The flowering almond is done. And you know we have never had lilacs for Mother's Day in other years. The hedge is in full growth. Joe is on his knees behind the toilet cutting the grass with the hedge clippers. You know how high you let it get last year in the fall. That one piece is waist high and we can't get a lawn mower through it. Otherwise, the rest is under control. Joe has it nearly done. He has two more nights work on it left.

I've done very little work today again; lazy. Rog will soon be home. How are you? Well, I hope. We sure are looking for mail. Hope you get ours. All is well.

Love,

Mom & Dad, Rog, Joe

Wednesday, April 25th, 1945

Dearest Son,

Here at home, it is raining hard since early this morning; so hard that I had to go to the bus to meet Roger. No mail again today from my sailor boy, but I know he writes. All I hope is that he is getting my mail.

We got the radio back last night. It cost $5.85 to fix it. Today, I got the check from the bank for $116.45. I guess you know Heinel's will get most of it. That ties us down for a while again, but those bastards will never jerk me around again. At least Dad will get the title. They sent a shitty letter to Dad about paying up by April 20th. When he goes and pays in full and gets the title, then he will tell them off, so I hope. He is sore about this, but you know Dad. Bill Bender's word is tops with Dad.

Aunt Lilly had a phone call that a girl got a letter from Edwin B. She is so thrilled. Edwin has been made a F.C. Private. Don't you think it took him a hell of a long time to reach that? Ted U. is a corporal in the marines. I wrote to Uncle John. He sent me two letters written March 30 & 31st. I do neglect to write him. I should write every week, but I never know any news.

I sure have put in three lonesome days. I can't go out tomorrow because the wash man now comes on Thursdays. It's 4:30 now and I have the cabbage on cooking, smoked butt, and fresh asparagus. Roger has gathered asparagus every night since Sunday. We sure had a fine dinner Sunday with Mrs. Spence. She enjoyed it so much. Dad and I told her what you said about the allotment. That, of course, did not please her too much. But we know it's right. Joe's wife, Thelma, is expecting the stork in September. Mrs. Spence says she doesn't know what she will do with Donald; he's so bad now.

Aunt Minnie got Ruthie home from the hospital, so Aunt Lilly told me. Margaret is a nurse there. Esther's boyfriend is home from the Pacific, Joe Reeser. So she has two different fellows now.

Aunt Lilly is all broke up with worry. She got a job at some eating place nearby, a few hours a day. Bill Bissinger rented a store for a repair shop and he wants Esther to come live with him. Of course, Esther likes her Dad best, so she is acting up. Aunt Lilly doesn't know where she stands. Fred refuses to come back. Esther went to see him last Sunday night. He said, 'No, I gave her three chances.' So Aunt Lilly asked me if I would write him a nice letter. So I did and Dad sent it off this morning. I asked him if Dad or I could do anything to make the marriage a go. I told him as I was a witness at God's altar, I heard him promise for better or worse, sickness or health until death do us part. We all make mistakes and perhaps he could forgive, as God always forgives those who ask. Aunt Lilly says Esther was too fresh and caused a lot of upset. Of course, she sided with Esther. You know. That Uncle Paul stuff. It's born in you. You have some of it.

The damn lousy Uncle Paul wrote to the insurance company about his policy. So the man came and I showed him the two books where I paid on it for 4 years. And besides, Dad, Grandpop and Grandmom had paid it for years and Aunt Lilly will swear to that. The beauty part of it was when Joe used to collect on it; it became paid up when he was 65 and I didn't run to the truck shed for Paul to sign it. Joe said, here, you sign this paper, and I did. So you see, I will see that he gets buried. It's only for $180, but the damn sneak won't be able to get it and cash it in and then have the state bury him. So that's one time I won out. By all that's true, we will come out on top yet. So you do your stuff and I'll do mine. Lots of love. We'll show them yet.

Your own Mom

love and kisses

Thursday, April 26, 1945 (V-Mail)

Dearest Son,

The world powers are sending out their views at the San Francisco Conference. Russia's representative is now speaking in Russian, to be translated in English later.
Roger is doing his lessons and I am trying to write. Roger and I are having a job of it. Pop and Joe are holding down the couch and easy chair. There's no planting of tomatoes tonight as we sure had a fierce storm around 6 PM. I sent Rog to Frankford to pay the electric and get some pads for the front steps. Joe met him and helped him carry them. Dad and they all just got in. Was I glad. I put the chickens in and shut the hot bed and we had to shut off all the electric.

Well darling, no news, just housework. I painted the kitchen closet today. So I am tired and now going to bed. I hope you are well and God take care of you. All my love is the wish of your Mother.

Friday, April 27th 1945

Dearest Son,

Supper is over and Joe says to tell you he has the dishes under control. No outside tonight. The storm last night made a drop in the temperature, enough for your red flannels. I ordered a ton of coal to come tomorrow morning. I've got both fires going good. Dad is in his bathrobe. Joe is shaving. I will hurry this up before the Lone Ranger gets going.

Gallaghers are coming in; and so I have nearly all the weekend work under control. I put mats on every front step today and cleaned the parlor and sprayed with Larvex. Rog got his hair cut. Carl was in the paper and said his mother had a letter from Ed Baker; no news of Dot.

Rog is down looking after his chickens. One pigeon is on a nest and today he discovered an egg. He sure is happy.

Now darling, everything is news of War. Last night, Fords had their banquet. Some of the fellows were telling Dad they had to call out the police and get the place closed; there were so many drunk and wild. I am wondering if Kebe, Sam, and Granny were there.[110] Granny is still mad, I suppose, as I haven't seen her since the night you took one to Aunt Dink's. That's the longest time in all my life, but of course Granny is busy getting her house in order.

---

[110] This is a sarcastic remark about Kebe, Sam and Granny and their drinking. They would not have been at a banquet hosted by Ford.

Well, "Comrade" has been met. The Americans and the Russians have met in Germany. But, I guess you hear the news. Bill Baldy is with Patton's 3rd Army.

Well darling, I don't know any news, except to say I am thinking of you so much today. Are you all right? No mail, as yet. It's been two weeks now.

All my love,

Mom, Dad, Rog kisses baby

Saturday night, April 28, 1945

My Darling,

Here I am, 7 PM and alone. So I will talk to you for a little. I am all nerves. All I am doing is praying and all I have is War on my mind. The European War is getting nearer to its close by the hour and I keep saying, 'Oh God, make it end all over the world.' It would drive one crazy to listen to it all.

I heard a broadcast this afternoon of an interview with 2000 boys just home for their first meal in America after being rescued from German prison camps. The first good news they got was that instead of 21 days leave, they were granted 60 days leave. Oh! Boy, you should have heard the cheers. They were all crying. When the band struck up God Bless America, they screamed.

My darling, I guess I have a lot of explaining to do. At eleven o'clock last night the phone rang. Would I accept a call? Oh yes, Norfolk, Virginia calling. I thought, oh Edwin's ship is in port. It was Mrs. Bell. I said, "What's the trouble?" She said, "Nothing. The Underwood boy is here." So I had a terrible time. I said, "You got me out of bed." She said, "I thought I would." So I said, "When did Ted get there?" She said, "This afternoon." I asked when he was leaving. She said tonight. I thought that was so funny. I said, "Edwin has gone to work, what time is it?" She said eleven o'clock. I said, "Eleven o'clock? Morning or Night?" She said night. I said, "That's funny, it's morning here." She said, "What time are you on?" I said, "Eastern War Time." She said, "I can't see how you would be five or 6 hours ahead of us." So Mr. Bell got on the phone. He said, "What's the trouble, Helen?" I said, "I must be getting old." He said, "What do you mean old?"

Anyway, I thought it was six o'clock in the morning. I had gone to bed at 8:30. So I wrote to her right away this morning. I sure was half asleep and I was sure disappointed. Ted was here last Sunday and I gave him her address and phone number. He is quite near her, so he was with them last night.

They are playing My Buddy. I sent my regards to Dot today. She worked all day and has Wednesday afternoon off this week. I had a letter from Uncle John. He said he was at Ulithi last year. I sure filled up when I got his letter today. It had a surprise in it. I won't tell you until later, as you may send me the same thing for Mother's Day.

My dearest, I love you and think of you all the time. Saturday night is the loneliest night of the week. Do you know that song? Nighty nite.
Love,

Mom

Monday, April 30, 1945 (Mussolini was shot. Damn him. That was too easy.)

My Dearest Darling,

Well son, no mail again today. So I am like you were, looking. But, I know I shall hear from you. Here at home it has been cold the past week, down to 40. So today, I haven't done a thing outside of the usual work. Roger will be home from school at any minute now. Dad, Joe and Rog worked hard all day Sunday with cutting grass and the garden and the chickens.

Mr. & Mrs. McAdams came in about five and stayed until eight. I made high balls and sandwiches for them. Pop was so gay and happy, and yet he wouldn't give Mr. Spence a drink. It was so cold the Sunday they were up. He went in and went to sleep. But, not so with Mac. At any rate, they had just come from putting Bill on the train to go back to California. They are lucky, as he is in the service 7 or 8 months before you and still in the state.

Well Dear, I was getting on my knees, thanking God all Saturday evening. Then President Truman told the world that the peace rumor was false. Aunt Lilly called me up. She was so happy. I got my hair all done up and I am praying all the time. And I say, 'Oh God; let it be over in the Pacific too. That's where my boy is, God.' I never did give you up to anybody. I knew you had to serve, so I had to give you with God's grace.

Roger is home. He sent away for an electric pencil. It came today. What junk. Well my darling, how are you? Keep up dear, for my sake. Be a good boy. I love you dear. A hug and a kiss from all.

My dearest, love,

Mother

****END OF APRIL****

Chapter Eight

May 1945

Helen May Price

Wartime Letters Written from Mother to Son

Tuesday, May 1, 1945

Dearest Son Edwin,

Here at home it's raining and is not a pleasing day for May Day. I am not doing a bit of work. I have all the home fires going. The cat is crying. I am mighty sure we will have extras before night. When I went down to fix the heater, I had an awful time. She looked at me as if to say, 'Won't you help me?' I said to her, 'I feed you and fixed a bed for you and you must take care of yourself.' So here I am for our little chat.

I am thinking of the May Day when I took sugared waffles down by the creek to you and Aunt Minnie, and a bottle of milk for Roger. Then when we got up on the meadow hill, we crowned Auntie with the waffle plate on her head. All the powdered sugar went in her hair. We threw buttercups on her and danced around her. I can still see you and Roger. I used to wish in those days that Roger was nearer your age. Now, I am so thankful he isn't.

Last night, Roger wanted to go to the sale at Penn Valley. I told him, if Dad takes you, you can go. He wanted to go on the bus with Carl. Pop stopped. But it turned out that the Ems' were going with another couple. Poor Carl had to stay home with Tommy and his Grandpop. Dad did not see Dot.

Rog and Dad are in the car, all started and I went to the back door. I said, 'Wait a minute,' no matter, how much of a hurry you were in, Dad would say, "Did you kiss your mother?" If you said, no, in you came running. I don't think you ever went out without kissing me. So, Rog got out of the car and came over smiling with a sailor hat on. So I smoothed his face for you and gave him a double kiss. He is now getting so big and at the age where he doesn't want mother kisses.

Darling, they are the only true kisses you will ever get. Yes, girls do remain true, but a mother's heart is always true to her children. We are not supposed to write and say we miss you. But I don't think a little soft love hurts anybody. There is so much nasty stuff in this world and so many "she devils", that I often wonder how good boys and good men can tolerate it; Women who only think of self, lazy, dirty, or else clean and beautiful and wicked. They say, 'Oh, times have changed. You're old-fashioned.' But dear, morals never change. I like to think that I have told and tried to teach you respect for women. I know you are clean. I never told you anything but what was clean and good.

Whenever I tried to tell you any personal things, you smiled and said, 'I was using what you said. Mom, use your stuff to find out what you knew.' I told you we all know certain things. But nice mothers don't talk about them.

So as Mother's Day draws near, I hope I am the kind of mother you would like me to be. I know I love you with every inch of my flesh. I press you close to my heart and ask God to return you to me and to keep you safe. Don't ever shed any tears over what I may write or say. You are part of my heart, close and dear to me, and so I want you to chat with me and understand.

Rog and Dad bought the flag for me at the sale and a picture of Roosevelt, somewhat like that one Mrs. Bell sent of Pearl Harbor, only it's square.

Wherever you are, Mother will say, Hello Son, on Mother's Day. I will stand beside you. Wherever you will see me, as you look, say, love me a little mother. I will say, my son, my darling, I will always love you, want you and pray for you. Smooth your face, and write 65 letters in two months.

Your Mother, love, kiss.

Wednesday, May 2, 1945 (V-Mail)

My Darling,

The cat had four kittens yesterday during the rain. It was worse than taking salts to hear her, but now that it's over, all is well. That's the biggest scandal I know of.

Just as soon as I can get out to Frankford, I will get the things you want. You can be sure I will mail them off by Saturday, May 5th or at least by Monday, May 7th as soon as I can get out to get them. I sent you Ted's letter this morning. I don't know any news of Dot except that Nutsie said she was roller skating on Monday night with a bunch of girls. You know, dear, true love never dies. To keep the spark lit, it must always have oil of gladness. Keep your chin up. Faint heart ne'er won fair lady. All is well.

Love,

Mom

Wednesday, May 2, 1945 (V-Mail)

Dearest Son,

Just a few minutes ago I got two letters and Dad got one, written the 15th, 16th and 17th of April. I was so happy and glad to hear from you once again. We are all okay and we miss you just as you miss us. We know like you say we got a job to do and God will see us through. I am so glad you put your trust in God. At all times, God will walk with thee. Open the door of your heart and God will shine in you. Have faith and then you will have strength and courage to carry you through, no matter what the odds. I told you that you are not alone. Look up. Look up, son. Grandpop is your watchman, the best old guy ever. So, don't be homesick. Courage, son. Old Nut looks out for Old Bum and Old Bum for Old Nut. Keep up the good work.

Love,

Mom

Wednesday, May 2, 1945

Dearest Son:

I sent two V-mails and the town paper mail off to you this afternoon to your new address. It cost 24 cents. I read your letters to Dad and Joe. Dad is going out to pay Bill B. on the car. Dad tells me tonight that from now on he is to work only 5 days a week. Eight hundred are to be laid off to look for other jobs.

Well, the world sure is in some mess. This week we got the news that Mussolini was executed. On top of that, Hitler is supposed to be dead. I still don't believe it. At any rate, three world's men supposed to be dead in three weeks time. Of course, our own President is the only one who died with honor; and cannot be classed or written about with those two rogues. They got off too easy. But you know dear, God is the Judge.

Anyhow dearest, please don't worry over us. You know Dad and I are of good old hard stock. We are not the flim-flam kind. We stick thick and thin, feast or famine, apples or gold. Dad and I can carry on. You know, I crawled up the railroad bank on Christmas Eve and I fell down on my knees and I thanked God.

On Christmas Eve, my dear boy had a light burning and I knew the house was warm. I knew the turkey and Christmas tree were there and Dad was getting better and I had my boys. That is the way you must always think of home. You know mother never fails. The flowers are on the table, the fires aglow and only waiting for the day to see those two long legs come home. I watched you go to school. I watched for you to come home and I watched you go out over the field to Dot and Mary B. I could hardly realize you were so grown, but like what I write, you are close to my heart. I am so proud of you. Yes, I know all the heartaches of being homesick. I suffered from it for twenty years. I never got over it until Roger was born. My mother came and took care of me. I knew that no one could ever do anymore for me than she did.

God put peace in my heart where I used to be dissatisfied and never quite happy. I went to church. I found God was the only one who never fails, no matter what is next to my heart. I talk to God and so I have comfort. I think my Dad and Grandpop tell God to look out for us. All my prayers have been answered. Your letters tell me what I want to know. All I can see is love in every line. It's nice to be loved even if it's only by your mother. Your day will come. So give love and you will get it in return.

Your Mom & all

Dear Son,

I sent the hair curlers back to Dot by Carl tonight. I put them in the envelope with your new address. So, I know she won't have any excuse if I see her and ask her if she wrote to you as on Easter when I saw her last. She said she had a picture taken and was waiting for your address.

She was to come over Easter Sunday to show me her new suit, but I haven't seen or heard from her since. Bob Underwood is up in Connecticut, so Ted told me. I wrote to Ted this morning and sent your Housatonic address, but I will write again and give him the new one. He gained 10 pounds and his nerves are better. He looks good. The town paper will tell you pretty much of the news. Uncle John said he was at Ulithi a year ago and he was at Vella La Vella also.

Can you tell me any news of where your brother might be? Bill is still out there somewhere, same ship, U.S.S. Starr and Uncle John still on New Caledonia. Give my love to all. Are you still with your boot pal? Be good son. I hope you are feeling well. I got two big maps. I study them all the time. It keeps me near to you.

Cheerio.

Mother & Dad & All

Thursday, May 3, 1945

Dearest Son,

Joe is home. It's 5:15. Dick Tracy is on full force. Here at home, it is pouring rain. You know, I always told you the first week in May, when the flowering almond was in bloom, we had a three day rain. And so darling, it has rained all day ever since Dad went to work. Joe is home early. I am not quite ready.

Dad will be real late. He is coming to Frankford with his riders and then he has to track back to Heinel's to pay them.

Supper is over and here I am to chat with you while Joe is doing the dishes. You know they can't work outside when it is raining, so the dishes get done in a hurry.

Well darling, I cleaned upstairs and painted the inside of the dish closet in the kitchen. It sure looks pretty. Tonight, I threw out all the junk on the top shelf, the glass rolling pin, the silver bread tray and all the things I have hoarded these twenty years. I have three basketfuls at the back door. When it clears, I will dispose of it all.

This pen is awful, can just about write. I hope you can understand it. Carl has not brought the paper yet. I called up Mrs. McAdams today. She said William called her up from Chicago on Monday on his way back to California. Dad wanted me to especially invite them up for dinner on Sunday. We never had them up except at that picnic that time. I hate the prospects, but Dad is very fond of them and so it suits us for this Sunday. Dad got an 18 pound fresh ham from the man he gets the turkeys from, so of course when you get this letter it will be long past. But my darling, your mother will think of you. They say when you write letters, you should not tell the boys what you have to eat nor to tell them you miss them, but honey, I would have no heart if I didn't share it with you.

Dad is coming, so I will leave this space to see what news he has. Edwin, Dad had bad luck with a tire this morning. It went flat and all the inside went apart. Edwin, Dad got all the things you wanted and we will send them off Saturday. In a separate box we will send you your watch and a new strap. So be on the look out for it. Now dearest, I have an overseas box and I will send it off on Saturday.

All our love

Mother, Dad and all, big hug and kiss my baby, I love you.

The Home Fires

Friday, May 4, 1945 (V-Mail)

Well Son,

Here it is nearly supper time. Joe is home. Rog is listening to the radio and I am all ready waiting for Dad. He is supposed to have Saturday and Sunday off. We will get your box mailed out tomorrow.

There is no news I know of. Mr. Gallagher was in. He asked for you. Aunt Lilly also asked about you today. She is working at some eating place near her home. I have a little ironing and a little wash to do. They say the war in Europe is getting near a close, but I can't celebrate until it is closed in the Pacific and all my loved ones are home. Betty Hattel wants Ed Bissinger's address. Joe Reeser, Esther's old boyfriend has a date with her tonight, but she also has another fellow, Bob, and is quite in love with Bob. So long for now.

Love,

Mother & All

Sunday, May 6, 1945

Dearest Son,

Here at home, it started out with a little shower about 7:30. It's just wet enough to keep Dad in from the field. He went down to Foers' for asparagus and took Joe and Roger along. When he got back about 10:30, he was picking our first crop of radishes. No, it's not the first crop, as we had rhubarb last Sunday. Then a man and his son came in. He is one of Dad's riders and he is moving up to Trevose this week. He wanted to see where we live because he is going to park his car here each day and continue down with Dad. He now lives in the city, but has one of those small places up in the sticks. He has a stepson, twenty-five, who got mustered out of the Army last week. He was here with him. Joe cleaned up your car and now for a change he doesn't have to go back to work today. He has left to go to Frankford and it is 2:30. I am just getting a breathing spell as I told you yesterday; I am looking for Mr. & Mrs. McAdams for dinner between 3 & 4. I baked two pans of your birthday biscuits and so I must have my chat with you. Because you are not here to say, 'Mom, what time are you going to eat?' Well son. I only wish and pray you were here. It turned out to be a fine day. After the shower, everything is beautiful and green. I have everything shining and it cost Dad plenty to put up this dinner, $8.00 for the 18 pound fresh ham. If I could only put on the seven league boots, or get on the magic carpet, I would take you your dinner like Uncle Bill took us that day to the Frankford Hospital to give Dad his Christmas dinner. But, no such fairy is to come flying. You know my thoughts are with you on this Sunday afternoon. Pop is going to serve high balls to McAdams' before we dine. Edwin, this is the new pen I got last night and look how it's writing. It must be the paper or new ink and new pen. I will finish later.

Sunday Night

Dearest Darling, Here I am, our big dinner is over. Dad went up to your room and looked in your carry all bag and got the cards, so here we are in the dining room and they are playing pinochle. Of course, you know me, I can't play. Dad and Mr. McAdams took Shirley out to the trolley. She did her lessons and helped Rog and he is out hunting asparagus. It's about 7:30 now. Brownie left after supper and when he came back, he had a fine dose of Fisher's cow plop. Mrs. McAdams was down to Smith Street yesterday and bought Shirley a dress for $20.00 for the Frankford High School dance. The June Prom is being held at the Benjamin Franklin Hotel this Friday night.

Pop sure is having a good time playing cards. Well dearest, we are patiently waiting for V.E. days. I am going to listen to the "Good Will Court". So I guess I will say so long for now. I loved all your letters. Please keep on sending them. No matter what you write, I am so happy to hear any news. No matter what you write, I love you and am with you always.

All our love,

Mother & All

Monday, May 7, 1945

Dearest Son,

This is the fourth letter I have written today to you and I tore each one up. I will wait to tell you why. I was so excited all day with the news coming in on the radio. I was looking for Roger at any minute and I ran out with the new flag. I was crying and praying. Roger came and he had a paper. I was at the window. He came all smiles, pointing at the reading and he went out and put the flag on top of the iron clothes line pole, so it's flying from there now. They say that Churchill will announce it at 9 tomorrow morning, Philadelphia time. I heard a broadcast at 11 AM Philadelphia time, 1 AM Guam time, and darling, I am happy for the sake of all mothers of the Pacific area boys. Now you boys will get more supplies and thank God, the air support will help end the Pacific war sooner.

I think of you all the time. When you talk about being homesick, I think of when I was your age and I only was a few miles from home at Bristol and Germantown. You inherit homesickness from me. It has been a curse for 20 years in my life. I guess you have it worse for my part. I could never go anywhere, not even overnight. I used to nearly die when Dad left me to go overnight anywhere.

Dearest, it's 5:45. Dad just called me up. He had a flat this morning. He paid $1.50 to have it fixed today. Now he is at Bruggerman's with another flat. It's one damn thing after another. Dear, this is my new pen and it doesn't work any better than the old one.

Well honey, Nutsie came in. I said, "How is your Mom taking the news?" We are so happy that the European slaughter is ending, yet our joy is not complete because our boys are in the Pacific. Times Square, N.Y. went wild. The baker told me that the paper was ankle deep at City Hall. Well son, I will write later and maybe tomorrow we will have the real formal news. Until then, Cheerio. All our love

Mom & Dad

Tuesday May 8, 1945 10 AM

Well Son,

As usual Bustleton is the slowest place on earth. At 9 AM today our President proclaimed the end of the war in Europe. The only sound I heard in Bustleton was one short blow on the siren. Not even the Baptist church bell sounded. Here in America, our joy is still mixed with tears. God always is good and kind to me as you know I am alone. Those who love me think of me. I was standing at the back door with a little flag, waving it and blowing a whistle and I thought of how that lady down next door to Uncle Bob's blows the whistle. As I was waving the flag, the phone rang and a joyous laugh saying, 'Aunt Helen, you are not alone. I am here to speak to you while the bells are ringing. Aunt Helen, I sold papers announcing War Declared and I am selling papers saying Germany Surrenders Unconditionally.'

Bill Long flew from San Pedro. It cost two hundred dollars. He has 8 days all together. So it took two to fly here and two to get back. He was at Iwo Jima, Okinawa, Guam, Pearl Harbor and lots of other islands. His ship was hit by one of those Jap suicide planes, so he is in port for repairs. I said, 'Bill, did you see Edwin.' Oh he said, "Aunt Helen, if I only knew what ship he was on. I looked my eyes out for every sailor I knew."

I think Roger will get home from school at 12. It's now 10. I am all powdered and curled, but how can I get out? Edwin, the heavens are crying. Buckets of rain are beating against the dining room windows. The President told us all that we should go to church on Sunday, May 13th. He proclaimed that day as one of worship and thanksgiving.

We all feel very close to you today. Now darling, they sing a star took my place in the window, but I'm still in your heart. So now darling, Aunt Lilly, and Aunt Dink can rejoice. And I rejoice for them. But Aunt Dink and I still have a war to fight. I stood at attention. I spoke to you. So dearest, I was with you.

Edwin, I think I have heard every General and leader; Patton, Hatch, Simpson, Montgomery, Churchill, Pope of Rome, and Truman. Governor Martin closed all liquor stores and tap rooms and ordered all flags out. Now Mrs. Roosevelt is speaking.

Wednesday afternoon, May 9 1945

Dearest Son,

Roger got out from school at noon on Tuesday. The rain was falling in buckets. He had on a new pair of pants and went all "slicked up" as usual for a special occasion. He then came home slip, slop, mud and soaked. He changed his clothes and off we went to Holmesburg. We had a good supper.

Wartime Letters Written from Mother to Son

Governor Martin closed all the tap rooms. Bill didn't know that as they have no radio. I heard it on the radio before I left. Jeano's pop sent in a case of quarts of beer, a case of orange and root beer, and a can of pretzels and potato chips. In the morning, they took all the neighbor women in from the Joe Brown School Services and gave them coffee and cake and absinthe. So dear, Howard Baldy, Pearl, Aunt Dink and I went to services at the Holmesburg Methodist Church. I'll write you later about it. I walked out of the Methodist church a bride, 25 years ago this next Christmas. It seems like fate sent me back to the same altar as a Mother 25 years later to pray for my son in the Pacific.

Howard Baldy and I went 35 years ago to that altar and took Jesus in our heart, and we had never been at an altar together since. He shed tears and so did we all. The color guard and standard bearers were all boys I knew when I was young like you.

Dearest, I got this far and Aunt Minnie came dashing in, asking if I would mind Ruthie and Danny. Little Elmer is in Nazareth Hospital with pneumonia. They took him in an ambulance yesterday. But he is a bit better today. The baby cried and screamed for four hours. I was near nuts. The dear little thing didn't want to cry. But, he sobbed. So now Aunt Minnie has left.

Dad went to pay Benders. I had three letters from you today. That makes 13 from the Pasadena. The last one was dated April 25th with the church blue sheet. Honey, I am anxious about you all time. I sent one box off to you today for 65 cents mail and will send another box and your watch off this Saturday. I have sent you stamps and so I hope all is well with you. I hope and pray for you all the time. We all send our love to you and tie you on my apron string tight. All is well.

Mother and all

Thursday, May 10, 1945

Dearest Son,

As I begin to write, I wonder how you are getting my mail. I have numbered all my letters since not hearing from you when you left the States. During March, April and up to now I wrote you at least 80 letters. I sent one every day and then stuck in V-Mail in hopes that somewhere you would have luck. You have not mentioned if you got my Easter card or Dad's, so like you say, there is still nothing I know about.

After a fine day yesterday, it is raining just like V.E. day. It is so cold that I went down and started up the heater. Everything is lush and green, growing fast. Dad has 450 tomato plants in. He put all new ones in on V.E. Day as I told you it rained so hard. After Dad had about 150 of his own plants in, the frost was a little strong on their tops, so they pulled them all out and replanted with good, strong, vigorous plants. He got down at "Ninety-Foot" from Billie Foehr. You know where you went to play "Tarzan". I guess swinging the ropes will be to your liking, for you sure used to be a tree climber when you were little.

I have a strong cup of coffee here and I am not doing anything as yet. I am going to clean around upstairs, as soon as the house warms up a little. You know, I can remember when the King of England was crowned on a May 12th and I was doing some spring sewing and we had the radio that is now in your room and I couldn't sew for shivering. Grandpop had his ear up to the radio and my hands were so cold, I couldn't sew. I always remember that and not to put the Passion Vine out until June 1st. This Sunday will be Mother's Day. Rog is going up to see Uncle Bill. So he said this morning, "I haven't been to any movie since we saw Meet Me in St. Louis." Aunt Dink and Aunt Dot went to see "Blossom Time" on the stage. I would like to see "Anna Lucasta". I think that is the way you spell it or "Oklahoma", which is a swell show. It's on the stage here in Philadelphia for $4.14 a ticket. Of course, the matinee is cheaper.

Timmy told me that Dad thinks Timmy is tops and Sissy is like a China Doll. Timmy waited on Dad. He sat a quart of beer beside his chair and ran and filled up his glass. Jeano upset the dish of potato chips and then knocked over his glass of beer. Aunt Dink made him get the scrub cloth and clean it up. Bill said, "Now boy, let me take over, the Navy Way." Jeano, you know, is so fat and Bill so tall and thin. Bill put his arm around Jeano's neck and some boy played the piano. Don't Fence Me In. Rog sang loud and we said, that's Edwin's piece. (Pop said that's the one the boy liked). Howard Baldy cried and tears came in Pop's eyes and then the piano banged out, "Over There" and we all cheered. So Dad said, "Helen, get your coat, it's 9:45."

So then yesterday after taking care of Aunt Minnie's babies, I was all tuckered out last night. Today is such a gray day. I am going to get on the phone. When I came back from the Methodist Church on Tuesday night, they kidded me. Yap Yap Yacka, that new song. I guess you haven't heard it yet. When he wanted to love, all she wanted to do was talk (yap-yacka).

I met Nell Travis, our old sewing teacher, and Dink said to her, if all the girls in Holmesburg or Bustleton darned their husband's socks as she showed us how, there would be no complaints. So, I said I know one person who learned to do it perfectly the way you taught. That was my husband's sister. Aunt Mary was an expert. She just weaved it without skipping a thread. But you see, one can cook, one can bake, one can draw, and so the world goes. All kinds to make it.

I had three letters yesterday. The last one written April 25th, so, I will say so long for now and will write more later. It's 9:30 and I have the beds made and

The Home Fires

the kitchen done. I must look at the fire.

Dear Son. It's now 12:30, the home fires are going full force. The rain is pouring down in rivers, running through the fields. Charlie Shep was here yesterday to collect on the chickens we had on Thanksgiving, so I paid him. He said he expects Buggy home for the first time after 15 weeks training out in Arkansas, so he wants to have a big party. The girl works at Budd's and the oldest girl came to live at home the other night. Her man is in the service; so she has to come back to the farm.

Mr. McAdams was down to see his nephew, who was reported missing but turned up as a prisoner of Germany. He is being sent to the England Hospital at Atlantic City. His arm is still bad, but he was in a hospital in England since his release from Germany. He looks fair, but thin. Mrs. McAdams has a cold. Shirley is home for today with a cold. Her school prom is tomorrow night and going in Wayne Babington's car. That is Katherine Baldwin's married name. You know big fat Wayne looks like a tub of -

Bill said to ask you if you ever ate "Shit, on the shingle". He said the "old man" was a heavy drinker, but was sober the night the Japs rammed them. Bill has a card as an expert swimmer from the Navy He got that in boot. So long for today.

Love,

Mother & all

Wartime Letters Written from Mother to Son

Friday, May 11, 1945 (V-Mail)

Dearest Son,

Here, it is Haber de Gundy, one more day, then comes Sunday and as you know, my busy day to clean up for the weekend. I guess Dad told you that he got a turkey for Mother's Day. Last Sunday, when the McAdams' were here, I couldn't eat thinking of you. So with this letter, I send all my love close to my heart. I hope to have this Pacific war over soon. That is my Mother's Day prayer. Darling, with this letter I am sending you package number two, also, a package of funnies, and a separate package with your watch. So, in all, two 5 pound packages, one funnies, and one package with your watch. Let us know if you get them.

Love,

Mom & All

Monday, May 14, 1945

Dearest Son,

Here I am, way behind. I have a wash out and the day is beautiful and warm. The fires are out for the first time in weeks.

Saturday, Dad took me to Aunt Dink's at 10 o'clock. Then we went to the Mayfair 5 & 10 and who did we run into but Marion and Sister Funk. Sister is as big and as fat as Mrs. Spence and she's 17 years old. I almost passed out. She went on, "Oh, Uncle Eddie, Oh, Aunt Helen," and kissed us. I gave Sister your address. Marion is married for 3 years to a 6 foot 2 inch Texan out of combat since last January. I said, "Oh no, you aren't married, don't tell me." She said, "If I ain't, I had better be." (She's expecting.)

From there we went to Kensington to see Granny. Uncle Bob and the kids were there. They were papering and getting the place fixed up just big enough for Granny. I took a gift for you, Rog and me. Then we came home. It was 4 PM.

I got all the groceries, produce and meat. One piece of meat to a customer. Pop had a few words with Deiner. He said we bought there for 7 years and can't run in every day. It didn't do any good. We got a small piece of lamb. But we had the turkey. It looks kinda sick this morning. Granny and Mrs. Spence had supper here at 6:30. Mr. Spence came about 8, then I gave him something. What a shit, messed up day, no more Sunday cooking.

Honey, I had your picture surrounded by flowers in the dining room. I talked to you. I held you close. I took your picture to Dad and he kissed you.

Mrs. Spence bought me a nice box of handkerchiefs and Granny gave me perfume. I had a card Saturday "To my Sweetheart's Mother", your Daughter Dottie". Dad and Roger met her Saturday night. Dad brought her here and she did my hair. She had a bunch of red peonies for her mother. They cost $2.00 a dozen. After she had my hair done, she went to Mayfair. Dad took her as she forgot to get her mother a pair of stockings. Dad also gave her two coupons. She said, "Mom, when you write Ed, tell him "His Wife" was here.' I said I will.

Sunday night, Dot, Rog, and Carl went to the Circle. Dave and Joe worked in the garden all day. Roger went to church with me. Dad had too much to get done. Mrs. Ray Wenker was in 8:30 this morning to collect for the Town Paper. So I gave her your address. She was sure surprised to hear you had left the States in February. She thought you were in California. So you see darling, an old house dress covers an anxious heart, for I sure think you are in the battle. I am always listening.

I took your hand yesterday on Mother's Day and I said, 'Son I am beside you. I went to church and prayed for you on Mother's Day. I prayed for all everywhere. They gave us a corsage in church. I gave money in your envelope and I gave it to Roger to give. So I said, 'Son, these are your flowers.' I gave them to Mrs. Spence. Dad bought me a gardenia and Rog bought a nice pink geranium. The flowers are sky high.

A man has been leaving his car here and going down with Dad. This morning he didn't show up. Rog went up to Uncle Bill's on Saturday. He got $5.00, so the feed just came for the chickens. Then Rog took a girl from Shelmire Street to the Mayfair on Saturday. He had 4 cents left. Mrs. Spence gave us $1.50 and Dot said you sent her a beautiful poem. She learned it by heart and told it to me.

Dear, Bill Long got three days extension and also Uncle Bob. I guess she is wild, but the secret is between you and me. So long for now, my dear little boy in blue. All our love. God take care of you. Please God is the wishes of Mom and Dad. hugs kisses.

Tuesday, May 15, 1945

Dearest Son,

Here at home it is 7:30 PM. Dad discovered the front tire leaking, or at least Roger did. Now it's Tuesday and Pop says Jonesie is closed Tuesday. So he has to hunt some other place. Today is quite warm for a change. I am sitting here in the dining room, with a screen in the window, the first this season and I am sweating. This afternoon, I heard some noise at the back door. I went and I saw the sweetest, long-haired, brown pup; a lady. So I called her "Lady", gave her a drink and something to eat. I sent Roger to lose her in Bustleton. He brings her back in Carl Ems' paper sack. She is crying now for Roger. He went with Dad. Joe is setting up the ice cream tonight. Mom is making hot apple cake to go with it. Sure wish you were here. Outside, I have some yellow tulips in bloom. Dad's row of peas, etc. look lovely and green. Today, a beautiful big Mother's Day card came in my name for Granny. Enclosed was a $25 check from California and a short note from my Brother Bill. Also on Friday, I had a nice letter from June. I answered it today, before I got the other one.

Well son, I guess I have told you all I know for today. I have ironed all day and I'm getting the clothes in order before it gets too hot.

Edwin, I am writing you with my old pen and it writes perfectly. So, I say it's the paper and not the pen. This is new paper. Now dearest, I hope and pray you are getting some mail and that you will get the watch safely. My prayers are for you. I am fighting this war alongside you. So help me keep up my spirits. Your letters are better than medicine for me and Dad. You sure have written us some nice ones. Dad sent the cats to sleep tonight. That's one mess out of the cellar. And now we have a new B----- around.

Darling, Joe helps Dad well. He keeps the car beautifully clean. He shines it up every Sunday. So long for now. As ever, with all our love,

Mother, Dad, Rog, Joe.

Wartime Letters Written from Mother to Son

Wednesday, May 16, 1945

Dearest Son,

It's evening and here I am for our little chat. Like you say, time gets me mixed up. I guess you are asleep and will soon be getting up when we are going to bed. Pop is getting shaved and is going out to Bender's. He pays Bill every Wednesday night.

Granny just called up. She said Bill left for Washington at eight o'clock this morning to fly to California. Uncle Charlie, Aunt Violet, Uncle Bob, Aunt Dot, Granny and everyone were down to Aunt Dink's last night. They had coffee and cakes. I hear Bill expected to buy his girl a diamond, but he got in a crap game and LOST $200! So, of course, Aunt Dink was out money as the trip cost $430. You better save up. But, I don't think the trip is worth that much money. I know it's nice to come home, but that's a lot of money.

Well dearest, Counter Spy is on with David Harding. Pop was pushing the wheel hoe all evening.

I guess we keep the new dog, "Lady". She sure is a heart breaker; so pretty. Well my dearest, I will close for now with all my love.

Mom & All

Trust you are well and keep smiling. Cheerio

Mom & All

The Home Fires

Thursday, May 17, 1945

Dearest Darling,

How are you? You know I am like you, sure looking for mail. But I am writing every day. We had two real warm days and we sure are trying hard to get all the grass cut and the place in shape. It looks nice and so green. Dad's rows are all showing up fast. He pulled a big pan of radishes tonight. Roger is eating a radish sandwich and the two dogs are spread out. Dad and Joe have gone down to Food Fair to see what they can get. The meat stores in Frankford are all closed. Deiner's is open two days a week. One piece of meat to each person and so things are getting scarcer and harder to get. But you know us, asparagus soup, potato soup, or any old thing will suit us so you boys get enough. I am listening all the time. I am with you. So my dear little boy, hold tight. I love you.

I just washed my head; itch, itch, all day. Rog was home today and we sure cleaned up outside a lot. You know, Mom had to be right behind. So, I sure am all done in. Tonight, I washed and put out the Navy sweater and so many odds and cleaned upstairs. I planted out the two geraniums Roger got me and I put out three passion vines and dug around. So I'll call it a day as soon as Dad gets in.

Now darling, the new dog wouldn't let our "old rag man" open the door today. Rog made 50 cents. Rog is to be made a "tender foot" Scout tomorrow night. He needs $2.00, which includes a camp trip of two days. I send all our love. Please God to keep you safe for us.

Mom & All

Wartime Letters Written from Mother to Son

Friday, May 18, 1945

Dearest Son,

Here it is 12 o'clock, and the rain is sure coming down. You know I can't work when it's raining. I just heard a program and it was pouring rain and the guy yelled, "Where's the O.P.A[111]?" and she said, "What good would the O.P.A. be?" he said, "Ceiling." So though I am under a ceiling, I am wondering where you are and what the weather is like. I just made a fire to take off the dampness. Yesterday it was so hot. I got to sleep last night and I thought I felt something touch me. I woke up. I thought it was Dad's arm. Then I heard the little stool move. I shouted, "Ed! Something's in this room!" Dad jumped out, put the light on and Miss Lizzie Bit stuck her head around the corner of the door, "Meow". Dad said, "That's why we couldn't find her last night." So Dad had to come down and let her out.

Edwin, it's pouring so heavy that water is starting to run in the cellar window where we put the coal in. I can't go out, as I would be soaked in a second. The two dogs are curled up here. They try to get as close to me as they can. "Lady" is behind my chair. "Brownie Baby" is in front. He watches every move. You sure would love Lady. She has bowed front legs and she puts up her little paw. She was alive with fleas. Rog took tweezers and picked them off. We bathed and powdered her. She still has them so I guess we have our hands full. Lady's hair is just like silk. She is real tiny; half as big as "Baby".

Now dear, I don't know any news of interest; only of what we eat and work is all I know. When I woke up, I was saying, U.S.S. Housatonic, U.S.S. Housatonic. Dad said, 'The boy's not on that ship.' I said, 'I know, but that is going through my head.' So darling, I will say good afternoon and hope you

---

[111] In 1941 the Office of Price Administration (OPA) was created. It could fix prices deemed to be "generally fair and equitable." The OPA could also sue companies and retailers for damages if they violated the set price limits.

are getting our mail and that you are well, as you have all our love and we miss you lots.

Cheerio, Smile.

Mom & All

Friday, May 18 1945 - Letter No. 2 today

Dearest,

Here I am baby. I just got five letters including the one with the church program and book. And oh! If only you are getting some mail. I got the letter back that I sent out with Dad. It had 9 cents on it and needs three more. Now Roger is home and he will take the three letters out.

Yes. The rain had stopped. The sun is out. I sent you the watch and a new strap. I sent you two boxes. The previous letters told you all about V.E. Day. The news is coming thick and fast. I hope you will soon be home and all is at peace again. I hope and pray for all.

My darling, I know about the horror of war. Paul Bell told me many things and wrote me letters like you do. Growing up, you know what I used to say. But, God knows best. I gave my life and thoughts to God. He will see us through, so baby dear, I am your best girl. You have a part of my heart. Though Roger looks like me, he is slow and peaceful like Dad. You are impulsive, explosive, and those long legs are in a hurry like me. I hope you get along in your job. To do your best is all you can do.

Never worry over Bustleton. There is only one circle in the world for you and you know they care for you and want you to succeed. Be good. Forget money worries. I told you that Dad and I had feast and famine. We get through because we stick together.

Now darling, I am so happy to hear from you. And like I told you, I have you at every port and every battle. I felt your hand in mine on Mother's Day and I said, God, make him a good, strong son. I love him and I am very proud of him. He will be a man of experience when he comes home. He will know why mothers turn gray. Those we love are ever close to us.

Rog said he is in a hurry to meet Carl. Until we meet again, God be with us.

Your Mom & All

Friday, May 18, 1945 - Letter No. 3 – (MISSING)

Friday, May 18, 1945 - Letter No. 4 today

Darling,

Here it is night, and Dad has gone up to Uncle Bill's to try to get a little meat. Two of the Hattel boys came to go with Roger to the Scouts as tonight Dad had to give him $2.00. He and Carl are to be made "tender foots" in the Bustleton Scout Troop.

Joe is here. Dad read all of your letters before he ate supper. I finished up my ironing while waiting for Joe and Roger while Dad read the letters. Dad went through the patch and respotted the peppers and tomatoes and also planted more cabbage.

We got your letters from April 24th to May 5th inclusive and the part that worries me is when I read that you had no mail since March 10th. My dear son, I know I put the address on you gave me. Also, I have enclosed so many stamps and sent you several snaps. I only wish you get our mail. I never miss a day and if I do, I write extra. You will know if any were lost because I numbered all my letters since you left the States. Honey, it is only natural for a mother to have anxious moments. I had 9 letters today. They were like sweet music to my ears and medicine of love to our hearts. Dear old Dad had his heart in his eyes when he was reading them. I got five in the box at 2 o'clock. I sent Rog to the post office and he brought back four more. So, I sure was busy for a while.

We are getting news in on the radio telling us of the battle out there. Please my baby, keep calm. I live through all the terror of battle when I read the stories. I start to shake. But darling, say, 'God, I am ready.' He is the only one I will trust you with. Keep God in your heart at all times. I know he will be your guide. His Will be done. I am so thankful to know you think of us. I know your work and duty is long and hard. It's like I told you; look up. The tiny star that blinks at you is where Grandpop sits. He is proud of you. So nothing else in this world matters. We miss you, but all will be well. We are proud you are our son.

Lots of love.

Mom & Dad, Rog, Joe

Sunday, May 20, 1945

Dearest Son,

Here, it is time to go to bed. It was a lovely day. It was a little on the cool side. It had gotten real chilly and raw Saturday, so we had a fire going in both places. But tonight, we let them both go out. Dad worked in the garden all day. Roger and I went to church together.

Aunt Minnie came in for an hour or so. The baby sure is lovely. Little Elmer is now home. Aunt Minnie said she had your letter and was so pleased to hear from you.

Aunt Violet also had two letters and a card from you. Roger went up there today.

Buggy Shephard is home on boot leave. His father has pneumonia.

We went out to Aunt Dink's on Saturday. At least Dad and Joe left me there. Howard Baldy came and took Dink, George, Timmy, Sissy and me down to Uncle Bob's and Aunt Dot was not ready. Bob was asleep, but managed to carry the birthday cake home from Holmesburg. When the lady gave it to him, she shook her head. But, he carried it safely and two chicken feeders besides.

Dad came with John, who lives at 90 foot. We stayed until 10 PM. Joe, who was with Byron, was home also. He became a nervous wreck since Byron was lost, and is in a hospital at Springfield, Massachusetts. Roger went to the Circle with Mildred and Carl, so we stopped at Ems'. Mr. Ems came to the door. But, we didn't see anyone else, so we went down to Fulmer Street. We waited one whole hour. The three squirts came up on the 12 o'clock car, so we sailed around and took the Ems' home. I was sure tired today. After our dinner, I took myself off to the couch.

Now it is nearly 10. Pop is having his usual coffee and I will get mine and off we go. We listened to Walter Winchell and Gabriel Heater on the news. We heard that anyone eating in a restaurant must give red points. So, I guess you know Dad and Joe will not be able to dine at Rialto's. Come Saturday, things are sure getting tight, but dandelions and grass still grow on the farm. Okay, darling.

Loads of love, hug, smooth your face,

Mom & all

Monday, May 21, 1945

Dearest Son,

I started this letter a little while ago. So here I am once again for our daily chat. The man and woman came up to see about the peonies and I sold the two rows for them to cut for $50.00. Maybe Pop will think that is not enough, but I figured I was glad to get any price. Last year I got $35.00 from them for 85 dozen, so I made the quick guess at 100 dozen and split the difference. With the weather and cutting them, etc., I was glad to get that much, although they are selling at $2.00 a dozen. On top of that, I locked myself out. I had to get Roger's feed bucket to stand on to get to the window, as my legs are not as long as yours. Even at that, I had a time getting in.

Edwin, I had started another letter to you and it had so many blots on it. I was ashamed of it. I will finish this later.

Monday afternoon

Well son, there isn't a thing new to write about that I know of. Dot did get two letters from you in our last batch of mail. Aunt Minnie and Aunt Lilly got one.

Wartime Letters Written from Mother to Son

Aunt Lilly is now all concerned that her Edwin will get sent to the Pacific. I think both he and the insurance man, Wilson, are misfits somewhere, as they have not seen any action so far. Edwin is in two years. Her Fred is still away. I wrote him a nice letter telling him come back if Dad or I could help in any way. But, so far, no news. So Aunt Lilly got a lawyer on his tail this week. Dad said he is getting off too soft. But, I guess there is something wrong somewhere. She is close and doesn't tell all. You see, no matter what you do in life, it all catches up with you. She had a fine man, but she was a hot tamale and John Budd was the guy. After eight years, he roamed to a new pasture. It sure was a blessing that she has no children with him or else things would sure be mixed up. They say don't worry. But I also have her worries and I try to keep them. She makes me so darn mad. I give her good advice and she doesn't listen to me. Then I must be burdened after it's over. I begged her not to get married. I thought maybe she had herself in a jam and while she had the chance that maybe it was for the best. I still think that, but I can't say it. She called me up a while ago and said she had a headache. I told her to go and lie down for awhile. She said she had to scrub the kitchen and shed, etc. I said that her head must not be very bad.

Mine is real bad this afternoon. I laid down awhile, but Roger is home. I must get supper on the go. I have pork and sauerkraut cooking. Stinks like... I must peel potatoes. I have a nice bowl of flowers on the table. They look pretty. I always think of what you said, "You're showing off." etc. But I still put them on with no one to show off to but myself. Dad did admire them the other night. Well darling, a cool breeze is blowing the wash dry. The baker will soon be in. I hope you get my mail and that you know I love you forever and ever and miss you most at mealtime. So darling, write when you can. Your letters are my love and so here is yours from us.

Mom & All

Tuesday, May 22, 1945

Dearest Darling Little boy in Blue:

You know you still are the two long legs going out at 7:30 across the fields. It's hard to realize you are so far away when I feel you so near my heart; but then the bed is empty and no more can I say, "Yes, he's in because I see his feet." How are your feet when no Mom is around to holler at you, "Wash your feet, put on clean socks!"? I know that tender feet are a real trouble. Since I got big, I took care of my feet and my teeth. Now that I am heavy and old, I don't have any troubles with my feet.

You know son, I don't know any news.

June 3rd is Pennypack Sunday. This year I am in hopes that I won't have to walk it as I did several years now. Dad says the car is running quite good. I just laugh because it sure cost enough. I got a nice dress to wear and that is all I care about. I have been sewing collars on shirts and let Roger's blue suit pant cuffs down and opened up the seat and let out the extra inch. He is growing. I fixed up Dad's pants for work for the summer. I have the two brown blankets on the line as Roger is going to Camp Morrell this Friday. I guess my family will soon be down to me and Dad. Joe is no bother. They finally got the grass cut in back of the toilet. I sure miss you and your long legs going with that lawn mower. Joe has a big round flower bed made over by the iron fence and that piece in back of the barn dug up. We expect to spot out the marigolds, asters, etc. there.

We have loads of radishes and by Sunday, the first cutting of spinach. I got two pounds of limas and two of string beans from Patton today. Pop planted limas three times. A good many rotted with all the rain we had, so he is going to put in another lot. It cost $1.70. I just sent Rog off to Frankford to pay the electric and the first $4.03 phone bill since you went into the service. We got two tons of briquettes and two of coal in, so we got a starter.

It's quite warm and a high wind is drying things up pretty hard. They asked Dad when he is going to take his vacation. He said, 'I won't take any time off until my boy comes home. Then I will take my vacation and I know my boy will take care of me.' I tell you, it does Pop's heart good when you write him. He always takes his letter to work and I can picture him sitting at his little shanty reading it or showing it to Clarence. So write him all you can or are allowed to about your work. He is so proud of you. He offered more blood to the Red Cross, but Dr. Powell at Ford's said, "No, Price. You need all you got. Maybe some other time," as he did give a pint.

They would not take mine, as Dr. Roseman said if the needles I got did not help me, I would need a transfusion. But I am better because I rest more. I would still love to do those two front rooms, but I will wait for you to help me. Oh, honey. I'll be looking for you to help me do them. So, it's a date, a promise that God will keep us close. And so, I'll be a seein' you. Cheerio.

Love,

Mom & All

Wednesday, May 23, 1945

Well, Darling,

Here I am once again, tired and busy. But it's 4:45 and the pot of bean soup is cooking away. The table is set, kettle on, and so now for a rest and a chat.

The Home Fires

I took the spread off of your bed, washed it, and after it was on the line, a bird left his trademark on it. I had to get the basin, take it out in the yard and wash the spot out. Even though you are not home, the black coal dirt gets over everything. I took down the curtains in your room and they were black. I put them to soak. I cleaned up all around and my feet are tired now.

Mr. Spence's brother, Clement is dead. He gets buried tomorrow. I used to like him, but have not seen him since I came up here. He had no children and was about 65. That is Mr. Spence's last brother. His wife is too high-toned, and they sure got rid of him quick. Died Tuesday, buried this Thursday. A laundry man came in to see Sam and asked him how he was. He said okay, but Clem was pretty sick from a stroke. So in a few minutes the laundry man went and was back again. He said, 'Sam, where does your brother live?' Sam said on Pulaski Avenue. Well, the laundry man said, "Not any more. His death notice is here in the paper." Mr. Spence nearly passed out. He was around the corner to see him on Sunday. Clem's wife never notified them until this morning. I read it in last night's paper, so I called up because it didn't say any viewing. So, Mrs. Spence said, no, no one to view him. Service is at 2 PM, Thursday, funeral private. I guess Dad will be glad he won't need to make that trip tonight.

Then Grace Long called me up. Her mother, Aunt Katie, wants some addresses she said. Howard Lewis was at a base in Rhode Island. He still has the same girl. He gets liberty every other weekend and every other night. So he was out with a girl he met up there. They only wish some other girl will steal him from the one we met.

Roger is at Shibe Park to see the Athletics play Detroit[112]. It's cool, but nice. We had a most awful storm last night. It tore the chicken house door off and took the sash over the field. Nutsie and I ran and got the sash. There was

---

[112] The Philadelphia Athletics lost the game 7 to 1.

lots of broken glass. Rog got in 2 minutes before it came. Nutsie and Muttie got drenched. The old Grandpop Ems is not good. They had a letter and Mothers' Day card yesterday from George. Okay for now.

Love,

Mother

Thursday May 24, 1945

My Darling,

Here it is 8 PM. I have the apple cake in the oven and out and getting on the last lap. I sure did some work today. I washed the windows in your room, put the curtains back up and ironed all day. Now I'll call it quits. When Dad comes in, I will get him to go for a little ice cream because tonight is pay night. It doesn't mean much, only working 5 days a week. It cuts out time and a half, which is always such a needful help. I guess we can manage along. Meat is very scarce. For the first time with rationing, we have to do without. Somehow, I can't get down to it. But, we are satisfied. We had all kinds of dishes and liked them. All we want is the boys to have enough.

We follow every bit of news. A young sailor, after two years in the Pacific, got married. He was in Los Angeles on his honeymoon and some dirty thief held him and his wife up and stole $100 from him. He put up such a fight that the damn skunk shot the bride in the knee. The sailor was at the hospital and he was comforting his wife. He said, "Just think how I sweated for two years and for this to happen." Every time I think of it my blood boils. I could just stone that thief and stick hat pins in him. So, let all the boys be careful. Even skunks are still at large on main streets.

My darling, I asked Nutsie tonight if Dot heard from Edwin. He said yes and she got Edwin's gift for her birthday. Dad and I will send a nice card.

My honey, Mrs. Rupert and Nina Lott were over here last night to ask me if I would have the Bible class on Tuesday night. I said no. Any church that can't ring its bell on V.E. Day is of no use to me. They knew it was awful. Even the air raid siren was out of order. I said put it in "Our Town". Bustleton, as usual, is asleep. So, I guess I will be off the list. All is well.

Love,

Mother & All

Friday, May 25, 1945

My Darling in Blue,

Yes, here I am again. Dad is stretched out in your old spot tonight with both dogs. I said, you remind me of Edwin. He said to hell with the garden, I am going to stay here. So, I said, Edwin, come on now. Get up. Get your work done. He said, no. 'I am waiting for the boy to come home.' So, you see honey, we are two old fools alone where we started. Dad said we better "start over". No, I said. Here's where the grandmoms come in.

Roger, you know, went to Scout camp. It took me all afternoon to get him ready. He and Carl were worn out before they left. We packed a blanket, leather jacket, sneaks, towel, soap, wash cloth, sugar, potatoes, bread, tomatoes, bacon, baked beans, coffee, lemon, knife, fork, spoons, turner, dish cloth, pad, flash light, and pen knife. Dear knows what else; bathing suit. They also gave two dollars for the other food. They were loaded, but they only had to go as far as Grant Avenue with most of it. There they have a big push cart. But it's four miles with a hungry gut, so I told them to sing, it's not the pack you carry on your back, nor the gun upon your shoulder. March on. Eddie and all the boys in blue know what endurance tests are. "Keep going." God be with you all. I cried when I saw him go, but I kept laughing and saying, "Oh! I had a good home and I left it, but experience makes us know the value of Home." The knot mother ties in the navel cord keeps tied to her heart and the knots loosen and tighten as the years roll by, but all roads lead to Home and Mother. Until that day darling, endurance, patience, perseverance, and then you know what it takes to make a good Mom. One who doesn't give up. Carry on my darling. No news. I've told you all. That's my motherly chat today.

Lots of love,

Mother & All

Sunday, May 27, 1945

Dearest Son,

Here it is 7:30 PM and just about getting through. It rained most of the day. Dad didn't get too much done. We had two lots of company. Billie Foehr and John from down "ninety foot" came up for some pepper plants. He offered Dad a horse. He begged him to come get the cultivator tractor and told how Pop used to do in school. A certain teacher they had would make Pop go along tied to her apron string. Pop would untie them and say, whoa! All the kids would roar laughing.

Then the fireman, Fred H., and Mrs. Dietz came in for about two hours. We had a nice visit. Joe had to stay on the job all day as they were going up to

Reading. While they were out last night, someone cleaned the place of all the flowers, especially the peonies.

Lou Heim was up to see about buying the peonies. When Dad said the Mrs. had sold them for $50.00, he said that's a lot of money for them, Ed. Lou said he only gave $35.00 to Brous for all he had. Dad said, they had all pink and the demand is for red and white. Every year we gave them away. So I have my $50.00. I gave Dad ten for work clothes and I bought $12.00 worth of groceries and the balance for the rent.

We didn't have enough flowers to go around to all the graves. So, I fixed a big basket of red and white peonies and blue corn flowers. Dad and I placed them at the honor roll. When we came back, another big basket was there.

We went to Aunt Lilly's Saturday evening for supper. Tom White came while we were there. I have a nice beautiful card to go out to Dot with this letter. We had to make a fire today in the heater and kitchen, but it's warming up now. So long, angel.

Lots of love,

Mom & All

Monday, May 28, 1945

Well, Son,

May is drawing to a close and I wrote you faithfully and I only hope by this time you have had mail. I guess you know we spend anxious moments when we hear any bit of important news. I sat in church yesterday and I talked to God from my heart. I always come home knowing that for one hour my mind is at peace. Here it is a new week. It was quite hot this morning in the house as Dad had started up the fires. It rained lightly again today. The air has gotten fresher, not that heavy kind.

Aunt Lilly just called up. She wants to know what I am doing Wednesday, May 30th. I said I don't know yet if Dad has to work. She said Esther is going to a U.S.O. dance at a camp in New Jersey. So, I said, 'Let her make her plans and you make yours.' The days for feeding a gang and cooking all day and getting my house full of flies and mud are over. Let each one take care of themselves. I'm not so foolish any more to invite all. I say we are going to the movies and that ends it. That way the next day, I am not all tired out from hauling out the mud.

Well, son, there is no news. Roger is going to cut some lawn over on Welsh Road and is asking $3.00. I told him to. Charlie Stevens charges $5.00 and only half cuts it. So Rog will have his holiday spending money. No Uncle Bill bringing in the watermelon. Hope you are well. Lots of love.

Mom & All

Monday afternoon, May 28, 1945

Hello, Honey,

Am I glad. I had just finished the first page when Roger came in from school and he said close your eyes and open your hand. Boy! Twelve letters. Two to Rog, one to Joe, and some to Dad and me. Yes, we understand all you write. Nothing so far has been cut out and we also got the girl's picture.

Well my dear baby, I have told you, once a man, twice a child. You saw it proven with Grandpop. When you left you were a boy. When you come home you will have forsaken boyhood ideas. Your old Mom always wanted you to see the kind things of life. Experience is the world's best teacher. If you can absorb what you see of life's good things, you can rock on the front porch and tend the flowers and fatten the chickens and the Seven Seas will be memories. The comfort of the old feather tick and Mom to steal in and cover you over were the best days you will ever know. A hurt will be in your heart from what you have seen and how other people are so mean, but hold fast with the faith and love I told you about. God rewards you.

I miss you so much that I sometimes think, oh why, why and then I think how for 16 years I worked so hard. But, God put me at the station where I was needed most. I did my duty like you are now. I am rewarded; a wonderful husband, 2 fine sons. God's reward. Lick those Japs. You'll get home.

Love,

Mom

Monday, May 28, 1945

Dear Son,

I am back again as I did not finish our chat. I can't think of anything else but all the nice things you told us in your letters. I just feel if I could take you up in my arms and love you, we would be so happy. I look at the old green rocker and I think, how can he be across the world and yet such a few short years ago he was getting a fan tail behind the pig pen, the little devil. What next? Maybe if you got the hairbrush more often, you wouldn't have messed up your lovely fine skin with circus girl ads. But now that's done.

Years are long and see that your sons get strap oil when they disobey. We were weak because I had a hard job to get you and then to raise you. Mother's day was nine months after Father's day, but I had to doctor fifteen months to get you. No wonder I thought your skin was the loveliest thing I had ever touched.

I used to think how I would go without shoes to send you to college. You would be educated. All I know is how to cook, sew, mend, wash, iron, and scrub. I wanted to be a school teacher. But with only bread and salt to carry in my lunch, and an onion or a pickle, it was a hardship.

When I was 28, my pop had 26 of us to sit to Christmas dinner with a 26 pound turkey and 5 big chickens. I manage to get along in this world so much so that I can get up on the altar and preach a sermon and know what I am talking about. But, I learned it the hard way too.
Circumstances always alter cases. If we have good in us, it will show up with effort. God puts us at the station he wants us to be at. So, always look up. There is none better than the watchman you have.

Everyone is well. Rog got home in good time from Scout camp. He enjoyed it, but was tired out. He is out now, I guess, cutting that lawn. Supper is nearly ready. I was going to see A Tree Grows in Brooklyn, but it was so wet through the fields. Maybe I will go tomorrow. Dad is getting his ears lowered tonight.

So long for now.

Mother & All

Supper is over. It's raining and no work outside tonight. Dad inspected the garden and the rabbits ate off eleven cauliflower plants. They chewed them down to the roots.

Nutsie was here with the paper. He said Dot got some letters from you. Buck Simon was up at Ems'. He is home from being a German captive wounded with shrapnel. He was so starved, his intestines have shrunk so that he can only eat a little at a time. He worked for Morrissey the contractor and he bought him a brand new car.

Russell brothers have a bulldozer going and it smells like they are using fuel oil. There is some smoke coming from it and boy, they are cleaning out the woods with the finest biggest trees. Today, I saw about 5 of those largest trees. They had them on a big truck about a freight car length. It went over the road with them towards Bustleton Pike. I guess they were taking them to the saw mill in Somerton as they were too big except to cut up for lumber. What's next?

Joe did the dishes for me tonight as he can't work outdoors in the rain.

Now, darling, about the war, there is still a great deal to be done in Europe. The devastation of the land makes it virtually impossible to get a good start to produce food, which is the first and foremost requisite to exist and rebuild. I do feel that they showed they should be conquered so that this awful upheaval will not occur for your children. They have a job on their hands, which the regular army should control. Now as for the Pacific, once the supplies get going to you boys and fresh troops get coming in, they will make short work of the Japs. I can't see how war-weary boys can be rerouted from

Europe to the Pacific without a certain degree of disgust and fatigue. But if you read Luke 1:37, you will know the answer[113].

So for now my dearest son, I think of you. I am proud of you. I am with you at all times and love you forever. I am your best girl who misses you more than mere words can tell. Keep smiling. Look up, no matter what, carry on.

Glad you liked the little pictures of Rog and me, and also Doris' picture. We thought it was kind of a short dress, eh? Oh well, be good and enjoy whatever you can. Rog has his chickens. They are doing good. No meat all this week, but you know how Mom can make up dishes. I have an eggplant and asparagus and I will cook you anything you want when you come home. I used to be starved for my mother's cooking too and still like it.

Tuesday, May 29, 1945 (V-Mail)

Dearest Son,

Here I am for our daily chat. This is the only paper I have on hand. I will get some on Saturday. I surely hope by this time you have the two boxes, the watch, and the roll of funnies. I was so happy and glad to hear from you. Please don't say you can't write well. We think it is like sweet music to hear you are okay. That is all Pop and I live for. I told you that if you only write Mother or Dad, we know you are alive. It has been wonderful and far more than we expected to hear from you. My son, may God be with you at all times. Tell the boy who gave you the paper that if he is from these parts, that I will pay him back when he comes home. He can just come to the farm and I will cook him a fine meal for that paper. All is well. I hope you are too.

---

[113] Luke 1:37 (King James Version) For with God nothing shall be impossible.

All our love,

Mother & All

Wednesday, May 30, 1945

Darling,

It's 10:30 and Aunt Lilly, Esther and Tom White just left. Dad took them to the trolley and is not back yet, so I will dash off these few words. Of course, we talked about you all day. The Boyds were here also for supper. She brought me the enclosed picture.

Well, Dad is back. I hope that you are well and I pray extra hard for you. We heard Dad's brother was around Okinawa. We are praying for all. Lots of love to you darling. Hug and kiss my baby.

Mother & All

Thursday, May 31, 1945

Dearest Son,

I'm back to writing on school paper until I go out to get some. Now, sweetheart, we got five more letters today and just as I was reading them, in came Dot. I took her in my arms and kissed her three times and smacked her bottom and gave her a good whipping. We had a good talk and so perhaps you will hear from her. I told her a thing or two, no bones about it. I gave her a big bag of spinach. She has been eating hot dogs all week. She said they didn't have any for a week and all plants are growing sky high. No French fries because lard is going for 10 points for one pound. My dear boy, speaking of sugar, we get 5 pounds for each person for four months. So, no rice pudding or cherry pie. The worst blow is 3 red points per dozen eggs. We have not had a taste of butter since you were home. But, we didn't care, dear. All we want is you boys home. I won't get so fat. But, what burns us up is who is getting it. If our boys get it, that's where we want it to go.

Now, baby, I wrote you a V-mail this afternoon and here I am for the last day of May. Tomorrow is June 1st. The garden looks fine. Dad put in a new crop of limas in tonight.

It's 9 PM and Gabriel Heater is blowing off. My darling, I am at all the battle fronts. Your cousin, Jackie Moore, is in the First Division Marines fighting at Shuri. The fleet must help those boys at Naha also. We hear that the battle fleet is giving them all the help they can. We also get the news about all the damage done to our ships, but not the names of them.

So, my dear son, my prayers, my love and my hopes are to you and God. Dearest, keep up. I am writing every day. I am trying to keep up your spirits in my letters and I hold you close to my heart. Dearest, I am listening to the radio and so I have told you all I know. Your darling looked like a little baby. She didn't know you were going to tell stories to Gail. She laughed at that. Nightie night, darling. I love you.

Mom & Dad & Rog & All

Darling, the check was wonderful. Dad is proud of it. It will go to the bank for your first foundation stone. So, do your best so you can get a good start.

Love from All.

Thursday, May 31, 1945 (V-Mail)

Hello, Dear Son,

Of course, as usual, no news, just here for our little daily chat. I always feel better after we talk each day. I feel you near me and so I always write to tell you that I am thinking as much about you. Because of the important news we are hearing, I say, Son, I am with you. I may not know how to load a gun, but I can help pass the ammunition. So, keep your spirit up and then mine will carry too. If your Dot only loved you one little finger as much as I do, she would write you. Words are not needed, for love is so natural that it is like eating. I could do no more without you than I could without eating. I will fill you up when those two long legs come dashing across that back porch.

Love for today,

Mom

Thursday, May 31, 1945

Dearest Son,

Roger came in from school and brought me five letters. One letter contained your money order for one hundred dollars. Son, that took six months for you to save. It took heartaches, fears, sore feet. It took and put something in your life that only you and God know about, but that Dad and I also felt. So now, that is the laying of the foundation stone like they lay a corner stone in the erection of a new edifice. I will carry that check with pride and honor to the Corn Exchange Bank at Oxford Avenue and Frankford Avenue.

You keep up your good work and try very hard to save all you can. Then, with the allowance you get and what you can borrow from the government, you can own a fine farm where you can always be your own boss. I used to watch Grandpop stand on the bank at the daffodil hill with his arms behind him and you running around him and I used to say, "Master of all he surveys, owner of none." He had no schooling and could not take advantage. But, if you listen to me and carry on, you will be free and independent and when you want a pork chop, you won't have to haggle over a red point. Nothing worthwhile comes easy in life. The sweat of your brow earns your bread and the lady of your choice either helps or hinders.

My opinion is that Dot is a good, fine girl, but not smart enough and not your type. That was why I wanted you to be sure of yourself and (this is as far as I got when Dot came in, but now son, it's a new month)

****END OF MAY****

Chapter Nine

June 1945

Edwin Charles Price, USN.

Wartime Letters Written from Mother to Son

Friday, June 1, 1945

It's 9 AM and the dishes are done, but I am still in my curl papers and night clothes. Dishes are done and the fire is fixed. I am going to sail off today for Frankford.

Edwin, I got 2 white slips and 2 night gowns for $10.95 and there is not enough material in them to make one good one. There is lace in the front on the slips and none in the back, so the top of the pink corset shows out the back. Now I must try to get some ribbon or lace to put a strip across the back. I tell you, it's a joke today trying to wear the damn junk they put out. The damn Hollywood rips, who can pose for pin-up girls are okay, but a good mother who cooks and works on a farm can't wear that junk. The first stone gets in the shoe on the knee. Well, try it in the field. On the couch it may be okay.

Of course, we know where Rog is. Pop took the letter to work about his brother.

Now, darling, you see how we know where Jackie Moore is. We know what outfit he is in and the papers and radio tell what companies are taking over. When we hear a certain fleet is helping with a naval landing of marines, etc., we say, I wonder if our boy is there. We scan every word. When we found where Ulithi was, we knew it was hot and then got cooler. We knew you must be in a certain place. If we knew what Naval Division you were in, we could tell better as the news will say, "The – under command of --." That was only a Jap rumor, not confirmed by the U.S., that because the news reels are always telling the news that we are fighting extra battles. We are anxious, but we fully understand you can't reveal your whereabouts and we wouldn't want you to.

Johnny Ems said he was going to the same place as George, so they are in your parts. He told his mother he would be sure to look for you at every turn. Bill has gone back. That was tough. I would rather you stay until you could come home for good. One of the Russells is home. Rog didn't know which one, but he saw him in the car.

I paid for the town paper again, so that you will get more news. Uncle John has not been heard from for over four weeks. He said he didn't pay the rent and was getting kicked out. I sort of think he may be sent to Luzon, Manila, or Okinawa to help get things under construction. You know it is as much a heartache for us to know how you all want to come home and yet the job must be done. So, keep up your spirits and God will take care of you all, whatever his will. Keep calm, dearest, keep calm. Have faith in God. My dear baby, I love you so. Smile for me, my sailor son.

With all our love,

Mother, Dad & All

Saturday, June 2, 1945

Dearest Son,

As I told you Friday, I was off to Frankford. I got the money order cashed at the Frankford Post Office. I went to the bank and got the cards for a checking account. That would be the quickest way to get it out in case you needed it in a hurry, as I put it in a joint account. Then I stopped at Mrs. McAdams' as I got a big carry all bag full of meat groceries. I stood at McGee Street to flag Dad down and he went right past me at 5:30. I could see the baby shoes swaying even though I got out waving the pocket book. He was looking straight ahead doing 50. For twenty minutes, I tried the telephone and that guy was in at Rhawn Street with his Dutch boss, Schaupp, getting a beer. So, finally, I got all of them and they came down for supper to McAdams'. I had a bad spell of headaches, so that was why I stopped there. I had the Saturday shopping all done and so much work to do. Dot came over to do my hair. I told her to wait until I got home, so I rushed away. When I got here, she had left, as her pop came for her because there were three girls there for her. She said she would be over tonight. I hope so, as I want to be smart for Pennypack Day tomorrow.

Darling, Dad and Rog will go up to Uncle Bill's to get chicken feed, so they will go to the bank and also mail a package to you with this letter. We did up the package last night. That makes three 5 pound packages we have sent. The extra package with the watch and a bundle of funnies will be four. So baby darling, I hope they touch the spot because I tried to send things that would keep. I got the paper also, the Rose Bowl. Just lovely, mail is coming regularly every two weeks.

Lots of love and prayers,

Mother, Dad & All

We understand all you write.

Sunday, June 3, 1945

Hello Honey,

Dad is taking Mr. Spence to the trolley. It's 9:30 and he went to church with us. We had a big day. Dad went to each service. It's so cold. I shivered and Dad made a fire in the heater before we left. The pastor said it was the first time in 21 years at Pennypack that people came in topcoats.

The Home Fires

Dad is back. We had our cake and coffee, so I will write a big letter tomorrow my darling.

All our love,

Mom, Dad, Rog

(Enclosure – Item 7)

Last year you took me. hope you can next year. love mother

"The Church of the Living God, the pillar and ground of the truth."
(I Tim. 3:15.)

IN OBSERVANCE OF THE

257th Anniversary Services

OF THE

LOWER DUBLIN BAPTIST CHURCH

AT

"YE OLDE PENNEPACK MEETING HOUSE"

KREWSTOWN ROAD BELOW WELSH ROAD, BUSTLETON, PHILADELPHIA

Sunday, June 3, 1945

1688 -:- 1945

WILLIAM H. TUMBLESTON, B.M.
Director of Music

ROBERT T. TUMBLESTON, D.D.
Minister

Wartime Letters Written from Mother to Son

Monday, June 4, 1945

Hello Son,

Here I am for our little chat of the day after three busy days. I am now back to normal. It's noon and I had my lunch and now for my cup of coffee and to talk to you. I wrote you Saturday and told you we were sending off a box with that letter. But, Dad had to bring it back. So now I have just finished packing you two boxes. Dad will tie them up tonight and get them mailed out tomorrow, Tuesday, June 5th.

Now, son, as usual there is nothing new outside of this important item; today a parade leaves the new airport with several important generals. Although it is close by, I don't feel like going to see it.

(Enclosure – Item 8)

RECORD, Monday, June 4, 1945

Generals Fly From Europe for Parade

ROUTE OF TODAY'S PARADE. Gens. Omar N. Bradley, Carl Spaatz and the 50 officers and enlisted men with them will arrive at 2 P. M. today at Northeast Airport. From there they will be taken in automobiles by the route shown (dark lines) to Independence Square, for exercises at 4 P. M.

The day is dreary and cool. I am going to rest up for a few days. I sure will be glad when school is over. Then my real vacation will start. I am not going to paint the back room until the fall. Most of the screens are up. The garden is under control. Joe is working hard on the back lawn. Between the wheat and the weeds and Dad not using the path to the car line, it's over my head. Joe tried to cut a little of one side yesterday.

Pop did not do much Saturday and yesterday. He didn't get in the garden at all between rain and church and yet he didn't get any rest to speak of, it seems. We were at McAdams' Friday night. Then Pop was running all day Saturday. He went up to Ems' Saturday night at 8:30, but Dot was not home yet from work. So, I said if she wasn't home not to worry about my hair as I wasn't home on Friday eve when she was here. But, I did phone her. She gets off Thursday. On Saturdays, she must wait until all the drivers get in off the route, so Mrs. Ems was still waiting with her supper. She said George got his wings and he earned them the hard way too. You see, he didn't have a college degree like Fred Dollenberg.

Pop said Fred Baker is supposed to have gotten two thousand dollars from the government and gone down on a farm in Texas. Of course, that's the story told. Dad says he doesn't believe it, but I pass it on.

The speaking at Pennypack was poor. The crowd was slim in the morning, but there was a better turnout in the afternoon. Lou Heim was there with the red car. We went to visit Aunt Mary's grave. Aunt Lilly planted quite a few things on them (Mal's mother & dad) and the three graves were in good shape.

We will be going to William Penn Cemetery this next Sunday.

So then son, take care of yourself. I love you very much. I hold you close, smooth your face and kiss you.

Until then, cheerio.

Love,

Mother & All

(Enclosure – Item 9)

CITY READY TO HAIL BRADLEY, SPAATZ, 52 OTHER HEROES

Bad Weather Prevents Flight and They'll Arrive by Train

AT NORTH PHILADELPHIA

Poor flying weather caused a last-minute change in the arrival plans of the 54 European war heroes who will parade through Philadelphia this afternoon.

Instead of the 2 o'clock arrival at the Northeast Airport, the 54 visitors, led by two four-star generals, will arrive at North Philadelphia Station of the Pennsylvania Railroad. Little change, however, was made necessary in the parade route.

Tuesday, June 5, 1945

Dear Son Edwin,

I am here early today, 9 AM. The fires are fixed and the dishes are done and now for our chat of the day. Yesterday, I planted my new flower garden behind the barn. In the back row, I put holly hocks, next row marigolds, next row stocks or wall flowers, larkspur and ragged robin, next row some sort of a daisy, next four rows straw flowers border of petunias, and in each corner a fire bush. By the scrub oak tree, Pop had Joe plant one of the passion vines. Then all along the barn (at the sink hole that is filled in), Pop put climbing nasturtiums, the pink rambler rose bushes, blue larkspur, pink holly hocks, red scarlet runner and blue morning glories. So, by next fall, we hope we have it nice looking back there beside the big round flower bed of cannas. Last night, Dad got the ground ready all along the lane for asters, zinnias, marigolds, and dahlias. At 1 AM, it started to pour rain. It has rained real hard ever since and everything is sure plenty wet and green. The lawn looks beautiful. Roger's pansy bed is a picture and topped by the new American flag, which he puts out every morning and takes down every night. I said to him, 'That is your job. Keep it flying in honor of your brother.' All my life I have wanted a flag pole and flag and on V.E. Day, I did queer things. I went out there and saluted it. I blew that whistle, one toot for each boy I knew and 3 for all those I didn't know. Then I got on my knees and thanked God and said, 'Flag, you're the most beautiful of all, long may you wave. My boy is out there to keep you flying over the land; over the 25 acres of wheat as tall as me; the bread of life.' Son, I was surely thankful and grateful. My nerves have been very bad ever since. But, the past two days, I have just called a halt. So, this morning I feel better. I can't remember if I said goodbye to Dad. I don't know if I answered when he called because I woke up and looked at the clock, 6:15, so I don't know if I answered or not. I was up at

2:45 and he asked me what time it was. I told him it was raining and he said yes, he heard it at 1 o'clock.

Well son, just picture three thousand or more school boys and girls from Wilson marching in double file and standing in double file lined along Roosevelt Boulevard at Cottman Street to give General Spatz and General Bradley and fifty other heroes a greeting. Your twelve-year-old brother will remember that as long as he lives. The General saluted and the children cheered. All the teachers and Dudley were there. The course of the parade was changed at the last minute. Due to bad flying weather they could not come to Northeast Airport, so they came by train to North Philadelphia and then came up by car through Mayfair over Cottman, etc. Well, the day my General comes home, I will parade our lane looking for him. That will be my happy day. What say, "General Manager"?

We have the two boxes ready to go out. But if it's raining, we won't get them out tonight. I will let you know when they are mailed so you can look for them. I guess Dad and Joe will be real busy getting in the flowers tonight. Dad hasn't the ground marked out for the celery, but this would sure be the time to plant it. I guess it will get hot so sudden it will knock us out, but it has been 44 degrees and it was sure raw on Sunday. The pastor said for the first time in history, he wore a topcoat to Pennypack. I could just see you jumping over the wall, nearly losing your watch. There are all sorts of happenings in life. We must take them as they come. I used to think how young I was. But, I am beginning to think how short and yet how long since I came here. Now it's your turn. Well dear, I wrote so much, so all my love for today. May God watch over thee and me while we are absent, one from the other.

Mom

Wednesday, June 6, 1945

My Dear Son,

Here it is 10:30, and I have sure had a busy day. Today we had our missionary meeting at Mary Butcher's and there were 34 ladies there, the pastor, and a wonderful speaker, Mrs. Davies, who spent 35 years in China. She sure told us some tales. Then tonight, Dad and I went to church to hear a Chinese Principal of Wayland Academy, Hankow, China speak. We sure had some meeting, singing, and then ice cream and coffee. Dad had Margery Dudley serve him coffee twice.

Now son, I will write a big letter tomorrow.

Guess who was here tonight just home from the Pacific (shot in the foot and ankle at Saipan)? Russell Peters. He sure had a fine crop of wavy hair. He has been in the hospital a good while. He got 30 days furlough. He is a gunner 2/C, 2 ½ years.

Son, I had good luck when I got home. There was a check of refund from your income tax for $75.06. I am going to use some of it towards the bills and put the balance in the bank for you with your others. I am so happy you will now have a start. Will write more tomorrow.

Lots of love,

Mother & All

Wartime Letters Written from Mother to Son

Thursday, June 7, 1945

Well My Dear Son in Blue,

I am tired, but it's only 1 o'clock. I was sitting by the window, eating a bite and I said, 'Well, Grandpop, this was your seat and I wonder what you saw or what you thought about as you sat here.' But I got a feeling right in the middle of my heart that there was a letter in the box for me from our sweet darling sugar tulip plum. So, I got up and hip, hop over the stones. It's a beautiful day with a cool breeze and hot sun. When I got halfway down there was the heavenly smell of the honeysuckle, oh! So, I go on down and there is one letter from my boy in blue. I tore it open and read a few lines to see if you were alright and then I picked some honeysuckle, oh! I could see the times when my Dad would bring honeysuckle to my mother and so I have flowers all over the house.

Roger's pansy bed and that American flag and the beautiful green lawn are sure a perfect sight. If two long were coming along yelling, 'Mom, I'm home,' then I would say; truly, what is so rare as a day in June? My dear boy, please don't say you are homesick. Just as true, you know that no one on God's green earth loves you any more than I do. Say to yourself, 'Oh! Mother dear, smooth my face,' and God will watch over you because I have never known God to fail me and so I am close to you in spirit. When you are tired, I say, Edwin, March On. I talk to you all day long. I look at your picture. I kiss it. It sure was a hard blow to me, but I wanted you to go. I think you will grow up better because you did not obey. You knew how much Dad was against a tattoo and writing with ink on your flesh, but in spite of it all, you did it. So maybe the Navy will teach you how to cooperate.

Son, don't worry about us. Dad and I have gone through many trials since we have been married. You make plans for you. All Dad and I will need in a short while is one room. It's up to you and Roger now to look after yourself. Dad and I will try to help you to get a start. We are so pleased and so proud that you have two bonds and $100 in the bank. We know that if you "obey" or listen to us, you will have a good start. So, relieve your mind of all worries. You are young. You are strong, so carry on for my sake. I know you will be a credit to us. You know you had me worn out from worry for six months. That car was sure a headache and still is. But Dad is like all the John Bulls with English determination. It's wonderful to possess at times, but I know it and I have a battle to make him see things for his own good too. When it's too late, he wishes he had listened to me. My darling, this letter sounds like our usual battles, but I write you what I think. You know that no one understands you like I do.

Old Grandpop went away four years ago today and so he sits at God's window now and he says, Old Nut, Old Bum is watching you. So, do what you can and show them what a good farm boy you are. Old Grandpop was your teacher, so make good and then I know Eddie and "the girl" will be happy. So you feel how close I am? Never be homesick.

Love,

Mom & All

Friday, June 8, 1945

Dearest Son Edwin,

Oh, what a beautiful morning! All the cattle are standing like statues over in Fisher's meadow. A beautiful day in June and, of course, I am thinking of my boy in blue. You know I loved my Dad very much and he loved me also. On a June day a few years ago (ten), he was celebrating his forty-first wedding anniversary. He said to me, dear, when you were home and still belonged to me before I gave you to Ed, you used to sing so nice. Annie Clift was there with me. He put his arm around me and Annie and I sang Mother McCree. Then we did another that puts your mother's sails down, "by the time she gets through". We did the Oceanic Roll. So when you go to listen or make a request for your band to play The Oceanic Roll, instead of the "Alabama", sing Pasadena. Now I know you will say, "Mom, I can't do that."

I am just telling you my thoughts on this beautiful June day here on the farm. Memories take me home very often and you don't need to be young nor in the Pacific. Home is where the heart is and so my heart is ever home in the Valley of the Pennypack with June days and honeysuckle, old dog Nell, sport fishing, watermelons, lima beans, corn and with Dad with his beer keg with no ice. He would put the keg down in the spring house and then when it was tapped, he would put it in the run where the ripples of water kept it cool in the forest at the Rowland Shovel Works. I had no thoughts that another war would take my boy and my brother and his sons away.

Russell Peters told us that the Sea Bees at Guadalcanal took and gave their Christmas dinner to the marines.

Do you remember how you always wanted to leave home and how I took you and pushed you out the back door? I think you were about seven. Do you remember the day you were going to run away and you got as far as the railroad tracks and I said, go ahead. In five minutes, the cops will pick you up. I was all stove polish and I made believe I was talking on the phone to the police.

Edwin, while I was writing this, Mrs. McAdams called me up. She said William was all packed and ready to go and the barracks was full of bed bugs, the first ones he had ever seen.

The Home Fires

I thought the Navy was particular. If a chocolate spot caused an order to rip off a pillow case and throw it on the floor, where was the inspector there? Not only that, but a Navy cook told me where he was up in Washington State, the roaches were so bad, they dropped off the wall into pots of food. Something is wrong somewhere. I never can solve the problem, so I guess that's why we have war. Keep clean.

We haven't gotten your last two boxes off yet. We will mail them Saturday the 9th, so disregard the other letter saying I had mailed them. Roger had to carry them home the second time. One was 8 ounces too heavy and the other ten ounces too heavy. Dad will mail them tomorrow.

Remember the day the teacher took you to the Zoo and you and John McCullough decided you wanted to go to New York? You got to Sears & Roebuck as Dad went by. I guess you know now why I always ran and looked for you. I am still looking. Lapergola told me Wednesday that John is in Germany. Jimmie's Camile is in Belgium. Jack O'Lone is home since Tuesday night. Me, I guess Caroline will soon push around two. Let them have them; more cannon fodder for twenty years hence.

Well son, I got off track. I still have plenty of work to do. Roger said music and math today. He made 60 cents last night. That lady pays him forty cents per hour on Welsh Road. I told him that you said you guess he is getting big. He said to tell you he will take you over when you come home. He's the boss of the shack now and he rules the bus. He is 5 feet 1 and he has me nuts with the dogs. He said, 'Oh Mom, you're nuts anyway.' The "Lady" has her basket full, but not from "Baby". Dad said maybe he called on her when he was away and that was why he was sick. I suppose I should not write those things.

I have my second cup of fresh coffee and my chat for the day, so, "Mom, hurry up and Mom make me something to eat."

Pop gave me $18.00 pay last night; two days out. Where is all that big money they say is around? I never see any of it. All the food is very high and very scarce. Mrs. Spence and quite a few can't get any toilet paper. She asked me for some and I said what Dad always says, "Use a corn cob, but the last S.B. stole ours." "Bad Mom." Well, they are so near the stores and yet they don't provide. The "hicks" who weed the beets are the suppliers, but son, the shelves don't get full.

Rocking in the rocker on the front porch or in the playsuit and my "Popeye" won't get canned if I keep on writing. Dad's spinach is wonderful, so I must do some up for that cold day you come home.

Lots of love forever,

Mother

Saturday, June 9, 1945

Dear Son,

Here it is 9 AM, and Dad has me up cooking his breakfast and now he is getting your boxes ready. What a time we have had trying to put something in. I had to take out all I had put in as everything is so heavy, but maybe they will have some little thing to touch the spot.

You should hear what Dad is calling me. I said I was going to tell you and he said, "My boy would agree with me."

Roger wanted a piece of watermelon and Dad said they are too expensive. I bought one small piece, enough for him. Fifty-nine cents. They weigh them now at six cents per pound. You know the rind is so heavy, that one ordinary watermelon cost $2.50. So, Uncle Bill won't be here to carry them in. Roger was going to go up to the pool today and stop in, but it's too cold.

We saw Dot on the way from work. She showed us the ring her mother got her for her birthday. It was quite pretty. She invited us to stop on our way home. So Pop jerked me around in a hurry. No looking at hats, etc. When we got back, she wasn't home, only the three young-uns. Mr. Ems is supposed to come over here today. He asked Pop for a scythe handle because Dad has one extra. Dot also said, 'I will call you up and come over from work tonight, good night, Mom and Pop.'

Well, that's all for today. Dad is nearly ready with the boxes and I still have breakfast dishes to do. Lots of love, hugs and kisses. Will write tomorrow, Children's Day Sunday. Cheerio.

Mom

Sunday, June 10, 1945 (Missing)

Monday, June 11, 1945 (V-Mail)

Yes, son, Dad got the small piece you sent. Some of your letters were censored. Not much, but where you told how hot it was, was out. The newspapers tell a little more news. I think you are in the Third Fleet. So we get news of it every once in awhile. I fully understand your letters and no matter what the censors think, that is all forgotten by them. I love you, I love you, means the same the world over. Write all you can. You do perfect. I love you and hope you are better.

Wartime Letters Written from Mother to Son

Mother

Monday, June 11, 1945 (V-Mail)

Dear Son,

My dear boy, I got nine letters and Rog got one today dated up to June 1st and you are still in sick bay. Now my dear son, all you told us in the letters we understand. My darling, I have been through the same thing working for the big bugs and things stuck with me that I could never forget. But, they make better characters of us. We get kinder and more gentle. As the years pass, all will be well. I sure hope you are better. I sure hope you get my mail. I write every day, sometimes twice. It's hot here today, eighty degrees.

Love,

Mother

Monday, June 11, 1945

Dearest Son,

I just wrote you two V-Mail letters, as they say they go the quickest. We get all of your letters because you date them in that way. I keep track of them. But I also number mine as to date. When you get three letters, you will know when I wrote them.

Son, I sure knew and felt something was ailing you and I kept worrying about it. I do hope you are lots better. Of course, I do think the needle made it show up. A good rest will give you a chance to get back. But, as you say, as soon as we feel better, we want to be at the job. Dad got the small piece and so we know you are our good boy. You used to make fun of me and say, 'Oh! That was 40 years ago.' But sweet memories linger.

I gave your address to the Town paper. I gave $1.00 also. I guess it will be in the next edition. Now, dear, we have all the maps and we are learning too.

It was quite cool here all during the first week of June, but today it hit 84 degrees; quite a change. You are a little ahead. Your mail reaches us in record time; 9 days for this last lot. I sure thank God you write. I am grateful to you that in your spare time you write us.

Dot and Mrs. Ems were here Saturday night. We had a nice visit together. Dot had dinner with us Sunday. I wanted her to meet Mrs. Spence, but they did not get up because it rained. Dad took her home about five as Buck[114] went fishing. He came home on account of the rain. Dot and Mrs. Ems were going to the movies. Someone must always be with old Grandpop. He's in bed 13 weeks. Mrs. Ems said she had a telegram from New Orleans, Louisiana asking for $100 for fare home, signed Johnnie. But the telegram was sent to Jake Ems in Somerton, so they are worried about it. Dot phoned Juanita, but did not hear anything yet. I will let you know when I hear anything. Dave Tumbelston was home with his new baby girl Jean Elizabeth, and they had it dedicated yesterday, as it was Children's day.

Son, that's all I know for today. It's 3:30. I guess Dad will not like to hear you've been sick. Good old Mom didn't wait on you this time, only in thought. You are ever near me. I love you lots. So does Dad and Rog.

Mother

---

[114] Buck is nickname for Roger, a reference that he often asked for a "buck".

Dear Son Edwin,

Wasn't that just wonderful that the doctor knew Bustleton people? It is often good as medicine to talk to someone about home. I know it made you feel better. An old Irish lady used to tell me, "People meet where mountains won't." It took me a long time to understand what she meant, but as I grew older I know now. People meet, pass by but sometimes they are tied with the same knot; "lovers knot". I hope you get to see something pleasant while in port and tell the doctor that here is a mother who says thanks "for the talk to her boy."

The thing that goes the farthest, costs the least and does the most is just a pleasant smile, so smile for me.

Love,

Mother

Tuesday, June 12, 1945

My Dear Son,

Be calm and keep up your spirits. All is well at home. We sure are happy to get so many letters from you. I was out to see Doctor Roseman last night. This morning I took a dose of salts and am doing nothing else. Of course, I did the dishes and made the beds, etc. I had no fires to fix today. Yesterday was our warmest day. The doctor said I am anemic. That, you know, means not enough red blood and that in turn causes my headache and no strength. I don't think I am as bad as in the winter. I told him to shoot me and finish me off. He said no coffee, tea or cocoa, 2 eggs every day, one piece of dry toast, plenty of spinach and green vegetables, fruits, no potatoes, gravy or sweets.

The Home Fires

All is just fine, but the coffee part, but because it is summer, I can drink fruit juices and love them.

The question of no butter is easy; haven't had any since Christmas anyway. It's 24 points. A pound of lard is 10 points (6 eggs to a customer per week). Meat is out of the question. We are eating so much fish that I never want to see it. I like fish, but not if you get too much. But you know us darling, we are never hungry. I have 75 quarts of tomatoes yet and all kinds of relish, beets, dried beans, and carrots.

When you come home, the table will be like I used to cook years ago for Jake Arlen and the harvesters. Mrs. Leiby and Mrs. Davis would come and Mrs. Patterson would help cook for 15 men. I'd have 14 quarts of Betsy's milk in the pan, 6 kinds of pies, roast beef, a 14 pound rib roast, 6 chickens, baskets of limas, and fresh corn. Grandpop would sharpen up the knife and I would stand beside him and pass plates that were so hot that I had to use the tail of my apron. Ted Ramsden, Mr. Brous, Wenkers, would be here. Then Grandpop would say, "Girl, have you got an extra leg under this table? If you keep on, you will need it." Everybody would laugh and then they would talk about how Grandpop always had a full table. The same old cook will do the same for you, only Pop won't have Old Betsy to milk and when I passed the cottage cheese say, "No white wash for me." Uncle Paul would say, "Pass the bowel remover (rhubarb) and hand me the commission men (beets)." Damn the war. All we want is peace and a chance to work and have enough to eat.

The doctor asked for you. Pop was at Benders. The carburetor went south. Then we went to Rhawn Street and couldn't get what we wanted there. So, we went to a drugstore in McAdams' block. Then we stopped at Mrs. McAdams'.

This morning, I woke up and saw that it was nearly light. I looked at the clock. It was 5 o'clock and Pop was snoring away. I said, 'Eddie. No work today?' He said, "What?" Up he got, so I rushed down, made the dried beef hot and his coffee, so he still had until 6 o'clock to leave. A man who lives in Trevose brings his Ford here and goes with Dad. Yes, Dad is okay with gas. We never go any where except to the store once a week and to church.

Bill, of course, has left. I don't know where he is now. I did tell you that Russell Peters was at Leyte last year. I also got the two pieces and also the religious books. They are just wonderful. I hope you are better. All our love, hugs and hopes for your return,

Mother & All

Tuesday, June 12, 1945

Dear Son,

Are you getting the stamps in the letters okay? I sent out three letters last night; two V and one air and this is the second one today. I just walked down for the mail. There is a nice air going, but it is real hot. Now, honey, I got four more letters today and mail is coming in fine and wonderful. Last week we got mail up to May 24th, and then yesterday got mail from May 20th. Today were two on May 22nd and one for June 2nd and one for June 3rd. I have mail now for all those days past in rotation. I sure am glad Aunt Violet writes you and all is well at home. As you know, you can read more home news in Our Town than I know.

Son, don't worry over anything. I hope you got ashore. It will bolster your feelings. I write so much advice, it's only from my heart, so don't ponder over it. You ask about Dot and in my previous letters I have tried to tell you. But some day, you might say things I said, this or that, and cause me trouble. You know me; what I have to say, I say it. Yes, you answered your own question. When you are 17 to 21, you learn. When you are 21 to 25, you wonder how you got so old and about all the things you've learned whereas you thought from 14 to 18 you knew everything. Then from 25 to 50, you live all your life put together. The clock never has enough hours on it and time has silvered your hair. You realize that you have sons away or about to marry and then you sit and write them your thoughts or you gaze out the kitchen window and think and think; Abergavenny when I was a boy, Leyte when I was a lad. Life passes us by in a different way for each of us. Plans and hopes are what keep us young. I took a pleasure and pride in my looks and my teeth. Any guy who gets a wife to do for him, like I did for your Dad, will be lucky. Your father always kept his word. He was a gentleman to me always and I knew that. I had seen what other women had. I had hard work. Flora Beyer says it's not the hard work that kills you, but the worry. So, I try to tell you, don't worry. The world passes us by. We get along because we have a will to do so, God to have faith in, and hope for our children at the post where God wanted us. So, until I clasp you to my breast, I put all my love in warm lines here to you and say, my son in blue, heed the advice of thy father and mother. When thou art old, thee will not turn from it and so that is our chat for today. All the questions are answered. How can I judge a girl by hello and goodbye? Background has a lot to do with a girl. When you are young, you can always improve. Looks are pleasing and kindness not bought. Wrist watches and such won't mean a thing if true love that never dies is there. Dad likes Dot. I do too. But, War is Hell and time will tell. Darling, I hope you feel better. Save your money. I hope you got all my other mail. Lots of love. Hugs, my baby.

Mom

(Enclosures – Items 10 and 11)

Hitler Reported To Be Father of 2

LONDON, June 11 (U.P.).—An unconfirmed dispatch from Stockholm said today that two children—a boy and a girl—were born to Adolf Hitler and Eva Braun during their long, illicit love affair.

Hitler's 11th-hour marriage to Eva just before Berlin fell was undertaken to legitimatize the children, the dispatch said. The marriage first was reported reported by Marshal George K. Zhukov, Soviet conqueror of Berlin, last Saturday.

BOY IS 5, DISPATCH SAYS

The Stockholm dispatch, which appeared in the London Daily Express, said the children—the boy now five years old and the girl four—were the object of a widespread search by American and British occupation forces.

The dispatch said the story of the children was told by Erik Wesslen, who was attached to the Swedish legation in Berlin and was in close touch with Hitler's headquarters during the siege of the German capital.

Mercury Soars To Year's High

Philadelphia area residents sweltered, discarded coats and loosened ties yesterday as the temperature, after remaining well below normal for the last two months, climbed to the highest mark reached so far this year.

Coupled with an unusually high humidity, the mercury rose rapidly in the late forenoon and early afternoon to 88 degrees in the shade at 4 P. M. in the central-city area. Previous high was on March 29 when, in an unseasonable rise, the mercury climbed to 87.

SHOWERS PREDICTED

The Weather Bureau's early forecast predicted a continuation of the heat and humidity today with thundershowers this afternoon.

Wednesday, June 13, 1945

Dearest Son,

Here I am, like you, with nothing to say. Of course, I am not in the middle of water, but here in the most charming spot in the world. I have beautiful music on the radio and a perfect June day with peace and quiet. So here I am wishing for my boy in blue. Then all would be complete. The next best thing is to chat with you and that is my pleasure now. I am through the daily routine, have the pansies, blue robin, and gorgeous brilliant nasturtiums all arranged prettily around the house. The shades are lowered and the birds are singing. I am so thankful to God. Lord, I thank you for so much;

friendship, love and a dream to hold. I see you write some of your dreams. That is wonderful to share your thoughts. Of course, being your mother, God gives a gift that always enables me to know exactly what your desires are because you are part of me.

I can also tell exactly about Aunt Lilly. She was to go down to Judge Brown yesterday. I called up last night to find how she made out. Esther talked to me. She said her mother was in the cellar doing her ironing. I said to never mind calling her. But, Esther did anyway. So, I waited and waited and finally I said to Esther, "Listen, I got work to do and I will talk to her again." After I hung up, I said to myself, damn it, she had more in the cellar than ironing. The night before, she told me all her troubles and I told her what to say in court. So, a little while ago, she called me up. Fred and Tom White were in the cellar with her. The court ordered Fred to pay her $10 a week. He came out with her, took her to dinner, went to the bank, and went there for supper. Now I believe he is going to court her, but not live there. In July, they may go away together for a new honeymoon. So, you can never tell Aunt Lilly. She also got a V-mail letter back, written in February to Edwin. They had his complete address on it. They have not heard a thing about him since our English cousins wrote that he was there in February. Aunt Lilly didn't write him for two weeks and she is going to take your advice and not write to him. Then she is going to go to the Red Cross. She sure is worried about him. I say, thank God that my son sends me and Dad the most beautiful letters.

Edwin, when I say this home is the most beautiful spot, it sure is true. It is a seven minute walk from the trolley, yet back off the road and no neighbors to annoy you.

Edwin, a beautiful fat rabbit is sitting by the red maple. I am writing this letter at the dining room window and all you can hear are the birds. Also this morning, I saw a hen pheasant with about ten babies marching across the lower end of Dad's garden. The wheat and rye are beginning to ripen and Joe has sure got his hands full on the back lawn. The grass grows fast. Roger's chickens are doing wonderfully; growing fine. Dad put in four rows of asters along the drive, so I guess I will have enough to cut and maybe sell some.

Well dear, I must run along. I sent a card to June[115], as it's her birthday on the 19th. I think she will graduate, and is going to college.

Roger bought two pedigree pigeons last night and he and Carl went to the Somerton Pool. Now, tell me any news you know of your "brother" or "Dad's" and that will be the best I know. I told you all the news for today. Dad is so pleased with his letters. He takes them to Ford Tank Depot for the fellows to read. He is sure proud of the way you write. And so, my dear, I will say I trust you are feeling better. I got everything you sent, money, the paper, and so all I can say is be a good boy. Do your best.

Mrs. North, the teacher at Jacob's, asked Rog to ask you the name of the doctor. She rides on the school bus every day with Roger. Maybe the doctor would like to know that school is over the 22nd and Mr. North teaches at Wilson where Roger goes. So long for now. Love from all.

Mother

Thursday, June 14, 1945

Dearest Son Edwin,

---

[115] June is Barbara June Long, daughter of Helen's brother, William Howard Long (Uncle Bill). June is Edwin's first cousin.

The Home Fires

Here it is Flag Day, so I did salute Old Glory. It is hardly moving. It is one of those hot, sultry days. But, I keep saying, it is nothing like the tropics. I have my corset off and I am making myself comfortable. So, here I am for our usual chat. It's 12:30 and I am about through the usual work. I am going to take life easy all afternoon.

Pop had the car passed for inspection last night. Tonight is pay night, so Pop is stopping at Food Fair to get fish and potatoes. I see three of the chickens are out, cleaning off Dad's head lettuce. They started to put up a higher fence, but last night we had a storm and Dad was at Bender's so, Joe took care of the dishes. I went to bed. I got up when Dad came back. I woke up with a terrible headache this morning. Rog cooked his own eggs and brought me a drink to the couch. I got up at 7, but I had to lie down again.

Edwin, it's now late afternoon. Rog went to the Boulevard Pool. He brought up two letters, one to Dad and one to me written June 4th. Yes, I got the two letters June 1st etc. and everything was in fine shape. Edwin, you said you got five letters. You should know if you are getting all my mail because I number them according to the date of the day. I write every day and send V-mail extra. Pop is tired when he comes in from the field and he will write when he can.

Now, son, maybe Dot got mixed up to try you out. The last two times she was here, she did not have the ring on. I didn't feel good, so I didn't ask her where the ring was. She had told me she would wear it forever and ever. They didn't say what they bought with the money you sent and I didn't ask, but Mrs. Ems said she paid $21.00 for Dot's birthday ring. It's very pretty with five reddish pink stones in a nice setting.

Betty Hattel sent for Edwin Bissinger's address and I also gave yours. Roger and Carl will give it to Hattel on the bus.

I am glad you are better. I took my medicine and by nine, I was okay. I have a big wash on the line right now and must hang out my own "funnies". So, until supper, I will be lady of the farm. Pop thought he heard a "meow" in the car one morning last week on the way to work and he heard it three times. Finally, he stopped near the Frankford High School. He raised the hood; no cat. She must have crawled in that hole in the back deck and away she went. We looked around the school that night, but couldn't see her. She was so well-trained and now we have no cat again. The two dogs are rip snorters. The new one, Lady, won't let the wash man, the baker, or anyone carrying a bundle in the door. Pop is tickled that she is such a sharper to take care of me. She is beautiful, but has a full basket. She is real tiny and looks like a big collie dog but is real small, about half as big as "Baby". They are barking now, outside.

Well honey, I got an invitation to June's graduation on June 22nd at Richer Field, Los Angeles. That means a present. Also this morning, Aunt Katie and Uncle Freeman called me up from Keller's house. Howard Lewis was home last weekend. Aunt Katie brought down two chickens, nearly 14 pounds and two pounds of butter. She is here to buy some clothes. She said she got a beautiful dress at John Wanamaker's and all the rest to go with it as she and Uncle Freeman are celebrating their golden wedding on July 28th. It's 130 miles each way to her home, which is 30 miles west of Harrisburg in Liverpool, PA. She wants us to come up for the weekend. Maybe we can. I was at her silver wedding anniversary and at my great grandmother's golden and my grandmother's golden. First I was age 3 months, the second one, 20 and now if I get to this one - - - . I often heard my Dad tell the story of how they put the gold under their plates and how happy his parents were when they found it. They invited all the children and thought that no one brought a gift. But when the plates were turned over, there were gold coins. This Christmas, I want you home for our silver wedding. I want a set of dishes, two service sets of 8 alike and a set of silverware if the war is over.

Edwin, I hope you get your watch. We insured it, but they tell us that is only good in the States. Freemont Long is at Honolulu in the Army. I got all your letters in date to June 4th. The two I got today were written June 2nd. But, I also got up to the 4th since Monday. Today is Thursday; Flag Day. I got 15 letters and Roger got one, making 16, which is wonderful. As you know, any addressed to Pop, I read and then read them to Pop before he eats supper. He says I can read them quicker and then he reads them when he comes to listen to Gabriel Heater. I don't think he ever hears him. I say, 'What did Gabriel Heater say?' and he says, 'I don't know.'

Love,

Mom

Friday, June 15, 1945 (Missing?)

Saturday, June 16, 1945 (Missing?)

Sunday Night, June 17, 1945

Edwin dear,

It's 10 PM and so this letter is short. I have a cup of coffee. It's ninety degrees in the dining room and what a day I have gone through. Aunt Katie and Uncle Freeman came Saturday morning and left this morning after I went to church with them in Holmesburg. Edwin, I will finish this letter tomorrow and tell you the rest. I am too hot to write and it's getting near eleven. We got in from Uncle Charlie's at 9:10. Mrs. Spence called. I cooked and I tried to write this letter between times because I chat with you every day. I talked of you all day and will write a big letter tomorrow. Darling, good night.

Wartime Letters Written from Mother to Son

Lots of love,

Mother & All

Monday, June 18, 1945

Dearest Edwin,

Well son, last night I wrote you a few short lines because of the lateness of the day and the heat. Here I am for a finish of the chat. I told you of Aunt and Uncle being here. Dad went to Tacony at 9 AM for them. I was up half of Friday night cooking because of the day's heat and I was on the spot for Saturday with the company and then them wanting to go to Holmesburg Church. Dad had his suit coat on sitting in church at 95 degrees. I had on my blue hat that I bought when you were with me. Every time you were mad at me, you were going to tell Dad that I paid $12.75 for a hat and when I showed the ticket to Dad, he said he couldn't see it. We went from church to Grace Long's house. She bought that house on Craig Street that Dad and I looked at. I could sure kick myself for not buying it. She is a dream of a housekeeper (Well, Grace and her family of 4). She had Dad, Rog, me, Uncle Freeman, Aunt Katie, Ruth Long Keller, her son Howard Lewis, and a sailor from the Navy Yard and back from the Pacific for dinner at 1 PM. He was coming back from the Pacific when you went out. He is from Detroit and was quiet. He said, I looked like Easter and Uncle Freeman, said, "Yes, isn't she beautiful." Dad said, "Yes, my favorite." So, I guess they were all struck with the heat. What do you think about your best girl? Then we had a good dinner and Aunt Katie and I went around the corner to see Aunt Dink. Her father was there, as you know it was Father's Day.

I gave Dad a white shirt and two summer undershirts. I bought 2 nice cards and I put one with your name and one with Roger's and one dollar in each.

The Home Fires

Dad brought one dozen roses and "put his heart in beside them". There were three yellow, three bronze, three red and three pink. He told me last night he had a fight (by words) with the guy he bought them from. He wanted to give Dad all one color and Dad wanted them mixed. He got them.

It was Keller's birthday and Aunt Katie was down here to buy a new dress. I think I did tell you. Well now, we got it all arranged. They had to call on me to help with the plans for Aunt's Golden wedding. It is to be held in the town fire hall on Saturday, July 28th from 4 to 8, so the invitations read. Two hundred people are invited. The ladies of the fire department are to do all the serving and of course, we girls are to help in the preparation of the food. That's where I come in. We'll have 50 chickens for chicken salad, potato salad, potato chips, olives and pickles by the gallons. There on top of that, 20 pound hams and Dad is getting a turkey, which is our contribution for me, Dad, Rog, Aunt Dink and Sis towards Sunday dinner.

Roger and I are going up on Friday morning, July 27th. Dad will take us down to Grace Long's when he goes to work in the morning. Grace and her two little girls, Rog and I, are going up with Ruth (she drives). Ruth is Howard Lewis' mother. Then at 9 o'clock on Friday night, Dad and Grace's and Ruth's husbands, Dan and Owen, along with Bob Lewis, Aunt Dink and Sissy will come in your car. Dad is not pleased with three in the front, but I think we can figure it out somehow. It's 30 miles west of Harrisburg, which makes it approximately 130 miles, but all those men are war plant workers and each contribute toward the trip. Ruth says her car makes it on 15 gallons of gas. The new gas tickets will be in. With the men not working on Saturday that makes enough gas for Dad's trip for 72 miles. I shall think of you all the while if I get there on the banks of the Susquehanna. I will never forget when I last saw that river. I am planning on a good trip. I think if I could stay away from home for a week's vacation, I would. But, Rog has the chickens to worry over and the dogs. Maybe by the time you get this, we will be in Liverpool.

I made out the menu for them yesterday and how much to buy. You know that's an old story with me to feed people. If you know how much it takes for 20, it's easy to figure it up, especially when I have had so much experience. And you know Mother, none of this tablespoon full. You know how Granny handled crowds.

In the heat after we left Aunt Dink, her father was up from Delaware. No news now for six weeks from Uncle John. We went to Aunt Katie's sister's on Rhawn Street (Moyers). Then we came home at 5 PM. We got out of our clothes and put on our comforts and we ate. I picked some blue and white larkspur. I took the red roses and I made a nice bouquet with a card and $1 in it and away we went to brother Charlie, whose birthday it was also (35). Granny, Al, Sam, Kebe and one of their friends were there. We stopped on our way up for Dot. No one was home but Mr. Ems. Granny and they were getting ready to leave on the 7:15 bus. For once, "no bottle". Violet gave me a slice of ham and a bunch of pink roses.

Then we went down to Aunt Minnie's. She had loads of company. It was hot, 95 degrees. Her three little babies have the whooping cough. Little Elmer is a wreck. They are taking him for a special needle today. So, we left and as I told you, we were home at 9 when Mrs. Spence delayed me.

I fried the ham. It was the first ham I had since the night at Mrs. Ems when you and Dot <u>weren't there</u>. On the way home, we also stopped at Dot's. Mr. Ems was sitting at the stand. Peg S. came with a note while we were there. It said, "Meet me at 10 AM tomorrow (that's today). George." Whoever took the message didn't say where to meet him, so I am waiting to hear the news tonight from Carl.

The Home Fires

Here is more news, I told you last night that this letter will be a big chat. Johnnie Ems got home okay and pulled into New Orleans and his wife is with him. He was here alone Saturday night. I loved and kissed him and he talked to Aunt Katie. He was serving the papers in the station wagon with all the kids. He is in from Okinawa on 27 days leave. Oh boy. Can you picture Mrs. Ems? She wasn't home then either, so I knew George was coming home before her. We all shook hands. Oh boy! Mrs. Ems said, "Here's where Dot will take two weeks vacation now."

Down at Aunt Dink's across the street at the brick house, a big sign across the front with two big flags says, 'Welcome Home Collie 2 ½ years in the Pacific.' They got word he was to get home and the spaghetti and barrels of red wine were rolling in ever since. It was so hot and every Italian lady from Frankford Avenue on was out. Old Mr. Barnes said, "I can hardly wait till I see that mother." She was pacing up and down the front porch for 2 ½ hours while I was at Aunt Dink's. Mr. Barnes (past 80 years old), said, "I'm gonna run across when he comes." So, my darling, It's that way in homes all over the world. Pops and moms and wife and sweetheart, boys and men, it's all the same when we love.

You know I would much rather go up with Dad, because Dad treats me good when we are out; the best food, etc. But all the men don't want any days out or any vacation. So, on Saturday they won't work as the production is over the quota. Then Dan and Keller can drive. If Pop gets too tired, someone will take over. Keller and Dan know the easiest way, as they have been up there many times. Ruth has driven to Florida and all over, so I think that is the best arrangement to make.

I am going to Lane Bryant as I want to "show off" too. Aunt Dink is going with me. Then, the first cool day, I will get a permanent. So my son, for now it's cheerio. It's too hot. I am not doing much today. Okay. My darling, General

"Ike" Eisenhower is getting his royal welcome today at the War Department. We are praying. Son, read Isaiah Chapter 41, Verse 10. I have your picture at that verse[116] and that brings you near me.

How did you like this chat today? Be a good son. I love you.

Your best girl.

Roger left now with Carl. He said you ought to hear how George spent Easter Sunday. He was at Okinawa and Tokyo. So long for now,

Mother

Dear Son,

It's 4:30 now, so here is the added news. You will say, Mom you sure did chat today. But, son, my arm is sticking fast to the paper. I have ice cubes and the electric fan and it's still hot.

Mrs. Ems missed George at the station. The train was three hours late, so they went back again. A cab pulled in. There was a knock at the door. Carl answered, as he had to stay home from school to mind Grandpop. There was George. Roger says he looks swell. George said, "I spent my Easter afternoon torpedoing those G.D. Japs." He had $300 in cash and he put a check in Roger's hand for one thousand dollars. So, Johnnie said, "The house is drunk tonight, Mom." Mrs. Ems is so happy. Dot, Peg S., Juanita and her daughter are all home. You know money talks. He is an officer now;

---

[116] Isaiah 41:10 (King James Version) Fear thou not; for I am with thee: be not dismayed; for I am thy God: I will strengthen thee; yea, I will help thee; yea, I will uphold thee with the right hand of my righteousness.

four years the hard way, but he made it. Roger and all are going swimming at 5:30.

You would shine tonight if you were home. Nutsie called his pop so he can get off work tomorrow. I have a big devil's food cake baked in case they come in and plenty on ice. My darling, I miss you too. I am hugging you right now. I wrote you a big letter today. May God please end this war and send <u>all</u> home. I must get supper and am going to the doctor tonight. I am better now again after my usual ailment for the week. But I will get a check up tonight.

Love,

Mother

Tuesday, June 19, 1945

My Dear Son,

I wrote you such a big letter yesterday that today, as usual; there is not much news of interest for our chat for the day. But, here I am. It's 12:30 and I am about through until the supper hour when I always look for you coming in at 50 miles per hour, dust going to Russell's.

I went to the doctor's last night. Pop went to Hermann's. He met Major Bill Tumbelston in there. He is at the Navy Yard. His arm is pretty bad and he is able to be out now. He is back from Iwo Jima. The doctor said my blood pressure was 15 above normal and better than last week. The anemia was also a little better and so on with the same medicine. We had a little shower last night while I was in the doctor's. We also had one through the night, which gave us some relief from the 95 degree heat. Now it is cloudy. The humidity is high and everything is sticky, which, I imagine is somewhat like the tropics. The grass, the foliage, the trees, and the weeds, are growing sky high and so heavy. I thought this is a good day to get an early start in my flower garden, so by 9, I was out there. I worked one hour and then the old ticker and my head started to thump. I must take salts every day before breakfast. Doctor's orders are to eat two eggs, one piece of dry toast, and no coffee. I ate the toast, no eggs. I took the salts and I got so sick out there. I made for the house. I just got in with the sweat pouring out of me. I vomited. I said, "Oh! Here alone. I'll call the doctor." But, I couldn't even do that. In a half hour it passed. So, I am cleaned up and doing nothing for the rest of the day. The doctor said I should not overdo things. I think stooping over did it. Of course, at this time of life, changes take place and that is the cause of my troubles. It is nothing serious. It just comes and goes in spells.

On the way home we stopped at Ems. They had a full house and were ready to go up to the sale, all except your sweetie, Dot. She has a beautiful case of sunburn and nothing on it. She could hardly move, so they were going to get some tannic acid for her to put on it. Now son, if you could see those two brothers; one a complete officer and the other - - - - - - - -, you would never think they were of the same family. George will go places in life. The southerners were up and John and Juanita were going back last night. I offered Mrs. Ems your bed for them to come and occupy as her house was full. But you know a mother finds room for all the chicks. It isn't so bad when they are little. Peg S. and all the Simons were in the station wagon and off to the sale. What a happy family they were. Mrs. Ems got the check for one thousand dollars from George to put on a home. We saw all the pictures of the squadron he is in and the flat top he is on. His ship was next to the Franklin when it got hit. He gave his mother a wing with three stars on it. I also saw ten yen, Jap money. He said his crew did perfect work. He is in the States now for one year and he reenlisted for four more years. Johnnie hit an officer on the way home. He is now rated an apprentice seaman. George gave him his tailor-made uniform. He had it on last night. That was the first time they met in three years. Johnnie has leave until July 7th and George until the end of July. Well son, that's all for now. I will write more later. Dot got your letters. I wish and hope to see you soon. I trust you are feeling lots better.

As ever, with all our love,

Mother, Dad, brother, Joe

Wednesday, June 20, 1945

Dearest Son,

I am thinking of you a lot this morning; what is on your mind, did you get the boxes, have you left port? Are you alright? That's only a few of the things I am thinking of. We got your letters telling us that you got 25 letters from the Housatonic and then four more, so I guess you know how much we think of you. I do hope that you got your watch. It would be a shame if it got lost. I know that a watch would only be a small item to lose. I hope that by this time some of your thoughts have been answered in my letters. Honey, don't save my letters. Save any others you want to. Those letters are meant just for you and me.

I don't know any news today. I am here just doing my usual work. I feel better than yesterday. We had quite a few thunderstorms and plenty of rain from 5 to 7 last night. Dad managed to get in two rows of celery, 305 plants in each row. That will give us a chaw on a few stalks. There are still plenty more to put in; just one planting and not much time after work.

Well, dearest, the Gardeners came up last night. She helps me out as they don't eat meat at any time. We met Caldwell at the Baltimore Market. He is a butcher. His father told us to go see him, so we did last Friday night. Okay, it's not what you know, but who. I guess the doctor winked his eye at the "old man" to pick you out; now that the boots are on board, maybe you will get one step ahead. I hope so. I send all my love and good wishes to my boy in blue. It's hard not to have you home, but I love you more for helping the U.S.A.

Love,

Mother

Thursday, June 21, 1945

Dearest Son,

It's 1:30 PM and now for our daily chat. I have no news whatsoever today except that, at last, Okinawa is ours; but at what a price; not worth it. It is still quite hot, but it suits me better than the kind of day you left. You say you can still see Dad the day you left for Bainbridge. I live the last morning over and over. I wanted you to love me that last morning, but you didn't want to. I took your hands and smoothed them. I can always see you. God knows what is best for us all.

Evening 8:10

Son, it got so hot that I left off and now it's time to call it quits for me. Dad is still on the job and Joe is head over heels in work. Dad put in two more rows of celery and Joe is hilling it up. Dad put in 36 rows of dahlia roots and wants to get in the marigolds. Then the flower bed along the drive will be finished.

Rog had to carry water tonight and Dad wishes it would rain. So life goes on for us during our busy season.

I painted the big bench outside white this afternoon, and I can see it's full of those fine blossoms that blow from the weeping birch tree, the one you used to climb. I hear a squirrel chirping in there every morning. It must have its home there.

I got your letter of June 10th today telling us you were ashore. I was not going to show it to Dad. But, when you said you had three ribbons and some stars, I was happy and proud. Dad said he is worried over you for fear you will do something, as you wrote about taking too much to drink. He is afraid something would happen to you while out on a lark.

We can't help but see the difference in the two Ems'. Dad said he doesn't want you like Johnnie; foolish and never have anything. So dear, please write us the news and let us know how you are.

The stars are for battle; the ribbons tell where, am I right? I will say good night for now.

With all our love,

Mother & All

Sunday, June 24, 1945

Dearest Son,

Here it is Sunday, June 24th. Now that I see the date, it brings to mind that Dad lost his mother 19 years ago today. Here at home, it sure is a nice beautiful day; a little on the hot side, but a nice cool air is blowing in the dining room window. Dad has been ready for breakfast hours ago. He has dusted the cauliflower, cabbage, etc. with lime and rotenone. He put in 11 hours in the garden yesterday. For once, he had a good break with the celery planting as we had a swell rain after the planting.

Now son, Saturday night at 7 o'clock, Mr. Stork flew around and today, "Lady" has 5 puppies. Edwin, you sure would love her. She is the sweetest thing. As soon as we can find any film, we will get her picture with the puppies.

Edwin, I don't know if I am going to church or not. It takes Dad's time. The same old story is going on at the table. Roger is on school vacation and he is getting orders on what needs to be done. He must keep my flower bed in condition. I planted it all, but I simply cannot weed it. I have a little more strength since taking the medicine.

Yesterday, we received two letters from you. You said you had to go on mess duty. Is that a must with your training; or did you do something? Dad was so happy that you were progressing in your line. If mess duty is just routine, maybe a change will be good for you and a better chance to get eats. Whatever the reason, keep in mind that where you are posted is where you are needed most. I sure would love to have you and five mates for dinner today. No need to tell you, the table seats 12 nicely with room and Deiner's sure handles good meat. I went in there Friday evening at 8 o'clock. All the trays were washed. Slim said, 'No meat, we are going to be closed all day Saturday,' and Eddie asked, 'What do you want?' I got two pounds of beef cubes, one pound of dried beef and a pot roast beef that took every ration point for two weeks, but I got it while the getting was good. To a lady next to me, they said, no meat madam. Edwin, I could see the refrigerator was full, but only for regular customers. The baker told me yesterday that

The Home Fires

Uncle Bill got a machine for hamburger. He is going to handle beef. I bet he is coining money.

Edwin, you can see in the few months since Christmas, the difference in the displays. It's tough trying to get size 44, but Mrs. Spence is just out with 52. Snooky told Roger that her mother was sick and we started over on Friday night. We came near a mansion at Harrison and Jackson Streets. Then he saw a sign. Bill Bates and he showed up because people were in the lawn. He said, 'Hello Billie,' and he came down to the curb. He insisted on us pulling in. He has his second wife and he sure took us all through the place. His wife treated us swell, so we didn't get to Uncle Bob's. I haven't been in such a magnificent place since bygone days. I sure wish Dot could see that place.

The "babies" are crying. I have not seen them yet. Edwin, I hurried through the dishes, got the flowers fixed, and the dinner on. The baker brought me two nice chickens; 9 pounds, two ounces for $4.45. These are the first we have had in months. Roger's chickens will soon be ready, although we want to keep them for winter.

I miss going to church, but I just can't rush.

Joe is not back yet. I gave him - - - - on Friday. He doesn't have a stitch of underwear on his back and he is still wearing Grandpop's flannel shirts. Baldwins' has 19 pigs, 6 or 7 steers, and several hundred chickens, turkeys and ducks. Joe sure is working and cranky as hell. I get sick of him and Dad and their simple ways. But, like I put up with you, I must with them too.

The day you left, you put your arms around me and said a kind word. You know, it hurts when you hear someone tell you that Edwin said, 'My Mom doesn't love me.' Well, if you don't give love, you don't get it. That's a true saying. Yes, I am sick and tired and would rather lie down than write. Dad and Dot have time if they want to do it. But you see, in this letter you will find my heart. When it's old, it will ever be true, so I seal it with tears and send it to you. You ought to know by now if I love you. It warmed my heart yesterday when you said, "Mom, I love you." You know son, life is not roses for some mothers. The worry of every day life settles as the years go by and they take a toll. I hope that when you return, things will be different in hopes for the best.

I am going to leave off here and go get cleaned up. Joe is home now. I hope you got our boxes and the watch. Write what you can. All is well.
With all our love,

Mother, Dad & all

Monday, June 25, 1945

My Dearest Son Edwin,

Here at home it is high noon. Carl brought in eight of your letters from the mail box and he said two for your brother. It is awful hot here and so I am not doing a thing. Roger must go to the post office with a money order, so I will stick this letter in as an extra.

I got the letter with the picture of the ideal farm. I heard of a man in these parts who had 32 rows of lettuce and made $800 off of them. The farmers are making out good this year. As for farm life, it's the only life if you like good food.

Now, as for any pal whom you want to bring home to entertain, your mother would be real happy to put an extra leg under the table for that day, from soup to pie. If it happens to be September for your birthday, you would be lucky. Boy, I can't say any more. That is too good to be true. In September, we will see that Dad puts in a late corn planting so that we can have corn on the cob, corn pudding and corn, as you like it; steamed in the husk. Not just one ear, but the wash boiler full, out of the field and into the pot. That is corn at its best. So, son, if there's any way we can get together, your mother and Dad would be pleased to have anyone who served our country to offer them the best we have whether it's corn or turkey, French fries or "poor man's potato soup".

Edwin, Dr. Roseman said, "How's Eddie?" I said he's down at the barber shop. Then he looked at me kind of funny. Later, he said, "Where is Eddie?" I said, you mean Edwin? That still goes. You know we and Grandpop never called you anything but Edwin.

Edwin, this sure seems to be a family year. Outside the window, in the spruce tree almost at the top, a robin has a family. I can hear her gibbering and them squawking. We have a lot more birds about since we don't have the cat.

George Ems is sure having a good time. They went ocean fishing yesterday and caught 125. Last night, they came with a dozen for us. I guess you know we will surely enjoy them. They only caught 2 flounders. Roger and Carl have gone to Somerton Pool. I packed his lunch; 3 fried bologna sandwiches and two slices of jelly roll.

We had a half bushel of fresh peas yesterday for dinner. Dad got a horse from Mr. Foehr at Ninety Foot and he and Joe went through the patch. We have no watermelons this year, but Dad did put in some cantaloupe. It's 90 degrees now and too hot for me. Rog weeded my flower bed yesterday.

None of us got to church. Howard Lewis' mother was here with her husband and sister Grace and family all afternoon.

Howard got home Saturday night for 8 days. Then in 30 more, he expects to ship out. He is in the Sea Bee outfit training at Davisville, Rhode Island where Uncle John trained. No news now for seven weeks from Uncle John, but we keep on writing. Bill has left for Pacific ports. John and George Ems were off Okinawa on Easter. George took part in the air battle that day. Elmer Tattersdill is out there also, although he got back a couple of times to San Pedro. George Long got laid off from Budd Field. They are making a turnover again to making Pullman cars. George was up at Bill Wenker's two days on the tractor. He is nothing but a frame.

Charlie's baby was christened yesterday, the 24th. Aunt Dink and George stood for it.

Well son, I have loads of work to do, so I will say keep up the good work. God bless you and keep you safe. When the golden sun is setting and your mind from care is free, and of absent friends you're thinking, don't forget to think of us (me).

With lots of love baby,

Mother & All

Tuesday, June 26, 1945

Dearest Son Edwin,

It's 12:30 here at home and the Northeast Airport is getting opened. The keys are being handed over to Mayor Samuel. The police have been going up and down Bustleton Avenue since early morning. Rog and I saw the plane coming in from New York's LaGuardia Airport to Northeast. It took 27 minutes. Now we can get to New York easy. My desire would be to have enough money to fly to Norfolk to see Mrs. Bell.

Edwin, the mayor said he accepts the key to open the lanes of the World of Tomorrow. Save all your money so you can fly home like Bill did. Roger cleaned the fish. Mrs. Haltzapple sent Rog a beautiful fish knife and so, I cleaned the first fish to show him how. He did a good job. There were just 13 fish. Now son, all planes were grounded today by Army order as a hurricane was sweeping the Atlantic Seaboard from Florida to Cape May. I now heard that it has gone out to sea. The wind here was quite high. It went from 95 degrees yesterday to now just 78 degrees. That is a welcome relief. I couldn't sleep all night. It was so hot my hair was soaked. Toward morning the change came.

Last Friday night we stopped at Ems' and we met Dot at the corner. Dad asked her to go along, but she said no. It was the hottest day we had and she was coming home from work. She said she would call me up Saturday afternoon to do my hair, but I have not seen or heard from her since. Of course, they are very busy going places with George home. George is going with Peggy S. and they went to Willow Grove last night. Dot and her Mom stayed home. Granny called me up from Delheim's yesterday and there is nothing new.

The planes are low and noisy. Edwin, what is your skipper's name? We get news over the air, but of course, only about the big shots. The airport has cost three million, three hundred thousand dollars. The poor farmers who owned that land didn't get it. Edwin, in speaking about farms and your dreams, did you know that this farm cost $10,000 in 1890? A farm of any kind around this section costs in the high figures.

The hurricane went out to sea over Norfolk at 40 miles per hour, so it wasn't as bad as expected. I guess you will say, 'Mom sure jumbled this letter.' I had the news on and I can't write when the radio is going. I ironed some fancies and cleaned up around. It's one o'clock now. I have several jobs to do, so I think I will stop here and finish up later on.

Roger went up to see Carl. He has to hoe some tomatoes. Pop's garden is doing fine. It cost seven dollars and fifty cents for 50 pounds of Rotentone. Ray brought it last night. You see, with the $50 I made on the peonies, it takes care of all the garden expenses.

Edwin, the only big letter I got was the one in the roll. Your mail is coming in swell. Be sure and date every letter. Sometimes I get the last ones first. For instance, June 17th came before June 10th, but they are all in order up to June 17th, which came on the 25th. That sure is fast time. George Ems said he hasn't gotten the box the church sent him in September yet. One box we sent cost us nearly $15.00. I sure hope you get it and I hope you get your watch. Dot also sent you a box, so you will have a good time with the contents. I don't know any news. It's now 4 o'clock. I took the radio room apart. I got some Kemtone for the ceiling. You know you promised to help me put it on. Maybe some cool day I will get the ambition to do it. I would have done it, but the step ladder was not safe enough and Dad is determined not to fix it because he doesn't want me to do it.

Two guys are going through and Brownie and Lady are getting after them. The puppies are crying as I left Lady out. She sure is proud and so busy. She only leaves them long enough to eat, but I put her out. She is scratching on the door now to get in. They sure are cry babies. I haven't seen them yet. Dad speaks to her so sweetly. He loves her. One of them left a big trade mark in the parlor this morning. Rog cleaned it up; not a word out of him.

Well dear, I will close for now. Be good.

Love and hug,

Mom and all

Wednesday, June 27, 1945

Dearest Son Edwin,

Here, it is 10:30 in the morning. Roger is scrubbing the kitchen for me. I have a big pot of peas shelled and that is a job. The dogs are fed. Howard Jones is on the air trying to give away $100. I sure wish he would call me for $105; no such luck. Rog was over for more pigeons last night. He has 16 now. He leaves them out and they don't come back. He has had over 30.

There is no news whatsoever at this writing, so when Rog gets through the kitchen, I will stop as I still have lots of work to do. It's 72 degrees now and it is nice! I just can't stand 95 degrees nor 4 below.

Howard Jones pulled the slip, "Supreme Motor Freight Lines", $105. Damn, damn. Some people have luck, but they don't give the prize to any businesses, only private people. Good, eh?

Rog is now finished. So, I will see you later.

Well son, I am back again for our chat. I got things pretty well cleaned up and was doing a little washing of towels and table cloths. The wet wash sure has me cleaned out and robbed. I fight with them every week. I threaten to call the O.P.A. and I sure have my trouble with them. They lost my good big white table cloth and they rob me of my pillow cases and towels every week.

I had so many dish towels; I didn't know where to put them. Now, I have only a few that I must wash out every meal. But this war won't last forever. Then we will get that farm with everything modern. We will tell them all to kiss our "fanny".

Four beautiful woodpeckers are outside the dining room window.

It's now 3 o'clock and it's warming up. I was down for the mail (electric bill), not worth walking down over the stones for. Both dogs went along. Edwin, I am scared to go anywhere in the field or in my flowers, as last Sunday on Russell's side of the road up near the drive, Pop and Joe saw a four foot black snake as thick as a tea cup curled up in the road. Before Dad realized it was such an enormous snake, it got over towards the field where Dad couldn't run over it because the bank and blackberry bushes are there. Dad warned Rog not to pick the berries along there as Mr. Ems said they are dangerous snakes. I pick honeysuckle along there. I just can't walk in the weeds or anything these last few days.

I hope to do up some beets this week and string beans. I didn't have a piece of bread in the house for lunch, so I just baked a big pan of biscuits. I sure wish you were here to have some with me. I am not supposed to eat bread, except 1 slice of dry toast and two eggs for breakfast and no coffee. But I do drink coffee for breakfast. We haven't had any butter since Christmas. It is 24 points a pound and we each get 50 points a month. I come across a good many women who have not turned in their son's ration books. In fact, Aunt Dink still uses Byron's. I guess I am too damn honest. That's why I never have anything. But, honesty is the best policy. Poverty is no disgrace, but it is awful unhandy. So I am waiting for the day to sit by the fire and sing to Gale all the love longs I sang to you and the biscuits will be hot. Mom will smile and think of all these letters.

All my love,

Mother & All

Thursday, June 28, 1945

Dear Son,

Ten years ago today, my Dad passed away. I often think of the days along the Pennypack and our old friend, Mr. Jones. You know old Bill Jones and my Dad fished and gunned together and they wanted a lot side by side in the cemetery. Now they are both there, as well as Mrs. Jones. And so my thoughts turn back the pages of time. I could fill a book with memories of them and the farm. So, here's standing beside you and singing as I did for my Dad and Mr. Jones. God bless them; Down by the old millstream where I first met you. Love – love – love.

Tonight, Dad and Joe are putting in my last row of flowers along our drive. Edwin, it's so hot here and it's 8 PM. I must get cleaned up. I am awful tired. Joe is getting water for the plants and we need rain again. Roger wrote you a letter this afternoon. He used my pen and I can't write with it tonight again.

Now here is some news for you. What do you think? Friday night from Ford's, Dad is expecting to leave for South Carolina to drive in a convoy. You know what they make where he works. Fifty of them are going and it will take two days. He gets $20 and all expenses for meals, etc. He is quite thrilled. Of course, if he goes, the man who leaves his car here will drive Dad's home. Dad can't tell about his orders, so I am going to be a lonesome Mom. Rog and I will go to church and maybe the movies if it's not too hot. I will let you know all about it later when I find out.

It's thundering. Dad got us six pounds of watermelon tonight for 42 cents. Rog is at Ems. Joe and Dad are coming in. It is thundering real heavy. I hear the kettle boiling.

I wrote to Ed Bissinger's chaplain last night trying to find out about him. Aunt Lilly is worried.

Dad said there are three male and two female puppies. We are only going to keep the three boys as we have homes for them. Tell me what you think of all the stuff I write.

Bad – Mom – no

Lots of love

(Enclosure – Item 12)

PHILADELPHIA
Port of the Air World

AVIATION WEEK
JUNE 25 – JULY 1

Special AVIATION WEEK Events

Monday, June 25—PHILADELPHIA CIVIC AVIATION DAY
City-wide celebration to mark the opening of Aviation Week.

Tuesday, June 26—PHILADELPHIA NORTHEAST AIRPORT DEDICATION DAY
Demonstration of Air Mail Pickup—Arrival of Airlines' planes, welcoming of officials—Official Dedication ceremonies—Glider flight by Captain Barnaby, U.S.N.—Flight maneuvers by Army-Navy planes—Display of Military Aircraft—Demonstration of "Flying Wing" aircraft—Demonstration of Helicopters, Autogiro.

Wednesday, June 27—COMMUNITY AND SERVICE CLUBS DAY
Observance of Aviation Week by Community organizations and service clubs throughout Philadelphia.

Thursday, June 28—HISTORY OF AVIATION DAY
Demonstration of the dramatic story of man's conquest of air from the Wright Brothers to the present in the hall of aviation at the Franklin Institute which is open to Museum visitors every day except Monday.

Friday, June 29—MILITARY AVIATION—WAR BOND DAY
Display and exhibition of Army, Navy and Coast Guard Aircraft—ATC Hospital Evacuation Plane (C-54)—Display of B-29 and other planes—admission to view these by War Bond purchases at field—Red Cross Blood Bank Unit—Air Show.

Saturday, June 30—CIVIL AVIATION—WAR BOND DAY
Model Airplane competition—exhibition—Display of civilian "sportsmen's" planes—CAP demonstration and inspection—Air Scout review and ceremonies—Display of C-54—B-29 and other planes—Flight of Curtis pusher airplane.

Sunday, July 1—AIRLINES' DAY
A program of ceremonies marking the inauguration of flights out of Philadelphia's Northeast Airport.

(OVER)

Wartime Letters Written from Mother to Son

Friday, June 29, 1945

Dear Son,

Today Bustleton is sure on the map. Every type of plane is doing its stuff over our town. Northeast Airport is putting on a show and since early morning a Navy Blimp, K-1-9 is sure sailing over our town. When it arrived, he was on a line with the railroad and only 500 feet up. I know it was 500 feet because they are broadcasting a two-way conversation from blimp to radio. It is a thrilling sight to hear and see at the same time. Roger has the binoculars and we are running every minute. I grabbed the American flag and waved it and I have saluted it hundreds of times; U.S. Navy. There is a tailless plane and a B-29 Super Fortress. I guess you know that we are on the map and on the air. So I will be watching the show all afternoon.

I have a few pieces to iron. We didn't get up until 10 AM. It's now 12:30. So, I will ring off here and finish up later.

Edwin, it's now 3:45. I don't know where the time goes. It seems as if I haven't started yet. I made Roger his dinner. He has been gone since 11 o'clock. He was up at Ems'. He is washing up to go see Uncle Bill. He said to tell you that he is the boss of the house for the first time because you are away. We expect Dad to be away until Sunday. I told Dad this morning not to fall in love with any of those South Carolina pistol packin' mamas.

Roger left on the 4:05 trolley and the baker has been in. It's very hot here today after a fierce rain and thunderstorm last night when I wrote you that letter about Bill Jones.

Well son, be good. That's all for now.

Lots of love,

Mother and All

Saturday, June 30, 1945

Dearest Son,

You know the old verse; thirty days hath September, April, June and November. So, here we are to the last day of June. I know I have written you thirty letters in June besides the extras I stuck in along the month. I have always considered it a pleasure as it was our daily chat like we used to have every day. I even used to come over in my nightie to sit and find out the news from you.

Now it's 9:30 and the Breakfast Club is on the air. Boy, is it hot. It's already 84 degrees and heavy. My feet are burning and I am not all geared up as Rog and I are sure having a holiday.

Dad got the trip to South Carolina. Of course, I don't know a thing about it until he returns. I think it's entirely too much for Dad. He still thinks he is young enough to work like a brute. The old darling would be afraid he wasn't doing his share toward ending the war. So, he volunteered to go in the convoy of fifty drivers.

Mrs. McAdams called me up about 5:30. She said her husband was home and to look for Dad back on Sunday. I know it will be hotter going south, but he can sure stand the heat and sun. He's tough, but not as tough as old Grandpop. But then, Dad had so much sickness.

We worked hard last night. Rog sure went over that grass. Joe gave him a buck and Uncle Bill gave him $5.00. Today he has a date. He sure has grown. We want to surprise Dad with how nice the place looks. Joe and I trimmed all the low branches from the willow tree. I painted the two benches white. Now, darling, this is where you come in, the hedge. Nothing has been done to it and you can't see over it. The rye and wheat are now golden yellow and almost ready to harvest.

Roger just got up so I will finish this later. I still have lots of work to do.

Edwin, it's now 3 o'clock and I won't write much. It's awful, awful hot and I am sure sweating. It's still better than the cold. I still have to iron Dad's work pants and shirt. I have everything ready for Sunday. All kinds of good things are cooked and our ice box is full of cold drinks and good food. So, I am going to call it quits.

Roger is off to the Mayfair movies to meet his girl. She called him up at eleven. He's wearing new blue trousers and your blue silk shirt, the last one you bought. It would be too small for you.

We got a $27.52 check in the morning mail for Dad's return. Boy, did we need it. Dad gave me $23.00 and the rent is $32.00.

So long.

Love,

Mom

****END OF JUNE****

Chapter Ten

July 1945

Joe Johnson (l) and Pop Price (c) and the mule!

Wartime Letters Written from Mother to Son

Sunday, July 1, 1945

Dear Son,

All I can do is write a line. What a heat spell, no relief since Thursday. It has me cooked. So far today at 2:45, it is 94 degrees. Yesterday, oh! What a Saturday; 99 degrees and me so lonesome. I guess it was a good thing that I didn't have to cook. I told Carl that if Dot would like to come over Saturday night and stay, as I would be alone. He said they were putting on a big party for George. Pop and I didn't even get a bid. But, I hear George got a load on. So I guess they had a party. I pity Mrs. Ems in that heat. Rog and I did our best to keep cool. We had the electric fan going all night. Rog slept on your bed in Grandpop's room.

Rog and I got up at 6 o'clock and the heat was still going strong. We came down and got coffee and the papers and fed the dog and chickens. Then I made dried beef about nine for Rog.

At 10, the back door opened and a poor, forlorn, old darling came in with a brown sweater over his arm all done in. He stood up for six hours on the train. It left Fayetteville, North Carolina at 6 PM on Saturday evening and got to Broad Street at 8 AM on Sunday. He changed trains three times. There were 70 in his convoy. He was third (10 wheel job) in an Army truck for Fort Bragg, North Carolina. The first convoy went off the road. Three others piled up on it. They were in convoys of ten and so Dad was in the third line.

He made $25.00 minus taxes and $3.00 for food. He was starved, had nothing but sandwiches. He said they couldn't get a meal anywhere. A Red Cross girl in Washington station gave Pop a drink of ice tea. She said it was only for servicemen. Pop said, 'I am a civilian,' but he showed her his paper

The Home Fires

from Army Ordinance Headquarters and he got the tea and a sandwich. He was black and sweaty.

I gave him roast beef, brown gravy, baked Idaho potatoes, fresh new peas, fresh hot buttered beets, lettuce with French dressing, chocolate pudding topped with marshmallows, jelly roll and iced grape juice. Did he eat?!

Now, he sure is snoring. He took a bath and he has on shorts and is on my couch in the parlor. Joe is out under the maple tree and Rog and Carl went to the movies. Here I am, with no shoes and no corset.

So long for now. Pop said. 'Look at how hot it is where the boy is.' I said, 'Yes. All I have done for two days is sit alone and look at his picture.'

Love from all,

Mom

(Enclosures – Items 13 and 14)

Philadelphia Inquirer
PUBLIC LEDGER
An Independent Newspaper for All the People
PHILADELPHIA, SUNDAY MORNING, JULY 1, 1945   B   PRICE, TWELVE CENTS

New High of 99 Sets Record,

Mercury 99 on Hottest Day in 5 Years; Crowds Jam Shore and Bathing Pools

Yesterday was the hottest day in five years. Two Philadelphians died as result of the train and bus terminals here and in Camden. But the temperature on the beach at Atlantic City at 2 P. M. yesterday was 98.

Wartime Letters Written from Mother to Son

Monday, July 2, 1945

Dearest Son,

This will sure be a hurry up chat for I am a child's nurse to three kids[117] with whooping cough aged 7 years to nine months. With the 90 degree heat at 10 AM, you know now my hands are tied, but I can't go through the day without saying hello. Ruth is here in the rocker looking at the funnies. Danny is asleep and Roger has Elmer on the bike giving him "the works".

I woke up and looked at the clock and you know my eyesight has failed me awfully and I can't see at times. The doctor said that it is due to anemia. I looked at the clock. I said, "My, oh, my!" I sure must have slept since Dad left. It was 10:30. I thought it was 5 of 5 when I said goodbye to Dad and he asked me to wash his sweater. So, it was 25 of 11 when I got up and went over to the clock. I said, 'My God. I bet Minnie has been here and couldn't get in.' Elmer called me last night. So, I said, Roger, come quick to water and feed your chickens in this heat. I hurried downstairs. Elmer said he would be here early. I saw no sign of anyone being here. I put the coffee on and I looked at the clock. It said 6:30. I said, 'Oh, what a relief.' I said to Roger to look at the other clock and it said 20 of 11. Either Dad advanced it or the hands fell, I don't know. I sure thought it couldn't be that I would sleep that long and not wake up. Aunt Minnie was here by 8 o'clock with a high chair, playpen, eggs, milk, diapers, and all. When Danny wakes up, he will keep me busy. He sure is an angel.

You tell those (boys) men on the Pasadena that I am their mascot. I pray for them all and I hold that flag high. I salute it every day. When they are at their work and need courage and strength, say Mother Price, we are listening to

---

[117] The three children are the children of her sister Minnie, married to Elmer Irons. The children are Ruth, Elmer and Daniel Irons.

you. Hold fast. March on for Uncle John. We sure are worried about him. We think he is a prisoner of the Japs. So son, give them hell; spare none. Aunt Dink wrote to a lady from Jersey whose husband she knew was with Uncle John. She said her husband got a note out. Minnie told me that, but Minnie didn't know what it was about and we wouldn't want Granny to know. As soon as I hear anything, I will let you know. But Pasadena, do your stuff for the N.C.B. 82nd Co. C. Plat 6. Yes, Pasadena, I love you so. March on. March on to Victory. Sail and give them all you got.

Pop is 55, but he took supplies to Fort Bragg, 429 miles away. Besides that, he worked all day and drove all night without any sleep and no hot food. If he can take it, so can you younger boys. We are Americans inside the heart, not on the surface. Sail on Pasadena.

All my love,

Mother

Tuesday, July 3, 1945

Hello Son,

Here it is 12 noon, and Roger is here for his lunch. He has a pigeon and calls him Carrier Joe. So he put a message in the aluminum capsule and took him on the bike to Ems and then let him go. So Carrier Joe is home before he is. We sure did have a storm yesterday afternoon. Today, you can live and breathe in comfort. It's 74 degrees. What a change from 96 and three sick babies! I went through the house and got things all in order for the 4th of July; no fuss, no picnic, but just a quiet stay at home. I don't know what the day shall bring forth.

Wartime Letters Written from Mother to Son

Well son, your one lonely letter of June 21st came today. Dad's and Roger's and two others from you came yesterday. The one from today darling, I shall keep in my Bible. When you are home and snooping in it, you will say I was out in the Pacific when I sent that to mother.

Your hair now is the color that Dad's was when I first knew him. You know son, I never build up my hopes on any special time of your return, but if God hears prayers and I know he does, you will come home.

I'll never forget Christmas Thursday last year. I simply couldn't wait another minute to see you. I told Granny that if I knew you were coming for sure, I would stay up all night to have the tree trimmed. I baked the cake and "Mom, are these biscuits hot?" for your birthday. I always love to make a fuss for my family. "Mom, you show off too much and Mom, you try to show off to Dot." Dot is only a poor girl, but you know dear, that's my way; to have things nice and pretty even if no one sees them but me. I love lace and flowers. I have sure had love, lace, and flowers in my life. I often think how I could do if I had better financial conditions. And so I told you, it's life. You are man enough to do what you want with your life. I told you all I know in many letters. Not even the Navy can untie the knot I tied in you.

Edwin, Elsie Ford came in and she has left now to go to the hairdresser in Frankford. I hear John Ems and his wife are up for the 4th. The insurance man told me. I wish my hairdresser would come and pretty me up for the 4th of July. I will write tomorrow.

Love,

Mother

Wednesday, July 4, 1945

My Dearest Son,

It's a beautiful peaceful day. Here on the farm you would never know there could be such a thing as a war going on, but in your heart, you can't forget there is.

Roger and I put a table out under the tree and we fixed a lovely picnic. Dad and Joe have been in the fields since sunrise. Roger is in my flower garden. I got all prettied up and put a red, white, and blue ribbon in my old gray hair. The sky is a picture. We four sat there and Pop said, 'The boy is a day ahead of us.' I guess he heard all the guns.

I could see you sitting on the step and from 6 AM until breakfast would be ready, you would be shooting off the caps with old Grandpop, who was as bad as you. Finally as you got older, you'd hit a half dozen with a hammer on the cement. Then I would get you in to breakfast. You would manage to shoot the pistol and scare me a couple of times. I guess you know thoughts are in a flash and take longer to write. You were not a big boy in my mind as you are now, but just a fair-haired baby and not the fellow of chestnut brown hair flying away to Bristol with Johnny Welker to swim in the Delaware on the Fourth of July. Remember how on the Fourth of July on the farm we'd have 25 to 30 people and Mother not getting time to eat? Now there is no ½ cow or pig getting roasted and bake beans on the outdoor fireplace that I showed you how to build; no gas, no company. I'm not satisfied. I would sooner have dry bread and black coffee and say we are together. You know I loved all my brothers and my Dad always brought us the watermelon for the 4th of July. In later years, Uncle Bill always saw that we had the fireworks and the watermelon. He would go over the county line and put them among the loaves of bread so you would have the caps. I would put them in the oven so you wouldn't find them until morning.

Dad brought us a big watermelon last night and I still have some jars of preserved watermelon rind that I made from the ones you grew. So my dear son, Fourth of July in the Pacific is not as nice as Fourth of July on the farm. The old hicks will write more tomorrow. It's 72 degrees and just a beautiful day. It's 2 o'clock and I have the coffee on and all is well. Cheerio. I miss you. I smooth your face. I love you.

Love and kiss,

Mother

Thursday, July 5, 1945

Hello Son,

Yes, I am taking a rest. It's raining real hard; thunderstorm. It blew out the 100 watt bulb on Monday and now again today. I am canning string beans today and have about eight quarts done. I am wondering because I saw the times I had five men and two children and did 24 quarts in one day while cooking three big meals and taking care of diapers and bottles. Your best girl sure must be slipping.

Edwin, we had the best and finest 4th of July weather I have ever seen. It was perfect; sun and breeze and 74 all day. I told you we had a picnic lunch out under the tree. Around 3, Mr. McAdams came. They had been over to see the airport. The air liners of five lines came in. They sure are a sight to see. When they take off, they nose right up over Baldwin's house. They come over our land between the barn and Herman's and then turn toward

Wenker's, just directly over Krewstown Road and roar away to the west. Atlantic Air Line, United Air Line, I can read them real plain. At night, the beacon is flashing in all directions and the plane is making its lights blink. As it is coming down, you can see the shaft of light for its landing. They sure make a noise. Mrs. McAdams said you should see them pick up the mail. Do you know I got a letter today that you wrote June 28th? I think that is just wonderful. If those boys who don't write home only knew what they were doing to their wives and mothers, they would write just like you do. If you had not written, I guess your Mom and Dad would be ready for Forrest Hills Cemetery. It is tough and this is war, but first in my heart is mail to you just like I have my morning coffee. I must have my chat with you every day.

Time is fast flying. I must press Dad's brown pants. He is going to take them along in your blue bag as he is driving the Army truck to Fort Jackson, South Carolina approximately 650 miles. I think that is too much, but he needs the money. The Army pays 5 cents a mile, tax deducted, $3.00 for meals, and for transportation home. It gives Dad a change from the farm. To work all day and drive all night and part of the next day without any sleep is tough on old fellows, but Dad can do it.

So, Rog is boss again this weekend. Now, save all you possibly can and then you can fly in our back door and as you come in, I will wave the flag. I know the time now of some of the regulars. I stand on the back step and wave the flag and the dish towel or the broom. The troop trains are coming through this way loaded. I can see how clean the boys are and I know they have gotten prettied up for their folks. I will be hoping for the day when our ship sails homeward and for all on board.

That clipping you sent of the Prices of the Illinois Prairie; they may be some of Dad's folks, although Dad's people in the west are in Boone, Iowa. They would be your second cousins; Jim Price's grandfather's children. Jim's grandfather was your grandfather's brother, John Price. He settled in Boone, Iowa and had a real big family. The children could be that age, because your Grandpop was 92 when he left us and he was the youngest of his family. You know Sarah Rowley and Aunt Mary are in their 80s and they are Dan Price's children.

Now son, the last batch of beans is about finished, so I must run along and get them out of the cooker.

After McAdams left yesterday at 4:30, we went up to Jones for gas. We stopped for Dot. There was no one home but Mrs. Ems. She was in the field getting some onions for supper. I asked her to come along. We went up to Uncle Charlie's. Granny and Al were there and Aunt Kebe and Tom. They had beer and a big picnic. They had a fire going and were spearing hot dogs for the roast. Uncle Charlie got all dressed up in Aunt Violet's clothes and sneaked through the trees with a suitcase and bare legs and a red scarf. I screamed as he came upon us. I thought it was a gypsy woman. The kids lifted the tail of the dress and he had on white pants. He sure carried on and made us laugh.

Cheerio. Keep smiling. I will write tomorrow. All my love. Rog said Dot got two letters from you today.

(Enclosure – Item 15)

THE FIRST United Airliner to arrive at the reopened Northeast Airport had on board a collection of new fall hats created by California designers. And these will be included in a fashion show to be held at Strawbridge & Clothier's today. Getting a first-hand peek at them are two of the airline hostesses, Helen Dettero, left, and Betty Wade.

Friday, July 6, 1945

Dear Son,

It's 2:30 and I call a halt to have my daily chat with you. I am alone except for my two guards. One is outside and the other one is with her family. Roger is up at Ems'. We had a terrific storm yesterday afternoon again. For the second time, it blew the wiring and now there is no lighting in the cellar. I called the Electric Company and they came. They said our own electrician would need to take care of it, so I called Charlie Burns.

What do you think Mrs. Neamand told me? Bill has been in the Philippines since April, but this is the news: her girl is 17 past and she has two babies. One is two years old and one is seven months, both boys. Uncle Mal's son, Bill, has T.B. and is in Jefferson Hospital for ten weeks now and expects to be sent to a sanitarium. I sure thought that was some awful news to hear. She said she thought how lucky you were to get so close to home. She thought you were still at Philadelphia Navy Yard. I said you left the States in February. Her son didn't leave until April. I guess it's a lucky break for her that her son is in the Navy and can get help for her. She always had to work at the school. Now with 2 babies and a sick father, young Bill can get government assistance for her. I guess we don't know when we are well off. Charlie Burns, her brother, won't see her want for anything.

Now son, it's hot and damp here today. It takes the starch out of you. It's showering off and on.

Johnny Ems leaves again tomorrow. Dad is going to Fort Jackson, South Carolina tonight, so he kissed us goodbye this morning. What a weekend. It's too hot for me to go anywhere. I can't drive and there the car sits parked beside the door. When Rog is sixteen he says, 'I'll take you Mom.' I say, "Oh yes! Just like Edwin did mad every time he had to take me anywhere."

You would be surprised how things have changed. I couldn't get a piece of meat in four different stores last night. They are putting out a lot of stuff they call Polish sausage filled with garlic. I guess they are using so much garlic in it that you can't tell what you are eating. I hear tons of butter are getting rancid in the warehouses because the housewives can't give 24 points per pound for it. Now after it's spoiled, they are going to release it and give each

¼ pound. All I worry about is this damn murdering ending. So, hurry up. Get the job done and I will get a new herd and make our own butter.

So long for now. Lots of love baby dear,

Mom

Monday, July 9, 1945

Dearest Son Edwin,

At last I am here with you for our chat of two days. Over Saturday and Sunday, I did not write, although I sent you a V-Mail Saturday afternoon.

And now to tell you the weekend news; first of all, Dad did not come home Friday night. After his day's work, he left at 4:20 from Chester to Fort Jackson, South Carolina in a large convoy of Army trucks. He went along miserably as the truck he had could not keep up with most on account of the governor being set below 40. At any rate, somewhere in the south, Dad got three hours behind. He missed the gas station where they gas up and along some lonely road he ran out of gas. So a guy came along and Dad hailed him. He said they were looking for him, so Dad got back to another part of a later convoy of 5 other trucks.

When the six of them were going through Fairfax County, Virginia at 10:30 at night, a traffic cop held up the leader and all of them. He said they were doing 45 and arrested the whole six of them. The Justice of the Peace fined them each $10.25. They had to pay it or else. So, one fellow said here is the truck, where is the nearest Army camp? So he said to hell with the truck. Take it to any Army camp. I got just enough money to get home from here. That's the cream of the trip.

I am going to write our State Senator, Lou Farrell. What a scandalous, money-making scheme. Pop could not make that truck do over 40 and he has proof. To think that men like Dad who worked all day in a tank depot and volunteered to drive 650 miles at night to get the goods delivered on the home front for our boys and there's a money-making schemer to make six men each pay $10.25 and delay them. They are not patriots. I am going to write Henry Ford and the six men will sign it. I bet they will get their money back. The men were so tired, so hot and hungry, they wanted no fight. You know the Southern don't like any sass from the Northern. So the men wanted to get the trucks where they were wanted and get home. Dad got on the train on Saturday at 4 o'clock and got home here Sunday to 30th Street at 10:10 AM. He had a long ride and did not change trains on the trip. It cost 10 cents to use the toilet, 10 cents for water, and 10 cents for use of a comb. By the time Dad got home, he was moneyed out. Now he is worried because for the first time in his life, 55 years, he was arrested and he might not get any chance to drive again for volunteer Army work as that arrest is a record. I guess you know I am going to do all I can to clear those men. I know Ford will also. You see it is not Ford work, but Army Ordinance with orders from Detroit.

While I am on the same subject, I know I wrote you about Bruce Culp. I hope you got those letters. Now I hear he got a six month sentence in Holmesburg Prison, at age 17. Fred is one unhappy person that he wouldn't sign for Bruce to go in the Navy.

Now for some good news: Saturday, Aunt Dink and Sissy came up and they stayed with me until Sunday night. Uncle John is okay as far as we can tell. Aunt Dink got a V-mail on Saturday. It read, 'Here it is. I am okay.' Then it was all blacked out. Then at the bottom it said, 'I sure have been at sea a long time, but did not get seasick. Will be home to stay by your birthday. I am

The Home Fires

on the water wagon. John.' Her birthday is November 17th, so we are at ease again.

Dad took us down to Aunt Dink's to take them home and then took us to Reardon's. He spent $3.50 for slop. We got home at 10:30. Pop went outside and we heard some girl's laughter. Here, it was Mil and Carl on their bikes bringing 2 big fish, about 10 pounds for Dad. Johnny Ems left for New York on the 7th, but came right home. He said 700 were called for the draft for the Pacific, but as yet he didn't know his assignment. He had to be in New York today again, this morning. George is going to Oklahoma on the 16th. Aunt Dink and I are going in town this Thursday to see if we can pick up a nice dress for the golden wedding celebration. Pop has the car in Bender's again today. The brakes grab and the light's out. Well son, it's hot here today. It's 12:30. We had a luscious dinner of home grown food Sunday; killed four chickens, roasted them split down the back, new potatoes, new green beans, new buttered beets, peas, salad, and all else, filling, gravy, homemade devil food cake, pears and homemade ice cream. You should have seen Dad and Aunt Dink eat.

Well dearest darling, I hear all the news of the task force on the radio. I am not doing any work today, just the usual. I am going to look at the paper and get a cool drink. We saw Dutch Heller and the Kelly girl in Reardon's. They didn't speak to me, but only to Dad. I haven't seen or heard from Dot for over two weeks. I did tell you we stopped twice for her, but she wasn't home. Bill Long is in your parts on the U.S.S. Starr. Okay darling, I love you. I miss you too.

All is well.

Mom & All

Wartime Letters Written from Mother to Son

Monday, July 9, 1945

Hello Son,

This is the second letter today. It's now just after five and I am looking for you to dash in the lane. But here I am to talk to you while waiting for the rest of the family to return. I made some peach ice cream and some chocolate for Dad when they get done in the field and come in to hear the 9 o'clock news. I will surprise them.

I had one letter from you and in it you spoke about not hearing from Dot. I have asked her several times to write you all she could. Now, I told you that you are young and when you come home and plan a future, then it is time to pick a mate. You know son, if anyone loves you, it is never any trouble to tell it because you wait to hear their footsteps and you fall in line with all their desires. Doris Moser writes her sweetheart every day, so the old man Engle told me. He mails one for her everyday to him. So, if Dot loves you, she would do just as you do, write every day. Pop likes her. So do I. She is a nice home good girl. If she loves you, you won't need to coax. You know, son, that I know all your faults and she knows some of them too. We have discussed you and so, perfect yourself all you can. You know drink is one drawback there and she knows your weakness too. Then you know you never have any money. So, deny yourself all your little wants. Then maybe when you come home, you will know exactly where you stand. I am sure thankful that God heard my prayers and that the knot was not tied before you left. It was best for everybody concerned.

Now, as for that ring; Aunt Dink said she knew who took it, but she wouldn't say who. I am always upset about it. She said Snooky did not take it and at first she thought it was her. Byron and Snooky were the only ones in her house that day. When I see Dot again, I am going to say, 'Dot, I see you don't wear the silver ring anymore,' just to see what she says. I never did mention the story to her about what I heard. That is between you and me.

As for your letters, darling, we understand them perfectly and Dad's brother is just fine. Look for him if you are anywhere around Japan waters or Leyte, and keep on the lookout for my brother John, 82nd C.B.

Whatever you write is for you and me and Dad alone. I don't read any of your letters aloud except what I know is okay to do. All your secrets are mine. I read all your mail first, even what you address to Dad unless you say not to.

Love,

Mom

Tuesday, July 10, 1945

Dearest Son Edwin,

Here it is 11:10 and Tom B. is on the air. Rog is eating fried tomatoes and I had to get two Bonds ready to send off. Now we have two left outside of your two, Rog two, Joe two. But we will get there. We still owe Heinel's $50.00 on the repair bill. So it goes with that car. I don't know a thing. Tom has three old ladies, one from Wales. I hear Dot didn't work yesterday. They are sure celebrating for John and George. He sent us two big fish and we are going to have them tonight. Roger is going to the post office so I will tuck this in as an extra and maybe tonight I will know more news. All we hear is war and we are quite interested in the Fleet. The lady from Wales homesteaded in Dakota Territory on 160 acres, 63 years ago. They had to stay there for five years then they owned it. Our government is a fine one from beginning to now, and that is why our boys are protecting it.

Cheerio darling. All for now. My best love.

Mother

Tuesday, July 10, 1945 – Second letter

Dearest Son Edwin,

Well son, here it is 5:20 and along about this time everyday I look for dust sweeping across the highway and then I know it's you turning the bend at 50 miles per hour. "Oh, that boy!" But here I am alone and looking for the rest of the family. The supper is a-sizzling and only needs the finish. We have just had a terrific thunderstorm. I had to lash the porch rocker down, shut up the chickens and hold tight, because you know Mom doesn't like thunder.

With all the war news, I guess you all have a job keeping calm. I sat in my rocker and said prayers for you all and myself too. So now it is calm and wet and I am talking to you on paper for the second time today. I have a slight earache, sore eyes and tomorrow night I will go to the doctor's again. I felt much stronger for two weeks. Since I took care of Aunt Minnie's children with whooping cough, I really believe I got some of the cold germ, for my nose has run and my throat's sore. I have been using Listerine and now I put camphorated oil and laudanum in my ear. It feels a little better, but I only wish I could get some of my old strength back. It's always something lately. Well darling, I don't know any news. I don't know where Rog is in this storm. They tarred the road this afternoon. I bet it's a mess now. Do you remember when you used to walk in it and then wipe it on your pants!? Oh, those were the days. Come home and be "little boy" again for Mommy and then I will give you the hair brush, eh!

Love,

The Home Fires

Mom

Saturday, July 14, 1945

Dearest Son Edwin,

Here it is high noon at home, and I didn't get up until 10 o'clock. Dad has been on the job since seven. I see he has all the tomatoes and cauliflower sprayed. He has to get caught up. He wasn't in the patch for two or three weekends. I wrote you about the six in the convoy getting arrested. None of them can drive again. That's against the rules. Dad can drive as I told you Dad was called to the office and the boss told the girl clerk to fix up Mr. Price, as he knew him for years, etc., etc. You must have a special license to drive the vehicles, so they got Dad's license on character and also that he made two successful trips. They wanted to send him last night again, but he said, no, he lived too far away and he couldn't notify his wife. What a poor excuse. He wanted to get in the garden to get another planting of spinach and corn in. He has corn in case the boy gets home in September.

Well dear, Roger told me Peg S. or Dot was not at work all week. Other than that I know no news. I was in town on Thursday. Aunt Dink, Doreen, Roger and I tramped through every store on Market Street; 5&10, Wanamaker's, Gimbels, Snellenburgs, Strawbridges, Frank & Ieders, Blauners, Lerners Select Shop, Lane Bryant. We didn't get a dress. I tried on one foundation in Lane Bryant, $11.98. It was too long and too big. I couldn't get a thing. Cotton dresses are $14.95. A common slip is $4.95. I said I won't go to town until the war is over. I saw women in line to get one Turkish town. I'll cut the tops off all your white socks and sew them together like Grandma Price used to do before I'll stand in line.

George Ems was in every store from Frankford to Mayfair. You can't get any beef; no hamburger. Nor last night could I get a piece of bologna. You know how I used to buy a big one in Deiner's. He said, 'I'll give you some sliced, but none in the piece.' Deiner's turns away everyone who is not a customer. I got some veal for stewing and a cross cut pot roast of beef, a piece of liverwurst; not like we used to get but some "shit" ground up for $6.00. There were no eggs in Deiner's. The stores, if they get them, sell them by the ½ dozen. Pop gets his eggs.

The Black Market is flourishing. Sugar stamps are 25 cents a piece. Red points are $120 for 100. Everywhere you turn, people approach you. Business men can get anything. The women are at the ration board howling for sugar. You have to show a receipt that you have the peaches or pears or berries. Al wrote one out for me for 4 baskets of peaches and we have one peach tree by the lilacs. But when you pick up the paper and read the war news, I would hate to cheat. Uncle Charlie said the rich are getting all they want and getting richer besides. People like us are too honest. I say I have a son and I would be afraid God wouldn't hear my prayers.

Now son, I went to the doctor's. He wants me out every week on the dot. I had an awful earache. He said there was a blood streak in my ear and sore throat. He sprayed it. My blood pressure was higher at 164. I was a wreck in town, but I held up better than Sis and Rog. The muscles in the calves of my legs were sore all day Friday. I slept good last night. Gardeners came as we were ready to go to the store. She gave me fifty red points and Pop gave them salad, beets, and cabbage, as they don't eat any meat.

Well darling, I must make Pop a bite to eat. It's 1 PM now and Rog went to the movies at the Tyson to see Hotel Berlin.

So long, darling.

The Home Fires

Mom

Sunday, July 15, 1945

Hello Son,

We have had a nice gentle rain practically all night. Dad's plans have changed. He did intend to work the mule today. He spent all of Saturday in the patch.

Tomorrow, I am going to order four pounds of string beans seed and white turnips. Al will buy from Dad any surplus we have. The cabbage is the finest and the beets are plentiful. In fact, I think the weather is ideal this year. Dad sprayed everything with Rotenone yesterday, so now it's washed off. It must be done over again. So farming goes.

Now it's 11:30. We had a big pan full of hamburger that Dad managed to get in the American store next to Nevins in Frankford. Pop and Rog went to town at it, being the first we had in a long time. I must go make my bed. I have the dishes done and dinner on. Rog has gone to Ems to play Monopoly. I believe the elders went up country to Abberta. Nutsie and Rog are keeping house for Grandpop. Thomas went south with Juanita for a vacation. I hear Mill earned $7.00 for brushing and cleaning 25 ponies for some stable on the boulevard. She is a worker.

Joe is out under the willow tree with a mile long face. The steers got out somehow, and at 5:30 AM were over at the Airport again. Someone leaves the gate open at night. Joe is mad because it is so wet this morning and he had to ride through a pouring rain hunting them.

I am trying to persuade Dad to take me to the Tyson to see Hotel Berlin or to the Circle to see A Song to Remember, but he is here in his brown bathrobe writing to you. I will close here as I want to get fixed up pretty and will write more later.

I hope dearest you are well. I did not get any letters this week and we are all thinking of you. The papers and the radio are giving out news of action in the Pacific. So we send our love, faith and hopes to God to give you all strength and courage to carry on. I love you heaps and heaps.

Mother & All

Monday Morning, July 16, 1945

Dearest Son,

Here I am for our chat. It's hot and sticky after a weekend rain. Dad took me out, but Hotel Berlin was not at the Tyson, so we continued on and saw A Song to Remember. It was alright if you like that type of picture, which of course, I do, but not Dad. We took Rog to Ems' and Joe with us and went over to see the new airport. All I kept thinking was, 'Oh! If only Edwin was only on board.' Won't that be the day. It sure is some wonderful place. Then we left Joe out at Tyson Street and we caught up to the trolley and the "hill" wouldn't get off. So Pop and I sailed along. When we got to the Circle, it was jammed. We waited until the show was over and there stood Joe. Pop and I went and got a seat. After a while, he came and sat down by Dad. Then we came out. We went in Horn & Hardart's and Joe got a 10 cent "cottage cheese" sandwich and a bowl of soup. Dad paid for it because Joe now pays us $15.00 a week. But he was so stubborn that Dad and I didn't pay any attention to him. Then we got Rog and came home. It was 9 PM so we listened to Walter Winchell and got some coffee and went to bed. I called Al up this morning to take beets and cabbage, so Dad will have to get busy tonight. I also called Patton for the bean and turnip seed. Roger is cutting the grass, but left off and is up at Ems' now. George goes back tomorrow. Now darling, I don't know any news. I sure am praying to God for all. The news is sure coming over the radio. I am not calm, but I pray to God for strength to you and all the boys.

The "Big 3" are meeting in Potsdam to assure everlasting "Peace". But, my darling, we are such a peaceful quiet home that if I could not read or hear the radio, one would never know the awful things going on in different parts of the world.

My darling, keep calm. God is with you. When you get upset, say, 'God give me strength and Mom smooth my face.' Then your nerves will keep up. We are sure anxious these days. So my dear little boy in blue, I smooth your face and know you are a man. God be your guide.

Love from all.

Mother

Tuesday, July 17, 1945

Hello Dearest Son,

How are you today? Keep calm, darling. We are hearing the news, wonderful. They are broadcasting directly from the big battle. Norman Page is giving us eyewitness stories of the action and giving out the names of the ships taking part and the guns, etc. All I pray for is God to guide you and give you strength. I had an awful dream about you the other night, so please be a good boy. I trust you, but I am always anxious about you losing your temper and patience. You yourself can see the difference in how people live and their wants and dislikes, so choose a model to be proud of and calm yourself. I know God will hear my prayers.

The Sleepy Hollow gang is on and it's nearly 1 PM. Roger and I got up at 11 o'clock. It's been raining hard all night and all day, so I couldn't wash and Rog can't finish the lawn. Dad and I took the cabbage and beets to Granny's last night. The house is a little palace inside, but the street has a million kids and a tap room on every corner. Granny is in the height of her glory. Al carries her everything her heart desires. Snooky was there to stay a week. I hear Aunt Dot is going to Nazareth Hospital in September. I have not seen her since Uncle Bob's birthday. Sometime, if you have a minute to spare, write dear old Uncle Bob a line. His address is 7109 State Street, Tacony. I know he would sure be proud of it.

Rog said Lou H. hit home last night. Young Blake is home from the Merchant Marines. Dillon is home from the Navy. Have you had any news of Jimmy Beck?

Patton was in and he left the seeds we ordered.

Dad won't know until Thursday if he gets a convoy job.

Yesterday, we got the invitation to the golden wedding printed in gold. We are planning to go on July 27th. Rog and I may stay a week. If Pop will stay over Monday, I will come home with him.

(Enclosure – Item 16)

The Home Fires

> 1895   1945
>
> Mr. and Mrs. Freeman Long
>
> request the pleasure of your company
>
> in honour of their
>
> Fiftieth Wedding Anniversary
>
> on Saturday, the twenty-eighth of July
>
> from four until eight o'clock
>
> Liverpool, Pennsylvania

The man who leaves the car here has a flat in the rear. I guess he will be sick when he sees it. He has no spare.

Well darling, I don't know any news. Rog is going down for mail, so I will wait and see if we get any from you.

No letter today love, no letter today. You did say I may not hear from you for awhile. I sure have been proud of the way you did write.

George Ems came in with the paper yesterday. I bid him so long. I hear they had a big party last night. The house was full. I have not seen or heard from Dot for three weeks. We stopped by several times. Pop and Rog went in, but she wasn't home. Fourth of July, I think was the last time we were up on our way to Charlie's.

Well dearest, I am hoping and I will write tomorrow again. Flora Boyd and the McAdams' were here Sunday when we were out. I was glad we were out. They left a note in the door. Flora was in the hospital, so Dick wrote. What for, I don't know. I sent her a card. I have a big pot of vegetable soup on. That's all for now.

Love,

Mom & All

Tuesday, July 17, 1945

Dearest Son,

Well honey, it's early evening, 8 PM. Dad was going to get his hair cut, but Joe's was closed just as we were ready to go. Oh boy! It sure did rain. It has rained for three days straight. When it let up a bit, we went. Just as I was coming out of the doctor's, it started again. The doctor said to sit down, so I did. It soon stopped again. The doctor gave me a needle and so I hope to get more strength.

Honey, I don't know a thing. Harold Wenker Sr. was in the office. I asked him where Bud was and he said Newport News, in and out on a destroyer escort.

Dot saw Joe this afternoon and said she was coming over to see me, but it rained so much all afternoon, I guess she couldn't come over. George left.

Dear, I am going to bed now. The doctor asked for you. Two of my letters to you came back today, not enough postage. So, Rog took them right out.

All our love, baby darling. I love you.

Mother

Thursday, July 19, 1945

Dearest Son Edwin,

Last night, I wrote you a short one page letter and I am sure I put on it Tuesday, 17th, where it should have been Wednesday, 18th. The pen took a fit again and won't write, but excuse all mistakes. You know the boys used to tell us "old ladies" to count all mistakes as love. If there weren't any, we knew they didn't love us, eh! At home it has rained six straight days. It's about getting me down. I am sitting in Roger's place at the kitchen table. It's just 5 of 2 and it sure is raining. Last week's wash came home today. It's piled up on the stove. The starch is made.

The mail came today and there are 8 letters in the lot. Dad sure will be glad when he sees them tonight. We are getting news over the radio about the action in the Pacific. "Bull" Halsey's Third Fleet is sure doing their stuff. We are all anxious for it to end.

Dearest, I told you in one letter how I had such a bad dream about you. It was about a fight and the thief. The thief was up to more mischief, but I stood aside you. You tried to chase me away and didn't want anyone to know I was there. But I said, 'Son, I am aside of you.' I wonder what Dad would say. I said if harm comes to you, your mother stands by and you were motioning for me to go back. I woke up screaming Edwin, Edwin! I looked and there I was in bed with Dad. I did not tell Dad the dream, but I said, 'Oh! I had such a dream about Edwin. He needs me.' Dad said, 'Mother, go to sleep. The boy is alright.' But for three days it was heavy on my mind.

Now dear, I have two sons, but you are the closest because you never wanted me. It was Daddy, Daddy. But God is good to mothers.

The doctor gave me a needle last night and I must go again tomorrow night for another one. I can't say it helped any today. The weather is so oppressive. That has a lot to do with it too. My nerves are shot and my blood pressure is 180.

Last night, did I tell you that Thelma Spence has a son, James, now ten days old?

Yes son, I am looking forward to going up to Liverpool, 30 miles west of Harrisburg. My aunt said that a lady in the country was going to bake homemade bread for me. Pop has a turkey promised like the one we had Christmas. It is 24 ¾ pounds.

You tell your marine pal that the good coal miners are the finest people on earth to me. My dear Dad, who loved me very well, told me hundreds of stories of coal mining. He was a breaker boy when he was eight in the Henry Clay Colliery and at 25 was foreman. He left the coal region during the 1902 strike. With what he learned, he qualified as an engineer at Torresdale

Pumping Station. He could teach the chief, but because he didn't have a diploma, he couldn't rate Chief Engineer. I have his certificate framed and in our radio room. He was an experienced Anthracite coal miner in Schuylkill and Northumberland Counties. When my old Grandpop died, they put his coal miner certificate in his pocket. He was as proud of that as he was our Flag. I am proud of my people. They produce the best cooks, housewives, and kind respectful men. In Philadelphia, they can't equal the upstate people for hospitality. So now that's how your pal will rate high if he is a true coal miner's son. God Bless you both as you lie there talking. Mommy is singing that piece for you, when the curtains of night are pinned back by the sash and the beautiful moon sails the sky.

Say dearest, I am proud of you all and as you sleep, God guide and protect you, but his will be done. I gave you in God's care to Uncle Sam the day you left with the brown shirt on, and I gave a piece of my heart that day and another piece on January 25th. That was the hardest of all. As the days pass, I say like you did that you're one day nearer to home. God gives me courage and strength. I truly have never had it so good in my life. Roger is real good and nice to me. Joe and Dad do all they can for me. I have three beautiful dresses I got for Easter that I haven't had on. I have a beautiful white hat with a great lavender or pale lilac colored rose and one bud on it, to wear at the golden wedding. I ordered five dozen gladioluses from Mrs. Chandler, the lady with the beard down by the "Old Pennypack".

Your letters were all of great interest. I have answered most of your questions. We got word that Uncle John was at sea. I told you about it. Dad's brother is at Saipan and was at Okinawa and now the circle goes around as he is now at Saipan again. I sent you the latest town paper. By now, you should have it with the hometown news.

We did your boxes and watch up and put your name and address on twice and also inside. It's a shame to lose all that money. I sent you powder in one. That would help the heat rash. So life goes.

(Secret) From my one glance, she kept herself out of my sight (Juanita). The stork looks due to me. It is none of my business, but interesting.

So long for now "General". Long legs come home. Love and smooth your face,

Mother

Thursday, July 19, 1945

Dear Old Nut,

Here I am for our second chat today. The rain has ceased a little and soon I must rustle something up for supper. Yesterday, I made five quarts of pepper cabbage. I got Grandmom's old chopping machine out and Rog and I sure make it chop. I put it in pint jars as they pile up on the shelf. I am thankful. I had the sewing machine humming yesterday patching and mending. I sure do hope the sun shines tomorrow. I did intend to go to Frankford early and take in the show and shop for the meat, but the doctor didn't want me to walk out. Dearest, don't worry over me. I haven't an ache or a pain. I'm just weak due to the change in life.

Now dearest, like I told you before, if you are man enough to go and fight, you can choose your own wife. You still have plenty of time and I am sure glad you are not chained. After the war, when you come home is time enough for you to be ready to be a home-maker.

Your dollar is your only friend. They are earned by the sweat of your brow. We never had any handed us for pastime, but labored for all we earned. We gave our best efforts to you and Roger. So carry on so that we can feel secure in your happiness. Patience and perseverance wins every time.
All for now.

Love,

Mom

Thursday, July 19, 1945

Dearest Son,

Here I am with the third letter today, but we won't say letter. We say here's Mommy again to talk to her General. Oh yes! You are a General. You command my heart. We sailed her main for 18 long years come storm or calm. We sailed together. Though the rollys have come between, we still drift together. Thoughts can't keep us apart. Dad is ready getting the new hubs ready. Now he and Joe are in listening to Gabriel Heater. Soon, I will be going to bed. I'm not a bit sleepy. This weather sure is on my nerves. I can't keep the kitchen clean. Now darling, I just said hello. Did I tell you Rog told me Don H. was home? Little shy Lou is getting married, so I read and so is Norman Sharp. I don't miss many.

Love, love. Nighty Night.

Mom

Wartime Letters Written from Mother to Son

Saturday, July 21, 1945

Dearest Son Edwin,

Here it is Saturday afternoon and soon time for you to be turning the corner with dust going to Russell's at 50 miles per hour. The pots are on cooking and I guess for one Saturday night Pop will eat at home. I have one of his special dishes (brains). For Joe, Rog and me, I have veal stew. It's hot, not too hot, 80 degrees. The sun at last has shown all day for the first time in a week. That is all everyone is talking about.

As soon as I was to leave for the doctor's last night at 7, in comes an old Ford. Johnny, Carl and Rog got it running. There was no license on it. Johnny as usual was all smiles, with a cud of tobacco. I kissed him. I said 'Tobacco & all.' He said, "That's right, Mom." He was home for the weekend and is going to Maryland today. He is on the Franklin, the aircraft carrier that was hit and is in for repair. From his last trip in, he is reassigned to the place you used to drive supplies to from Supreme. He looks just wonderful. I told him all the news about you. He said to tell you to study hard, boy and good luck so you pass for first class 1/C.

Now darling, this is to be a short note. Pop and Joe will mail it out. I must iron a white sport shirt for Dad as I couldn't get the wash dry. I will write tonight when I am alone and tell you the news of the day. I sent three letters to you yesterday. I am like you, anything new, nothing of interest, but I want you to know your best girl is thinking of you. Darling, I love you heaps and heaps. You should see the puppies. The one we are keeping we named "Bum". He sure is one. He grabs the tit and rules all the rest. One is awful ugly. Bye for now.

Love,

The Home Fires

Mom

Sunday, July 22, 1945

Dearest Son,

Now it is 4 o'clock or after. I can't tell. All the clocks are off. We had a terrific electrical storm. I have no lights, no stove, no coffee, no ice box and no radio. Oh boy! I am all alone. Pop and Rog took Joe over to work. He and Pop worked all day with the mule. They had the garden looking swell. It was so hot and so damp. I heard on the radio where a hurricane was sweeping north. The tail end must have hit here about 3 PM. Joe got as far as Hermann's with the mule and the heavens broke lose. The patch looks like a mud flat and the two poor dears worked so hard. I sent out big pitchers of ice lemonade. Just a while ago, I heard the ice box go on, so I came out and the stove was on and I put on a pot of coffee. But now it's off again. There was no light in the house anywhere while they were on, and the coffee didn't finish cooking. I called the electric company over an hour ago, but no one is here yet. The fire company went up the pike.

I wrote you a short letter yesterday. I promised to write you last night when I would be alone. Well, I washed up the supper dishes and went out to get a few flowers for today and a car came in: Aunt Minnie. It was 8 o'clock. I was tired and I had intended to get bathed while Pop was out. To make matters worse, they had no supper. Elmer Irons said, 'Helen I have some fish. Will you fry them?' So I fried the fish and served them stewed tomatoes, etc. What a mess. They left at 11 PM. It was 1 AM when I got to bed. Then with the roar of the airliners, I couldn't sleep. I had another needle on Friday evening for my nerves. Oh boy! I hear the ice box. The house lights are all real faint and dim, so it must be on the line. We can hardly hear on our telephone.

Pop is back here. Maybe they will know some news. Joe is back with Dad. Baldwin came home, so Dad was talking to Mr. B. while Joe did up the work. Son, I don't know any other news. I got the coffee on, so I will say love, I am thinking of you and miss you.

All my love today and always,

Your Mom

Monday, July 23, 1945

Hello Honey,

It is hot, damp, and sticky at 5:30 and supper is on cooking. Ruth Keller called me up and I let the elbow macaroni scorch. So now I have more on cooking. I guess they will be ready for 6 PM. I have been ironing all day. I'm hot, dirty and tired. My hair is still up in curlers. Gardeners phoned that they are coming up for cabbage tonight. I have orange jello made with honeydew and peach slices in it topped with marshmallows, and then frozen. I have cream jelly roll and a cool drink I will give them. I like her.

Well dear, I called Al up this morning about cabbage. He said, 'Did you get a letter from your mother?' I said no. He said John is in California and will be home. Aunt Dink called me on Friday night, but I was at the doctor's. I guess she wanted to tell me the news

Supper is over now and Joe is shaving. Pop has gone to the barber so he can pretty up for the golden wedding.

Well dearest, I hear the news coming over; announced five minutes ago about the U.S. Navy, big news. Oh, God, let those Japs surrender. They say

The Home Fires

it's big news. I am all worked up. Doolittle is ready with his air fleet. Oh! Darling, I hope it's over soon.

Well dearest, Lewis was home yesterday. His mother said he can't get home for the Golden Wedding. She and Keller are going on to Virginia for a vacation. She makes $100 a week in Budd's Navy Department. She got the fat upper part of her thumb caught in a machine last week, so they are going to put a special splint on it so she can drive. She paid $15.00 for <u>one</u> white orchid for her mother's corsage. She has a big golden bell for them to stand under and all gold lace paper doilies and crepe paper. I did tell you I ordered 50 golden gladiolas. Pop got a 24 pound turkey ordered and promised. We will take beets and cabbage and salad. Gladys Moore and her sister Katie and her girl are going up Thursday. All the neighbors are offering their homes. Aunt Katie's brother is coming in from Ohio and one of her sisters from far off.

Edwin, my father had a brother Howard, who died young and left a wife and "baby". The baby is like Aunt Minnie. She is my Aunt Frances. She married a Navy man high up and she is coming from Newark, New Jersey.

Well dear, it's 7:30 and the Gardeners are not here yet. I made a date with the hairdresser for 11:30, Thursday and Dad will pick up my corsage Friday night. I am going to wear my blue lace dress that I wore for Aunt Lilly's wedding. Lilly hasn't heard from Edwin, and she gets $10.00 a week from Fred through the court. He came to call for a week again and then sent the key back. He drinks heavy. Dad met Mrs. Fetters. She said he drank so heavy that Lilly was about to leave him. So I stick to dear old Dad and you, my honey. Don't drink. Be good.

Lots of love,

Wartime Letters Written from Mother to Son

Your Mother

Wednesday, July 25, 1945

Dearest Son,

Here it is Wednesday, 11 AM, and I am about one day behind in my work. Before I try to crowd it all in, I must have our daily chat; because I am full up with news. The first and the best is that Granny raised the new flag and put the Welcome Home signs in her front window and door and all the little flags on the pavement. There are 42 kids in the one block where she lives. I guess she had them all and not one touched the flag. All her neighbors ran over when she hung the flag and they danced and cried, all the fat women, thin women, and old women. You can't beat Kensington when it comes for news, good or bad. They rally to help. The telegram came last Friday, $1.50 collect; "Am in the States, will be home soon, John, San Francisco." I guess you know Granny is one happy mom. She keeps saying, 'My John will have a home to come home to.' Thank God. She won't leave the doorstep, but Aunt Dink is going to venture with Dad to the Golden Wedding.

Aunt Dink came up with Sis and George and a boy from lower Holmesburg. He was a prisoner in Germany, three months (too long), and weighed 90 pounds. He spent 6 days traveling 20 miles in box cars, 70 to a car with two slices of black bread a day and hardly any water. He was liberated by the 6th Armored Division near Frankfort on the Rhine. He was brought home here to Valley Forge Hospital by plane. He now has 30 days leave. He is not injured, just starved. When his Dad heard he was missing, he died of a heart attack and left him his car. In our yard he got a flat. It was the tube, so they worked and worked, but couldn't fix it. So, I made them a wonderful supper. He bowed his head and said, "Thank God for this banquet." It just so happened I did have everything lovely, but you know "Mom". Good old Dad loaned him our spare and he and George went on. Aunt Dink was in the back of our car with three crates of cabbage and 50 bunches of beets with Sis, me and Dad in the front. We crawled along and took Aunt Dink down to Granny's and picked up the spare on Torresdale Avenue.

Bill Long is, at last letter, at Guam where Bill McAdams flew by plane too. They (McAdams') came in the lane last night as we were going out. He is on two weeks vacation. They left for the Poconos, Saturday and had to come home Sunday. They couldn't get any place to stay.

Flora Boyd sent me a card from Weir Lake. I think that is up in the Poconos some place. Tonight, Dad gets the turkey. It's 60 cents a pound, 25 pounds. Then we are putting $10.00 in a nice card and $2.00 for you and Roger in another card. Son, I am real proud of my family. I have attended three generations of golden weddings, as a baby age 3 months, as a girl 20, and now as an "old lady". I can account for 6 generations in my time; four living at the same time. So Pennsylvania stock, I am proud of you all. Fight on son, to help preserve Wonderful America.

Edwin, the Kensington Mills are going full force. All four and five floors are lit up brightly and all electric signs going and cars and buses. You can hardly get packed into. Stores (especially food stores) have the people carrying loads of bags that are overflowing. Things are harder to get, but with so much food, you never need be hungry.

The black market and the robbers are flourishing. Poor old Dad gets $1.50 for a crate of cabbage with 16 to 18 big heads. In the stores, the damn crooks weigh it. Each head costs 48 to 52 cents; they get those extra odd pennies besides.

When you come home, that's what you want to do; open a produce store. Dad will do the buying on the wharf and raise some. Forget about the big farm, just a gentleman's farm. Get on Dock Street or Callowhill and be a robber for a change. Al said his company has 32 trucks on the road buying and selling, hauling produce and fruit. Two honeydew melons are $1.02, if they sell. One hundred for $102 that's 100 x 2 cents, that's the extra profit.

Now darling, I have much to do. Aunt Lilly and the Roxborough girl had a letter in May from Edwin B. and he is in the Infantry. Aunt Lilly is sure now that he no doubt is shipped, or will be, to the Pacific zone and so I guess, like Uncle John, they get home. It's two years on July 6th since Uncle John left California.

Darling, it takes 22 hours from L.A. and costs $145 one way. I wave to all the airliners and I just pray for the day when V.J.[118] comes. I can't sleep half the time for thinking. But the good old Doc R. has my nerves calmed a little. I must go tonight again. We have had to turn in our bonds in order to keep going. Dad only gives me $25.00 a week and I have hard scratching to make ends meet with high insurance and the cost of living. Dear, we haven't had steak since you were home.

So now my dear little boy in blue, I must go. The weather is lousy; damp, moldy and wet, and I can't get anything to dry. It's awful.

So long for now dearest love.

Mom

---

[118] V.J. means Victory over Japan.

Liverpool, Pennsylvania, U.S.A.
Friday, July 27, 1945

Darling,

I can't pass the day without one little chat. I'm here. I had a marvelous trip up. It took from 9 AM to 4:30 PM. I was up at 4 AM. I am tired, but will wait for Dad. I hope to see him at 1 AM. Honey, it's a beautiful, lovely place and comfortable and clean with plenty to eat; a perfect welcome. I will write all the details at the first moment.

Dad got the turkey and they killed 25 chickens.

Monday

My Dearest Darling,

Now dear son, I haven't had one moment to write and it's now 9 AM Monday. Dad got in around 2 AM and in a few hours he is leaving for home, just him and Sissy. Aunt Dink and Sissy were just stepping on to a trolley at Welsh Road to go to Frankford on Thursday at 11 AM when a yellow taxi stopped for the trolley. And my God, out jumped Uncle John. He grabbed her in the middle of Frankford Avenue and held up traffic. He was mad. He had been home and no one was there, so he was going to the Navy Yard. He was black, dirty and tired. He sat and stood five days from San Francisco. He was at Okinawa to set up the water system. He had off only until 8 AM Sunday at the Yard and that would not allow him to come here. So Aunt Dink could not come.

Edwin, it was everything of the finest and most perfect, but it rained from Friday until Sunday morning. There was so much rain that the roads and rivers are overflowing.

Ruth Keller has just left for their farm in Virginia. Howard Lewis got here for the celebration. He gets shipped to California. His brother is here, but he is going ten miles out this afternoon to his Aunt Florence. Dad and Rog have gone out to the country now in an old 1928 Ford. Uncle Freeman would not let Pop take his own car. He insisted he use his instead. Pop is going to buy eggs and chickens to take home. He is going home about noon. I may stay two weeks. Edwin, it is a grand place.

My baby, I love you. Dad will send me any mail from you. All my love, I will write tomorrow to make up for the lost time.

Mother

****END OF JULY****

Chapter Eleven

August 1945

From l to r, Edwin Price Jr., Freeman Long, Catherine Long and Helen Price.

Wartime Letters Written from Mother to Son

Liverpool,
Perry County,
Pennsylvania
Wednesday, August 1, 1945

Dearest Son,

Here it is 6 o'clock in the morning. I have been awake since 4:45. I went out in the kitchen, but the household is still asleep. The house has a real large kitchen, dining room, living room, den, 3 swell bedrooms and a bath all on one floor and on a level like the second story, 2 entrances and 2 pairs of steps up from the highway with a porch entirely around the four sides of the house. There are large lawns around and the Susquehanna River to the back and beautiful mountains. The view up the river is beyond my description. The food and everything is spotless and perfect. The trucks fly by so fast and the house is on the highway. At night, it seems they go right through my belly, as I am not used to the noise yet.

The neighbors are real friendly and a real pleasure for me to talk to them. They fell in love with Roger and everyone just can't speak highly enough of Sissy. I sleep in a big double bed and Grace Long's girl, Cassie, age 9, is sleeping in a cot in my room. I still like "little boys best"; they are not half as much bother as girls. She is a nice polite child and sensible, but I can't be bothered with children. My Auntie said, "Patience" is the highest tree in Heaven, so I might be able to catch on to the lowest limb. I wrote Dad a letter yesterday and said, it's 25 years and that's a heap long time between those letters you and Dot read, but he will miss my kicking.

Now darling, a mosquito woke me up and now a fly is pestering me. It has rained continually since July 15. Last night, it poured. I do hope today it clears up. It's so sticky and moldy. Roger's shoe molded in the bag. Now, dearest, I pray you are okay. The news is big. I have not heard a radio since I came here. All my love, baby dear, My General.

Love,

Mom

Friday, August 3, 1945

Dearest Son,

Here it is Friday, and I have been here a week today. The home is peaceful and beautiful and all that I can wish for, but like wishing for you, I also miss Dad; because he is good. He sent me a letter with your mail (4 letters) and also one from Padre Micheli, which I am very proud of. You are a Christian boy, dear, and a Protestant, so their good teaching has been given to you. Stick to it. Kind words are better than medicine. One of your letters said, 'My leg is sore today where I got hit.' Does that mean you got wounded in battle? Answer, yes about my leg and I will know. Also in that letter, you said I expect to go--- and that length from here to the bottom was cut out by censor and almost as much on the second page, so I figured you were in action again. Pop's brother sure gets around, doesn't he? I guess all the boys do.

Now, sweetheart, today is Friday and they have a maid and she is busy. Uncle Freeman is going to take us to the store and he is now taking pictures of the house. When I get the pictures, I will send them to you.

Dearest darling, I wrote to the Padre, as he sent us such a wonderful letter of encouragement. For him to take his time to write us is appreciated by Dad and me. I don't know any special news. I think Lewis' mother will be up from Virginia by the weekend. I am hoping Dad comes up. I suppose he will if the car and gas are okay. I will try to catch up with extra letters when I get home. I pray for you and all. I prayed extra special for your safety and welfare and all on the Pasadena last night.

As ever,

Mother

Sunday, August 5, 1945

Dearest Son,

It is now 7 PM and I am still on vacation, first day of the second week. Dad brought Doreen up Saturday and got here around eleven o'clock. What a busy weekend we had. We went out to a big farm and I bought 21 ½ pounds of lard. Aunt Katie bought 7 pounds and five dozen eggs. I ordered eggs and 2 pounds of butter for next week. She is Aunt Katie's cousin and they have over 100 acres, corn, wheat, oats, potatoes, several dozen of honey hives and are real up country Dutch.

Edwin, the stoves in each house are more beautiful as I go along. Never have I seen such wonderful housekeepers. They speak in a slow tongue. The man had been a school teacher. When he bought the place, they tore out the fireplace and found a sack of gold, thousands of dollars worth and they are so Scotch. She makes her slips out of feed bags. We left there and went to a country picnic. Pop and I sure fell in line. Boy oh boy! There is a family that has eight girls and 1 boy. He is in the service. Another has 14 girls, and man oh! The tables were loaded with everything you could eat. They sold all sorts of wonderful eats at a big tent and Dad and I sure fell for the chicken, twenty cents a bowl and homemade ice cream. The country is in the Juniata Valley. It is hilly and I don't know how they farm. We had a

The Home Fires

twenty mile ride this afternoon in Uncle Freeman's Ford (like Uncle Paul's model) and we went into the virgin forest...deer bountiful...huckleberries...and squirrel. We saw a large buzzard feeding on a groundhog. The pine tress and the forests are a sight to see, Shade Mountains. Dad had a marvelous Sunday dinner. He got here at 11 AM Saturday and he had a broken heart.

One month ago, Edwin, a hailstorm hit up here and ruined all the gardens and wrecked most of the roofs. I was in the Liverpool Methodist Church this morning and they gave out the repair bills, $1675 for the repair to the roof and $200 for the broken windows. Everyone has stored furniture here and there to save it from the water from the damage done the roofs.

Friday night the same kind of a storm hit our northeast section. Hailstones 2½ inches around ruined Pop's tomatoes, cucumbers, eggplant, etc., but the path where the corn was planted escaped the cloud and the corn is standing. It made the tomatoes look like they were frozen, big soft holes in them. Pop brought some up to show us. So, I loved him and told him to forget it.

He had Doreen with him and today he left at 2 PM. He took Grace's girl, Cassie, home and Bob Lewis. He is coming next week and may bring Joe if he would come.

Uncle John gets mustered out of the service on August 11th. He is going to take Aunt Dink down to Atlantic City for 2 weeks.

Now Darling, Uncle Freeman is in the cellar teaching Roger woodwork. Aunt Katie is writing a letter. Edwin, we had a 16 pound home cured ham today. Pop sure went to work on it. Dearest, the picture of Jim and wife is just lovely. I love you all. I say special prayers every night for all on the Pasadena and ask please, God, to hear all of them. I love you darling. I hope you are okay. I will write tomorrow.

Mother & All

Monday, August 6, 1945

Hello Darling,

This letter is to be short. It's 9 PM. I am tired. We washed today and Ruth Keller came back this afternoon and Dad had taken Bob Lewis back to Philadelphia yesterday. He left about 2 o'clock and so I have not heard back yet about his return trip. I feel lots better since Saturday, seeing Dad and getting nine letters from you. I was surprised when Dad told me Bill Neamand was buried on Friday, He died from T.B. I know young Bill is in the Pacific. Did you know that he left Bill and the girl, 20 and 18, and 2 small babies, 1 ten months old and one 2 years old? Now I guess the Navy will have to help them out. Just like Mal. Oh! Well darling, I don't know any news. Rog is tired and has gone to bed. So has everyone else. But, they are busy around here so I can't miss writing to you. I miss you. I understand all your letters. I know you have seen action and I pray for you all. Your letters have been so helpful to me. God will watch over you and so darling, I close for now. I send all my mother love to you and the knot pulled a little tighter so to keep you. May God's blessing be upon me and thee while we are absent one from the other. Unto you, dear son, I hold you close, kiss you sweet and say nighty night for now.

Love from,

Mother & All

Edwin; a ship was sinking and on board were an American, a Jap, a German, and an Italian. The Jap said, me sink, me can't swim, me eat too much rice. The German said, Got, I drown. I can't swim, I eat too much kraut. The Italian said, Me drown too. Eat too much spaghetti.

What did the American say?

Answer: Put frt. Put, buir. Good Old Boston Baked Beans.

Thursday, August 9, 1945

Dearest Son Edwin,

During this vacation trip I am all mixed up as to days and date. So, if your letters miss out in numbers, you know the reason. This morning, I had happy news brought to me. Aunt Katie knocked on the door. I was dreaming I was down at the Ford Tank Depot in my nightgown and I couldn't pass by the men. Aunt Katie woke me up saying, 'Come on. Here's mail from your boy.' Dad sent four letters to us and one to Roger from you. The last one was dated July 26th telling us you got your watch and the packages. I knew you would enjoy what I sent you and Dad got you the wallet. Did you get the box with the canned tomatoes? I am so glad the ice mint did the rash good. As soon as I get home, I will make up another box for you. Now darling, all we think about is you. We know all the boxes are doing their best.

Bill Long is out there also. No word from Ed Bissinger nor from his chaplain, to whom I wrote. I guess they are on the move. Uncle John gets mustered out this coming Saturday, August 11th. He had no decent clothes and no money. He is wearing Byron's things, but I guess by Saturday he will be fixed up. He has to report at the Navy Yard every day. You see, if he got 30 days off, that would mean more expense for the Government. So, he must report every day until the papers, etc. come through for his discharge. I am real anxious to see him. He refused drink and Granny was mad. But, he claims he is off of it. I hope so, and you too stay away from the card sharks. They play the game on boots all the time and poor boys like you are the losers.

Roger is sure a busy boy, making ducks and birds on the jigsaw and Uncle Freeman is pleased. He is sick today. He is lying down.

Now dearest, did you hear the news? I know you did. Russia against Japan. Mr. Ritter, a neighbor, came across the street and told us the news had come from Harrisburg. Uncle Freeman's radio is out of order since the last hailstorm, so I didn't hear a radio until last night when they asked us to come over to hear the news at 8 PM. This sure is a lovely place. The air is so different. The place has a gorgeous view, mountains and river, looks like Christmas pictures.

Now dearest, it's 11 o'clock. I had a lovely permanent before I came up here and my hair cut short. My hair is all curls.

Darling, I am so proud of you and I give all my love and prayers to all on the Pasadena. Keep the good work up. The Atomic Bomb sure made a hit. This is all for now.

Love,

Mother

The Home Fires

Friday, August 10, 1945

Dearest Son,

I got up at 9 AM. Rog at 10. What a quiet peaceful place. The view here is beautiful and I sure have enjoyed my visit. Tomorrow is Saturday, and I will look for Dad and Joe. Roger is in the cellar and he has made some wonderful things since he is here. He made a big duck and six little ones. I am going to put them on the lawn at home. He made a pin wheel, a jockey on horseback for a weather vane and two quail with revolving wings. Uncle Freeman is selling him a saw. The day before we came away from home,

Rog went up to see Uncle Bill and he gave him $50.00 for our vacation. It soon went and I got nothing, but I did buy the lard and the chickens. Also, we bought the gas and our lunch on the way up, and plenty of groceries and food Dad took down last Sunday for him and Joe for the week.

Edwin darling, there are no points on olives, but on the sardines, tomatoes, and canned fruit. I always have plenty of blue points. I am going out in the country to a big farm tomorrow. I ordered two pounds of butter and four dozen eggs. Also, last week I bought a big steak, which cost 40 points.

Now dear, what do you think of the news; Russia against Japan? The Atomic bomb will sure do its work. So, my darling, I pray for you and peace.

I am much, much better and sure wish we had a nice place like this with a bathroom. Did you get Aunt Violet's box yet and the one I sent with the can of tomatoes? I will write tomorrow. Love to Jim, Joe and all.

Mother

(Editor's Note: Item 17 is an account from the News-Sun, Newport, PA – August 1945)

Mr. and Mrs. Freeman Long Celebrate Golden Wedding

Saturday, July 28th, the Fire Hall was a scene of a beautiful golden wedding anniversary celebration of Mr. and Mrs. Freeman Long, who were married 50 years, and who spent a very happy life. The hall was tastefully decorated and in the center of the ceiling a beautiful golden bell hung, which was made by Dennison Company of Philadelphia, the gift of their son-in-law and daughter, Mr. and Mrs. Owen Keller, Philadelphia. Table decorations were two large baskets of gladioli, presented by Mr. and Mrs. Edwin Price, Philadelphia, niece and nephew of Mr. and Mrs. Long and Mr. and Mrs. Arthur Crawford, their neighbors. The center piece was a large wedding cake, very nicely decorated and on it were a miniature bride and groom and a gold bell. Although the weather was not so fair, the many friends of the happy couple called at their home and extended congratulations on this occasion. At 4 P. M. the guests began to arrive at the fire hall in honor of the occasion and although the rain came down very fast, a large number of relatives and friends gathered there. Warren Stailey acted as master of ceremonies and paid a beautiful tribute to the bride and groom, having said how long he knew these folks and what a pleasure to have such good folks in our community. The guests then sang "Praise God From Whom All Blessings Flow," after which they were seated at the tables and Harry Ritter, Sr., made a beautiful prayer. A delicious luncheon was served, which was heartily enjoyed. Before the wedding cake was served the groom very lovingly asked the bride to stand and then placed on her finger a beautiful white gold wedding ring, explaining the meaning of the ring ceremony, she in turn presented the groom with an amethyst birthstone ring, which was a surprise to each one.

The groom was attired in a lovely Palm Beach suit while the bride was dressed in a beautiful light blue gown of marquisette and wore an orchid corsage. They presented a lovely appearance. After the ceremony the guest then partook of the luncheon, during which time many old time songs were sung, among them were "Silver Threads Among the Gold," and "The Old Grey Mare Is Not What She Used to Be" was enjoyed by everyone and created a lot of fun. The Rev. E. L. Ritzman, pastor of the happy couple, made a short address, then all sang "God Be With You Till We Meet Again." There were three couples present who were married 50 years and celebrated their golden wedding anniversary, viz: Mr. and Mrs. Jacob Erlenmeyer, Mr. and Mrs. Harry Ritter, Sr., and the bride and groom. Wedding anniversaries celebrated, Mr. Longs' grandparents, his parents and his aunt, which is remarkable. The Longs received many nice cards and gifts and are deeply grateful to all who helped in any way to make the occasion such a happy one, and everyone present had a delightful evening. Everyone is cordially invited to the Long home to see the gifts they received. The Longs have a son, Freemont Long who is serving in the services of his country and is overseas and unable to be present; their son Howard and daughter Mrs. Robert Smith were also unable to be present. Their three daughters, Mrs. Owen Keller, Mrs. Dan Reale of Philadelphia and Mrs. Clayton Marks, Richfield and their families were present.

The folks who took part in the celebration of the golden wedding of Mr. and Mrs. Freeman Long, Saturday, July 28, at the Fire Hall in Liverpool were: Mr. and Mrs. Edwin Price, Roger Price, Mr. and Mrs. O. B. Keller, Philadelphia, Robert and Howard Lewis, Rhode Island, J.F. Cassidy, Mrs. Minnie Fulmer, Mrs. John Moore, Gladys Moore, Mrs. Edward Cannon, Mr. and Mrs. Dan Reale, Catherine Reale, Carol Reale, Miss Doreen Long, Mr. and Mrs. Robert Davidson, Mrs. Ruth Kernan, Fred Keiter, Edward Keiter, all of Philadelphia; Mrs. Charles Tiley, Miss Lillian Tiley, Shamokin; Mrs. Joseph Radcliff, Mrs. William Kautz, Harrisburg; Mr. and Mrs. Clayton Marks,

Richfield; Mr. and Mrs. H.E. Ritter, Mr. and Mrs. J.W. Stailey, Miss Annie Stailey, Miss Zella Flickinger, Mrs. Jennie Dodge, Mr. and Mrs. Alvin Grubb, Mr. and Mrs. E.C. Mengle, Mrs. Anna Connell, Mrs. J.K. Holman, Mrs. Alma Cook, Mrs. George Reisinger, Mrs. Russell Hoffman, Miss Mellie Shuler, Mr. and Mrs. Jacob Erlenmeyer, Mrs. Annie Bair, Miss Maud Knisley, Mr. and Mrs. Edward Brink, Mr. and Mrs. John Mailen, Mrs. Maggie Linn, Mr. and Mrs. Alvin Williamson, Bruce Williamson, Mrs. Frank Morris, Mr. and Mrs. Howard Coulter, Mr. and Mrs. S.M. Shuler, Mr. and Mrs. H.A.S. Shuler, Mrs. Arthur Crawford, the Rev. and Mrs. E.L. Ritzman, Mr. and Mrs. Edgar Beigh, Miss Gertrude Shuler, Mrs. Howard Arnold, Mrs. Walter Wert, Mrs. G. DeHaven, Mrs. John Charles, Mrs. Maurice Deckard, Mrs. M. Grubb, Miss Dorothy Hoffman, Miss Geraldine Miller, Miss Susan Shumaker, Miss Alma Crane, all of Liverpool.

———

*Edwin Price Junior and Helen May Long Price
in Liverpool, PA in 1945.*

Monday, August 13, 1945

My Darling,

Well, son, here I am at home after two weeks away. They were the first two weeks I have ever spent away from the farm since I went to buy you from

"Mr. Stork". Now, all jokes aside, the place looks worse than I have ever seen it. It looks like a grown up field where no one lives. The weeds are higher than me and the lawn grass nearly to my waist. I sent for Carl and I told him if he helped Roger, I would pay him. But, I think when you get two boys together you get none, like you and Baker. The house was in pretty good shape. Joe gave it the once over, but it smelled very moldy. I have it all aired out; and the flowers are gorgeous and the colors are radiant. We have had so much rain, and shower drops are starting now. Rog has gone to pull corn for supper.

My darling, I saw my brother today. I stopped at his home last night after a 151 mile drive and he wasn't home. So, today he came up for ration books and gas. Howard Baldy brought Johnny and his new baby, Donna. It is the first I have seen her. Uncle John looks marvelous. It took Uncle John 53 days to get home from the time he left. He has his papers, W. T. 1/C, Honorably Discharged, November 12, 1942 to August 11, 1945, Physical Card, Perfect. So, he deserves a good rest.

Bill is in your territory, or maybe you are in his, off the coast of Japan. Darling, we are awaiting the full surrender news. I fell on my knees last night when I heard the news, but it turned out to be a false rumor. Now son, send those things home that you have for us, as you can't bring a thing home. Dad said he would be so pleased if you could get him any war souvenir. He is so proud of you. He is always saying he only hopes you will have sense and settle down. He said he knows you are young. When you return, he wants you to prosper and not have to worry and work like we did, and then have no home and no one to want us. I tell him what we always said. 'Our children should never be burdened with us.' The he says, 'Yes mother, someone must look out for you.' But, if going away for two weeks makes Dad and the place look the way it does, well then, Heaven help Dad if he ever gets alone. I have three weeks clothes to iron and so I will write more later. By that time,

The Home Fires

I hope I can say thank God, six more months to go and my "General's" two blue legs will top that railroad and he will be in my arms.

Love,

Mom

Tuesday, August 14, 1945

> God Bless America.
> Tues. Aug. 14, 1945.
> Just Wonderful News.
> Peace.

Philadelphia
United States of America.
To the
U. S. S. Pasadena.

Thank You All.
for your service to
our country. Praise
God - and may you
all come home to your
beloved land soon.

Just a country Mother.
in the kitchen waiting
Once again thanks to
a fine ship - Pasadena.
Helen M. Price.

U. S. America;
    Winner—
Thank God; and
    May God be with thee all.—
            Mother.
Aug. 14th. 1945.
I'm so happy. that I can't write. but you are plenty close to my heart, dear son— I kissed dad. special for you; and we patted each

other and cried - six more months to go - but at least you can rest easier. Be good - we are two proud parents. My darling I thank you for your service to our country and my heart is overflowing Tonight. Joy to all on the Pasadena - and hopes To see you all soon. Oh. God - I have prayed for this day - May we see each other soon - My general - I want to see you soon - Praise God. With all my love our love. Mother & aa

The Home Fires

Thursday, August 16, 1945

All our love.
All our thanks.
Mom, Dad, Rog & Joe.

Dearest Son Edwin,

Along about this time you usually come in at 50 miles per hour, but tonight the car sits by the truck shed door and Dad has been in the onion patch since 7 AM. What a happy look on his face as when he came home on Tuesday evening. Little did he think he would not have any work until next Monday. Yes, orders came, first for two days celebration of the good news, Peace. Then as the official military news is awaited, we are told the actual signing is to take place on the Missouri and then President Truman will speak to us.

Dear, it's 4:45. I have a great big meat pie in the oven, a big cake baked, and Aunt Lilly and Esther are here. Esther took sixteen snaps today and if they turn out, you will see the cake I baked. Gas has gone off rationing, also all canned foods. We left after 8 o'clock when the whistles ceased blowing on Tuesday night and went to McAdams'. Five girls were there and many neighbors. We sang, waved the flags, rung bells, and McAdams got drunk and so did the man next door. Joe and Pop sure were sweating. I was glad when Pop got the car in the yard. Now today, I could shout all over Bustleton. Halsey's Third Fleet has a big write up in tonight's paper and the name of your ship, U.S.S. Pasadena is listed and all the praise that is due the Third Fleet. It tells how many ships they have and tells where they are off of Japan to keep order. Also, it said they had their picture taken. I sure am proud of you son; not only for my sake, but Dad's smile is my (our) reward.

Now dear, I don't know any special news outside of the fact everyone is smiles. Granny paraded with Peachey on Market Street until 3 AM. Market Street was roped off; no cars or buses. The people danced, loved, girls got in line and kissed all the wounded sailors who were around City Hall and old guys counted how long the kiss lasted until they were out of breath. I did expect to hear from Dot, but no call. Everybody is busy. Pop is as happy and prays you are well. He is the proudest Dad in the world. All he can say is, the boy, the boy, I wonder how he took the news.

Mom & All

****END OF AN ERA****

The Home Fires
Epilogue

My grandmother wrote other letters to my father after the ones in this collection, up until Dad received his Honorable Discharge from the U.S. Navy in June of 1946. I also have in my possession the letters that he wrote to her and Grandpop. Additionally, I have a great number of letters written to Dad from other relatives and friends.

My father heeded his parents' advice; he saved his money, followed orders, and learned as much as he could. For his naval tenure, Dad received an American Campaign Medal, an Asiatic Campaign Medal (two stars), a WW II Victory Medal, a Navy Occupation Medal (Asian Clasp), and a Philippine Liberation ribbon (one star). Throughout his life, my father was hard-working and honest. He could be abrupt in his manner, but he was, nonetheless, a very loving parent.

While I was a senior in high school, I had an assignment to interview a person I considered to be a hero. I interviewed my dad. During the interview, I asked him, "Which was the happiest day of your life?" He quickly answered, "The day I got out of the Navy!" He then immediately amended his answer to, "The day I married your mother." It gave me a great deal of insight into how he felt about the Navy.

Grandmom died in March of 1958. Although I was less than two years old at the time, I do have one vivid memory of her. That memory is one of kindness and love. Those traits are ones that she had in common with my own mother, and my wife, Deborah.

♦

About the Author

The author of the letters contained in The Home Fires was Helen May Price, born in Shamokin, PA, the eldest of ten children, in 1897. Because of the violence of the Coal Miner's strike of 1902, she moved to the Philadelphia area with her parents, Norman and Minnie Long in that year. Helen left school before the age of 15 to work as a servant in the home of the former Pennsylvania State Senator Grundy and the home of Caspar Wister Morris, two prominent Philadelphia area families.

It is known that as an adult, she worked in employ of the L.H. Gilmer Company, a manufacturing firm, in the Tacony section of Philadelphia until October of 1921.

In 1920, she married Edwin Price Junior, whose family roots can be traced back in Philadelphia to 1685. Helen's own ancestors included many early Pennsylvania German immigrants, whose arrival also predated the American Revolution.

Sometime after her marriage, she moved to the Price Family Farm in Bustleton. In 1924, her first child, Norman Francis Long, survived only a few minutes after birth. Edwin Charles Price was born in 1926 and Roger Daniel Price was born in 1932. The Price family lived there until 1954.

Helen died in Philadelphia from heart disease in 1958 at the age of 60.

Gregory Edwin Price, the editor, is the grandson of Helen Price. Born in Philadelphia in 1956, Greg grew up in the Delaware Valley and later attended Temple University, majoring in Communications.

Greg's career has included being a radio broadcaster in several capacities, as well as general manager for an Internet service provider. Greg currently is sales manager of television advertising in Vermont, where he lives with his wife, Deborah, and three children, Jonathan, Elizabeth, and Matthew. This is his first venture into the world of publishing

Greg also has an avid interest in American history and is an amateur genealogist.

Gregory Edwin Price

♦

Sources and Permissions

Item 1- Chapter 1, Pages 15/16, 1944, Campaign Apple - Front Side/Reverse Side, Printed by Trades Council Union Label, Allied Printing, Philadelphia.

Item 2- Chapter 1, Pages 28/29, 10.24.1944, Wilson News Front/Back Page, School District of Philadelphia.

Item 3- Chapter 2, Pages 76/77, 11.8.1944, USN Visitor Pass - Front/Back, Source: U.S. Navy.

Item 4- Chapter 3, Pages 140/141, 1944, Forget-Me-Not Greeting Card - Front/Interior, Forget-Me-Not Greeting Card, Reproduced by Permission. American Greetings Corporation. ©AGC, Inc.

Item 5- Chapter 4, Pages 145/148, 1944, Fold Four Pigs to Find Fifth One/The Fifth Pig, Allied Propaganda.

Item 6- Chapter 6, Page 284, 3.18.1945, Hottest Winter Day Baffles Men of Science, Source: Philadelphia Record.

Item 7- Chapter 9, Page 414, 6.3.1945, 257th Anniversary - Lower Dublin Baptist Church Bulletin, Reprinted by permission of the Pennepack Baptist Church, Philadelphia, PA.

Item 8- Chapter 9, Page 415, 6.4.1945, Generals Fly From Europe for Parade, Source: Philadelphia Record.

Item 9- Chapter 9, Page 417, 6.4.1945, City Ready To Hail Bradley, Spaatz, Source: Philadelphia Bulletin. Reprinted by permission of the Bulletin Company.

Item 10- Chapter 9, Page 433, 6.12.1945, Hitler Reported To Be Father of 2, Reprinted with permission from United Press International from The Philadelphia Inquirer.

Item 11- Chapter 9, Page 433, 6.12.1945, Mercury Soars To Year's High, Reprinted with permission from The Philadelphia Inquirer.

Item 12- Chapter 9, Page 460, 6.25.1945, Philadelphia Port of the Air World, City of Philadelphia.

Item 13- Chapter 10, Page 468, 7.1.1945, New High of 99 Sets Record, Reprinted with permission from The Philadelphia Inquirer.

Item 14- Chapter 10, Page 468, 7.1.1945, Mercury 99 on Hottest Day in 5 Years, Source: Philadelphia Record.

Item 15- Chapter 10, Page 476, 7.5.1945, United Airlines Picture, Source: Philadelphia Record.

Item 16- Chapter 10, Page 490, 7.17.1945, Wedding Invitation.

Item 17- Chapter 11, Page 517-520, 8.1945, Newspaper Account - Mr. & Mrs. Freeman Long Celebrate Golden Wedding, Reprinted by permission of the News-Sun.

All other photographs are the property of and from the personal collection of Gregory Edwin Price.

◆